THE A[R]E

General Editors: Richard Proudfoot, Ann Thompson
and David Scott Kastan
Associate General Editor for this volume:
George Walton Williams

THE
MERRY WIVES
OF
WINDSOR

THE ARDEN SHAKESPEARE

ALL'S WELL THAT ENDS WELL	edited by G.K. Hunter*
ANTONY AND CLEOPATRA	edited by John Wilders
AS YOU LIKE IT	edited by Agnes Latham*
THE COMEDY OF ERRORS	edited by R.A. Foakes*
CORIOLANUS	edited by Philip Brockbank*
CYMBELINE	edited by J.M. Nosworthy*
HAMLET	edited by Harold Jenkins*
JULIUS CAESAR	edited by David Daniell
KING HENRY IV Parts 1 and 2	edited by A.R. Humphreys*
KING HENRY V	edited by T.W. Craik
KING HENRY VI Part 1	edited by Edward Burns
KING HENRY VI Part 2	edited by Ronald Knowles
KING HENRY VI Part 3	edited by A.S. Cairncross*
KING HENRY VIII	edited by R.A. Foakes*
KING JOHN	edited by E.A.J. Honigmann*
KING LEAR	edited by R.A. Foakes
KING RICHARD II	edited by Peter Ure*
KING RICHARD III	edited by Anthony Hammond*
LOVE'S LABOUR'S LOST	edited by H.R. Woudhuysen
MACBETH	edited by Kenneth Muir*
MEASURE FOR MEASURE	edited by J.W. Lever*
THE MERCHANT OF VENICE	edited by John Russell Brown*
THE MERRY WIVES OF WINDSOR	edited by Giorgio Melchiori
A MIDSUMMER NIGHT'S DREAM	edited by Harold F. Brooks*
MUCH ADO ABOUT NOTHING	edited by A.R. Humphreys*
OTHELLO	edited by E.A.J. Honigmann
PERICLES	edited by F.D. Hoeniger*
THE POEMS	edited by F.T. Prince*
ROMEO AND JULIET	edited by Brian Gibbons*
SHAKESPEARE'S SONNETS	edited by Katherine Duncan-Jones
THE TAMING OF THE SHREW	edited by Brian Morris*
THE TEMPEST	edited by Virginia Mason Vaughan and Alden T. Vaughan
TIMON OF ATHENS	edited by H.J. Oliver*
TITUS ANDRONICUS	edited by Jonathan Bate
TROILUS AND CRESSIDA	edited by David Bevington
TWELFTH NIGHT	edited by J.M. Lothian and T.W. Craik*
THE TWO GENTLEMEN OF VERONA	edited by Clifford Leech*
THE TWO NOBLE KINSMEN	edited by Lois Potter
THE WINTER'S TALE	edited by J.H. Pafford*

*Second Series

THE MERRY WIVES OF WINDSOR

Edited by
GIORGIO MELCHIORI

The Arden website is at
http://www.ardenshakespeare.com/

The general editors of the Arden Shakespeare have been
W.J. Craig and R.H. Case (first series 1899–1944)
Una Ellis-Fermor, Harold F. Brooks, Harold Jenkins and
Brian Morris (second series 1946–82)

Present general editors (third series)
Richard Proudfoot, Ann Thompson and David Scott Kastan

This edition of *The Merry Wives of Windsor*, by Giorgio Melchiori,
first published 2000 by Thomas Nelson and Sons Ltd

Thomas Nelson and Sons Ltd
Nelson House Mayfield Road
Walton-on-Thames Surrey
KT12 5PL UK

Arden Shakespeare
is an imprint of
Thomson Learning

Editorial matter © 2000 Giorgio Melchiori

Typeset in Ehrhardt by
Wyvern 21 Ltd, Bristol

Printed in Spain

British Library Cataloguing in Publication Data
A catalogue record for this book is available from the British
Library
Library of Congress Cataloguing in Publication Data
A catalogue record has been applied for

ISBN 0–17–443561–4 (hardback)
NPN 9 8 7 6 5 4 3 2 1
ISBN 0–17–443528–2 (paperback)
NPN 9 8 7 6 5 4 3 2 1

The Editor

Giorgio Melchiori is Emeritus Professor of English Literature at the Università Roma Tre in Italy. His major publications include *Shakespeare's Dramatic Meditations: An Experiment in Criticism* (1976); editions of *King Henry IV Part 1* (1989) and *King Edward III* (1998) for the New Cambridge Shakespeare; an edition of *Sir Thomas More* (with Vittorio Gabrieli) for the Revels series (1990); *Shakespeare's Garter Plays: 'King Edward III' to 'The Merry Wives of Windsor'* (1994); and *Joyce's Feast of Languages* (1995). He is a Fellow of the British Academy and Life Trustee of the Shakespeare Birthplace Trust. He was awarded a CBE in 1990.

CONTENTS

SIR JOHN FALSTAFF AND THE MERRY WIVES OF WINDSOR 119

LIST OF
ILLUSTRATIONS

LIST OF TABLES

GENERAL EDITORS' PREFACE

The Arden Shakespeare is now over one hundred years old. The earliest volume in the series, Edward Dowden's *Hamlet*, was published in 1899. Since then the Arden Shakespeare has become internationally recognized and respected. It is now widely acknowledged as the pre-eminent Shakespeare series, valued by scholars, students, actors, and 'the great variety of readers' alike for its readable and reliable texts, its full annotations and its richly informative introductions.

We have aimed in the third Arden edition to maintain the quality and general character of its predecessors, preserving the commitment to presenting the play as it has been shaped in history. While each individual volume will necessarily have its own emphasis in the light of the unique possibilities and problems posed by the play, the series as a whole, like the earlier Ardens, insists upon the highest standards of scholarship and upon attractive and accessible presentation.

Newly edited from the original quarto and folio editions, the texts are presented in fully modernized form, with a textual apparatus that records all substantial divergences from those early printings. The notes and introductions focus on the conditions and possibilities of meaning that editors, critics and performers (on stage and screen) have discovered in the play. While building upon the rich history of scholarly and theatrical activity that has long shaped our understanding of the texts of Shakespeare's plays, this third series of the Arden Shakespeare is made necessary and possible by a new generation's encounter with Shakespeare, engaging with the plays and their complex relation to the culture in which they were – and continue to be – produced.

THE TEXT

On each page of the work itself, readers will find a passage of text followed by commentary and, finally, textual notes. Act and scene divisions (seldom present in the early editions and often the product of eighteenth-century or later scholarship) have been retained for ease of reference, but have been given less prominence than in the previous series. Editorial indications of location of the action have been removed to the textual notes or commentary.

In the text itself, unfamiliar typographic conventions have been avoided in order to minimize obstacles to the reader. Elided forms in the early texts are spelt out in full in verse lines wherever they indicate a usual late twentieth-century pronunciation that requires no special indication and wherever they occur in prose (except when they indicate non-standard pronunciation). In verse speeches, marks of elision are retained where they are necessary guides to the scansion and pronunciation of the line. Final -ed in past tense and participial forms of verbs is always printed as -ed without accent, never as -'d, but wherever the required pronunciation diverges from modern usage a note in the commentary draws attention to the fact. Where the final -ed should be given syllabic value contrary to modern usage, e.g.

> Doth Silvia know that I am banished?
> (*TGV* 3.1.221)

the note will take the form

   221 **banished** banishèd

Conventional lineation of divided verse lines shared by two or more speakers has been reconsidered and sometimes rearranged. Except for the familiar *Exit* and *Exeunt*, Latin forms in stage directions and speech prefixes have been translated into English and the original Latin forms recorded in the textual notes.

COMMENTARY AND TEXTUAL NOTES

Notes in the commentary, for which a major source will be the *Oxford English Dictionary*, offer glossarial and other explication of verbal difficulties; they may also include discussion of points of theatrical interpretation and, in relevant cases, substantial extracts from Shakespeare's source material. Editors will not usually offer glossarial notes for words adequately defined in the latest edition of *The Concise Oxford Dictionary* or *Merriam-Webster's Collegiate Dictionary*, but in cases of doubt they will include notes. Attention, however, will be drawn to places where more than one likely interpretation can be proposed and to significant verbal and syntactic complexity. Notes preceded by * involve discussion of textual variants in readings from the early edition(s) on which the text is based.

Headnotes to acts or scenes discuss, where appropriate, questions of scene location, Shakespeare's handling of his source materials, and major difficulties of staging. The list of roles (so headed to emphasize the play's status for performance) is also considered in commentary notes. These may include comment on plausible patterns of casting with the resources of an Elizabethan or Jacobean acting company, and also on any variation in the description of roles in their speech prefixes in the early editions.

The textual notes are designed to let readers know when the edited text diverges from the early edition(s) on which it is based. Wherever this happens the note will record the rejected reading of the early edition(s), in original spelling, and the source of the reading adopted in this edition. Other forms from the early edition(s) recorded in these notes will include some spellings of particular interest or significance and original forms of translated stage directions. Where two early editions are involved, for instance with *Othello*, the notes will also record all important differences between them. The textual notes take a form that has been in use since the nineteenth century. This comprises, first: line reference, reading adopted in the text and closing

square bracket; then: abbreviated reference, in italic, to the earliest edition to adopt the accepted reading, italic semicolon and noteworthy alternate reading(s), beginning with the rejected original reading, each with abbreviated italic reference to its source.

Conventions used in these textual notes include the following. The solidus / is used, in notes quoting verse or discussing verse lining, to indicate line endings. Distinctive spellings of the basic text (Q or F) follow the square bracket without indication of source and are enclosed in italic brackets. Names enclosed in italic brackets indicate originators of conjectural emendations when these did not originate in an edition of the text. Stage directions (SDs) are referred to by the number of the line within or immediately after which they are placed. Line numbers with a decimal point relate to entry SDs and to SDs more than one line long, with the number after the point indicating the line within the SD: e.g. 78.4 refers to the fourth line of the SD following line 78. Lines of SDs at the start of a scene are numbered 0.1, 0.2, etc. Where only a line number and SD precede the square bracket, e.g. 128 SD], the note relates to the whole of a SD within or immediately following the line. Speech prefixes (SPs) follow similar conventions, 203 SP] referring to the speaker's name for line 203. Where a SP reference takes the form e.g. 38 + SP, it relates to all subsequent speeches assigned to that speaker in the scene in question.

Where, as with *King Henry V*, one of the early editions is a so-called 'bad quarto' (that is, a text either heavily adapted, or reconstructed from memory, or both), the divergences from the present edition are too great to be recorded in full in the notes. In these cases the editions will include a reduced photographic facsimile of the 'bad quarto' in an appendix.

INTRODUCTION

Both the introduction and the commentary are designed to present the plays as texts for performance, and make appropriate

reference to stage, film and television versions, as well as introducing the reader to the range of critical approaches to the plays. They discuss the history of the reception of the texts within the theatre and scholarship and beyond, investigating the interdependency of the literary text and the surrounding 'cultural text' both at the time of the original reproduction of Shakespeare's works and during their long and rich afterlife.

PREFACE

Though cover and title-page of the present volume pay homage
to the title traditionally established by the Folio text of 1623, the
original conception of this play is much more truly expressed by
the form in which it appears on the title-page of the 1602 Quarto
edition and in the entry in the Stationers' Register: *Sir John
Falstaff and the Merry Wives of Windsor*.

This comedy is the last touch added to a figure created by
Shakespeare in the two parts of *Henry IV*. It turns that figure into
an icon; an image; an impression 'from the life of the mind', as
Walter Hodges says of the sketch of the fat knight that he jotted
down in my room in Clare Hall, Cambridge, when he visited me
there in the summer of 1985 to discuss his illustrations for my
edition of the second part of *Henry IV*. Now all those admirable
illustrations for a number of Shakespeare plays are collected in
his splendid volume *Enter the Whole Army* (Cambridge, 1999) but
I remain the proud possessor of that vivid image of Falstaff,
reproduced here for the first time (Fig. 10). It was the constant
presence of that image that encouraged me to undertake an
inquiry into the origins, the nature, the transformations, of the
Falstaff icon, the results of which I set out some nine years later
in my *Shakespeare's Garter Plays*.

My first acknowledgements must be to Walter Hodges, and
to the Presidents, the Fellows and the staff of Clare Hall, who
welcomed me summer after summer for so many years: their
friendliness and interest contributed to create the right atmosphere in which to carry on my work.

By far my greatest debt is to my old friend Richard Proudfoot,
who helped and taught me so much, long before he became the

General Editor of the Arden Third Series and entrusted to me the editing of *Merry Wives*. The time and patience he devoted to this volume, his many suggestions as well as much-needed corrections, together with the stimulating advice and substantial improvements and additions prompted by his fellow General Editor Ann Thompson and Associate General Editor George Walton Williams, make of this edition a collaborative work. For my own part, I claim all those mistakes that their scholarship and friendly care did not manage to make good. It was a privilege to have the extremely competent attention as copy editors, first of Jane Armstrong, and later of Hannah Hyam, and above all the constant, cordial, acute and indulgent support of Nelson's Jessica Hodge, without whose encouragement I should never have got to the end of my task.

Editing a Shakespeare play is an exacting craft, and I had the good fortune to be instructed in it in my previous undertakings by some exceptional teachers and friends as general editors, from Clifford Leech, David Hoeniger, Ernst Honigmann, to Philip Brockbank, and Albert Braunmuller. My gratitude goes to them, and even more to the previous editors of *Merry Wives*. I had no scruples in plundering their scholarly contributions and acute comments, especially in the case of George Hibbard (New Penguin, 1973), H.J. Oliver (New Arden, 1971), and T.W. Craik (Oxford, 1990), although my conviction that the play as it stands cannot have been written before 1599 may occasionally have obscured the extent of my debt to those who have argued for an earlier dating. I wish to acknowledge how substantial are my borrowings from their editions, and at the same time to express my gratitude to Jay Halio, who enabled me to publish my views, in the book I mentioned earlier, on the genesis, background and dating of the Falstaff plays.

Leo Salinger provided invaluable advice over the years, and Doreen Brockbank provided generous hospitality in Stratford, together with affectionate friendship. Patricia Parker's *Shakespeare from the Margins*, which I received from her unexpectedly

in 1996, opened for me new perspectives on this and other plays.

My daughter Miranda helped with the reading of print-outs and proofs, while to Barbara, my other self for many golden years, I owe my still being alive and happy. With her I share the recollection of so many friends and colleagues that have helped us in a variety of ways. Some (perhaps too few) of them are mentioned in the prefaces and dedications of our previous books, especially in the editions of *Sir Thomas More*, *The Second Part of Henry IV* and *Edward III*. But what stands out most in our minds in the present context is the Falstaffian figure of the Italian Shakespeare scholar Gabriele Baldini, translator of the complete works, walking back with us at night from the Rome opera house, in the deserted streets of fifty years ago, singing in his powerful baritone the Verdi arias we had just heard in the theatre.

Finally, I wish to dedicate this book to the memory of another writer, scholar and friend, Nemi D'Agostino, whose last work, or rather labour of love, was a translation of *Merry Wives* into an extraordinary blend of Italian linguistic forms from all ages and parts of the country – a true comedy of (Italian) languages.

Giorgio Melchiori
Università degli Studi Roma Tre
and Clare Hall, Cambridge

INTRODUCTION

This is Falstaff's play. The two entries in the Stationers' Register
(the book where publishers recorded the works they wanted to
copyright) for 18 January 1602 leave no doubt about it; in modern spelling they read: *an excellent and pleasant conceited comedy of
Sir John Falstaff and the Merry Wives of Windsor*.[1] This is confirmed by the title of the first edition published in the same year:
'A Most pleasaunt and excellent conceited Comedie, of Syr *Iohn
Falstaffe*, and the merrie Wiues of *Windsor*.'[2] Though his name
has disappeared from the title of later editions of the play,
Falstaff is firmly established as an archetypal figure in world literature, and this excellent conceited comedy is one of the most
popular plays of Shakespeare on the modern stage: it is hardly
possible to keep track of the numberless productions and adaptations staged every year, not only in the original but in all known
languages. Its appeal to English-speaking audiences consists
mainly in its being Shakespeare's only thoroughly English comedy – apart from the Histories, all his other plays are located in
settings distant in place or time – while foreigners appreciate
what they consider its robust English humour.

Until recently, though, *The Merry Wives of Windsor* did not
meet with the same favour in most critical opinion. Untold damage to it derived from the legend, circulated at the beginning of
the eighteenth century, that Shakespeare wrote it in a fortnight at

[1]   The first entry, to John Busby, spells Falstaff's name *S^r Io. ffaulstof*. This is immediately followed by a transfer from J. Busby to Arthur Johnson, who actually published
the book; in this second entry the name is spelt *Sir Iohn ffaulstafe* (see Greg, *BEPD*,
18 and 298).
[2]   Cf. Knutson, 74: 'The language both of the entry in the Stationers' Register . . . and
of the advertisement on the title page of the quarto (1602) indicates that the play was
to be called *A . . . Comedy of Sir John Falstaff* '.

1

the request of Queen Elizabeth[1]. In fact it can hardly be said that the comedy shows 'Falstaff in love', as the Queen supposedly requested, and crediting this narrative confines the play to the limbo of instant – albeit royal – pot-boilers, an impression confirmed by its being nearly exclusively in prose, apart from some passages of serviceable verse[2]. It was one of such passages, the speech of Mistress Quickly as the Queen of Fairies at 5.5.56–77 – a passage not in the Quarto of 1602, making its first appearance in the Folio of 1623 – celebrating the supreme chivalric Order of England, the Most Noble Order of the Garter, that, while confirming the label of 'occasional play' for *Merry Wives*, suggested that the occasion was of a most exalted kind. The play, as Leslie Hotson first suggested in 1931[3], vigorously supported with a wealth of new arguments by William Green in 1962[4], was conceived and written as a royal entertainment to be performed at the feast held in Westminster Palace on St George's Day, 23 April 1597, to celebrate the election of five new knights (one of them being George Carey, Lord Hunsdon, the patron of Shakespeare's company) to the Order of the Garter.

---

[1] John Dennis, in the dedicatory epistle to his adaptation of the play under the title *The Comical Gallant: or the Amours of Sir John Falstaffe*, published in 1702, wrote that '[t]his comedy was written at [the queen's] command, and by her direction, and she was so eager to see it Acted, that she commanded it to be finished in fourteen days'. In turn, Nicholas Rowe, in the introduction to his edition of Shakespeare in 1709, stated that Queen Elizabeth 'was so well pleased with the admirable character of Falstaff, in the two parts of *Henry IV*, that she commanded [Shakespeare] to continue it for one play more, and to show him in love.'

[2] Only about 12 per cent of *Merry Wives* in the Folio text is in verse, including Pistol's doggerel found here and there in early scenes (1.1 and 1.3, 2.1–2) – by far the lowest percentage of any Shakespeare play. The young courtier Fenton is the only character that speaks consistently in verse in all his appearances (3.4, 4.6, 5.5.208–39) except at 1.4.124–50, while Anne Page and the other Windsor citizens use verse only in his presence. 4.4 and the fairy masque at 5.5.37–102 are the other scenes in verse – possibly based on some kind of earlier court entertainment partly incorporated in the play. The comparative table of percentage distribution of prose in Shakespeare's plays in Vickers, 433, shows that the other plays in which prose prevails, though to a much smaller extent, are *Much Ado About Nothing* (69 per cent), *Twelfth Night* (59 per cent) and *As You Like It* (55 per cent), all written between 1598 and 1601, where prose marks a distinction in the social status of the speakers or between comic and serious scenes.

[3] Leslie Hotson, *Shakespeare versus Shallow* (1931).

[4] William Green, *Shakespeare's Merry Wives of Windsor* (Princeton, N.J., 1962).

Although there is no positive evidence of the nature of the entertainment offered the new knights on the otherwise well-documented Garter Feast of 1597, this notion has found a very wide measure of acceptance, with a few exceptions and a number of provisos, among recent scholars and editors of the play[1]. It is a view that not only affects, among other things, the question of the dating of *Merry Wives* and of the second sequence of Shakespeare's Histories, but obscures some of the subtleties of a play that occupies an isolated position in the Shakespearean canon. If we take it to be the stray offshoot – whether responding to a royal command or to the celebration of a more solemn occasion – from a man who was at the time busy writing the second part of *Henry IV*, then indeed the play is nothing more than a hastily conceived jolly prank to please a court audience that could appreciate certain topical allusions, and a popular audience fond of buffoonery.

THE ENGLISH COMEDY AND THE COMEDY OF ENGLISH

What gets overlooked is the fact that, even granting that Falstaff's play was written at command (either the Queen's or the box office's), its distinguishing feature and supreme merit consists in its being an extraordinary document of Shakespeare's skill in his 'mystery', the job of playwriting.[2] Whatever the

---

[1] It is taken for granted, for instance, in the recent editions by T.W. Craik (Oxford, 1990) and by David Crane (Cambridge, 1997), while the Oxford editors (*TxC*, 1987, 120) and the Norton Shakespeare (1997) suggest a date 1597–8, and so does Knutson (64–5), who maintains that '[n]ow, with the assignment of *The Merry Wives of Windsor* to the repertory of 1597–98, we see that the Chamberlain's men acquired a play with humorous characters within six months of the show at the Rose [of *The Comedy of Humours* (presumably Chapman's *An Humorous Day's Mirth*) in May–June 1597,]'. Riverside, 2nd edn (1997), 82, dates the play '1597 (revised c.1600–1)'. The most cogent and convincing rejection of 1597 as the date of the play is Elizabeth Schafer, 'The date of *The Merry Wives of Windsor*', *N&Q*, 236 (1991), 57–60. For a fuller discussion of the dating and destination of the play see the section 'Garter comedy: date, occasion and Falstaff's metamorphoses' below.

[2] In her memorable Clark Lecture of 1968 Muriel Bradbrook considers *Merry Wives* 'an example of craftsman's theatre . . . one of the most thoroughly professional jobs in the English theatre'.

occasion that suggested it, Shakespeare made *Merry Wives* into a joyous exploration of the main tool of his trade, i.e. the English language, or rather language as such. The pleasant conceited comedy of Sir John Falstaff and the merry wives of Windsor is the culmination of Shakespeare's experiment with English as a living organism subject to infinite individual variations. The consciousness of the instability of language would come naturally to a man of the theatre like Shakespeare, supremely aware of the instability of the texts he provided for his fellow players, in the knowledge that no two performances would be identical, subject as they were to the daily changes in the acting conditions, according to the varying times, places and dispositions of actors and audiences. A marked differentiation in the languages of the people appearing in the plays emerges in the late Histories, where characterization is based on the linguistic peculiarities of persons belonging to different social strata or of different ethnic origin. In the earlier plays the language vagaries of the clowns or the servants, including the Nurse in *Romeo and Juliet*, respond to current comic conventions, while as late as in the First Part of *Henry IV* (1596) Bardolph is characterized not by his language but by the redness of his complexion, and Hostess Quickly (here a married woman) is content to stick to her interjection 'O Jeshu' without any of her extraordinary malapropisms. In *Henry V* and still more in *Merry Wives* language manipulation takes a different turn.

The manipulation of language serves a double purpose. At the level of linguistic differentiation, *Merry Wives* is a unique example of representation of a cross-section of contemporary English social structures: as Walter Cohen puts it, the play creates 'the impression of life in an English provincial town as it is being lived at the moment of the play's first performance'; it 'retains a contemporary, domestic, and nonaristocratic feel unique in Shakespearean drama'.[1] Its uniqueness, i.e. the fact of being

---

[1] Norton, 1225. For similar approaches to the social implications of the play in the course of discussions of the origins of the Quarto and Folio texts see Siegel (1986), Marcus, 'Levelling' (1991) and Kinney (1993).

Shakespeare's one and only 'English comedy'[1] – though large sections of the plot and action derive from obvious Italian models – as well as his only 'comedy of humours',[2] is achieved through a subtle gradation of linguistic distinctions in a play where verse is used only in a very few scenes and individual nuances of social rank are established by the grammatical and syntactical usages of English by each speaker. In some of them, such as Shallow and Slender, the Host of the Garter, the servants Simple and Rugby, the linguistic peculiarities border on deliberate mannerisms, which make of them humorous figures – the whole comedy insists on the interplay between the natural speech conditioned by each character's social status and the verbal quirks that tend to transform them into 'humours'. It is this interplay that makes of *Merry Wives* a satire of the conventions of the 'comedy of humours', even apart from Nim's repeated tag line 'the humour of it'.

In fact *Merry Wives* is not so much an 'English comedy' as 'the Comedy of English', or rather 'the Comedy of Language'.

THE COMEDY OF LANGUAGE(S) AND THE LATIN LESSON

At the level of linguistic experimentation, the manipulation of language places *Merry Wives* side by side with *Love's Labour's Lost*: the latter is the most consistent and successful Shakespearean exploration of the language of rhetoric in all its aspects, while Falstaff's play is the most thorough exploitation of the potentialities of the English language in all its nuances.[3] *Merry Wives*, while on the one hand reviving and carrying to new

---

[1] The most comprehensive treatment of the Englishness of the play is Jeanne Addison Roberts, *Shakespeare's English Comedy:* The Merry Wives of Windsor *in Context* (Lincoln, Nebr., 1979). For a more specific contextualization see Leggatt, 146–9.

[2] See the section 'Translating: Italian into English – Falstaff's ancestry and the comedy of humours' below.

[3] Vickers, 142, sees *Merry Wives*, with its 'anthology of linguistic oddities', as 'an obvious development from the exuberance of *Love's Labour's Lost* with its fantastics . . . we must concede that [*Merry Wives*] shows a virtuoso control of styles'. Cf. Salmon for a thorough study of the language of Falstaff's plays.

extremes Falstaff's richly articulated verbal inventions in the two parts of *Henry IV*, plays on the whole gamut of linguistic variations peculiar to the characters of previous plays: from the bombastic language of Pistol and Mistress Quickly's involuntary equivocations (see *2 Henry IV* and *Henry V*) to Nim's verbal tags (*Henry V*), from Parson Evans's Welsh accent to Doctor Caius's Frenchified English (compare, respectively, Fluellen and the French characters in *Henry V*). In fact, *Henry V* is already, in a way, a comedy of languages: the meeting of the four captains (3.2), an Englishman, a Welshman, an Irishman, and a Scot, characterized by their accents, under the walls of Harfleur, marks the merging of separate nationalities in a common cause under British leadership, in preparation for the overcoming of linguistic and political barriers in the union of Henry and Katherine of France, anticipated by the English lesson imparted to Katherine by a French gentlewoman (3.4). While in the history play the comedy of languages is functional to the mood of celebration of a 'charismatic leader who . . . forges the martial national state',[1] in *Merry Wives* it becomes the central motif of the play, as revealed by what could be called its pivot scene, 4.1, Evans's Latin lesson to the boy William Page, interspersed with the grotesque misconstructions and salacious equivocations of Mistress Quickly – a scene absent from the earlier versions of the play and irrelevant to the development of the action, but providing the essential clue to its inner meaning, in the same way as *Titus Andronicus* 3.3, where the killing of a fly reveals the nature of the villain Aaron the Moor; *2 Henry IV* 3.1, the night musings of a sick king (both scenes missing from the first issues of the respective plays); or *Hamlet* 4.4.9ff., the hero's last soliloquy; and *King Lear* 3.6.17– 55, the mock arraignment of Goneril and Regan, passages suppressed in the final 1623 Folio versions. All these scenes and passages are expendable from the point of view of

---

[1] See Stephen Greenblatt's 'Invisible Bullets: Renaissance Authority and Its Subversion, *Henry IV* and *Henry V*', first in *Political Shakespeare*, ed. John Dollimore and Alan Sinfield (Manchester, 1985), 18–47, then in his *Shakespearean Negotiations* (Oxford, 1988), 21–65.

theatrical narrative, but they have a pivotal fuction at the level of the ideological structures of the plays in which they appear.[1] The Latin lesson in *Merry Wives*, though apparently patterned on the English lesson in *Henry V*, and undoubtedly 'intended for an educated audience'[2] who had some knowledge of Latin, carries much more complex implications because of the very fact of playing not on a living language but on the 'father language' surviving as a set of rules in a school grammar.[3] The word-play, mostly with marked sexual innuendos, on the terminology of grammar and on (mis)translation is by no means limited to this scene, but runs through the play like a hidden linguistic thread that links together all or most of the characters. The most obvious example is when Falstaff says to Pistol of Mistress Ford:

> I can *construe* the action of her *familiar style*, and
> the hardest voice of her behaviour – to be *Englished*
> rightly – is: 'I am Sir John Falstaff's'.

PISTOL   He hath *studied* her well, and *translated* her will –
out of honesty into English.

$$(1.3.42–7)^4$$

Again, Ford disguised as Brook tells Falstaff, referring to Mistress Ford, that 'there is shrewd *construction* made of her' (2.2.212–13), and speaking of himself he fears that he will 'stand under the adoption of abominable *terms*' (2.2.279–80).[5] In no other Shakespearean play does the word 'English' with reference

---

[1] See Melchiori, 'Pivot', 154–9, where I mistakenly consider *Merry Wives* 4.1 as a 'decorative' dramatic insertion in respect of the pivot scenes in *Titus, 2 Henry IV, Hamlet* and *Lear*.

[2] H.J. Oliver in Ard², 102.nn

[3] The grammatical and lexical expressions used in the scene are based on William Lilly's and John Colet's *A Shorte Introduction of Grammar . . . for the bryngynge vp of all those that entende to atteyne the knowledge of the Latine tongue* (1549, frequently reprinted) that Edward VI commanded to be used in all schools. See T.W. Baldwin, *Shakespeare's Small Latine and Lesse Greeke* (Urbana, Ill., 1944), 1. 557–68.

[4] Italics in this and the following quotations are mine.

[5] For an extremely perceptive study of the relevance of the 'Latin lesson' to an understanding of the network of wordplay in *Merry Wives* and its social, sexual and gender implications, see Parker, 116–48: '"Illegitimate construction": translation, adultery, and mechanical reproduction in *The Merry Wives of Windsor*'.

7

to the language and its misuse appear so frequently. Actually it is Mistress Quickly, herself an arch-equivocator and manipulator of language with a 'genius for unintended and unperceived obscenities',[1] who first calls attentions to the abuses of the English tongue by saying of Doctor Caius:

> here will be an old *abusing of* God's patience and *the King's English*.
>
> (1.4.4–5)

Page comments on Nim's verbal tic, 'the humour of it':

> Here's a fellow frights *English* out of his wits.
>
> (2.1.124–5)

The Host of the Garter, who takes pride in his rhetorical gifts and in his skill in preventing the duel between Parson Evans and Doctor Caius, says of them:

> Let them keep their limbs whole and *hack our English*.
>
> (3.1.70–1)

And in order to be reassured about the German gentlemen who wish to hire his horses he asks 'they speak English?' (4.3.6). In the end Ford, cured of his jealousy, cracks a joke with Parson Evans:

> I will never mistrust my wife again, till thou art able to woo her *in good English*.
>
> (5.5.132–3)

And finally Falstaff resents the Welsh Parson's jokes at his defeat:

> Have I lived to stand at the taunts of one that makes *fritters of English*?
>
> (5.5.141–2)

Though the linguistic vagaries of such characters as Doctor Caius and Parson Evans are emphasised also in the version of the play preserved in the Quarto edition of 1602, no such attention is drawn there to the misuses and abuses of English. For instance, Falstaff's last comment quoted appears in the Quarto (sig. G3v) as

---

[1] Gary Taylor, (ed.), *Henry V* (Oxford, 1982), 63.

'haue I liued to these yeares / To be gulled now, now to be ridden?', and Page does not say that Nim frights *English* out of his wits, but 'Heres a fellow frites humor out of his wits' (Quarto, sig. C1r).[1]

TRANSLATING: ITALIAN INTO ENGLISH – FALSTAFF'S ANCESTRY AND THE COMEDY OF HUMOURS

The much shorter version of the play preserved in the 1602 Quarto, by omitting the Latin lesson and most of the references to the manipulation of language, seems much more concerned with the presentation of 'sundry variable and pleasing humours' (as promised by its title page) than with the uses of language as the basic tool of Shakespeare's trade. The nature of the Quarto will be discussed in a later section, but this reduced attention to the linguistic factor should be taken in connection with another feature of the Quarto: as compared with the Folio, it is much less specific in pointing out the precise Windsor locale and its implications in the matter of class distinctions. The absence from it not only of the speech celebrating the Order of the Garter (5.5.57–74) but also of most references to the court scattered through the Folio text justify an acute scholar like Leah Marcus in asking the question 'Windsor or Elsewhere?'[2] and in drawing the conclusion:

---

[1] Most of the other passages quoted have no counterpart in the 1602 Quarto, except in the case of the exchange between Falstaff and Pistol at 1.3.42–7, but the omission in it (sig. B2r) of the mention of 'translation' renders it nonsensical: 'And euery part to be construed rightly is, I am / Syr *Iohn Falstaffes. / Pis.* He hath studied her well, out of honestie into English'; the Host of the Garter's remark about the prevented duel between Caius and Evans figures verbatim in the Quarto (sig. D3r: 'Let them keep their limbs hole, and hack our English') but is assigned to Shallow.

Further discussion of linguistic self-consciousness and the manipulation of language will be found throughout the commentary notes but especially at the following points: errors in Latin: 1.1.5–8, 1.1.113, 1.1.151 and 166, 4.1 *passim*; Welsh pronunciation: 1.1.16–17, 1.1.42–55, 3.1.63 and 70–1, 5.5.142; French pronunciation: 1.4.40ff, 1.4.101 and 110, 3.1.70–1 and 89, 3.3.220; archaic language: 1.3.19, 1.3.91, 2.3.67; specialist legal terminology: 1.1.34–5, 2.1.195; specialist fencing terminology: 2.3.21–4; linguistic affectation: 1.3.53–4, 2.1.116–23 and 127, 3.3.56–7; 'Quicklyisms' and other mistakings of words: 1.1.231–5, 1.4.139, 142 and 148–9. 2.2.39 and 58, 3.5.38, 4.5.42; sexual innuendo: 1.1.207, 1.4.75–6, 2.1.69, 4.2.133–4, 5.5.18; disappearance of accents: 5.5.37SP, 5.5.49, 5.5.128–9, 131.

[2] Marcus, *Unediting*, 84–8.

9

> The folio version of *Merry Wives* is a comedy of small-town and rural life, steeped in rustic customs and topography but also imbued with the "high" presence of the royal court; the quarto version is "lower", more urban, closer to the pattern of city and "citizen" comedy.[1]

In other words, the Windsor of the Quarto *Merry Wives* resembles London or any other town, the normal setting for a story of middle-class life whether in England or elsewhere. And in fact its main plot-line, like that of many citizen and 'romantic' comedies, is akin to that on which most continental and especially Italian story-telling is based, so as to justify the adjective 'Italianate' in respect of the background of the play.[2]

The question of the relationship between the Quarto and Folio versions of the play will be examined in a later section. What should be noted now is that the *'pleasant conceited comedy of Sir John Falstaff and the Merry Wives of Windsor'* is a multiple-plot play. There is first of all Falstaff himself, a character already familiar to English audiences who would expect to see him surrounded by his usual retinue of 'Irregular Humorists':[3] fiery complexioned Bardolph from *1 Henry IV*, swaggering Pistol and the page boy from *2 Henry IV*, and Corporal Nim from *Henry V*. Significantly they disappear after the second or third act of the comedy[4] and are not integrated in a consistent plot. Only Bardolph, no longer as Falstaff's follower but as a drawer in the Garter Inn, is involved later in the subsidiary plot of the horse-

---

[1] Marcus, *Unediting*, 88. See also Leggatt, *passim*, and cf. Slights, 152–70, pointing out the pastoral element in *Merry Wives*, within the context of Shakespeare's later comedies.

[2] See Campbell, 'Italianate' (1932). Cf. Bradbrook (1979), 85–6. Fleissner (1978) discusses in detail the problem of the sources of *Merry Wives* and finds the closest analogy in a novella in Boccaccio's *Decameron*. Miola (1993), 373, maintains that *Merry Wives* 'presents an Italianate appropriation of [Latin] New Comedic characters', especially from Plautus' *Casina*.

[3] The definition is from the list of 'Actors' names' appended to the text of the Second Part of *Henry IV* in the 1623 Folio.

[4] Only in the Folio version does Pistol improbably reappear in Act 5, rather incongruously impersonating Hobgoblin in the fairy masque.

stealing from the Host (4.3 and 4.5). Other characters who had figured in Shakespeare's Histories fit more precisely both the real main plot suggested by the title of the play (Falstaff and the merry wives), and its subplot, the Anne Page/Fenton love story: in both plot and subplot fairly substantial parts are played by Mistress Quickly – who shares the linguistic peculiarities of her previous Hostess-self, but has changed her basic role – and by Justice Shallow, unaccountably transplanted to Windsor from his Gloucestershire domain in *2 Henry IV*. And surely the Welshman Captain Fluellen and the pompous French characters of *Henry V* live again in the humours of the Welsh Parson Evans[1] and the French court-doctor Caius, for whom, beside their participation in main- and subplot, Shakespeare has devised the mock duel (2.3/3.1) as a further sideshow[2].

The characters originating in previous plays and engaged in secondary actions (the Caius/Evans mock duel, the horse-stealing episode) are in fact the 'humours' that the author presents as a deliberate take-off of the latest theatrical fashion, the comedy of humours[3]. These subsidiary episodes share with the

[1] The role of Fluellen was apparently created for Robert Armin, when in 1599 he replaced Will Kemp as the company's clown: Armin, as his own play *The Two Maids of More- Clacke* shows (see A.S. Liddie's introduction to his critical edition of that play, New York, 1979), specialized in the role of the comic Welshman. See Melchiori, 'Which Falstaff', 98–9, and *Garter*, 71–2 and 93, n. 2. This tends to confirm that the date of *Merry Wives* cannot be earlier than 1599.

[2] According to plot logic Caius should have challenged Slender, his rival in Anne Page's love, instead of Evans. Bradbrook, 81, observes that Shakespeare might have heard from his future son-in-law John Hall, a Cambridge graduate, that Dr John Caius, the third founder of Caius College, 'had such an antipathy to Welshmen that he forbade their admission to his foundation'. Cf. Cam[1], xxxiii. I suspect Shakespeare's choice of duellists was suggested by the comic possibilities offered by the linguistic Welsh/French confrontation, as a compensation for an opportunity missed in *Henry V*, where the Welshman Fluellen never comes face to face with the French.

[3] Dover Wilson, Cam[1], xxxi–xxxii, suggests that the character of Nim was devised to ridicule Ben Jonson. *Merry Wives* is treated as a humour comedy by Knutson (see note 1 on p. 3) and Tiffany, 'False Staff', 254ff.; but compare 'Fie on sinful fantasy: *The Merry Wives of Windsor* and *Every Man in His Humour*', in McDonald, 31–55, which deliberately does not discuss the theory of humours, but considers Jonson's comedy to place 'less emphasis on the story, more on peculiarities of character' than those that preceded it (31), and Shakespeare's play as a 'brief detour from the path of romantic comedy' (55).

main plot and subplot the central theme of the play, i.e. the hoax, the trick played at the expense of people who in their turn think they are cozening other persons. In fact 'cozen' and its derivates (cozenage, cozener, etc.) occur ten times in *Merry Wives*, more often by far than in any other Shakespearean play. The Host deceives Doctor Caius and Parson Evans by appointing different places for their duel, but is in turn deceived by the thieves disguised as 'Germans' who steal his horses. In the love subplot, while Master Page and Mistress Page think of deceiving each other by manipulating Anne's disguise in the fairy masque so as to have her 'stolen' either by Slender (Page's choice) or by Caius (her mother's favourite), they are both deceived by the young lovers, who get married with the help of the Host - a typical example of 'the deceits in love', an expression that occurs on the title pages of many plays, beginning with one published in 1585:

> Fedele and Fortunio. The deceites in Loue: excellently discoursed in a very pleasant and fine conceited Comoedie, of two Italian Gentlemen.

The hoax theme, implying both deceit and disguise, is the dominant feature of the main plot, culminating in the exposure of Falstaff in the emblematic disguise[1] as a buck at Herne's oak in 5.5, anticipated by his two previous experiences in the buck-basket in 3.3 and under the guise of the 'witch of Brentford' in 4.2. Ford in turn deceives Falstaff by appearing to him disguised as Master Brook, but is subjected to the 'honest deceit' ('Wives may be merry and yet honest too' – 4.2.100) intended to cure him of his jealousy, that is to say to translate him out of the stock

---

[1] Steadman connects Falstaff with Actaeon the mythical hunter who was transformed into a stag for spying on Diana's nymphs bathing, and was killed by his own hounds – a myth mentioned twice in *Merry Wives*, by Pistol with reference to Ford at 2.1.106 and by Ford with reference to Page at 3.2.39, in both cases alluding to the stag's horns as emblematic of cuckoldry. Roberts (*Context*, 76) sees Falstaff's disguise as representing a scapegoat for his threat to the social and sexual order and his dis-horning as a symbolic castration, an interpretation upheld by Cotton. Cf. Freedman, 'Punishment', and Hinely.

'humour' of the jealous husband into a sensible and sensitive human being.

While stories of lovers who deceive their parents in order to avoid the miseries of enforced marriage (see 5.5.223–4) are so traditional that it would be idle to suggest a specific novel or play as the inspiration of the Anne/Fenton subplot, source-hunters have been asking for a long time where Shakespeare could have found the major situations on which to construct the main plot of his play, particularly the lover or would-be lover who keeps a husband informed of his love-exploits, unaware that his mistress is the man's wife, or the ways he avoids detection when surprised by the husband in the mistress's house. Parallels have been found with stories in English collections: 'Of Two Brethren and their Wives', in Barnaby Riche's *Riche his Farewell to the Militarie Profession* (1581), where a wife gets rid of two lovers by persuading a third to beat them soundly, and then returns to the love of her husband, who is all unaware of her misbehaviour; or 'The Tale of the two Lovers of Pisa' in *Tarltons Newes out of Purgatorie* (1590), where Tarlton, transferring the action from Padua to Pisa and changing the names of the characters, adapts a novella from Gianfrancesco Straparola's *Le piacevoli notti*, in which a young student informs his teacher of his love for a woman without realizing that she is the teacher's wife; the teacher becomes suspicious, but the student, after avoiding being caught with her three times, induces the woman to run away with him, and the foolish old doctor, not finding her at home, dies of despair.[1] But the one really close analogue is not

---

[1] For a discussion of these sources and their texts as well as a translation of the novella from *Il pecorone* see Bullough, 2: 3–58. Cf. Oliver, introduction to Ard², lviii–lxv. The theory according to which *Merry Wives* might have been based on the lost *Jealous Comedy* entered in Henslowe's *Diary* as performed on 5 January 1593 (see Campbell, 'Italianate', 84ff.) is firmly rejected by Bullough (2: 5), and the same treatment has been reserved for Nosworthy's notion (*Occasional Plays*) that Shakespeare's play was modelled on Porter's *The Two Merry Women of Abingdon*, a merely hypothetical companion piece to his *The Two Angry Women of Abingdon*. See Bradbrook, 95: 'I do not think that he took an old play, whether the lost "Jealous Comedy" or the much more unlikely *Two Merry Women of Abingdon*, and rewrote it.' More convincingly, Gurr, 197–200, noting thematic and other affinities between *The Two Angry Women* and *Merry Wives*,

an English (or 'Englished') story but an Italian one. It is the second novella of the second 'day' of the collection *Il pecorone* by Ser Giovanni Fiorentino, a book not translated into English but certainly known to Shakespeare, who had borrowed from the first story of its fourth 'day' all the main situations and the plot-line of *The Merchant of Venice*. The second novella of the second day is once again a story combining the themes of a student who unwittingly deceives his master and of a young wife deceiving her old husband; as the title announces, it deals with Bucciolo, a student in Bologna, and 'how he asked his master to teach him the art of loving, and how he profited by it'. As soon as Bucciolo receives his first assignation from a young woman whom he does not know to be his master's wife, he reports it to his teacher, who becomes suspicious and follows him to the appointed house. He knocks at his own door as soon as the young man is inside, but the woman hides Bucciolo under a pile of washing, where the master in his search of the house does not think of looking for him. The master goes back to the school, while Bucciolo enjoys his wife, and the next morning the young scholar reports to him what has happened and informs him of his next assignation in the evening. This time the woman manages to let her lover out while her furious husband is breaking into the house, and when relatives and neighbours turn up at the fracas and find the master, sword in hand, cutting up a pile of washing, they think he has gone mad and put him in chains. Only the next morning, visiting the supposed madman with his fellow students, does Bucciolo realise that his lover was his master's wife and, pitying him, leaves Bologna for good with the comment 'I have learnt so much that I don't need any more schooling'. What is notable is that in transferring a plot with so many details in common from an Italian to an English setting Shakespeare has omitted the central point of the hoax, adultery: for all the talk of 'horns' in

places Porter's play, for the 'second part' of which the author received payments from Henslowe in December 1598 and February 1599, in the context of the rivalry between the parallel repertories of the Admiral's Men and Chamberlain's Men. This prompted a rejoinder by Roslyn L. Knutson, and Gurr's reply, in *SQ*, 39 (1988), 391–8.

Merry Wives there is no consummation. The roles of husband and lover in the play are reversed: not only is the husband not cuckolded (though he is subjected to a certain amount of deception in order to be cured of his jealousy), but he is also considerably younger than the would-be lover, who is the real butt of the tricks played upon him. Furthermore, the wife is no young thing married against her will, but a happily married matron, no longer 'in the holiday-time of [her] beauty'.[1] Though Falstaff, in 'construing' Mistress Ford's 'familiar style', is deluded into 'Englishing' it as evidence of her love for him, Pistol's already quoted comment 'He . . . translated her will – out of honesty into English' (1.3.46–7)[2] should be reversed. In fact Shakespeare translated the plot of Ser Giovanni Fiorentino's novella out of Italian into honesty.

Shakespeare, confronted with the task of writing, presumably at short notice, either an entertainment in honour of the Queen and of the Order of the Garter or a full-fledged comedy on the character of Falstaff, looked for the basic plot to those Italian models that, as Leo Salingar has convincingly demonstrated,[3] conditioned the writing of his comedies from the early 1590s to at least 1601, not only through borrowed plots and situations but also in dramaturgic technique. Salingar actually singles out *Merry Wives* to illustrate the strength of the Italian influence in the one play that, because of its firm location in Windsor, seems least amenable to it.[4] In fact the model in theatrical terms for

---

[1] See Bradbrook, 86: 'The Italian works, and many of the English comedies derived from them with likenesses to Shakespeare shew one startling difference – All are tales of *youthful* and *successful* adultery. None has more than one heroine; the cornuto may be an ancient professor, and the successful intruder one of his own undergraduates. This is the sort of comedy Falstaff imagines himself to be part of, with his scornful description of 'the peaking cornuto, her husband', and his own assumption of youthful energy.'

[2] For further sexual and social implications of the phrase see Parker, 143–7, 'Out of Honesty into English: Ingles, Angles, Englishmen'.

[3] 'Shakespeare and Italian comedy', Salingar, *Traditions*, 175–242. Cf. Louise George Clubb, *Italian Drama in Shakespeare's Time* (New Haven, CT., 1989).

[4] Salingar, *Traditions*, 228–38. In a later paper Salingar vindicates 'The Englishness of *The Merry Wives of Windsor*' through a revealing analysis of the play's language and by reference to ancient folk rituals and customs, echoed in Shakespeare's invention of the Herne the Hunter legend. I am grateful to Dr Salingar for his as yet unpublished paper.

Shakespeare's comedies that are now called 'romantic', from *The Two Gentlemen of Verona* to *Twelfth Night*, is Italian, but it undergoes a peculiar process of transformation. The earliest such model of a 'very pleasant and fine conceited comedy', going back to 1585, is the one mentioned before, bearing three alternative titles: 'Fedele and Fortunio', 'The deceits in Love', or 'The Two Italian Gentlemen'. It is an early work in elaborate verse by that extremely versatile writer, Anthony Munday,[1] meant for presentation to a literate court audience. In fact, after giving the title(s) of the comedy, the title-page advertisement goes on:

> Translated out of Italian, and set downe according
> as it hath beene presented before the Queenes
> moste excellent Maiestie.[2]

It purports therefore to be the English translation of an Italian '*commedia erudita*', *Il Fedele*, by the Venetian nobleman Alvise (or Luigi) Pasquàligo, first published in 1576. *Commedia erudita* was an elitist dramatic genre practised by eminent men of letters, fusing together classical allusions, stylistic refinements and for good measure unrestrained bawdiness. In fact *Il Fedele* is a story of rampant conjugal unfaithfulness in which Vittoria, a married woman (her husband has the emblematic name of Cornelio, alluding to his 'horns'), freely dispenses her favours alternately to her lovers Fedele and Fortunio and, when one of them threatens to reveal the situation to her husband, tries to have the lover killed by a boasting and ineffectual henchman whom she chooses as her third lover. The plan fails and she is reconciled with the 'unfaithful' lover when he manages to hoodwink her husband into believing in her married chastity. The whole is

---

[1] He was not only a brilliant playwright, but also novelist, pamphleteer, historian, translator of voluminous French romances, deviser of pageants for the London City Guilds, and government informer against Roman Catholics. See Celeste Turner, *Anthony Munday: Elizabethan Man of Letters*, University of California Publications in English, vol. 2, no. 1 (1928).

[2] Quotations and references to the play-text are from *Anthony Munday*, Fedele and Fortunio *1585: A Critical Edition* by Richard Hosley (New York, 1981).

seasoned with the sexual intrigues and menial loves of a number of other characters and lengthy tirades by a pedant on female promiscuity.

Munday's so-called translation is nothing of the sort: in the very pleasant and fine conceited comedy presented before the Queen's most excellent Majesty, Victoria is no promiscuous married woman but a maid uncertain in her choice between two suitors, and, after a number of equivocations, the story ends in no fewer than four happy marriages. In the process of moral cleansing of the bawdy Italian *commedia erudita* Munday created the first model of the genre of romantic comedy that Shakespeare so successfully practised in the 1590s – Munday in fact translated bawdy Italian into honest English. As well as a reorientation of the plot of *Il Fedele*, the 'translation' entailed a drastic reduction of the main acting roles. But the rule did not apply in at least one case: the small part of the henchman Frangipietra, rough in behaviour and language, sketchily presented by Pasqualigo in terms of *commedia dell'arte* rather than *commedia erudita* as the would-be hired assassin exposed for cheating and failing in his undertaking, became in Munday's play the second longest role. While all the other characters in *Fedele and Fortunio, or the Two Italian Gentlemen* retained their original Italian names, the disreputable braggart Frangipietra was translated into English as Captain Crackstone, a fully rounded character with his boasts, his arguments about honour, his devices used when caught red-handed, his high-sounding language, his new word coinages that anticipate the attitudes and the eloquence of the Falstaff of the Histories. He is no Italian *bravo* but, as he himself reveals, a dishonest army sutler who by his cheats and heroic boasts has usurped the title of captain. As I have suggested elsewhere,[1] Crackstone is Falstaff's closest ancestor. That *Fedele and Fortunio, or the Two Italian Gentlemen* was known to Shakespeare is proved by the thematic affinities

[1] Melchiori, *Garter*, 86–91.

between that play and *The Two Gentlemen of Verona*;[1] by compounding the *maschera* (it could be called 'humour' in English) of the Italian *bravo* with the Morality Vice and the Lord of Misrule of the native English tradition, Shakespeare did not 'translate' this compound figure into one of his romantic Italianate comedies, but promoted it to the role of leading character in two of his *English* Histories, the two parts of *Henry IV*. How Sir John Falstaff acquired his name and his Windsor setting will be discussed in the next section of this introduction.

GARTER COMEDY: DATE, OCCASION AND FALSTAFF'S METAMORPHOSES

It is clear, in view of the celebration of the Order of the Garter in the last scene of the Folio version, that, as Peter Erickson has argued,[2] *The Merry Wives of Windsor* can be considered a 'Garter play'. In fact the speech of the 'Fairy Queen' and its context, by quoting the motto of the Order, underlines one particular aspect of it: not the martial prowess expected of the knights, but their leading a virtuous public and private life – which is exactly what Falstaff does not do. The play could be taken as the comic counterpart of the military enterprises celebrated in the Histories – in other words as the comic jig that concluded all theatrical shows, whether tragic or comic.[3] The choice of the Garter as the name of the inn where Falstaff lodges is the crowning touch. But it should be noted that, though that name and the character of the Host of the Garter are also present in the Quarto version of the play, any other reference to the chivalric Order is absent from that text.

Attention to the problem of the mutual relationship between the Quarto and the Folio texts of *Merry Wives* has been to a

---

[1] Pointed out by Salingar, *Traditions*, 232. The affinities between Frangipietra (the original of Crackstone) and Falstaff are discussed in Daniel C. Boughner, *The Braggart in Renaissance Comedy: A Study in Comparative Drama from Aristophanes to Shakespeare* (Minneapolis, 1954), 88.

[2] Erickson, *passim*.

[3] See Melchiori, *Garter*, 132: 'The Garter Jig'.

certain extent diverted by what, at first sight, might appear to be a genetic approach to the play, since the first question all critics addresses is that of the dating of the play in respect of the other Histories where Falstaff appears, or rather of its origin as an entertainment offered on the occasion of the Garter Feast at Westminster on 23 April 1597. As already noted, the case was put so ably by William Green in 1962, after it was first broached by Leslie Hotson in 1931,[1] that most later editors accepted this explanation of the genesis of the play, with the notable exception of George Hibbard;[2] the Oxford editors[3] had some reservations not against the basic theory but against the exact date, which they moved to a year later. It is only by following a more comprehensive genetic approach that takes into consideration current practices relating not only to how plays were devised and grew by degrees through a work of collaboration, but also to how they were conditioned by their destination (for the court or for private or public theatres) that we can see how radically a play intended for the public stage differs from a court entertainment for a special occasion. It will be clear then that the comedy of Sir John Falstaff and the merry wives of Windsor could not possibly be the entertainment offered on the night of 23 April 1597 to the Queen and the old and new knights of the Garter. If such an entertainment ever existed (there is no documentary proof of the fact), it must have been a much shorter, masque-like affair, which was later partly incorporated in a full-blown comedy hastily devised by Shakespeare (whether commissioned by the Queen or by his fellow players for merely commercial reasons)

---

[1] See notes 3,4 on p.2 and 1 on p. 3. Curiously, all recent scholars accept the unproven proposition that the Westminster entertainment was a full-blown comedy.

[2] Hibbard; see especially the introduction, 49–50, quoted later in this section.

[3] *TxC*, 120. 'Queen Elizabeth's request for a play on Falstaff in love could have been made in anticipation of a later performance that Whitehall season (on 26 February 1598) . . . *Merry Wives* could . . . have recollected rather than anticipated, the Garter ceremonies of spring 1597.' Freedman, 'Chronology', after attacking and effectively demolishing with a wealth of carefully researched documentation the notion of the April 1597 performance at Westminster, finds that 'the most convincing argument to date is Gary Taylor's theory [in *TxC*] for a February 1598 date of composition and performance' (207).

some years later, when he had had time to present on the stage such entertaining characters as Justice Shallow and Pistol (in *2 Henry IV* – 1598) and Corporal Nim (in *Henry V* – 1599), that is to say not before late 1599 or 1600.[1]

The notion of 1597 as the date of the comedy, in spite of the fact that *Merry Wives* is not mentioned in the list of Shakespeare's plays provided in 1598 by Francis Meres in his *Palladis Tamia*, found acceptance because it seemed illogical to place it in the sequence of composition of the Falstaff plays after *Henry V*, where his death is announced. In fact it seems more reasonable to think that it was written to compensate for that death, which betrayed the promise made in the Epilogue of the Second Part of *Henry IV* to 'continue the story with Sir John in it'.[2] Having to 'revive' at the Queen's or the public's request such a popular hero after having 'killed him off' in the last of his Histories, Shakespeare had to devise a time for the action of the play which would fit with Falstaff's rejection at the end of *2 Henry IV*, where the king had enjoined him and his companions 'Not to come near our person by ten miles', but had immediately added 'competence of life I will allow you, / That lack of means enforce you not to evils' (*2H4*, 5.5.61–3). What other 'competence of life' could be offered a discredited and impecunious

---

[1] Schafer, 60, rejecting the 1597 dating which 'seems to have become orthodoxy because it has been repeated so many times', does not suggest alternative dates, except before publication of the Quarto in 1602. Even if Roy F. Montgomery were right in taking Ford's mention at 2.2.205-7 of 'a fair house built on another man's ground' as an allusion not to a current proverb but to the fact that James Burbage had built the Theatre on land leased from Giles Allen, who claimed it back when the lease expired in 1597 (see *SQ*, 5 (1954), 207–8), it would not help to date the play. At the end of 1598 James's son, Cuthbert Burbage, had the playhouse, which he considered his property, pulled down and the timber carried to another site on which the Globe was built the next year. Giles brought an action against Burbage, but lost it in 1600. The thought of the playhouse built (and pulled down) on another's land was a concern of Shakespeare's, as a full sharer in Burbage's company, throughout the litigation, from 1597 to 1600. Gurr, 198, maintains that Ford's words 'reflect Shakespeare's company's problem over the Theatre in the winter of 1596', but adds: 'It was a crisis the company had lived with for nearly three years by 1599 when the Globe plan was hatched'.

[2] It is tempting to surmise, accepting the legend about the play's origin reported by Rowe (note 1, p. 2), that the Queen's command 'to continue it [Falstaff's story] for one play more, and to show him in love' was caused by her disappointment that the promise made in *2 Henry IV* had not been kept in *Henry V*.

knight except a Crown pension and a place among those who were popularly known as the poor knights of Windsor? They were in fact retired soldiers who had to reside in Windsor, attending church twice a day, kept by a small pension and a clothing allowance. The status of Falstaff in Windsor as a 'poor knight' is never openly mentioned but is implicit in his financial distress and in what is said of him by the other characters, and would be immediately recognized by a contemporary audience.[1] The sequence of composition must be distinguished from the sequence of narrative or 'historical' action of the Falstaff plays: in the chronology of 'history' *Merry Wives* takes place between the action of the Second Part of *Henry IV* and that of *Henry V*. But Shakespeare could not have placed it there if, in the chronology of composition, he had actually written the comedy before the last of his Histories of the Lancastrian cycle.[2] The Garter celebrations of St George's Day, 23 April 1597 at Westminster – or possibly the solemn ceremonies for the installation of the new knights held in Windsor a month later – may have been the occasion for a masque or other entertainment, but certainly not for the full-blown comedy that we have now. This does not rule out completely the possibility that the comedy might have been privately performed for the Queen by royal command at Windsor on another occasion.[3] But the comedy could not have been written before late 1599, and is therefore a completely separate venture from the presumptive Garter entertainment.

I have argued the case at length elsewhere, offering at the same time a hypothetical reconstruction of the outlines of the

---

[1] The status of Falstaff is known to Mistress Quickly, when she, at 2.2.72–3, among the 'proudest' wooers of Mistress Ford, flatteringly places 'pensioners' above 'earls', a joke that the audience could not fail to appreciate.

[2] For a fuller demonstration see Melchiori, *Garter*, 106–12, 'Postscript: the dual chronology of the Falstaff plays'.

[3] George Walton Williams, noticing that at least in two scenes (4.2 and 4.5) the action requires repeated movements from an upper to a lower location and vice versa, possibly by a staircase in view of the audience, privately suggested that the play might have been first performed in the Vicars' Hall at St George's, Windsor Castle, and where, according to the former librarian, 'there indeed had been a staircase in that hall at the time of the play, going up to an upper storey of apartments'.

evasive 1597 entertainment.[1] In fact not only the Garter speech but all the Herne's oak fairy gambols at 5.5.37–102, as George Hibbard notes, are 'singularly masque-like. The Fairy Queen, the fairies, the Satyr, Hobgoblin – all these are exactly the kind of figures that are to be found in the Royal "Entertainments" that have survived.' Significantly in this scene Mistress Quickly and Parson Evans are totally deprived of their linguistic peculiarities. It looks therefore as if most of the passage was conceived as an independent masque, part of an entertainment offered to the Queen on some particular occasion (Fig. 1). After mentioning several such entertainments that delighted the Queen on visits during her annual 'progresses' to the houses of the most eminent noblemen, Hibbard goes on:

> It therefore seems a reasonable hypothesis that either Hunsdon or the Queen may well have asked Shakespeare and his company to put together such an entertainment for the Garter celebrations of 1597. It would certainly be something that they could do within a fortnight, and it would fit the occasion. Then later, when it was all long over, Shakespeare, with the economy so characteristic of him, salvaged the entertainment, . . . and used it for the denouement of his new comedy.[2]

In other words, the hypothetical entertainment of 1597 might have existed well before the comedy of *The Merry Wives of Windsor*, and the verse speeches improbably assigned in the comedy to Mistress Quickly, Sir Hugh Evans and Pistol (the latter does not appear in the Quarto version of the scene) were originally meant for the emblematic traditional figures in a royal masque, such as the Fairy Queen and her attendant spirits.

Taking into account that such entertainments were mainly in verse, it can be surmised that what Shakespeare 'salvaged' and

---

[1] Melchiori, *Garter*, 82–112.
[2] Hibbard, introduction, 49–50.

1 A typical private entertainment in Elizabeth's time: a wedding masque, detail from *The Life and Death of Sir Henry Unton*

adapted in his later comedy was not only the Garter masque in 5.5, in which the Fairy Queen (the allegorical projection of Queen Elizabeth) ordered the preparations for the installation

23

ceremony of the new knights, but also parts of what are now the only three other scenes of the comedy which are at least partly in verse (3.4, 4.4, 4.6; see note 2 on p. 2), and they may provide a clue to the nature of the original entertainment. Those scenes in their versified parts are concerned with the love plot of Anne Page and Fenton (3.4.1–21 and 65–93, as well as 4.6, where Fenton enlists the Host of the Garter's help for his marriage to Anne), and with the plans for punishing an unworthy knight 'corrupt, and tainted in desire' (5.5.90) during the fairy masque (4.4.6–15, 24–64, 67–77, 80–8; the prose speeches of Parson Evans or addressed to him in this scene look like late insertions to fit the new comedic context). Apart from the Garter speech of the Fairy Queen (5.5.55–76), all the rest of the versified parts of 5.5 are also essentially concerned with these two themes: the knight's exposure (37–54, 77–102; see Fig. 2) and the Anne

2 *The Herne's Oak Revels* (5.5) painted by Robert Smirke for the Boydell Shakespeare Gallery in 1789: Falstaff with buck's head on pinched by the 'fairies', Mistress Quickly as Queen of Fairies, Evans as a satyr

Page/Fenton plot (210–34). Two themes that would perfectly fit a Garter entertainment, round a central speech that puts the stress not on military values, but on loyalty and moral integrity. The Queen considered chastity as the supreme virtue both in men and women.[1] It therefore seems appropriate that a masque in her honour should be accompanied by an antimasque[2] underlining on the one hand the unworthiness of a lecherous knight and on the other the dangers to married chastity represented by parentally enforced marriage. Fenton's justification of Anne's disobedience to parental will at the close of the play is unequivocal:

> Th'offence is holy that she hath committed,
> . . .
> Since therein she doth evitate and shun
> A thousand irreligious cursed hours
> Which forced marriage would have brought upon her.
>
> (5.5.219, 220–4)

If the 1597 Garter entertainment ever existed, it existed as separate from a comedy that, as we saw, could not have been written at that date, if for no better reason than that it assumes the audience's familiarity with characters that made their first appearances on the stage only one or two years later. The general outlines of such an entertainment would be based on the honourable deception of parents practised by a pair of lovers, and on the punishment of a corrupt knight unworthy of his title and even more of the Order of the Garter, culminating in the celebration of the 'radiant Queen' who 'hates sluts and sluttery'

---

[1] On the Elizabethan cult of chastity see Philippa Berry, *Of Chastity and Power* (1989).

[2] Significantly Anne Barton, in her introduction to *The Merry Wives of Windsor* in Riv, 320, remarks: 'a comedy concerned, as this one is, with the punishment of a knight whose principles and behaviour contravene all the ideals of his rank would be appropriate, almost as a kind of antimasque, at a Garter feast'. What is suggested here is that Falstaff's punishment and the Fenton/Anne plot are in fact part of the antimasque included in a Garter entertainment. For instance, Falstaff, at the beginning of the antimasque, might have revealed to the Garter Host his plan for the seduction of rich Windsor women. See Melchiori, *Garter*, 104–5.

(5.5.46).[1] It should be noted that such a show would not entail the use of the Italianate plot of the jealous husband or the presence of such characters as Bardolph, Pistol, Nim, Mistress Quickly or, for that matter, Parson Evans and Doctor Caius. The only indispensable 'new' character in it would have been the Host of the Garter Inn, the lodging of the unworthy knight – the choice of name for the inn, which allows for the equivocation on his title as 'knight of the Garter', is surely deliberate as fitting the jocular spirit of an antimasque.

The presence of the Host suggests that there was a third strand in the entertainment that was strictly and topically linked with the Garter events of 1597, introducing an element of satire that only a court audience in the know could fully appreciate. This is the marginal episode of the pretended German noblemen who cheat the Host of three horses as well as of their board at the inn, an episode surviving both in the Quarto and in the Folio text of the comedy in two scenes: 4.3 and 4.5.61–86. There is general agreement[2] that the episode is meant to satirize the behaviour of a German nobleman who, when visiting England in 1592 as Frederick, Count Mömpelgard, had manoeuvred to be elected to the Order of the Garter, but when the honour was conferred upon him in 1597, by which time he had become Duke of Württemberg, he did not acknowledge it and failed to attend the investiture and installation ceremonies. The use of the expression 'cosen garmombles' in the Quarto version or 'Cozen-Iermans' in the Folio at 4.5.73 leaves no doubt about the intentional allusion – an allusion which would perfectly fit a

---

[1] For more detailed evidence and a fuller discussion of this point see Melchiori, *Garter*, 92–112.

[2] The dissenting voice is that of J.E.V. Crofts, *Shakespeare and the Post Horses: A New Study of 'The Merry Wives of Windsor'* (Bristol, 1937), who found that the Duke of Württemberg had been given a warrant to use post-horses without charge, so that the satire on horse-stealing Germans would be unfounded. He suggested that the satire was addressed to a Monsieur de Chastes, who in 1596 stole post-horses when rushing back to France to bring the news that the French king had been elected to the Garter. Freedman, 'Chronology', 206, finds that 'Crofts's argument for the importance of the de Chastes affair . . . deserves a new hearing.'

topical Garter entertainment, but is hardly relevant in the context of a comedy about Sir John Falstaff and the merry wives of Windsor. The only reason for its survival there, albeit in a ghostly form, is that it fits the more general theme of the deceiver deceived: the Host, who in the comedy has played tricks at the expense of Parson Evans and Doctor Caius, is in turn cheated, as they gleefully point out to him at 4.5.69–84.[1]

Assuming then that the figure of the knight was conceived for the antimasque of a Garter entertainment as the anti-hero, contravening the rules of the chivalric Order, the question is why did the author choose for him the name of Sir John Falstaff at a time (1597) when that character as we know him had not yet appeared on the stage, or if he had in the First Part of *Henry IV* it was not as Falstaff but as Sir John Oldcastle. The only other substantial mention in Shakespeare's work of the Order of the Garter and its values appears in an early history play, the First Part of *Henry VI* (before 1592, but first printed only in the Folio of 1623), where the English national hero, Talbot, asks for the degradation of a knight recently elected to the Order but guilty of desertion at the crucial battle of Patay:

> When first this Order was ordained, my Lords,
> Knights of the Garter were of Noble birth,
> Valiant and Virtuous, full of haughty Courage,
> Such as were grown to credit by the wars,
> Not fearing Death, nor shrinking for Distress,
> But always resolute in most extremes.
> He, then, that is not furnished in this sort
> Doth but usurp the sacred name of Knight,
> Profaning this most Honourable Order,
> And should, if I were worthy to be Judge,

---

[1] Dover Wilson, Cam[1], xiv, suggested that the horse-stealing had been arranged by Evans and Caius in revenge for the hoax played upon them by the Host.

> Be quite degraded, like a Hedge-born Swain
> That doth presume to boast of Gentle blood.
> (*1H6* 4.1.33–44, 1623 Folio, sig. 13v)[1]

In the Folio the name of the degraded knight is consistently spelled 'Falstaffe', though in modern editions he appears as Sir John Fastolf because the historical figure that he incarnates is named in the *Chronicles* of Hall and Holinshed 'Fastolf', 'Fastolfe' or 'Fastollfe'. It would be natural for the writer of the Garter entertainment, when looking for an anti-hero, a knight unworthy of the Order, to adopt for him the name (perhaps with a slight spelling variant) of the disgartered knight already known to Elizabethan audiences from *1 Henry VI*.[2] In other words the Sir John of the putative 1597 entertainment could only have been the Fastolf/Falstaff of *Henry VI*, not of *Henry IV*.

According to evidence which is now generally accepted, in 1596 Lord Hunsdon's Men (formerly Chamberlain's Men) got into trouble for presenting on the stage a play on *Henry IV*[3] in which the elderly 'misleader of youth' was called Sir John Oldcastle (a name found in the anonymous *The Famous Victories*

---

[1] I have modernized spelling and punctuation but kept the use of capitals in the original.

[2] Michael Hattaway, in his edition of *1 Henry VI* (Cambridge, 1991), 64, suggests that the Folio spelling 'Falstaffe' is 'a scribal or compositorial confusion with the famous character in *1* and *2 Henry IV*', but it may well be that, meeting 'Fastolf' in the chronicles, Shakespeare saw the allusive possibilities offered by a possible alternative spelling of the name, for Fastolf, Fall-staff or False-staff, branding him as one who let fall or bore falsely the staff or spear, emblem of military valour - a 'fall' that according to Roberts, *Context*, 48, in *Merry Wives* implies also impotence, while Tiffany, 'False Staff', associates the expression 'False Staff' with androgyny. See Melchiori, *Garter*, 96–9, reporting the debate on the significance of Falstaff's name (G.W. Williams, 'Fastolf or Falstaff' *ELR*, 5 (1975), 308–12; R.F. Willson Jr, 'Falstaff in *Henry IV*: what's in a name?' *SQ*, 27 (1976), 199–200; N. Davis, 'Falstaff's name' *SQ*, 28 (1977), 513–15; G.W. Williams, 'Second thoughts on Falstaff's name' *SQ*, 30 (1979), 82–4), to be seen also in connection with that of Shakespeare's own name (Shake-spear – see T. Walter Herbert, 'The naming of Falstaff', *Emory University Quarterly*, 10 (1954), 1–11; Harry Levin, 'Shakespeare's nomenclature', *Essays on Shakespeare*, ed. G.W. Chapman (Princeton, N.J., 1965, 87).

[3] Not necessarily identical with the text published twice in 1598 (reprinted in 1599, 1604, 1608, 1613, 1622) under that title (*The History of Henrie the Fourth*) and as *The First Part of Henry the Fourth* in the 1623 Folio. Possibly *Henry IV* had not been originally conceived as a two-part play; see Melchiori, *Garter*, 41–56, 'Reconstructing the ur-

of Henry the Fifth, an earlier play dealing with the same material) and two other of Prince Hal's boon companions were called Rossill, or Sir John Russell, and Harvey.[1] This caused the hostile reaction of William Brooke, Baron Cobham, who had become Lord Chamberlain after the death of Henry Carey, Baron Hunsdon, in July 1596; Lord Cobham had family connections with the historical Sir John Oldcastle, a former friend of Prince Henry (the future Henry V), executed for being a Lollard and therefore considered a proto-martyr of the protestant religion;[2] in view of this the powerful Cobham family, as well as presumably the Russells and the Harveys, objected to the presentation of their ancestors or namesakes as irregular humorists in the play.[3]

---

[1] Evidence for the original names is provided not only by punning allusions to Oldcastle in the texts of the two parts of *Henry IV* but also by the survival of the names 'Harvey, Rossill' in *1H4* 1.2.162, of the speech prefix *Ross.* in *1H4* 2.4.174, 176, 180, as well as of the speech prefix *Old.* in *2H4* 1.2.120 and of *sir Iohn Russel* in *2H4* 2.2.0. This suggests that the two plays were completely rewritten incorporating only some odd pages of the foul copy of the original 1596 version of *Henry IV*. The attempt by Gary Taylor to 'restore' such a version in the Oxford *Complete Works* (1986), by simply replacing with the original names those of the three characters in *1H4*, seems misguided and has not been followed by Stephen Greenblatt when reproducing the Oxford texts in the Norton Shakespeare (1997). RP remarks that, since the text of *Famous Victories* is a wretched report dated as late as 1598, the name 'Oldcastle' may have been introduced in it by the compiler 'as a result of its use in performances of [the early version of] *1 Henry IV*' (1596–7).

[2] The martyrdom of Sir John Oldcastle is celebrated in John Foxe's *Actes and Monumentes* (1579). But in order to justify his execution ordered by Henry V, Holinshed and other chroniclers implicate him in the Scroop/Grey/Cambridge plot (cf. *H5* 2.2). Discussing the Oldcastle/Falstaff question, Poole, 69, notices that 'in *Henry V* Shakespeare completely removes Oldcastle/Falstaff from this treacherous triad', adding 'we might speculate that Falstaff's premature death is an effort to avoid the awkwardness of the historical alliance of Oldcastle with these traitors'. Significantly Oldcastle is falsely accused of complicity in the conspiracy in *1 Sir John Oldcastle*, a play by Munday Drayton and others performed in 1599 by the Admiral's Men to vindicate his memory from the slur received in the first version of Shakespeare's history ('It is no pamperd glutton we present, / Nor aged Councellor to youthfull sinne . . .'). In the comedy *Falstaff's Wedding* by W. Kenrick (1760), Falstaff (not Oldcastle) is hired by the conspirators to assassinate the king, but repents at the last moment and offers his life to Henry.

[3] The most elaborate and fully documented discussion of the whole question is in Scoufos, *Satire*. See also Peter Corbin and Douglas Sedge, eds, *The Oldcastle Controversy* (Manchester, 1991). The polemical and satirical implications of the stage presentation of Sir John Oldcastle are thoroughly explored in the already quoted paper by Poole. In the two parts of *Henry IV* Falstaff inherits from Oldcastle the habit ironically attributed to the puritans of having frequent recourse to Scriptural phraseology. Poole remarks (65) that 'of the fifty-four biblical references identified [by Naseeb

So by April 1597, in spite of the fact that on the 17th of that month, following the death of Lord Cobham, Henry Carey's son George, second Baron Hunsdon, had been newly appointed Lord Chamberlain and elected to the Order of the Garter, Shakespeare must have been busy replacing the offending names in his history play. Rossill (Sir John Russell) became Bardolph, Harvey became Peto, and for the misleader of youth Sir John Oldcastle the choice fell on that of the unworthy knight disgartered in Part One of *Henry VI*, a choice the more justified if that character had been revived in the Garter entertainment of April 1597. In other words, the name of Falstaff as anti-hero in a Garter entertainment would have evoked the historical Falstolf who had been degraded from the Order of the Garter at the time of Henry VI, but the same name was used to replace that of Sir John Oldcastle, another historical character who lived in the earlier reigns of Henry IV and Henry V.[1] It is round the latter Falstaff, who had become a favourite of London audiences in the two parts of *Henry IV*, that Shakespeare later devised the comedy of Sir John Falstaff and the merry wives of Windsor, in which he apparently incorporated parts of an earlier text that had included a figure named after the unworthy knight exposed in two brief scenes (3.2.104–9 and 4.1.9–47) of the First Part of *Henry VI*. At all events neither version of the play that has reached us, the Quarto of 1602 nor the 1623 Folio, can possibly be identified *in toto* with the presumptive 1597 entertainment – actually the Quarto omits the lines on the Garter ceremonies in the masque-like part of Act 5 that would have been most appropriate to the occasion. It may be helpful to look next into the nature of these two texts.

Shaheen, *Biblical References in Shakespeare's History Plays*, 1989] in *1 Henry IV* twenty-six come from the mouth of Falstaff. It is perhaps symptomatic of the further removal of the Falstaff of *Merry Wives* from that of the Histories that of over thirty biblical allusions in the comedy only two, at 5.1.21–2, are referred to by Falstaff.

[1] The librarian Richard James, in an epistle of 1634/5 addressed to Sir Henry Bouchier, reports the puzzlement of a 'young gentle lady' who asked him how Falstaff, who died at the time of Henry V, could have been banished for cowardice under Henry VI. See Taylor, 'Oldcastle'.

QUARTO AND FOLIO: MEMORIAL
RECONSTRUCTION AND ACTING VERSION

The most authoritative text of the Falstaff play is no doubt that in the 1623 Folio edition of Shakespeare's dramatic works, where it takes third place in the section *Comedies*, pp. 39–60. Like *The Tempest* and *The Two Gentlemen of Verona* that precede it and *Measure for Measure* that follows it in the volume, it is based on a transcript made for printing purposes by the highly competent scribe Ralph Crane who, as it now appears, was responsible for preparing for the press, at least in part, some other Folio plays, notably *Othello*.[1] The reliability of such a text, though, is somewhat diminished not only by possible misreadings of the copy by the Folio printers, by the suppression of 'profanities' in accordance with the Profanity Act of 1606, and by other possible censorial interventions such as the substitution of *Broom[e]* for *Brook[e]* as Master Ford's assumed name (discussed in a later section of this introduction), but also by Crane's peculiar habits, such as his method of punctuation with a large use of parentheses and hyphens and, more important still, by constant use of 'massed entries', i.e. listing at the beginning of each scene all the characters that are to appear in it, omitting therefore all entry, exit and other directions for each single character in the course of the scene. Another habit of Crane's, pointed out by Honigmann especially in respect of *Othello* and *2 Henry IV*[2] is that of editing, improving or regularizing the text he was transcribing, by adding, omitting or replacing words and expressions not to his taste. It is very difficult to decide the extent of Crane's interference, while in the case of missing directions a certain amount of guidance may occasionally be found in

---

[1] Crane's transcripts of Shakespearean works have been studied by T.H. Howard-Hill, *Ralph Crane and Some Shakespeare First Folio Comedies* (Charlottesville, Va., 1972), and more recently by E.A.J. Honigmann, *The Texts of* Othello *and Shakespearian Revision* (1996).

[2] For the latter see Eleanor Prosser, *Shakespeare's Anonymous Editors: Scribe and Compositor in the Folio Text of* 2 Henry IV (1981), though for her Ralph Crane is not necessarily the scribe who provided the copy for that play.

the corresponding scenes (when they exist) of *Merry Wives* in the first Quarto edition of 1602. Besides, its overall structure is peculiarly uncertain, presenting a number of unnecessary side-scenes that break up and at times confuse the development of its plot or plots, which in the Quarto appear much tidier and therefore more effective in performance terms.

The 1602 Quarto differs radically from the Folio text. In the first place there are glaring omissions: 4.1 (the 'Latin lesson'), 5.1, 5.2, 5.3, 5.4 and the Garter speech at 5.5.55–76 are totally missing, 3.4 and 3.5 are transposed, and there are further transpositions of passages within single scenes or from one scene to another. Finally all scenes are radically reduced in length, so that the Quarto version is less than 60 per cent of the length of that in the Folio (about 1620 lines as compared with 2729 of the Folio Through Line Numbering), and the wording of the surviving speeches presents substantial variants. A number of other inconsistencies have been pointed out, inducing critical opinion to classify it, together with the first quartos of *Romeo and Juliet* (1597), *Henry V* (1600), *Hamlet* (1602), and possibly *The Contention between the Two Famous Houses of Lancaster and York* (1594, i.e. *2 Henry VI*), *The True Tragedy of Richard Duke of York* (1595, i.e. *3 Henry VI*), among the 'bad quartos', that is to say, those 'stolne and surreptitious copies maimed, and deformed by the frauds and stealthes of iniurious impostors' that John Heminge and Henry Condell thought to have 'cured' when collecting them in the Folio, as they state in their address 'To the Great Variety of Readers'. But in recent times there has been a growing feeling that the adjective 'bad' is an inappropriate definition for these works,[1] especially in view of their theatrical effectiveness, so that the debate on their origins and individual

---

[1] The problem had been faced in 1961 by Hardin Craig who, in the case of *Merry Wives* (Craig, *New Look*, 65–75), had come to the conclusion that 'with proper corrections and in the light of its history, the quarto text is both good and Shakespearean'. In turn Jeanne Addison Roberts (*MW* Q & F) supported in her lengthy study the theory of the Quarto as a memorial reconstruction. The case for a radical rethinking of the nature of the Quartos was forcibly argued by Werstine. But see Urkowitz, and especially Maguire, 73–94, 'Memorial reconstruction and its discontents'.

qualities is as open as ever. The greater suitability to stage presentation of the shorter texts preserved in some quartos which had been labelled 'bad' has brought about, now that Shakespeare is rightly seen as first and foremost a man of the theatre rather than as a literary figure and the supreme bard of a nation, a reconsideration of the merits of the 'bad' quartos.

Claims or vindications can be pushed too far, as by Eric Sams who, in his book on Shakespeare's early years, begins his chapter XXXI with the words:

> Some seventy reasons, together with dozens of source-references, have already been given . . . for rejecting the trumped-up charges of 'Bad Quartos' (BQ) or 'memorial reconstruction by actors' (MRA) made against *Hamlet* 1603, *A Shrew*, *Troublesome Reign*, *Contention* and *True Tragedy*, and restoring these plays to their previous Shakespearean status . . . . The same restitution is long overdue for other so-called BQ/MRA texts . . . , such as *Romeo and Juliet* 1597, *Henry V* 1600, *The Merry Wives of Windsor* 1602, *King Lear* 1608 and *Pericles* 1609.[1]

In other words, Sams wants to force us back to the discredited theory that all these are earlier Shakespearean versions of the plays, and his claim finds support in the editions by Graham Holderness and Bryan Loughrey of the first quartos of *Hamlet*, *A Shrew* and *Henry V*, presenting them as 'Shakespearean originals: first editions'.[2]

Performance features have been rightly chosen by Kathleen Irace as the touchstone for her recent thorough re-examination of the whole problem of 'Bad Quartos'.[3] She reconsiders the

---

[1] Sams, 173.

[2] As for *Merry Wives*, Y.S. Bains, 'Making sense of some passages in the 1602 Quarto of Shakespeare's *The Merry Wives of Windsor*', *N&Q*, 237 (1992), 322–6, argues that the Folio is Shakespeare's revision of his original text published in the 1602 Quarto.

[3] Kathleen O. Irace, *Reforming the 'Bad' Quartos: Performance and Provenance of Six Shakespearean First Editions* (Newark, Del., 1994).

main theories - revision, memorial reconstruction, adaptation - on the origins of the six 'bad' texts in the light of the fact that recent stage or film productions of these plays adopted the structural features (transpositions, omissions, stage business) characteristic of the early quartos, though at times the directors were hardly aware of the existence of, or showed no interest in, such versions; this demonstrates that Shakespeare is in the first place theatre, and his texts are by definition unstable, subject to the circumstances of stage presentation, the best judges of which are theatre professionals, actors and directors. The usefulness of Irace's book is in providing rich and carefully assembled analytical evidence in support of this principle, which she confronts with traditional approaches to the problem.

Sams, as we saw, took the shortcut of considering one and all as Shakespeare's youthful works, hallmarked by his mastery of the theatrical art at a very early stage, and therefore frequently preferable to the later stylistic sophistications. This also allowed for the inclusion in the canon, because of linguistic affinities, such plays as *Edmund Ironside*, *Faire Em*, *Locrine*, and even, from Nashe's and Lodge's vague hints, the ur-*Hamlet*.[1] This solution has been considered with great caution even by the so-called early-daters, whom Sams freely quotes in support of his theories,[2] and has found no favour with the revisionists, whose ideas of 'revision' have very different foundations.[3]

Different responses can be found for each individual 'bad quarto'. A reconsideration of the status of the First Quarto of *Merry Wives* must begin with the title-page advertisement, parts of which have already been quoted:

> A Most pleasaunt and excellent conceited Comedie, of
> Syr *Iohn Falstaffe*, and the merrie Wiues of *Windsor*. //

[1] Sams, 116–24 and 163–6.

[2] Especially Ernst A.J. Honigmann, *Shakespeare's Impact on His Contemporaries* (1982), where Shakespeare's early start as a playwright is advocated, in view of which 'the dramatic history of the Elizabethan age will have to be rewritten' (90).

[3] See especially Stanley Wells, *Shakespeare and Revision: The Hilda Hume Memorial Lecture* (1988).

> Entermixed with sundrie variable and pleasing humours, of Syr *Hugh* the Welch Knight, Iustice *Shallow*, and his wise Cousin M. *Slender*. // With the swaggering vaine of Auncient *Pistoll*, and Corporall *Nym*. // By *William Shakespeare*. // As it hath bene diuers times Acted by the right Honorable my Lord Chamberlaines seruants: Both before her Maiestie, and else-where.

Obviously this title-page was devised by the publisher to cash in on the fashion for the comedy of humours, and the fact that, on the strength of the title 'Sir', Hugh Evans is taken to be a knight rather than a parson confirms that neither author nor theatre company had anything to do with it.[1] The only certainty is that a play of that title was performed by the Chamberlain's Men both at court and in the public theatre, in London and/or 'else-where'; the text presented reflected in some way either one or the other of these occasions. It is tempting to assume that the Folio version reflects the text of the comedy as written (if we believe the legend circulated a century later by John Dennis and Nicholas Rowe) in fourteen days at the Queen's command and 'diuers times Acted by the right Honorable my Lord Chamberlaines seruants. Both before her Maiestie, and else-where'. It reflects but does not necessarily reproduce it: we cannot know what manipulations it underwent between the original presentation at court and 'else-where' and the time when the scribe Ralph Crane prepared the copy for the 1623 Folio, introducing his own 'improvements' and emendations in a text which had already been cleared of all oaths in observance of the Profanity Act of 1606. On the other hand the Quarto version may give an idea of how the play was presented 'else-where', to

---

[1] When, after Shakespeare's death, William Jaggard decided to reprint for Thomas Pavier several plays attributed to him but mostly spurious, he reproduced in the Second Quarto of 1619 the text of the First Quarto, but omitted the second paragraph of the title-page; obviously the mistake in Sir Hugh Evans's title had been detected and the popularity of comedies of humours had declined.

an audience that would not have relished the word-play of that
dramatically superfluous scene, the Latin lesson (4.1), and
would have preferred the homely gambols of the fairy children
to the more formal celebratory speech of the Garter virtues.
Even granting this, especially in view of the already-mentioned
basic differences in emphasis between the two texts (as noted by
Leah Marcus (see pp. 9–10 above), the court, though mentioned
in Q, is by no means a constant presence there as in F), the relationship between the two texts remains problematic.

The fact that the 1602 version makes no reference to Garter
ceremonies, but ironically mentions the Garter as the name of
the inn where the 'poor knight of Windsor' Sir John Falstaff
lodges, proves: a) that the original comedy had in fact contained
elements from the earlier entertainment, more amply preserved
in the Folio version; b) that Q reflects not an earlier authorial
version or the text as acted 'before her Maiestie' (as the title-
page claims), but an acting version for the public stage.

The Quarto, as William Bracy vigorously maintained, 'offers
unquestioned evidence of extensive adaptation and abridgement
for special production purposes'.[1] In other words, the suppression of substantial sections of scenes, and even more the transposition of whole scenes and the salvaging of particularly
effective passages or speeches from suppressed scenes by trans-
fers to other contexts seem the result of authorial decisions. One
example of this may suffice. In the Folio version, after the revelation in 4.5 of the cozening of the Host by the 'Germans',
Falstaff, left alone on the stage, comments:

> I would all the world might be cozened, for I have been
> cozened and beaten too. If it should come to the ear of
> the court how I have been transformed, and how my
> transformation hath been washed and cudgelled, they
> would melt me out of my fat drop by drop, and liquor
> fishermen's boots with me. I warrant they would whip

---

[1] Bracy, 97.

me with their fine wits till I were as crestfallen as a dried
pear. I never prospered since I forswore myself at
primero. Well, if my mind were but long enough, I
would repent.

(4.5.87–96)

Only the first and the last two lines of this soliloquy are preserved with slight changes (and the significant addition 'to say
my prayers' after 'long enough') in the equivalent scene in Q
(sigs F4v–G1r). But in that text Falstaff's comment on discovering he is the victim of the Herne the Hunter hoax, instead of,
as in F at 5.5.126–7, 'See now how wit may be made a Jack-a-
Lent when 'tis upon ill employment!', is:

> Well, and the fine wits of the Court heare this,
> Thayle so whip me with their keene Iests,
> That thayle melt me out like tallow,
> Drop by drop out of my grease.

(sig. G3v)

Where does Falstaff's notion of being made the laughing stock
of the court fit better - after the second or after the third hoax
at his expense? It looks as if whoever attempted to produce a reduced version of the play wished to preserve the
allusion to the court's attitudes but found that its presence
in 4.5 ran counter to the general process of streamlining the
action. This able streamlining process – another feature
shared with Q1 *Hamlet* – goes to show that Q *Merry Wives* is
essentially what we would call now an 'acting version' of the
play. It is not just a case of abridgement, but of restructuring the
whole, which – and this is true also of *Hamlet* – could hardly
have been undertaken and approved by anybody except the
author himself.

Granted this at the structural level, can we really believe that
the wording of the acting version, the confusions, the weak
paraphrases of the brilliant speeches that we find in F, are also

authorial? If so, this is not an acting version, but a first draft that the linguistically unskilled author sketched out not in 1600 or even in 1597, but a long time before, at the time in fact when (accepting Sams's narrative) he wrote *Edmund Ironside*. Which, in the case of *Merry Wives*, is manifestly impossible. The discrepancies in the use of language in the two versions are better explained by accepting that Shakespeare did provide side by side with his play a shortened restructured acting version suitable for current use on the stage (not necessarily for provincial tours only); but what we have in Q is not exactly this. It is in fact a reported text, restructured by the author but reconstituted by others (including actors). The discriminating factor between authorial and memorially reconstructed texts is language, one particular aspect of which, in Q *Merry Wives* as in Q1 *Romeo and Juliet*, seems to have been overlooked, but which sticks out particularly in the former because there is so little of it: versification. In F only four scenes are mainly in verse – 3.4, 4.4, 4.6 and 5.5, corresponding to scenes 12 (sigs E4r–F1r), 15 (sigs F2v–F3v), 17 (sigs G1r–G1v) and 18 (sigs G1v–G4v) in Q, which, though generally shorter than those in the Folio, and in one case (12) with notable transpositions and rearrangement of the action, are also mainly in verse. But it is a very different sort of verse. Its poor quality, and the introduction especially in scenes 15 and 18 (the last in the play) of a number of jingling rhymes where there are none in F, suggest not Shakespeare's hand but that of somebody who was trying to reconstruct the text. Aware that in those scenes several characters spoke in verse, but unable to recall the lines, he provided others of his own devising, throwing additional rhymes into the bargain. One example will suffice, the last section of 4.4 (scene 15 in Q), the planning of the trap set for Falstaff in Windsor forest. The Folio version is shown in Fig. 3.

Apart from the possible '*Broome*/come' rhyme in Ford's speech, only the closing couplet of the scene is rhymed. No fewer than three rhyming couplets (and one at the close of an

Mist. Page. The truth being knowne,
We'll all prefent our felues; dif-horne the fpirit,
And mocke him home to Windfor.
 Ford. The children muft
Be practis'd well to this, or they'il neu'r doo't.
 Eua. I will teach the children their behauiours: and I
will be like a Iacke-an-Apes alfo, to burne the Knight
with my Taber.
 Ford. That will be excellent,
Ile go buy them vizards.

 Mist. Page. My *Nan* fhall be the Queene of all the
Fairies, finely attired in a robe of white.
 Page. That filke will I go buy, and in that time
Shall M. *Slender* fteale my *Nan* away,
And marry her at *Eaton* : go, fend to *Falftaffe* ftraight.
 Ford. Nay, Ile to him againe in name of *Broome*,
Hee'l tell me all his purpofe: fure hee'l come.
 Mist. Page. Feare not you that : Go get vs properties
And tricking for our Fayries.
 Euans. Let vs about it,
It is admirable pleafures, and ferry honeft knaueries.
 Mif. Page. Go *Mist. Ford*,
Send quickly to Sir *Iohn*, to know his minde :
Ile to the Doctor, he hath my good will,
And none but he to marry with *Nan Page* :
That *Slender* (though well landed) is an Ideot :
And he, my husband beft of all affects :
The Doctor is well monied, and his friends
Potent at Court: he, none but he fhall haue her,
Though twenty thoufand worthier come to craue her.

3 Folio sig. E4v

earlier speech by Mistress Page) are introduced at the end of the
scene by the reporters of the acting version[1] in Q:

[MIS.PA.]   And then to make a period to the Iest,
   Tell *Falstaffe* all, I thinke this will do best.
PA.   Tis excellent, and my daughter *Anne*,
   Shall like a litle Fayrie be disguised.

---

[1] The same happens in *Romeo and Juliet*, where for instance 2.6, the scene between the
Friar, Romeo and Juliet containing in Q2 (1599) only two rhyming couplets in 37 lines,
is completely reversified in Q1 (1597) with the introduction of no fewer than seven
rhyming couplets in 28 lines.

MIS.PA. And in that Maske Ile make the Doctor
    steale my daughter *An*, & ere my husband knowes
    it, to carrie her to Church, and marrie her. (boyes?
MIS.FOR. But who will buy the silkes to tyre the
PA. That will I do, and in a robe of white
    Ile cloath my daughter, and aduertise *Slender*
    To know her by that signe, and steale her thence,
    And vnknowne to my wife, shall marrie her.
HU. So kad vdge me the deuises is excellent.
    I will also be there, and be like a Iackanapes,
    And pinch him most cruelly for his lecheries.
MIS.PA. Why then we are reuenged sufficiently.
    First he was carried and throwne in the Thames,
    Next beaten well, I am sure youle witnes that.
MIS.FOR. Ile lay my life this makes him nothing fat.
PA. Well lets about this stratagem, I long
    To see deceit deceiued, and wrong haue wrong.
FOR. Well send to *Falstaffe*, and if he come thither,
    Twill make vs smile and laugh one moneth togither.

Exit omnes.
(sig. F3v)

The introduction of new and rather obvious rhymes where there are none in the more authoritative text seems to be evidence of memorial reconstruction. The slack, repetitive, commonplace language of most of Q is not Shakespeare's language: it is a patchwork language alternating one or two actors' parts more or less correctly reported with what they remembered of the speeches of their fellows and with reconstructed passages intended to render the meaning rather than the exact wording of the speeches pronounced on the stage, padded out with the repetition of such tags as 'so kad vdge me' (five times) for Evans, and 'O Ieshu' or 'By Ieshu', which Evans shares (twice in the form 'Ieshu pless me') with Doctor Caius, Mistress Quickly and even Mistress Page. It can be argued that the disappearance of such expressions from F was due to the Profanity Act. But this is certainly not true of Nim's most conspicuous verbal tic, 'and

theres the humor of it' (already present in *Henry V* – five times in the Folio, eight in the Quarto version – as 'that's the humour of it'): there are five identical repetitions of it in Q (sigs A4, 1.8; B1v, 27; B2v, 16; B3, 1; C1, 21), while in the equivalent passages in F we find respectively: 1) 'if you runne the nut-hooks humor on me, that is the very note of it' (1.1.155–6, sig. D2v); 2) 'He was gotten in drink: is not the humour co[n]ceited?' (1.3.20–1, sig. D3); 3) later in the same scene, though Q and F have in common the expression 'I will keep the hauior of reputation', it is not followed by the usual tag in F (1.3.75, sig. D3v); 4) still in the same scene, 'that is my true humour' (1.3.95–6, sig. D3v); 5) 'Adieu' (2.1.123, sig. D4v). The explanation of the changes is simple: the reporter of Q replaced the imperfectly remembered varied mentions of humours with a constant formula modelled with a slight variant on the one consistently used in *Henry V*.[1]

Kathleen Irace, like many before her, had reached the conclusion that the *Merry Wives* Quarto is a memorially reconstructed text with the Host of the Garter as the main reporter,[2] and even a scholar like Laurie Maguire, who is disinclined to credit the theory of memorial reconstruction, singles out Q *Merry Wives*, together with *The Taming of a Shrew* (1594), *The Famous Victories of Henry the Fifth* and Marlowe's *The Massacre at Paris* as the only four 'suspect texts' for which 'a strong case can be made for memorial reconstruction'.[3]

The clinching argument, confirming Gerald Johnson's plea for a fresh reappraisal of the relationship between Quarto and Folio in view of '[t]he probability that the Quarto represents a memorial reconstruction of an alternate, adapted version of the play',[4] is provided by the introduction of four rhyming

---

[1] Other mechanical repetitions of speech mannerisms in the Quarto text are pointed out by Laurie Maguire (Maguire, 185): Quickly's 'all goe[s] through my hands' (twice) on sig. B3r/v, Falstaff's 'cuckally knaue[s]' five times on two consecutive pages, while on two other pages Falstaff prefaces two speeches with an exclamatory 'Well'. Such repetitions in the Quarto incline her to conclude that the text is probably a memorial reconstruction.

[2] Irace, 115-17, 122–3, 136–7 and chart at 180.

[3] Maguire, 324.

[4] Johnson, '*MW*, Q1', *passim*.

verse lines in a lengthy prose scene. At 4.2.99–102 Mistress Page, setting the 'witch of Brentford' trap for Falstaff, comments:

> We'll leaue a proofe by that which we will doo,
> Wiues may be merry, and yet honest too:
> We do not acte that often, iest, and laugh,
> 'Tis old, but true. Still Swine eats all the draugh.
>
> (Folio sig. E3v)

These lines, which are indeed a moral epitaph for the whole play, are not found in the corresponding scene 13 of Q. But in the Quarto equivalent of the earlier scene in which Falstaff is carried away in the buck-basket (3.3 in F, 10 in Q) the wives' comment is:

MIS.PA.   Nay we wil send to *Falstaffe* once again,
    Tis great pittie we should leaue him:
    What wiues may be merry, and yet honest too.
MI.FOR.   Shall we be co[n]demnd because we laugh?
    Tis old, but true: still sowes eate all the draffe.

(sig. E1v)

Whoever recorded this passage was aware of the relevance of the central line ('Wives may be merry . . .') in the context of a hoax played on Falstaff, but mistook its place in the play and garbled the surrounding lines.

It is safe to conclude that the Quarto is a reported text, a memorial reconstruction of an authorial acting version. It is authoritative in that it throws light on how Shakespeare could restructure his own work for the common stage, and it may well offer guidance to directors for 'streamlining' the play's action for modern audiences, provided they don't assume that its language is Shakespeare's. A comparison of the text of this edition, based essentially on F, with that of Q, reproduced in a reduced facsimile in the appendix, will make the linguistic differences clear.

UNCONFORMITIES AND COMICAL SATIRE

Confusions, inconsistencies, loose ends in the subplots of both
the Quarto and the Folio versions of the comedy of *Sir John
Falstaff and the Merry Wives of Windsor* are so glaring that no
critic has failed to notice them. For instance, the play opens with
the quarrel between Justice Shallow and Falstaff, who is accused
of stealing ('stolne' in Q) and killing (in F) Shallow's deer. But,
leaving aside the question of how a Justice of the Peace and
Coram '[i]n the County of Gloucester' (1.1.4–5, a detail ignored
in the Quarto version) could have owned a deer park in Windsor,
and in spite of the fact that Parson Evans, Master Page and the
Host of the Garter are accepted as the 'three umpires in the matter' (1.1.127–35, cf. Q sig. A3v), actually the 'matter' itself is
pursued no further, while the Host, not informed of this particular quarrel, is appointed to act as umpire in a different dispute,
the duel between Doctor Caius and Parson Evans (1.4.109–10),
a duel for which, as noted before, the doctor, discovering in his
rooms Slender's servant Simple, should have challenged not the
Parson but Slender himself, his rival for Anne Page's hand. This
is only one of the many 'unconformities' pointed out by Kristian
Smidt in the play.[1] Others which are particularly notable are the
confusions as to the colour of Anne Page's costume in the fairy
masque and the question of who is to impersonate the Fairy
Queen, or the working of the time scheme of the play in connection with Falstaff's different assignations at Ford's house.[2] Even
the name of Master Page remains uncertain: he is Thomas at
1.1.41 but George in the rest of the play (at 2.1.134 and 142, and
at 5.5.197. Page's first name is never mentioned in the Quarto).
Finally, as Smidt puts it,

> The lack of connection between the Falstaff of Windsor
> and the Falstaff of Eastcheap, apart from their appear-
> ance and habits, and the new identity of Mrs Quickly

[1] Smidt, 141–55, 'Windsor Humours'.
[2] All these points are noted and discussed in the relevant places of the commentary.

compared to that of the history plays, remain the most puzzling problems.[1]

Indeed, when at 2.2 Mistress Quickly turns up at the Garter Inn with messages for Falstaff from the merry wives, there is no sign of recognition between the two, in spite of the knight's familiarity with the Eastcheap Hostess in the two parts of *Henry IV* and of the fact that she retains the speech mannerisms she had acquired in *2 Henry IV*; she introduces herself not as a 'goodwife' but as a maid 'as my mother was the first hour I was born' (2.2.36–7), and she fails to recognize Pistol, silently present at her interview with the knight, together with Robin the page (reassuringly described by Falstaff as 'mine own people', 2.2.48–9), completely oblivious of the sequel of insults with which she and Doll Tearsheet had gratified this 'swaggering rascal' on his first appearance in a history play, in *2 Henry IV* 2.4.71–207. Pistol, after her exit, describing the woman that he has now seen for the first time as 'This punk is one of Cupid's carriers' (2.2.127), makes a comment, before following her out, that suggests a connection with the Histories: 'Clap on more sails, pursue, up with your fights, / Give fire! She is my prize, or ocean whelm them all' (2.2.128–9). These are in fact the final exit lines of Pistol in the play in the Folio version, except for his incongruous reappearance disguised as Hobgoblin in the masque at 5.5,[2] and they would have been meaningless to an audience unaware of the result of Pistol's pursuit of Quickly recorded in the Histories, not in the earlier parts of *Henry IV*, but only in *Henry V*, where, rather surprisingly, Quickly, once again a Hostess, has become the wife of Pistol. This is further evidence that the comedy, at least in the version presented in the Folio, can hardly have been written before *Henry V*.

[1] Smidt, 155.
[2] Smidt, 145. The prefix *Pist* before the three short speeches at 5.5.42–6, 83, 88 in F may be either an indication that Hobgoblin should be impersonated by the same actor who had previously appeared as Pistol, or a last-minute change made by the author in adapting a pre-existing text; see note to 5.5.36.3. Pistol does not appear at all in 5.5. in the Quarto version, and in the equivalent of 2.2 is dismissed by Falstaff before the entrance of Mistress Quickly.

There is scarcely any allusion to the Histories in the play, but what there is is perplexing in another sense. The 'wild prince' or 'the Prince of Wales', i.e. Prince Hal, the future Henry V, in the two parts of *Henry IV*, is mentioned both in the Quarto and in the Folio version, but in different contexts. In the Quarto equivalent of 5.5.103ff. Falstaff, at the entrance of the merry wives and their husbands (sig. G3r), instead of exclaiming, as in F, 'I do begin to perceive that I am made an ass', wonders: 'What hunting at this time at night? / Ile lay my life the mad Prince of *Wales* / Is stealing his fathers Deare. How now who haue we here, what is all *Windsor* stirring?' implying Falstaff's acquaintance with the Prince's misbehaviour in his youth (though deer-stealing in Windsor Royal Park is not mentioned among his exploits in the Histories – while the stealing of Shallow's deer is attributed to Falstaff himself in the first scene of the comedy). In F the reference to Prince Hal occurs at 3.2.64–6, when Master Page explains to the Host the unsuitability of Fenton as a husband for Anne: 'The gentleman is of no having, he kept company with the wild Prince and Poins. He is of too high a region'.[1] The allusion to Hal's boon companions led by Falstaff in *1* and *2 Henry IV* is obvious, but significantly the only one of them mentioned by name is Poins, who in the Histories is not so much Falstaff's as the Prince's personal friend and confidant, playing tricks with him at the expense of Falstaff and the other 'irregular humorists', such as the Gadshill robbery (*1H4* 1.2, 2.1, 2.2, 2.4), or the tavern scene where the Prince and Poins disguised as drawers watch Falstaff's pranks with Doll Tearsheet (*2H4* 2.4);

---

[1] While the rest of Page's speech is substantially similar in Q (sig. D4r), instead of this passage and the next sentence (3.2.64–8, from 'I promise' to 'substance') it has only the words: 'the gentleman is / Wilde'. In F the reference to the misbehaviour of the Prince is in the past, suggesting that the action of the play takes place when he had reformed, i.e. after his accession as King Henry V, and the play itself may well have been written after *Henry V*. Q's wording, with no mention of the Prince, leaves the possibility open that the king at the time of the action is still Henry IV. This finds support in the only mention, already quoted, of the Prince in the last scene of Q. Either the Quarto version is based on an earlier text written before 1599, or, more probably, the passage in it about the Prince's deer-stealing is a survival from an earlier court entertainment or masque later incorporated in the comedy (see pp. 52–5 below).

but in neither play does Fenton appear either as the Prince's or Falstaff's follower. There is, though, in the two parts of *Henry IV*, one character that could at a pinch be identified as Fenton: it is Peto (originally called Harvey[1]), who takes part in the Gadshill episode, but never boasts or tells lies like his companions and is the first to acknowledge Falstaff's cowardly behaviour (*1H4* 2.4.304–8); he also makes a brief appearance in the second part (*2H4* 2.4.354–66) as a messenger calling the Prince to his duties. He definitely sides with the Prince and Poins rather than with Falstaff and Bardolph, in spite of the fact that, while preparing the Gadshill hoax, Prince Hal had said: 'Well, for two of them [Falstaff and Bardolph], I know them to be as true-bred cowards as ever turned back, and for the third [Peto], if he fights longer than he sees reason, I'll forswear arms.' (*1H4* 1.2.183–6). This comment, presenting Peto not exactly as a coward, but as a person devoid of martial pretensions, must belong to the earlier version of the play of *Henry IV*, in which he bore the name of Harvey and, with Sir John Oldcastle and Rossill (Sir John Russell), was one of the figures conceived as part of a general design of comic satire at the expense of past and present eminent figures in Elizabethan public life. In his case the allusion was to the recently knighted (June 1596) Sir William Harvey who, to improve his fortunes, wooed the considerably older widowed mother of the Earl of Southampton, Shakespeare's patron, and therefore represented a threat to the young Earl, only heir to the family fortunes. In other words the character of Harvey was included in the history as representing, among Hal's followers, a fairly common type of courtier: the unscrupulous fortune-hunter.[2] When the resentment of the satirized families led to the removal of the offending names (Oldcastle, Russell, Harvey) the role of Harvey, transformed into Peto and redeemed from any

[1] For the reasons for the name change see pp. 28–30 above and the discussion later in this section.
[2] For a fully documented treatment of this view see Alice-Lyle Scoufos, 'Harvey: A Name Change in *Henry IV*', *ELH*, 36 (1961), 297–318, later elaborated in her *Satire*, chapter 8.

charge of money-grabbing (except in the case of the Gadshill robbery), could have been considerably reduced, accounting for the
scarcity of his appearances in the two parts of the history and for
his transfer from Falstaff's followers to the Prince's retinue: in *1
H4* 2.4.545–6 the Prince, left alone with Peto, tells him, 'We
must all to the wars, and thy place shall be honourable', and in *1
H4* 3.3.199–200, when Hal and his followers are called to arms,
the Prince selects Peto as his escort: 'Go, Peto, to horse, to horse,
for thou and I / Have thirty miles to ride yet ere dinner-time'.[1]
Devising either a hypothetical court entertainment or a full-
blown comedy that presented Falstaff as an unworthy knight who
degraded the passion of love to unashamed fortune-hunting (of
Mistress Ford he says 'she has all the rule of her husband's purse'
and of Mistress Page 'She bears the purse too', 1.3.49–50, 65),
Shakespeare in the love subplot contrasted him with the figure of
the repentant fortune-hunter who frankly acknowledges:

> Albeit I will confess thy father's wealth
> Was the first motive that I wooed thee, Anne,
> Yet, wooing thee, I found thee of more value
> Than stamps in gold or sums in sealed bags.
> And 'tis the very riches of thyself
> That now I aim at.
>
> (3.4.13–18)

Fenton's plight must have recalled to Shakespeare's mind that of
Harvey, originally conceived as a satire of the fortune-hunter,
forcibly redeemed in the character of Peto, like Poins the wild
Prince's companion – Fenton had told Anne about Master
Page's opposition to their marriage:

---

[1] Poins is strangely absent from this scene in *1H4*, and 'Poins' would be metrically more
correct than 'Peto' in line 199. Possibly the lines were originally written with Poins in
mind, and Shakespeare replaced him later with Peto both here and in the earlier scene
at 2.3.506–50, to mark the final redemption of the latter from his previous misconduct,
or, as Proudfoot privately suggests, to make the actor impersonating Poins available for
the role of Lord Mortimer in *1H4* 3.1. It should be noted that 3.3 marks the last appearance of Peto in Part One, while in Part Two he figures briefly only once (2.4.354–66),
again in a military context.

> He doth object I am too great of birth,
> And that, my state being galled with my expense,
> I seek to heal it only by his wealth.
> Beside these, other bars he lays before me:
> My riots past, my wild societies –
>
> $(3.4.4–8)^1$

This analogy between Fenton and Harvey/Peto offers a possible reason for Master Page's statement that 'he kept company with the wild Prince and Poins', giving Fenton a place among those that Henry IV had called 'unrestrained loose companions [of Prince Hal] . . . / Which he, young wanton and effeminate boy, / Takes on the point of honour to support / So dissolute a crew' (*R2* 5.3.7, 10–12). The allusions to the legend of the wild Prince with reference to characters present in *Merry Wives* imply that the action of the comedy takes place shortly after the events evoked, i.e. either towards the end of the reign of Henry IV or at the beginning of that of the reformed Prince, crowned as Henry V. But the masque in the last act pays homage not to a king but to 'Our radiant queen', who 'hates sluts and sluttery' (5.5.46), and who cannot be other than Elizabeth.[2]

This is indeed a major unconformity in the play. It looks as if the masque and Falstaff's exposure, as well as the marriage trick played by the lovers, and no doubt the horse-stealing episode, belong to a different narrative – different in time and topical allusions – from that told in the rest of the comedy. Fenton, in his confession to Anne, speaks in very general terms of his past misdemeanours: the link with the Prince's dissolute crew is established only by Master Page's allusion in a prose speech that could have been inserted at any time, precisely in order to

---

[1] In the Quarto version (sig. E4r) Fenton's speeches at 3.4.4–10 and 12–18 are concentrated into five lines, with no mention of 'riots past' and 'wild societies': 'Thy father thinks I loue thee for his wealth, / Tho I must needs confesse at first that drew me, / But since thy vertues wiped that trash away, / I loue thee *Nan*, and so deare is it set, / That whilst I liue, I nere shall thee forget' (note the final rhymed couplet and see pp. 38–40 above).

[2] The direct allusion to the Queen is omitted in the corresponding passage of Q.

suggest a connection with the Histories that had not been planned beforehand. The masque and the other versified parts of the present play seem to have existed before the introduction of the anglicized Italianate plot of the jealous husband, as well as the early intrusion of characters known to the audience from the Histories: Bardolph from *1 Henry IV*, Pistol, Shallow and Falstaff's page from *2 Henry IV*, Nim from *Henry V*, not to mention the comical–satirical Welsh parson and French doctor modelled respectively on Fluellen and the boastful French characters in the last of the Histories. And the irrepressible busybody Mistress Quickly, a totally different person from the Hostess of the Histories, might have acquired her name only when the pre-existing narrative was rather awkwardly inserted into the framework of the newly-minted 'citizen' comedy of the merry wives of Windsor. Only at this late stage would she be cast to impersonate the Fairy Queen in the masque originally conceived as part of the earlier narrative.[1] The only way to solve these glaring inconsistencies would seem to be the acceptance of the metamorphosis of the Falstaff of the earlier narrative, akin to the unworthy knight of the Garter exposed in *1 Henry VI*, into the figure endeared to Elizabethan audiences from his first appearance as Sir John Oldcastle in *Henry IV*.

Another type of unconformity, not unconnected with the thin thread of topical satire exemplified in the Mömpelgard allusions

---

[1] Long, 'Masque', 39–43, leaving aside the question of the date of the play, distinguishes between the versions of the masque in the Quarto and in the Folio texts, finding 'the Quarto masque more suitable to the play from the standpoint of dramatic construction and freedom from textual problems' (41), such as the colour of Anne Page's costume, the repeated hints in Folio 4.4.69 and 4.6.20 that Anne Page should impersonate the Fairy Queen, the introduction of the Garter speech, the casting of Pistol as Hobgoblin. Long concludes that, after the publication of the Quarto, on the occasion of the presentation of the play at court before King James I on 4 November 1604 (a performance recorded in the Revels Accounts; see Chambers, *Stage*, 4: 171), Shakespeare rewrote the masque to make it more 'appropriate to the dignity and formality of the occasion. . . . The tribute to Windsor Castle, its owner, the Order of the Garter [the Prince of Wales had been installed in the Order the previous year] was assigned to Anne Page, the only suitable member of the cast, and Anne replaced Quickly as the Queen of the Fairies' (42). An ingenious solution, if we ignore the homage to Elizabeth after her death.

(4.3 and 4.5), cuts across the two printed versions of the play. In the Quarto version the assumed name of Master Ford, when enrolling Falstaff's help to conquer a married woman who is in fact his own wife, is consistently spelt 'Brooke', but in the Folio version, published over twenty years later, it is constantly spelt 'Broome'. That Shakespeare intended 'Brooke' as the assumed name is obvious from Falstaff's quibbles on current meanings of both the 'real' and the assumed name: after his ducking into the Thames, when Mistress Quickly tells him that she comes from Mistress Ford, Falstaff exclaims 'Mistress Ford? I have had ford enough: I was thrown into the ford, I have my belly full of ford' (3.5.34–5).[1] And when at 2.2.136ff. Bardolph announces the arrival of a 'Master Brooke' ('Broome' in F) with a present of 'a morning's draught of sack' ('a cup of sacke' in Q), Falstaff's comment 'Such brooks are welcome to me, that o'erflows such liquor' becomes meaningless in F, where Q's '*Brookes*' is replaced by '*Broomes*'. The substitution of the name seems to be the result of censorial intervention, like that of Oldcastle, Rossill and Harvey with Falstaff, Bardolph and Peto respectively in *Henry IV*. Brooke or Brook was the family name of the Lords Cobham, and William Brooke, seventh Baron Cobham, as Lord Chamberlain from August 1596 to March 1597, had apparently been mainly responsible for the removal of the offending names from the first version of the history play. It is attractive to suppose that the adoption of the assumed name 'Brooke' was meant to satirize the Cobhams, in revenge for their interference with *Henry IV*, and that its replacement with 'Broome' was caused, as in the case of Oldcastle/Falstaff, by a further objection raised by the Cobham family. But several other factors should be taken into account: 1) The satire would have been most inappropriate if the play had been performed for the Garter feast of April 1597, only one month after the death of William Brooke; 2) The name

---

[1] The speech is practically identical in the Quarto version, sig. E2v, except for 'I haue bene throwne' for 'I was thrown', and, to underline the quibble, the word 'ford' is spelt all four times with a capital 'F'.

cannot have been objected to before 1602, because it appears in the Quarto version of that date; 3) Ford's disguise is not part of the masque-like section of the narrative where most topical allusions occur, but it belongs to the main 'Italianate' plot of the jealous husband and the deceits in love. Once again we are confronted with the existence of two separate narratives: an earlier one concerned, as a homage to a chaste, 'radiant Queen', with the exposure of a fortune-hunting, unworthy knight 'full of lecheries and iniquitie',[1] in contrast to the honourable love stratagems of a couple intent on shunning the 'irreligious cursed hours' brought about by enforced marriage (5.5.222–4); and a later comedy based on intrigues derived from Italian models but transferred to an English middle-class setting, onto which the earlier narrative was grafted, where the 'corrupt' knight was identified as the Falstaff of the history plays, escorted by his retinue of 'irregular humorists'. In devising the new play Shakespeare took his revenge on the censorship of *Henry IV* suffered at the hand of William Brooke, Baron Cobham (who had died a couple of years earlier), by adopting the assumed name of Brooke for Ford, apparently an innocent word-play on common nouns, since a 'ford' is the place where a 'brook' can be crossed, but with a further joke at the expense of William's son and heir, Henry Brooke eighth Baron Cobham, who in April 1599 had been elected a Garter knight. It is surprising that the younger Brooke did not immediately raise an objection to the use of his name in the play; it may well be that he wanted to avoid calling attention to it:[2] the replacement of 'Oldcastle' by 'Falstaff' in *Henry IV*, deliberately publicized in the Epilogue of *2 Henry IV*, lent itself to further ridicule of the martyr's descendants. But the name *was* actually changed some time later, in years during which the influence of Henry Brooke was nil. In December 1603 Henry Brooke, together with his brother George, was tried for

---

[1] Parson Evans's description of Falstaff in the Quarto version, sig. G3r; cf. the 'Fairy Queen' in F, 5.5.90, 'Corrupt, corrupt, and tainted in desire!'
[2] For a different view of the case see Taylor, 'Cobham', 349–54.

plotting against the new King James I: both brothers were sentenced to death, but only George was executed; Henry was imprisoned in the Tower, where he died in 1619, and (like the Falstaff/Fastolf of *1 Henry VI*) was 'disgartered', i.e. expelled from the chivalric Order. It seems reasonable to think, with Alfred Hart,[1] that the name change from 'Brooke' to 'Broome' took place on the occasion of the recorded performance of *Merry Wives* before the King on 4 November 1604, in order not to 'revive unpleasant memories' of plots against his person. A further possibility is that the change itself from Brooke to Broome implied another malicious dig, not at the unfortunate Henry, but at his dead father William Brooke, the former Lord Chamberlain, who had died in 1597. It appears from recently discovered documents that in 1595, less than two years before William Brooke's death, the wife of a Mr Broome was, with her husband's consent, under the 'protection' of the Baron Cobham;[2] but this would be an allusion only for those in the know.

Other major inconsistencies loom large in the last part of the play, concerned with the preparation and the enactment of the Herne the Hunter hoax at the expense of Falstaff. Taking for granted that the fairies' masque adapts the text of a previous courtly masque intended as a homage to Queen Elizabeth, traditionally represented by the allegorical figure of the Fairy Queen, which character would be called upon to play that role in the comedy version? Would the Queen, when the comedy was 'Acted by the right Honorable my Lord Chamberlaines seruants . . . before her Maiestie', have appreciated an impersonation by such a character as Mistress Quickly, as both Folio and Quarto stage directions and speech prefixes unequivocally indicate? The appropriateness of such an impersonation must have been called in question on at least one occasion, and in fact in the Folio, i.e.

---

[1] Hart, 89–90. The explanation is supported by Oliver, Ard[2], Introduction, lvii.

[2] Honigmann, 'Oldcastle', 128–31. He concludes that the change 'added insult to injury . . . the Cobham–Mr Broome–Mrs Broome triangle is repeated in the play, with Cobham (i.e. Oldcastle, i.e Falstaff) offering to cuckold "Mr Broome"' (129).

the 'courtly' version of the play, in the course of the preparation of the hoax, Mistress Page, after saying 'Nan Page my daughter, and my little son [William, present only in 4.1], / And three or four more of their growth, we'll dress / Like urchins, oafs and fairies, green and white' (4.4.46–8) decides that 'My Nan shall be the queen of all the fairies, / Finely attired in a robe of white' (4.4.69–70) – a decision confirmed by Fenton when he reports to the Host 'Tonight at Herne's oak, just 'twixt twelve and one, / Must my sweet Nan present the Fairy Queen' (4.6.19–20). At some stage, then, not Quickly but Anne Page was cast for the main role in the masque.[1] No such perplexity arises in the Quarto, i.e. the 'public stage' version, where in the equivalent of 4.4 (sig. F3v) not Mistress but Master Page states 'my daughter *Anne*, / Shall like a litle Fayrie be disguised', and adds a few lines later 'in a robe of white / Ile cloath my daughter, and aduertise *Slender* / to know her by that signe'. Anne is to be just one of the fairies, identified by her being 'robed in white'. This is confirmed by Fenton's report to the Host of Anne's father's intentions in the equivalent of 4.6 (sig. G1v), 'And in a robe of white this night disguised, /. . . / Must *Slender* take her'; when asked by the Host how he will recognize her, Fenton replies: 'by a robe of white, the which she weares / With ribones pendant flaring bout her head, / I shalbe sure to know her'. It looks as if the real token of recognition is not the white robe but the addition of ribbons hanging down from the girl's head. Later we are told in the stage direction in the final scene (sig. G3r) that '*Fenton steales misteris Anne, being in white*'. So far the Quarto version seems fairly consistent. Why then, after the audience has

---

[1] The inappropriateness of having Mistress Quickly play the Fairy Queen must have struck Arrigo Boito when writing the operatic libretto for Verdi's *Falstaff* (1893), and in fact he gave the role to Nannetta (Anne Page). The problem did not arise in the case of the earlier opera by Otto Nicolai (1849): having dispensed with the character of Mistress Quickly altogether, the libretto writer H.S. Mosenthal had no choice but to cast Anna as the 'Feenkönigin' (Fairy Queen) Titania. Salieri's opera, *Falstaff* (1799), omits both Mistress Quickly and the Anne/Fenton love plot, so that the indefatigable Mistress Ford, not content with having pretended earlier in the story to be a German friend of the two wives, turns up in the last scene as 'Regina delle Fate'.

been repeatedly informed that Page had 'advertised' Slender that Anne would wear 'a robe of white', does the already-quoted stage direction state that Slender '*takes a boy in greene*', and, to make confusion worse confounded, when asked why he took the wrong 'Anne', Slender replies 'I came to her in red' (sig. G4r)? And it should be noted that at G1v Fenton had said that it was Mistress Page's intention that 'in a robe of red . . . the Doctor must steale her [Anne] hence' (sig. G1v). The compiler of the Quarto text seems at this stage to have become completely colour-blind, but the scribe Ralph Crane, who prepared the copy for the Folio, was no better judge of colours. At 4.6.34–41 Fenton tells the Host that Master Page, for Slender's benefit, means Anne 'to be all in white', while Mistress Page, for Caius's sake, 'hath intended . . . That quaint in green she shall be loose enrobed, / With ribbons pendant flaring 'bout her head': Anne is not to be recognized by the 'ribbons' about her head but by the colour of her costume. Both colours are confirmed in two scenes missing from Q: at 5.2.9–10 Shallow assures Slender 'The white will decipher her well enough', and at 5.3.1–2 Mistress Page is positive: 'Master Doctor, my daughter is in green'. But some sort of exchange must have taken place at this stage. At 5.5.194 Slender assures Master Page that he 'went to her in *green*', only to find out later that his 'Anne' was 'a great lubberly boy'; Mistress Page in her turn explains that, to cross her husband's purpose, she 'turned my daughter into white' (5.5.198), but when she asks Doctor Caius 'did you take her in *white*?' (5.5.204) she receives the indignant reply 'Ay, by gar, and 'tis a boy!'[1]

The confusions in the Folio text may well throw light on the origin of the copy that Ralph Crane prepared for it. It appears that Crane was assembling his transcript not from a single prompt-book or set of foul papers, but from more than one theatrical document, i.e. from manuscripts of at least two versions of the play itself and of the postulated antecedent

---

[1] Most modern editions since Rowe, including the present one, emend 'green' to 'white' at 194 and 'white' to 'green' at 198 and 204.

entertainment.[1] He was possibly confronted with on the one hand an earlier court masque amply modified for inclusion in a full-length 'citizen' comedy, in which the allegorical masque figures were impersonated by comic characters largely derived from earlier histories (Quickly, Pistol, Evans/Fluellen), and on the other hand a version of the same comedy or part of it modified for a courtly occasion, where the new young innocent heroine Anne Page replaced Quickly in delivering the lines of the Fairy Queen, and perhaps the allusive name of Brooke was replaced by the apparently innocuous Broome. Crane was thinking in terms of publication, not of performance, and introduced into the text a number of minor changes in diction, punctuation and regularization of the verse lines, but was unable to tidy up all the loose ends and inconsistencies. The Folio text, in other words, is certainly basically authorial, but is also a scribal reconstruction that does not necessarily reflect word for word any precise stage of the many through which Shakespeare's play of Falstaff and the merry wives of Windsor must have passed in its early private and public stage life.

The origin of the Quarto unconformities is of a different nature. As indicated before (pp. 35–42), the text seems to be based on an authorially reduced acting version that, by omitting most of the allusions to the court and Windsor as its seat, and all those to the Garter ritual, as well as to the Latin lesson, was intended to present a streamlined, unsophisticated middle-class comedy. The smoothing-out in it of some of the inconsistencies present in the Folio version – for instance the fact that in Q Anne Page is never cast for the role of Fairy Queen in the masque, or the transposition of 3.4 and 3.5 in order to establish a direct continuity between Falstaff's ducking into the Thames in 3.3 and his calling for sack to restore his spirits in 3.5 – would appear to

---

[1] Crane, Cam[2], 157–9, presents a stemma in which the transcript is assumed to derive from foul papers, used in an early private performance, in which the name 'Brooke' had been replaced by 'Broome', and which was further subjected about 1606 to the expurgation of profanities.

depend on authorial decisions; but the remaining unconformities are due to the fact that what we have in Q is not Shakespeare's own but a reported text. A typical reporter's confusion reduces to nonsense Caius's challenge to Evans in 1.4, when, instead of recalling Quickly's explanation that Simple has come on an errand from Evans to her (1.4.70–1), it makes Simple blurt out: 'I brought a Letter sir, / From my M. *Slender*, about misteris *Anne Page*' (sig. B4r). Worse still, in the fairy masque, when the reporter has only a confused reminiscence of Evans's injunction to the supposed spirits, he devises a new verse speech for him:

> Where is *Pead?* go you & see where Brokers sleep,
> And Fox-eyed Seriants with their mase,
> Goe laie the Proctors in the street,
> And pinch the lowsie Seriants face:
> Spare none of these when they are a bed,
> But such whose nose lookes plew and red.
>
> (sig. G2r)

In improvising a speech somehow reminiscent of the tricks played by Queen Mab on self-important citizens when asleep in Mercutio's famous speech in *Romeo and Juliet* 1.4.48ff. to replace Evans's three rhymed couplets at 5.5.49–54 about the punishment of careless sleeping maids ('But those as sleep and think not on their sins, / Pinch them, arms, legs, backs shoulders, sides and shins') the reporter sacrifices sense to rhyme and rhythm.[1]

STRUCTURAL UNCONFORMITIES AND TIME GAPS: THREE VERSIONS OF *MERRY WIVES*

A parallel reading of the two texts, noting the structural differences and their respective timescales, can bear witness to their different origin and destination, and can also account for the

---

[1] See the section 'Quarto and Folio: memorial reconstruction and acting version' above.

composite nature of each of them. Some of the most glaring inconsistencies have already been pointed out in the previous sections of this introduction, but it is worth establishing the length and time sequence of the action as it appears in either text. The general impression received is that the action develops over three or four days: the first presenting the initial situation, the interrelations between the characters, the different strands of the multiple plots, and those following devoted in turn to each of the hoaxes played by the merry wives upon Falstaff – his hiding in the buck-basket (3.3), the beating he receives when disguised as an old woman (4.2) and finally the Herne the Hunter disguise on the night between either the third and fourth or the fourth and fifth day (5.5).

Time and structure in the Folio

To take the Folio version first: there is no doubt that the action of 1.1 begins in mid-morning, shortly before lunchtime, which was normally eleven to twelve o'clock – the word 'dinner' was used indiscriminately to indicate both the midday and the evening meal. It is during dinner that Parson Evans sends Simple on an errand to Mistress Quickly (1.2). 1.3, when Falstaff, after the refusal by Pistol and Nim, dispatches Robin to take his letters to the two wives (76: 'Hold, sirrah, bear you these letters titely', i.e. 'straight away'), obviously takes place after the 'dinner' at Page's, i.e. in the afternoon of the same day. The action of 1.4, in Caius's house, seems to be contemporary with 1.3: Simple has just arrived directly from the dinner and the doctor, before returning on business to court, orders him to carry a challenge to Parson Evans.

The timing of 2.1 is more perplexing. The opening speeches suggest that the two merry wives have just received Falstaff's letters – i.e. it is later in the same day, an impression confirmed by the arrival of Pistol and Nim warning Ford and Page of Falstaff's schemes upon their wives, while the wives retire with Quickly, whom they want to employ as their 'messenger to this

paltry knight' (143–4), to fix an assignation with him for the next morning. Curiously, though, Mistress Page asks her husband 'You'll come to dinner, George?' (141–2). Either 'dinner' means the evening meal, or it is already about 11 am on the second day. Shallow's greeting to Page and Ford upon his entering with the Host, 'Good even and twenty' (177–8), though, confirms that the time is the evening of the first day – but shortly afterwards (185–9) Shallow invites Page to go with him and the Host to see the 'duel' between Caius and Evans, and the three of them leave together for this purpose. We must suppose then that the second part of the scene, from the entrance of the Host at 171.1, takes place in the early morning of the next day. Such sudden time changes in mid-scene are not uncommon in Elizabethan plays.

In fact the following scene, 2.2, supports the transition to the second day, and suggests even the time, about 8 a.m., because: a) Quickly greets Falstaff with 'good morrow' (32); b) she gives the time of the assignation at Ford's house as 'between ten and eleven' the same morning (80); c) Falstaff repeats the information to Ford disguised as Brook (251), and tells him to come for his report 'at night' (253) or 'soon at night' (269, 271); d) Ford, left alone, repeats 'Eleven o'clock the hour' (293) and comments: 'better three hours too soon than a minute too late' (295–6) – three hours being the difference between eight and eleven o' clock.

There is no doubt that 2.3 and 3.1, the mock duel between Caius and Evans stage-managed by the Host, involving Page, Shallow and Slender as spectators, takes place in the morning of the second day, and its timing overlaps, at least in part, with 2.2. Duels were fought shortly after dawn. Rugby's remark, at 2.3.4, that ''Tis past the hour' appointed for the duel, and later Caius saying that he has been waiting 'two, tree hours' (2.3.33) suggest that it is by now nearer ten o'clock than eight (though this is contradicted at 3.1.43–4 by Page's remark on 'this raw rheumatic day', suggesting very early morning).

3.2 is a transitional scene, marking the approach of all the characters to Ford's house. The hour struck by the clock at 40–1, which prompts Ford's remark 'The clock gives me my cue', is not specified, but Ford's invitation to Page, Evans and Caius to 'dinner' at his house where he'll show them 'a monster' (71–4) – an invitation declined by Shallow and Slender because they intend in the meantime to visit Anne at Page's house – implies that the time is close to eleven. There is no time problem with the next, the central scene of the play (3.3), the buck-basket hoax at Falstaff's (and Ford's) expense: the fact that it is the late morning of the second day is confirmed towards the end of the scene by a penitent Ford's renewal of his invitation to lunch (he tells Page, Caius and Evans 'I promised you a dinner', 208). Another invitation to be kept in mind is that of Page to Ford, Caius and Evans: 'I do invite you tomorrow morning to my house to breakfast; after, we'll a-birding together' (214–16).

3.4 is the first scene partly in verse in the play, located in Page's house (as Page himself makes clear at 67), beginning with the meeting of Anne Page with Fenton – a scene that deserves much closer attention, and which will be discussed later in connection with its Quarto equivalent. The entrance at 21.1 of Shallow and Slender fits in with their decision at 3.2.75–6 to visit Page's house while the rest are going to Ford's, making Slender's ridiculous wooing of Anne (3.4.36–64) partly overlap in the matter of time with the buck-basket scene there (3.3). Master and Mistress Page, entering at 64.1, apparently come directly from 'dinner' at Ford's (see 3.3.208), confirming that the scene takes place in the middle of the second day. The only puzzling element is Mistress Quickly's exit speech at the end, 'I must of another errand to Sir John Falstaff from my two mistresses – what a beast am I to slack it!' (106–8): apart from the fact that there has been no time for the 'two mistresses' to give her the errand (a new assignation with Falstaff), her words imply that she is going directly from Page's house to the knight at the Garter Inn that same afternoon.

The real confusion begins with 3.5: Falstaff is shown at first still suffering from his ducking in the Thames (Fig. 4), as if he were coming directly from it (20–1: 'Come, let me pour in some sack to the Thames water'), but immediately afterwards Mistress Quickly makes it clear that it is the early morning of the third day, not only by her greeting Falstaff with 'good morrow' (25), i.e. good morning, but also because the new assignation with Mistress Ford is fixed for when 'her husband goes *this morning* a-birding . . . between eight and nine' (42–4), and Falstaff, after making double sure of the time (at 50–1 he asks 'Between nine and ten, sayst thou?' and Quickly replies 'Eight and nine'), reports the information to Master Ford/Brook (118–21), who in turn remarks ''Tis past eight already' (122). A further serious inconsistency is that Ford/Brook was due to visit Falstaff not early in the morning of the third day, but 'soon at night' on the second, i.e. the previous, day (see 2.2.253, 269, 271). In any case,

4 Falstaff thrown into the ditch at Datchet Mead, suggested by Falstaff's speech at 3.5.4–17, illustration by George Cruikshank, from Robert Brough, *The Life of Sir John Falstaff* (1858). Nineteenth-century illustrations of Shakespeare are frequently based on descriptive passages rather than stage action

granting that 3.5 takes place early in the morning of the third day, then the action of 4.1, the Latin lesson, is contemporary with that of 3.5, since eight is the time for children to go to school. Mistress Page, at the end of the scene, sends William home and presumably proceeds directly to Ford's house.

The timing of the second trap set by the 'mistresses' for Falstaff, scene 4.2, is not in question: between eight and nine on the third day. It must be assumed that Ford had visited Falstaff before joining the party of Windsor citizens and visitors that Page had invited for breakfast at his house in view of going a-birding (see 3.3.214–17), and had persuaded them to go and search his own house for the supposed intruder. After Falstaff's escape in woman's disguise, and apparently while the men are still engaged in the fruitless search (at 188 Page comments 'Let's obey his humour a little further'), the wives decide to reveal their plots to their husbands and to devise further punishments for Falstaff (202–13).

There is hardly any time reference in the following scenes. Bardolph's request of horses for the 'Germans' (4.3) may well occur at the same time as the 'witch of Brentford' scene (4.2), while in 4.4 the wives' disclosure to their husbands of their plots, the devising of the Herne the Hunter hoax, and the decision to 'send quickly to Sir John' (81) for that purpose, should follow closely on 4.2, i.e. take place later in the morning of the third day. The same is true of 4.5, since we learn from Simple that Falstaff is just back in the inn still disguised as 'an old woman, a fat woman' (10). If this is so, the rest of the scene, i.e. the report of the theft of the Host's horses (61–86) and the arrival of Mistress Quickly, who goes up with Falstaff to talk in his chamber (97–120), are also meant to happen on the third day.

Inconsistencies in the timescale re-emerge in the following scenes, 4.6 and 5.1, the second of which has no counterpart in Q. In 4.6 Fenton asks the Host for his help in eloping with Anne, while 5.1 begins with Mistress Quickly taking leave of Falstaff after descending from his room (see 4.5.120), meaning that the

interview of Fenton with the Host (4.6) has taken place while Quickly was talking to Falstaff upstairs, at the same hour of the same day. Now, in the course of the interview Fenton informs the Host that the fairies' revels are to take place 'Tonight at Herne's oak, just 'twixt twelve and one' (4.6.19), i.e. in the night between the third and fourth day, and this is confirmed by Falstaff at 5.1.10–11 when he informs Ford/Brook that his assignation is for 'tonight . . . in the park about midnight, at Herne's oak'. What is surprising is Ford's reaction: 'Went you not to her yesterday, sir, as you told me you had appointed?' (13–14), to which Falstaff replies by telling of his unfortunate disguise as a woman and concludes 'tonight I will be revenged' on Ford (27). Ford's 'yesterday' means that the action of 5.1 (and of the rest of the play) does not take place, as was implied in the previous scenes, on the third, but on the fourth day.

The next three short scenes (like 5.1 with no equivalent in Q) are concerned not with the day but with the approaching hour of the fairies' masque. At 5.2.10 Shallow announces that 'It hath struck ten o'clock'; at 5.3.23–4 Mistress Ford exclaims 'The hour draws on. To the oak, to the oak!', and in 5.4 Parson Evans is ready to jump out from the sand pit with his fairy children. Time references are obviously unnecessary in the final scene, where the fairy dances are supposed to last 'till 'tis one o'clock' (5.5.74). What remains contradictory is the day, or rather night, of Falstaff's third trial – is it the third in the play's action, as appears from several allusions in the scenes following 4.2 and as is confirmed by Fenton in 4.6, or is it the fourth, as suggested in 5.1? It is the same sort of unconformity in the time sequence noted in the case of 3.5, where Quickly's and Ford's visits to Falstaff, scheduled for the evening of the second day, appear to take place at an incredibly early hour of the third. These structural faults in F run parallel to several other inconsistencies of a different nature pointed out in the previous sections of this introduction: for instance, the colour of Anne Page's costume in the masque, the question of who is to impersonate the Queen of

the fairies, or in whose reign the action of the play is supposed to take place.

Time and structure in the Quarto

It is significant that several if not all inconsistencies disappear in the Quarto.[1] It is expedient to look into Q taking note not only of its time sequence but also of other structural divergences from the ampler text. Beginning with the first scene (sigs A3–B1), the puzzlement created by the presence of Shallow in Windsor, where he seems to own a deer park, is avoided in Q, where: a) there is no mention of his being an esquire 'in the county of Gloucester, Justice of Peace and Coram'; b) his business in Windsor is stated very clearly from the start, when he tells Master Page, present from the beginning of the scene as a peace-maker, together with parson Evans, in Shallow's quarrel with Falstaff: 'M. *Page* I will not be wronged. For you / Syr, I loue you, and for my cousen [Slender] / He comes to looke vpon your daughter'; c) the fact that Shallow is a visitor to Windsor on private affairs is made clear in Page's reply – after promising that 'if my daughter / Likes him [Slender] so well as I, wee'l quickly haue it a match', he goes on 'In the meane time let me intreat you to soiourne / Here a while'; d) the possibility that Falstaff's deer-stealing and Bardolph, Pistol and Nim's robbery of Slender in a tavern may have taken place, not in Windsor, but at some other time and in some other place, is left open by the omission of any mention of Shallow's gift of venison to Page. The different structure of this scene, introducing Master Page at the beginning, has the advantage of foregrounding the triangular love subplot at the expense of the laborious heraldic jokes in F. The following three scenes do not reveal substantial structural discrepancies between the two versions, except for the fact that in Q the texts are ruthlessly shortened. The main inconsistency

---

[1] As noted before, some of them remain: Caius's challenge to Evans instead of Slender in 1.4 is even less justified in Q than in F (see p. 43 above), and the confusion about the colour of Anne Page's costume in the night revels is as bad, but at least there is no suggestion, as in F, that she should impersonate the Fairy Queen (p. 53 above).

concerning the cause of Caius's challenge to Evans has already been noted (p. 56), and the most interesting omission in respect of Folio is that of Fenton's visit to Quickly in Caius's house at 1.4.121–54, which seems to be a late addition as an afterthought to the Folio text, as it is the only passage in the play where Fenton speaks exclusively in prose. At all events in this scene the Quarto text is most helpful in sorting out the stage movements.

Though structured in the same way as 2.1 in F, its equivalent scene 5 in Q (sigs B4–C2v) manages to iron out the time discrepancies in the Folio text, where the scene presents a kind of seesaw between the afternoon of the first day (lines 1–140 and 152–71) and the early morning of the second (141–51 and 172–216). The action in Q is limited to the second part of the first day, because in it: (a) Mistress Page does not mention dinner to Master Page at 141–2; (b) Shallow says 'God den and twenty', confirming that it is the evening of the first day, and, what is more, though the duel is mentioned, there is no hint that it should take place immediately, as in F, and in fact Page does not join the Host and Shallow to see the 'sport in hand' but, while the other two 'wag' (not necessarily to the place appointed for the duel), Page remains with Ford and they go together to dinner – undoubtedly an evening meal. This means that the 'sport' may well take place early next morning.

Folio 2.2 opens early in the morning of the second day, but the Quarto version (scene 6, sigs C3–D1) leaves more than a margin of ambiguity. A first distinction between the two versions is the fact that in F Pistol, though dismissed by Falstaff, remains on stage till the exit of Quickly, while in Q he is got rid of ('Well, gotoo, away, no more') before her entrance, and disappears for good from the play. This simplifies the action. The only reason for Pistol's belated exit in pursuit of Quickly and his reappearance as Hobgoblin in 5.5 in F is the establishing of a connection with the earlier Histories, like Page's mention in a later scene of Fenton as a companion of the wild prince and Poins – another exclusive feature of F. In Q Quickly, instead of

'good morrow', wishes Falstaff 'God den' and he replies 'Good den' ('good evening', though the expression could simply mean 'good day'), and she fixes the assignation between eight and nine, which is the appropriate time for Ford to 'go a birding', without specifying the day, so it can be assumed that she is referring to the next morning, and that this scene is taking place in the evening of the first day. The real transition from the first day to the second in the course of a single scene occurs, as an authorial sleight of hand, after Quickly's exit. Bardolph's entrance announcing the arrival of a Master Brook, i.e. Ford in disguise, effectively marks the beginning of a new scene on a new day, and more precisely before eight in the morning. This is made clear when Falstaff, after informing Ford/Brook that 'between eight and nine' is the time for meeting Mistress Ford, and telling him repeatedly 'Come to me soone at night', goes out (apparently to keep the assignation); Ford, left alone, does not mention (as in F) eleven as 'the hour', but comments 'the time drawes on, / Better *an houre* too soone, then a minit too late', mindful that the fateful meeting should occur within an hour – and not three, as in F, where it was fixed for between ten and eleven.

Quarto scenes 7 and 8, the equivalent of 2.3 and 3.1 in F, show the attention of the Quarto compiler to the new timescale adopted in it: there are no remarks, as in Folio, about Caius having waited two, three hours for Evans – a deliberate omission, since, with Falstaff's assignation being for between eight and nine, the action of these scenes must take place at an earlier hour. Q is at fault only in the mention of Bardolph as accompanying the Host in scene 9 (sig. D3v: '*Bardolfe* laie their swords to pawne'), though he does not speak and is not mentioned in stage directions.

Scene 9 (sigs D3v–D4), the equivalent of Folio 3.2, omits the initial meeting of Ford with Mistress Page and Robin, and does not mention the clock striking the hour of the assignation; the apparent inconsistency of Ford (as in F) inviting Page, Evans and Caius to 'dinner' at his house, where he'll show them 'a

monster', is solved by considering the indiscriminate use of 'dinner' in Q for any meal in the day: eight or nine in the morning is correct if 'dinner' is taken to mean breakfast, in the same way that 'dinner' is correct in F if we take it to refer to a twelve o'clock meal, i.e. lunch. In both texts Shallow and Slender excuse themselves from going because they intend to visit Anne at Page's house, though Q erroneously includes them in an entry direction for the buck-basket scene (sig. E1v), where they never speak: this, like the mention of Bardolph at sig. D3v, seems to be an oversight by the compiler of Q.[1]

Quarto 10 is the central scene of the play, the buck-basket hoax (Fig. 5), corresponding to Folio 3.3. Neither text carries a precise indication of time, which, by all that has gone before, must obviously be in the morning of the second day, at about eleven o'clock in F, at about nine in Q – the latter being somewhat awkward because at the end of the scene (sig. E2) they all 'goe in to dinner' at Ford's – apparently, as noted before, a belated breakfast rather than a lunch; in fact immediately afterwards, Page extends his invitation for early the next morning to the other men with the words 'to morrow I inuite you all / To my house to dinner: and in the morning weele / A birding', which is certainly a more ambiguous way of saying, as in the Folio version, 'I do invite you tomorrow morning to my house to breakfast; after, we'll a-birding together' (3.3.214–16).

After this scene, Folio and Quarto part ways: Quarto scene 11 does not correspond to Folio 3.4 but to 3.5. In other words, the equivalents of Folio 3.4 and 3.5 are transposed, and Folio 4.1 immediately following (the Latin lesson scene taking place early in the morning of the third day) is totally omitted. The transposition establishes a different, and on the whole neater, time sequence. The first part of scene 11 (sigs E2–E3) leaves no doubt

---

[1] If, as it appears (p. 68 below), Quarto scene 12 – Shallow's and Slender's visit to Anne – takes place not, as in Folio 3.4, on the same day but early next morning, their presence in scene 10 (equivalent to Folio 3.3) is justified and the compiler's error consists in having retained at this point in scene 9 (sig. D4) Shallow's speech 'wel, wel, God be with you, we shall haue the fairer / Wooing at Maister *Paiges*.'

5 *Falstaff in the Basket*, painted by the Austrian artist Hans Makart, 1867

that Falstaff has just returned from his misadventure in the Thames ('Let me put some Sacke among this cold water'), and this is confirmed by Mistress Quickly announcing the new

assignation for 'to morrow . . . betweene ten and eleuen', with no mention of Master Ford going a-birding. The sleight of hand, as in the case of scene 6, corresponding to Folio 2.2, occurs when Ford/Brook visits Falstaff. Ford does not seem to keep his appointment 'soon at night' of the second day: halfway through his dialogue with Falstaff the time appears clearly to be early in the morning of the third day. Falstaff announces 'I haue receiued / Another appointment of meeting, / Between ten and eleuen is the houre' (sig. E3v), and Ford responds: 'Why sir, tis almost ten alreadie', at which Falstaff remarks 'Is it? Why then will I addresse my selfe / For my appointment', and exits after repeating twice 'M. *Brooke* come to me soone / At night.'

The main difficulty with Quarto scene 12 (sigs E4–F1), the 'transposed' scene corresponding to Folio 3.4, is in establishing its position in the time sequence of the play's action. The advantage of the transposition consists in showing the effect of Falstaff's ducking in the Thames shortly after the event on the second day rather than on the next morning (as in Folio 3.5). On the other hand, since the second part of scene 11 suggested a transition to the morning of the third day, the new assumption is that this scene is happening while Falstaff is on his way to his second assignation at Ford's house. This leaves the arrival at Page's house, first of Shallow and Slender, and then of the two Pages, unaccounted for, since the latter as well as Shallow figure in the scene immediately following at Ford's house. It should be noted, though, that Falstaff's visit there is supposed to take place not, as in F, between eight and nine, but between ten and eleven, which allows for their presence at Page's earlier the same morning. This scene, which in F is the first scene partly in verse, deserves much closer attention, because the verse speeches in the Folio version give the odd impression of belonging to a different kind of narrative, presenting some striking features in connection with the multi-layered nature of the text or texts of the play. This will be examined more closely after the completion of the survey of the time sequence in Q.

The omission of the Latin lesson (Folio 4.1) saves the embarrassment of moving back from mid-morning to an earlier hour. Scene 13, unlike its equivalent 4.2 in F, begins with Mistress Ford instructing her servants about carrying in and out the buckbasket, avoiding in this way the confusion engendered in Folio 4.2 by the sudden appearance of servants and basket and by their remarks about it later in the scene (103–8). The time of the action, ten to eleven of the third day, repeatedly stated in scene 11, is taken for granted, and the most serious loss, in respect of F, is Mistress Page's comment at 4.2.99–102, the only lines of verse in the scene, providing the essential key to a reading of the whole play and accounting for its title ('Wives may be merry and yet honest too'). As noted before (pp. 41–2), the gist of it is transferred in Q to an earlier, inappropriate, context. Also in the brief scene 14 (4.3 in F) there is no time pointer, and it must obviously be assumed that it coincides with the previous scene.

Scene 15 (sigs F3v–F4v), supposedly taking place on the third day shortly after the action of scene 13, corresponds to Folio 4.4, the second scene in the play written mainly in verse; but though the characters on stage are the same in both versions,[1] the more concise Quarto text (55 lines instead of 88 – for the difference in versification and its significance see pp. 38–40 above) gives a clearer account of the trap set for Falstaff at Herne's oak, so much so that in modern editions line 41 in the Folio version is borrowed from Q (see 4.4.41 t.n.). Besides Q avoids, as noted before (p. 53), the error of casting Anne in the role of 'queen of all the fairies', though the uncertainty about the colour of Anne's costume remains. Scene 16 (sigs F3v–G1) is structured and

---

[1] Actually the Quarto entrance stage direction includes, besides the two Fords, the two Pages and Evans, also Shallow and Slender, though they are mute throughout the scene. In this case, unlike that of scene 10 (Folio 3.3, see p. 66, note 1 above), their presence is justified in order to acquaint them with the plan about Herne's oak. In Folio their involvement in the plot is made clear in 5.2, a scene omitted in Q. Shallow is also included in the Quarto stage direction in the last scene, at the equivalent of 5.5.102.2, entering together with the Pages and the two Fords, and has a single one-line speech 'God saue you sir *Iohn Falstaffe*', while in F he is unaccountably absent from the denouement of the play, like the Host in both versions.

timed exactly as its equivalent 4.5 in F, except for the transposition of the entrances of the doctor and the parson telling the Host about the horse thieves – Evans first and Caius afterwards in F, Caius first and Evans after in Q.[1] Falstaff is just back from his second misadventure in Ford's house, indicating that the action still takes place on the third day, and at the end he retires with Mistress Quickly to his chamber.

A serious discrepancy in the time sequence of F is avoided in Quarto by streamlining the play's action through a series of omissions. As noted before, Folio 5.1 began with Quickly still in the Garter Inn as in 4.5, implying that the intervening scene, 4.6, when Fenton had informed the Host that 'Tonight at Herne's oak, just 'twixt twelve and one, / Must my sweet Nan present the Fairy Queen' (19–20), took place the same day as the 'witch of Brentford' episode; but this was contradicted immediately after in 5.1 by Ford/Brook asking Falstaff 'Went you not to her [Mistress Ford] *yesterday*?' (13). The absence of this remark and of any equivalent for Folio scenes 5.1 to 5.4 in Q makes it credible that the interview between Fenton and the Host in scene 17 (sigs G1–G1v, the counterpart of Folio 4.6) takes place not on the same but on the next day: Fenton's remark that Anne is to be 'in a robe of white this night disguised' not only establishes that the final hoax is to take place on the night of the fourth rather than the third day, but also that it is not Anne who will impersonate the Fairy Queen.

The substantial differences between the two texts of the last scene of the play – scene 18, sigs G1v–G4v in Q, 5.5 in F – have been amply discussed in the previous pages of this introduction, especially with regard to the absence from Q of the Garter speech and several other masque-like features, so as to suggest the intrusion in F of a fairly elaborate court masque including comic elements characteristic of an antimasque. Only the comic

---

[1]   A similar reversal of entrances occurs in the last scene with the two deceived suitors of Anne: in F Slender enters at 5.5.173.1 and Caius at 5.5.200.1, while in Q (sig. G4) the Doctor enters first and Slender ten lines later.

parts are present in Q, though in this case too, as in the equivalents of the verse sections of 3.4, 4.4 and 4.6, the verse and rhyming patterns differ considerably in the two texts.

The main differences between the two texts concerning the times of the action and the characters taking part in it are illustrated in the tables on pp. 75 and 76–7.

The third narrative strand

The impression that the play is a conflation of texts of different origin and the evidence of its multi-layered nature can be tested by subjecting to a close reading the first of the four scenes in F which are mainly in verse, 3.4, compared with its equivalent in Q (scene 12 – a scene which appears in it *after* instead of before the equivalent of Folio 3.5), taking into account on the one hand that the Folio scene has about 108 lines against 65 in Q, and on the other that in fact only 53 of those 108 Folio lines, i.e. nearly 50 per cent, are actually lines of verse, while all the rest is prose.[1] In the Folio the scene develops through six stages: 1) 1–21, all verse: Fenton courts Anne. 2) 22–64: Enter Mistress Quickly with Shallow and Slender (the only verse in this section at 31–3 is Anne's comment 'This is my father's choice. / O, what a world of vile ill-favoured faults / Looks handsome in three hundred pounds a year!'); then, while Mistress Quickly takes Fenton aside, Shallow encourages Slender to woo Anne. 3) 65–74, mainly verse: Enter to them Master and Mistress Page; he, after commanding Anne to accept Slender's suit, deplores Fenton's presence, but instead of sending him away, he himself leaves, together with Shallow and Slender, who have not said a word. 4) 75–93, verse except for Mistress Quickly's speeches: Quickly encourages Fenton to speak to Mistress Page, who first

---

[1] Of the other three Folio 'verse' scenes, only 4.6 (between Fenton and the Host) is completely in verse (with the exception only of the Host's four lines, 1–2 and 6–7). In 4.4 the verse lines are 70 out of a total of about 88 – the prose parts being represented mainly by Parson Evans's speeches. Finally in 5.5 the verse parts are some 100 lines out of about 240, limited to the Fairy/Garter masque (37–102) and the final revelation of the Anne Page/Fenton marriage (210–39).

tells Anne that she is seeking for her 'a better husband' than Slender, and then assures Fenton (89–90): 'My daughter will I question how she loves you, / And as I find her, so am I affected' – a surprising statement from a person who, as Mistress Quickly comments at 84, has in mind Doctor Caius as the 'better husband' for her daughter; finally she leaves the stage with Anne. 5) 94–9: a short exchange between Quickly (prose) and Fenton (verse); the latter, before leaving, gives her a ring for Anne and a gratuity for herself. 6) 100–8, all prose: Quickly, alone, declares that she will do her best for all three suitors and exits hurriedly on an 'errand to Sir John Falstaff from my two mistresses'.

The Quarto version of the scene (sigs E4–F1) develops through five stages: 1) Mistress Quickly is present from the beginning, listening to the conversation between Fenton and Anne and warning them of the arrival of Master Page. It should be noted that while in F Fenton never mentions his rivals for Anne's hand but only her father's opposition, in Q he begins by asking 'Shall foolish *Slender* haue thee to his wife? / Or one as wise as he, the learned Doctor?'. 2) Shallow and Slender are introduced not by Quickly, who is already on stage, but by Page and Mistress Page; Page, after briefly dismissing Fenton, whispers aside with Slender, Shallow and Anne, while Fenton, encouraged by Quickly, turns to Mistress Page, receiving from her a rather dispiriting answer: 'Ifaith M. *Fenton* tis as my husband please. / For my part Ile neither hinder you, nor further you', and Fenton leaves after giving 'a brace of angels' to Quickly, but no ring for Anne. 3) Master Page calls on his wife to go with him in order to leave Slender, in the company of Shallow, to court Anne; there is no mention of Mistress Quickly's presence, but no record of her exit. 4) The comic wooing scene that follows occasions Anne's remark 'O God how many grosse faults are hid, / And couered in three hundred pound a yeare? / Well M. *Slender*, within a day or two Ile tell you more', which is interpreted by Slender as a positive answer ('vncle I shall haue her'); the courting scene is interrupted not,

as in F, by the entrance of Master and Mistress Page, but by Mistress Quickly's announcement that Page is asking Shallow, Slender and Anne to come to him. 5) Quickly, lagging behind after their exit, protests 'I will do what I can for them all three' (i.e. Anne's suitors), without mentioning any business with Falstaff since in the Quarto version her visit to him (3.5 in F) had taken place in the preceding scene 11.

On the whole scene 12 in Q, though half the length of 3.4 in F, establishes a more logical sequence for the action: a) the presence of Mistress Quickly from the beginning makes her the real manipulator of the scene; b) the transposition of Slender's wooing scene to *after* the exit of Fenton, Page and Mistress Page avoids the awkwardness of having Fenton, albeit engaged in an unexplained conversation with Quickly, as an onlooker; c) Mistress Page's reply to Fenton's plea is more in line than that in F with her disregard for Anne's feelings in the choice of a husband; d) Page's behaviour in leaving the stage is justified: he exits in order to leave Slender free to woo Anne, while in Folio he unaccountably allows Anne to remain with Fenton and the unreliable Quickly.

The Quarto version, most of which is in irregular verse that bears little resemblance to the verse parts of the scene in F, suits the time sequence of the play action, provided it is assumed that it takes place not, as apparently in Folio 3.4, later in the second day, but early in the third, at the same time as Ford's visit to Falstaff in the second part of scene 11, at the end of which the latter leaves the stage to keep his assignation between ten and eleven. The entrance of Shallow and Slender together with the two Pages in Q also rules out the possibility, suggested in F, that they visited Anne while Page was at 'dinner' at Ford's on the previous day.

One question remains: what suggested the different arrangement of 3.4 and 3.5 in F and the introduction in that text of the additional – dramatically superfluous – scene of the Latin lesson (4.1)? One possible explanation could be Shakespeare's decision

to make use in the comedy, perhaps for some special performance such as a court presentation, of scenic material at hand from a previous courtly occasion. A different kind of dramatic narrative emerges if all prose speeches in Folio 3.4 are eliminated and only the verse parts of the scene are considered. In the first place, Mistress Quickly disappears from it altogether, as do Shallow and Slender, unless the latter, mentioned by name at 65, puts in a brief appearance as a mute. The resulting narrative is this: a young gentleman (Fenton) professes his love to a girl (Anne) and regrets her father's hostility to him (1–21). The sight of the father (Page), apparently accompanied by a suitor for the girl's hand, prompts a bitter comment from her (32–3). The father, a prepossessing figure determined to impose his choice of husband on a recalcitrant daughter, is very brusque both with her and with the gentleman in her company, and exits in a huff (65–74).[1] At this point the lovers turn to the girl's mother (Mistress Page), she pleading not to be married 'to yond fool', he asking for the mother's goodwill towards him. The girl's mother answers that she is prepared to second her daughter's inclinations, making no attempt to discourage a suitor whom the girl obviously prefers (76–83, 85–93). There is no hint that Mistress Page favours a Doctor (Caius) as a suitor for Anne, no interference by Mistress Quickly or Justice Shallow. Caius, Quickly, Shallow simply don't exist in the narrative implicit in the verse part of the scene, which tells a different story from the one on which the love plot of *Merry Wives* is based. This discrepancy engenders the suspicion that a dramatic narrative of a different kind, all in verse, has been grafted onto the basic comedy plot, and the process of adaptation has required a number of minor and major alterations in the structure of the comedy, including the transposition of two scenes.

---

[1] If the mention of Shallow at 73 is eliminated, the verse runs more smoothly:
PAGE   She is no match for you.
FENTON   Sir, will you hear me?
PAGE   No, good Master Fenton. – Come, son Slender, in. –
Knowing my mind, you wrong me, Master Fenton.   [*Exit with Slender.*]

TIME SEQUENCES IN FOLIO AND QUARTO

Folio Act/Scene	Place	Day	Time	Quarto Scene	Place	Day	Time
1.1	nr Page's	1	mid-morning	1	nr Page's	1	mid-morning
1.2	nr Page's	1	11/12 am	2	nr Page's	1	11/12 am
1.3	Garter Inn	1	afternoon	3	Garter Inn	1	afternoon
1.4	Caius's	1	afternoon (same as 1.3)	4	Caius's	1	afternoon (same as 3)
2.1	Ford's — 1st part / 2nd part	1 / 2	evening? / before 8 am	5	Ford's	1	evening
2.2	Garter Inn	2	*c.* 8 am	6	Garter Inn — 1st part / 2nd part	1 / 2	evening / before 8 am
2.3	Park	2	*c.* 10 am	7	Park	2	*c.* 8 am
3.1	Park	2	10 (or 8?) am	8	Park	2	*c.* 8 am
3.2	Street	2	10/11 am	9	Street	2	8/9 am
3.3	Ford's	2	*c.* 11 am	10	Ford's	2	*c.* 9 am
Scene transposed: Q scene 11 = F 3.5				11	Garter Inn — 1st part / 2nd part	2 / 3	late morning / 9/10 am
3.4	Page's	2	midday	12	Page's	3	9/10 am
3.5	Garter Inn	3	before 8 am **but at beginning contemporary with 3.4**	**Equivalent to Q scene 11**			
4.1	Street	3	*c.* 8 am	**Not in Q**			
4.2	Ford's	3	8/9 am	13	Ford's	3	10/11 am
4.3	Garter Inn	3	early morning	14	Garter Inn	3	before sc.13?
4.4	Ford's?	3	late morning	15	Ford's?	3	*c.* 12 am
4.5	Garter Inn	3	late morning	16	Garter Inn	3	*c.* midday
4.6	Garter Inn	3	4.5 continued	17	Garter Inn	4	**during day 4**
5.1	Garter Inn	3	4.6 continued **but for Ford morning of day 4**	**Not in Q**			
5.2	Park?	3 (or 4)	10 pm	**Not in Q**			
5.3	Park	3 (or 4)	*c.* 12 pm	**Not in Q**			
5.4	Park	3 (or 4)	12 pm	**Not in Q**			
5.5	Herne's oak	3 (or 4)	from 12 pm till 1 am	18	Herne's oak	4	from 12 pm till 1 am

Changes of day in mid-scene: Folio 2.1 (from first to second day);
Quarto sc.6 (from first to second day), and sc.11 (from second to third day).

CHARACTERS PRESENT IN EACH SCENE

Bold: Characters missing from equivalent scene in either text.
Italics: Characters appearing as mutes.

Folio		Quarto	
Act/Scene no.		*Scene no.*	
1.1	Sh. Sl. Ev./Pa.	1	Sh. Sl. Ev. **Pa.**
	Sh. Sl. Ev. Pa. Fal. Pi. Ba. Ni.		Sh. Sl. Ev. Pa. Fal. Pi. Ba. Ni.
	+ MrsF. MrsP. [*AP.*]		Sh. Sl. Ev. Pa. Fal. Pi. Ba. Ni. MrsF. MrsP.
AP			
	Sl. **Sim.**/Sh. Ev.//Sl. AP/Pa.		Sl. AP
1.2	Ev. Sim.	2	Ev. Sim.
1.3	Ho. Fal. Pi. Ba. Ni. **Rob.**	3	Ho. Fal. Pi. Ba. Ni. [*Rob.*]
1.4	Qu. Sim. Ru.	4	Qu. Sim.
	Qu. Sim. Ru. Ca.//Qu. **Fen.**		Qu. Sim. Ca. Ru.
2.1	MrsP./MrsF.	5	MrsP./MrsF
	+ Fo. Pi. Pa. Ni./Qu.//		+ Fo. Pi. Pa. Ni. (+ Qu.)
	Fo. Pa.		Fo. Pa.
	Fo. Pa. Ho. Sh.		Fo. Pa. Ho. Sh.
2.2	Fal. Pi./**Rob.**	6	Fal. Pi.
	Fal. Pi. Qu.		Fal. Qu.//
	Fal. Ba.		Fal. Ba.
	Fal. Fo.		Fal. Fo.
2.3	Ca. Ru./Ho. Sh. Sl. Pa.	7	Ca. Ru./Ho. Sh. Sl. Pa.
	Ca. Ho. *Ru.*		Ca. Ho.
3.1	Ev. Sim.	8	Ev. Sim.
	Ev. Sim. Pa. Sh. Sl.		Ev. Sim. Pa. Sh. Sl.
	Ev. Sim. Pa. Sh. Sl. Ho. Ca. *Ru.*		Ev. Sim. Pa. Sh. Sl. Ho. Ca. *Ru.* [*Ba.*]
3.2	**MrsP. Rob.**/Fo.	9	Fo.
	Fo. Pa. Sh. Sl. Ho. Ev. Ca. *Ru.*		Pa. Sh. Sl. Ho. Ev. Ca. *Ru.*
3.3	MrsF. **MrsP.**/2Ser./**Rob.**//MrsF. Fal.	10	MrsF. 2Ser./MrsF. Fal.
	Rob. MrsP. MrsF. Fal./*2Ser.*		MrsP. MrsF. Fal./*2Ser.*
	MrsP. MrsF. Fo. Pa. Ca. Ev.		MrsP. MrsF. Fo. Pa. Ca. Ev. [**Sh. Sl.**]

Folio	Quarto
Act/Scene no.	*Scene no.*
Quarto scene 11 = Folio 3.5	11 Fal. Ba./Qu.//
	Fal. Fo.
3.4 AP Fen.	12 Qu. AP Fen.
AP Fen. Sh. Sl. Qu./Pa. MrsP.	Qu. AP Fen. Pa. MrsP. Sh. Sl.
AP Fen. MrsP. Qu.	AP Sh. Sl./Qu.
3.5 Fal. Ba./Qu.//	Folio 3.5 = Quarto scene 11
Fal. Fo.	
4.1 MrsP. Qu. Wil./Ev.	Omitted from Quarto
4.2 Fal. MrsF.	13 MrsF. 2Ser./Fal.
MrsF. MrsP. Fal./2Ser.	MrsF. Fal. MrsP.
Fo. Pa. Sh. *Ca.* Ev. MrsF./MrsP. [*Fal.*]	MrsF. Fo. Pa. Sh. Ev./+ MrsP. *Fal.*
4.3 Ho. Ba.	14 Ho. Ba.
4.4 Pa. Fo. MrsP. MrsF. Ev.	15 Pa. Fo. MrsP. MrsF. Ev. **Sh. Sl.**
4.5 Ho. Sim./Fal.	16 Ho. Sim./Fal.
Ho. Fal. Ba./Ev./Ca.	Ho. Fal. Ba./Ca./Ev.
Fal. Qu.	Fal. Qu.
4.6 Ho. Fen.	17 Ho. Fen.
5.1 Fal. Qu.//Fal. Fo.	Omitted from Quarto
5.2 Pa. Sh. Sl.	Omitted from Quarto
5.3 MrsP. MrsF. Ca.	Omitted from Quarto
5.4 Ev. Children	Omitted from Quarto
5.5 Fal./MrsF. MrsP.	18 Fal./MrsF. MrsP.
Fal. Qu. Ev. **Pi**. Children//	Fal. Qu. Ev. Children
Fal. Pa. Fo. MrsP. MrsF. Ev.	Fal. Pa. Fo. MrsP. MrsF. **Sh.** Ev.
+ Sl./Ca:/AP Fen. Fen.	Fal.Pa.Fo.MrsP.MrsF.**Sh**.Ev./Ca./Sl./AP

Upon the evidence provided by the analysis of Folio 3.4, only one thing seems clear: the composite nature of the text preserved in it. Secondarily, such evidence, taken in connection with that provided by the other three scenes mainly in verse in the play, supports the hypothesis, already advanced in the earlier parts of this introduction, of the previous existence of some kind of script, mainly in verse, telling the story of the deceits in love of a young couple who, in order to avoid the miseries of a marriage enforced on the girl by an authoritarian father, take advantage of a hoax played upon an unworthy, fortune-hunting knight during the night gambols presided over by the Fairy Queen in Windsor and defeat through a secret marriage the parental plan. This might well be the basic subject matter of an antimasque devised as part of a masque celebrating the 'radiant Queen' Elizabeth and the Order of the Garter on some state occasion or other. How far and when this script, or parts of it, came to be incorporated in a hurriedly devised comedy concerned with the popular figure of Sir John Falstaff is mere guesswork.

If we accept the notion that the comedy of Sir John Falstaff was basically conceived as a vehicle for a new presentation of a comic character of great entertainment value to London audiences, following his appearances in *1* and *2 Henry IV* – in other words, as a sequel to those plays centring on the figure that had 'stolen the show' from the historical characters in them – then the story of its inception would run more or less like this. Shakespeare, as an experienced actor–playwright, would think first of all in terms of his fellow players and would devise roles suited to their individual gifts, involving 'humours' which they had already impersonated in his Histories, from the tercet of Falstaff's followers, the equivocating female busybody and the nostalgic justice of the peace, to the Welshman and the Frenchman with their linguistic quirks. They had to be fitted into a plot dominated by the figure of Falstaff, based on the hoax played on him by the merry wives; for this Shakespeare had

recourse to one of the many jealous husband stories available both in narrative and dramatic form, compounding it with the parallel plot of the honourable love deceit by a young couple, and adding some subsidiary incidents mainly to accommodate the humours derived from his previous plays, as well as the newly created character of the Host of the Garter Inn. It should be noted that if the basic plot framing the main action is ultimately derived, as we have seen, from Italian sources, the love deceits to avoid a parentally enforced marriage, as well as at least one of the subsidiary actions, that of the cozening Germans stealing the Host's horses, with its already noted topical implications, seem to have a different origin. It can be said at this point that the resulting structure is that of a middle-class citizen comedy reflected in the Quarto version. It is sufficiently coherent and viable, perfectly suited for presentation in public theatres.

The apparently insoluble question is whether this version (containing, though in a garbled form, echoes of some sort of stage entertainment serving a different purpose) was written before the version reflected in F, or whether it was an adaptation for the common stages of that ampler version, suitable for court presentation, in an attempt at straightening out at least some of the many unconformities in it. Such unconformities could be explained, though not justified, if we consider that in 1602, when the Quarto was published, the fuller text of the comedy may still have been in a fluid condition, subject to ever new changes and accretions in view of the varying occasions and destinations of its performance. This is turn could justify the surmise (see pp. 54–5 above) that twenty years later, when the scribe Ralph Crane was given the task of preparing it for the press, he was confronted with a composite accumulation of working papers rather than with an orderly script.

Whether we assume that Q is based on an early version and F on a later re-elaboration of it, or that the comedy was conceived from the beginning in a form similar to that reflected in F, and

that Q represents an attempt at simplification for the common stage, what remains true is that it is possible to detect, as in filigree, behind both texts a third shorter and earlier version that tells a different story.

The different versions of *Merry Wives*, as Grace Ioppolo puts it, 'represent one fluid text capable of being transformed for differing occasions, differing audiences, and different authorial forms and meanings'.[1]

CRITICAL ATTITUDES AND STAGE LIFE: THE MUSIC OF *MERRY WIVES*

The existence of two separate versions of the comedy of Sir John Falstaff, with marked differences in the matter of structure, length and especially language, each of them showing signs of various manipulations by those who prepared them for the press, and presenting a number of internal inconsistencies, as well as suggesting the presence of a third narrative strand emerging here and there in some of the scenes – in other words the general impression it gives of a play put together rather casually and possibly hurriedly – is responsible both for its disrepute in scholarly opinion and for its fortune on the stage – a bane and a blessing at the same time.

There is no reason to doubt the statement on the title-page of the First Quarto that by 1602 the play in some form – possibly more than one – had 'bene diuers times Acted by the right Honorable my Lord Chamberlaines seruants [b]oth before her Maiestie, and else-where'.

Casting and doubling
Even allowing for the different destination of the two texts, the Folio version reflecting court occasions and Quarto the common stages, the notion that the drastic cuts in the latter

---

[1] Ioppolo (1991), 120.

were meant to meet the requirements of a smaller cast is deceptive. All roles are severely reduced in Q,[1] but the only two speaking parts that disappear altogether are those of William Page[2] and of Robin,[3] two roles impersonated by a single child actor and therefore hardly relevant to the question of employing a reduced company for touring purposes, especially in view of the fact that, in the shorter version too, 'boyes drest like Fayries' had to be present and to 'sing a song about [Falstaff]' at Herne's oak in the final scene. The small troupe of untrained boys would be available for this purpose in any circumstances, and the skilled boy actor impersonating Anne in only three scenes in both texts (Folio 1.1, 3.4, 5.5, Quarto 1, 12, 18) could in the longer version double for both Robin and William. Apart from that, and taking into account that the two servants in Ford's house could be played by any actors strong enough to carry a buck-basket containing a fellow player and not otherwise employed in the two relevant scenes, for instance Simple and Rugby (but also Nim, Bardolph, Pistol and even the Host), what both texts require are fourteen adult actors and three experienced female impersonators, a number that could be further reduced by careful doubling. For instance the actor presenting Nim in 1.1 and 1.3 in either version of the play could put on a doctor's long coat turning him into Caius in 1.4, and have sufficient time to remove it for his last appearance as Nim in 2.1 and then impersonate the doctor again in the following scenes, from 2.3 to the end. But these are simply

---

[1] According to the comparative tables of the length of roles in the two texts in King, *Casting*, 252–4, the heaviest losers among the major characters are Shallow, minus 57 per cent of his lines, in spite of his appearing in two Quarto scenes where he is not present in F (the equivalents of 3.3 and 5.5), Mistress Page (minus 55.5 per cent), Mistress Quickly (minus 54.7 per cent), Fenton (minus 52.6 per cent) and Mistress Ford (minus 48.9 per cent), while those whose lines are cut least are Parson Evans (only by about 16 per cent) and the Host (by 9.5 per cent, which suggests that the actor impersonating the latter was the main 'reporter' of the Quarto version).

[2] The boy William has twelve lines in 4.1, a scene missing in Q.

[3] Falstaff's page figures in F (with a total of thirteen lines) in 1.3, 2.2, 3.2 and 3.3, while in Q he is present as a mute only in the equivalent of 1.3.

hypotheses.[1] The surmise that the cuts in Q were intended to accommodate the play-text to a smaller company was prompted not so much by the omission in it of 4.1 and of the first four scenes of the last act, as by the disappearance of single characters from scenes present in a shorter form. This is the case of the absence of Pistol/Hobgoblin from 5.5, which leaves 'Pistol' free for a different impersonation in the last three acts, of Rugby from 3.2, and, more interestingly, of Fenton from 1.4, which allows the actor to be cast in a different role in the first part of the play, up to 3.3. But is it really possible, as has been suggested,[2] that the bombastic 'Pistol' should not only alternate with Rugby up to 3.1, but also turn into the gentlemanly Fenton from 3.4 on? To burden a single actor with the impersonation of two such incompatible roles in the same performance is conceivable only as a device for a company desperately short of players, which was certainly not the case of the Chamberlain's Men. Shakespeare was a past master in the art of doubling, but the basic principle of his art appears to have been congruity in the different parts entrusted to any one of his fellow players.[3] For the same reason it seems improbable that Slender, whose name indicates that the author had in mind a particularly thin actor, should alternate in the role of the red-nosed Bardolph in the first four acts of the play.[4]

[1] David Bradley, in the cast lists appended to his study *From Text to Performance in the Elizabethan Theatre* (Cambridge, 1992), 233, postulates as probable the number of sixteen actors for both texts of *Merry Wives*, the only difference between the two being in the number of boys: seven for Q, seven or more for F. The speaking parts of more than three lines are twenty in F and seventeen in Q.

[2] Robert E. Burkhart, *Shakespeare's Bad Quartos: Deliberate Abridgements Designed for Performance by a Reduced Cast*. Studies in English Literature, 100 (The Hague and Paris, 1975), 83–95.

[3] See for instance G. Melchiori, 'Peter, Balthasar, and Shakespeare's art of doubling', *MLR*, 78 (1983), 777–92, and 'The staging of the Capulets's Ball: doubling as an art', in *En torno a Shakespeare* II, ed. M.A. Conejero (Valencia, 1982), 129–54.

[4] In this case, as in that of Pistol/Rugby/Fenton, Burkhart (*Bad Quartos*, 93) suggests 'trebling' rather than doubling: Bardolph/Slender/Ford's servant, which is contradicted not only by the physical incongruity of the Bardolph/Slender pair, but also by the fact that Q, unlike F, lists Slender and Shallow among those present – with Ford's servants – in scene 10 (the counterpart of Folio 3.3). This makes impossible a further doubling suggested by Burkhart, that of Shallow with Ford's other servant. A fourth suggestion in the same paper, the doubling of Ford with Simple, is just technically feasible according to both texts of the play, but very unlikely.

On the other hand it is idle to speculate on the original cast of *Merry Wives* on the basis of the Folio list of 'The Names of the Principall Actors in all these Playes'. The only reasonable guess involves an actor who does not appear in that list: the exceptionally lean John Sincklo or Sinclair as Slender.[1] The leading actor Richard Burbage, still in his middle thirties, is more likely to have taken the 'strong' part of Ford, rather than the more marginal one of young Fenton.[2] It is instead highly probable that the role of Parson Evans was devised (like that of Fluellen in *Henry V*), for Robert Armin, who in 1599 had replaced Will Kemp as the company's clown and is known for his skill in impersonating the character of the comic Welshman.[3] If that is so there would be some ground for believing that *Merry Wives*, like *Henry V*, was written after Armin's advent, i.e. in 1599 or later, and that Falstaff was not meant to be played by Will Kemp or, for that matter, by the new clown Armin. A further implication is that Falstaff's role may well have been taken by another member of the company – the names suggested are those of John Heminge, the future co-editor of Shakespeare's Folio, at first, and later John Lowin[4] – and that the former proved so successful in the

---

[1] See note on Slender to the List of Roles, as well as 1.1.120n. and 1.1.271–2n. Though not a sharer or half-sharer in the Chamberlain's/King's Men, 'Sincklo' was still with them in 1604, appearing in his own person in the Induction written by John Webster for John Marston's *The Malcontent*, when the play was transferred from the Children of Blackfriars to the King's Men in that year.

[2] According to the figures provided by King, *Casting*, Ford's is the second longest part in both versions of the play, 304 lines in F, 171 in Q, preceded by Falstaff (424 in F, 313 in Q) and followed by Mistress Page (279 and 124 respectively) and Mistress Quickly (252 and 114). Significantly the Host, who comes tenth with 115 lines in F, takes fifth place, with 104 lines, in Q; in both texts Fenton is only twelfth (95 lines in F, 45 in Q). See note 1 on p. 81.

[3] In his own play of uncertain date, *The Two Maids of More-Clacke* (critical edition by A.S. Liddie, New York, 1979), Armin reserved for himself the part of the comic Welshman as well as that of the clown.

[4] The statement by the late-eighteenth-century scholar Edmond Malone that Heminge was the first to play Falstaff has been questioned but never disproved. John Lowin, who joined the King's Men in 1603 at the age of twenty-seven, may well have taken over, on Heminge's death in 1639, the dead player's roles in the company, together with his shares in the Globe and Blackfriars, which he is known to have bought at the time. James Wright, in *Historia Histrionica* (1699), places Falstaff first among the parts that 'Lowin used to act, with mighty applause'.

part that shortly afterwards Shakespeare created for him similar roles in two later comedies: Sir Toby Belch in *Twelfth Night* (where Armin, a good singer, could impersonate the clown Feste), and Parolles in *All's Well that Ends Well* (whose relationship with Bertram reflects that of Falstaff with Prince Hal in *Henry IV*).[1] All these are mere hypotheses; recreating the original cast and doubling pattern of *Merry Wives* must remain a matter of speculation, and as such is offered in the table below.

ORIGINAL CASTING AND DOUBLING

Players	Number of lines in F	in Q	Original actors
Adult actors:			
1 Falstaff	424	333	John Heminge?
2 Ford	304	171	Richard Burbage?
3 Page	143	99	
4 Shallow	124	53	
5 Slender	141	59	John Sincklo
6 Evans	120	100	Robert Armin
7 Caius/Nim	127	86	
8 Pistol/Rugby/Ford's servant 1	72	40	
9 Simple/Ford's servant 2	49	31	
10 Fenton	95	45	
11 Bardolph	24	15	
12 Host	115	104	
Female impersonators:			
13 Mistress Ford	190	97	
14 Mistress Page	279	124	
15 Quickly	252	114	
Boy actor:			
16. Anne Page/[William/Robin]	54	21	

Source: Number of lines per player(s) from tables 62 and 63 in T.J. King, *Casting Shakespeare's Plays: London Actors and Their Roles, 1590–1642* (1993).

[1] This runs counter to the notion that (at least in the Histories) 'Falstaff is structurally the clown's part' written for Will Kemp, as David Wiles vigorously argues (*Clown*, 116–35). In other Shakespearean plays Kemp's appearances on the stage (documented by the mention of his name e.g. in Q2 *Romeo and Juliet* (1599), 4.5, and Q *Much Ado About Nothing* (1600), 4.2) are always brief, and his language is that of the professional clown, chiefly based on equivocations, lacking Falstaff's much wider range. On the whole, one could imagine Kemp better cast, in the two parts of *Henry IV*, as Bardolph. See Melchiori, *Garter*, 30 and 71–2.

Early performance and adaptation

In spite of the fact that the Quarto title-page does not mention, as in the case of many other published plays, that it was received 'with great applause', and that the allusions to Falstaff in contemporary writings may refer to *1* and *2 Henry IV* rather than *Merry Wives*, the comedy must have been fairly popular from the start. But, as usual, the only records remaining are of court performances. From the Revels Accounts for 1604 it appears that the King's Men performed in the Banqueting Hall at Whitehall 'The Moor of Venis' on 'Hallamas Day being the first of Nouembar' and 'The Sunday followinge [4 November] A Play of the Merry Wiues of Winsor'.[1] As for the payment to the King's Men on 20 May 1613 for fourteen plays including a *Sir Iohn ffalstaffe*, the Falstaff vehicle could have been *2 Henry IV* rather than *Merry Wives*,[2] since in the same season John Heminge was also paid for the play 'The Hotspur' (presumably *1 Henry IV*). There is a long gap in time before the next entry, when, on 15 November 1638, three King's Men, John Lowin, Joseph Taylor and Eliard Swanston, were paid for a performance of *Merry Wives* at the Cockpit-at-Court, in Whitehall Palace. There is little doubt that on this occasion Lowin played Falstaff,[3] while Taylor, who in 1619 had succeeded Burbage as leading actor in the company, may have inherited from him Ford's role.

Merry Wives, however, was among the first plays performed at the reopening of the theatres at the time of the Restoration, as testified by Samuel Pepys, who saw it at the Vere Street Theatre on 5 December 1660. He obviously considered it an old-fashioned play of humours: he found 'the humours of the country gentleman [Slender?] and the French Doctor very well done, but the rest but very poorly, and Sir J. Falstaffe as bad as

---

[1] Chambers, *Stage*, 4: 171 and 136–40. This performance is discussed on p. 49 note 1, cf. p. 52.

[2] Chambers, *Stage*, 4: 180.

[3] See note 4 on p. 83.

any'. In spite of his reservations, he attended another poor performance on 25 September 1661, and finally when, on 15 August
1667, he could not find a seat for a new play at the Duke's
Theatre, he sadly noted: 'And so we went to the King's, and
there saw *The Merry Wives of Windsor*; which did not please me
at all, in no part of it'.[1]

Pepys's strictures refer to the production rather than to the
text of the play, but by the end of the seventeenth century there
was a wide difference of opinion about it. John Dryden praised it
in 1679 for 'the mechanic beauties of the plot, which are the
observation of the three Unities, Time, Place, and Action',[2] and
John Dennis lists no fewer than eight 'men of extraordinary
parts' who 'were in Love with the Beauties of this Comedy'.[3]
But criticism of the text is implicit in Dennis's statement, frequently quoted, that the play was written in fourteen days,[4] and
in the reasons he gives for writing his adaptation, i.e. to 'correct'
the 'Errours' in the plot: 'there are no less than three Actions in
it that are independent one of another, which divide and distract
the minds of an Audience',[5] while the style in some parts is 'stiff

---

[1] Relevant passages and information from *Pepys' Diary Deciphered by the Rev. J. Smith*,
    edited by Lord Braybrooke (1906), 1.113–14, 195, 2.316..

[2] Reported in White, xxiii. What Dryden means is that, compared with the liberties
    taken with the classical unities in the rest of Shakespeare's plays, *Merry Wives* reflects
    a greater respect for them. Rowe too, stating that the play was written at the Queen's
    command (note 1, p. 2), wrote that 'the whole play is admirable; the humours are var-
    ious and well oppos'd; the main design, which is to cure *Ford* of his unreasonable jeal-
    ousie, is extremely well conducted'.

[3] All quotations from Dennis are from the Epistle Dedicatory of his adaptation of the
    play as *The Comical Gallant* (1702; Cornmarket Press reprint, 1969). Perhaps the exis-
    tence of a scribal transcript of the whole text, with the addition of the *Dramatis
    Personae*, datable to the second half of the seventeenth century, witnesses the interest
    of literary people in the play at the time. The manuscript, now preserved in the Folger
    Shakespeare Library (Folger MS. V.a.73), is based on the text in the 1632 Folio but
    curiously anticipates in a few places Dennis's adaptation and Rowe's edition (1709).
    For a full discussion see G. Blakemore Evans, '*The Merry Wives of Windsor*: the Folger
    manuscript', in B. Fabian and K. Tetzeli von Rosador (eds), *Shakespeare: Text,
    Language, Criticism* (Hildesheim, Germany, 1987), 57–79.

[4] See note 1 on p. 2.

[5] Compare Samuel Johnson's comment in the third edition of his and George Steevens's
    The Plays of William Shakespeare (1785), 1.404–5: 'the conduct of this drama is defi-
    cient; the action begins and ends often before the conclusion, and the different parts
    might change places without inconvenience'.

and forced and affected'. More damningly, Dennis anticipates objections to his adaptation from two different critical quarters: 'The one believed it to be so admirable, that nothing ought to be added to it; the others fancied it to be so despicable, that any ones time would be lost upon it'. As it turned out, Dennis's *The Comical Gallant: Or The Amours of Sir John Falstaffe*, presented at Drury Lane in 1702, was a complete rewriting of the play, an awkward pastiche, not only stiff, forced and affected, but also boring, with Fenton as the main manipulator of a plot where he is the nephew of Mistress Ford, while Mistress Page appears at one point disguised as a Captain, Ford in the last scene is pinched by the 'fairies' because, like Falstaff, he is dressed as Herne the Hunter, and Caius and Slender, deceived by Anne's costume and their own disguises, find themselves 'married' to each other by the Host of the Garter pretending to be a parson.

On the stage, *The Comical Gallant* was the failure that it deserved to be, while the original *Merry Wives* enjoyed the distinction of being presented by Thomas Betterton at court on 24 April 1705 with two of the most celebrated actresses of the time, Anne Bracegirdle and Mrs Barry, as the wives. Nevertheless, the play then disappeared from the stage for a time. No performances are recorded between 1706 and 1720.[1] Apparently its absence was due to the difficulty of finding a suitable actor for the leading role of Falstaff.

When in 1720 the manager of Lincoln's Inn Fields, John Rich, planned to revive the comedy, he was at a loss for a player in the leading role and reluctantly accepted the offer of a 27-year-old actor, James Quin. Quin, an actor of the declamatory, antinaturalistic old school, was so successful in the part, which he played no fewer than 153 times before his retirement in 1751, that his name has remained permanently associated with it

---

[1] Most of the information in this section comes from Odell, and for the eighteenth century from Mace. The records of performances are based on Hogan, and on *London Stage*.

(Fig. 6), in spite of his appearances in other major Shakespearean roles, from Richard III to Macbeth, from Othello to Lear. In the same period he also played Falstaff ninety-one times in *1 Henry IV* and thirty-four times in *2 Henry IV*, but, at

6 China statuette of James Quin as Falstaff. The number of eighteenth- and ninteenth-century china statuettes representing Falstaff with the features of Quin show how completely the actor was identified with the role (see Mace, 65, and R. Mander and J. Mitcheson, 'The China Statuettes of Quin as Falstaff', *Theatre Notebook*, 32 (1958), 54–8)

least with popular theatre audiences, he managed to reverse the current critical opinion that in *Merry Wives* Falstaff appears 'in general greatly below his true character'[1] expressed in the Histories – an opinion clearly shared by the authors of the two major studies of the figure of Falstaff in the eighteenth century: Maurice Morgann[2] makes no mention of *Merry Wives* and William Richardson[3] alludes to it only once. And in the twentieth century the Falstaff of *Merry Wives* gets short shrift from John Dover Wilson in his *The Fortunes of Falstaff* (1953).[4] It is significant that when William Kenrick in 1760 dedicated his new comedy *Falstaff's Wedding* to James Quin, who had retired from the stage, he presented it as a sequel not to *Merry Wives* but to the Second Part of *Henry IV*,[5] though the characters include not only Bardolph, Pistol, Shallow, Hostess Quickly and Doll Tearsheet, appearing in the Histories, but also Master Slender of *Merry Wives*. The two Falstaffs, that of the *Henry IV* plays and that of the comedy, rivalled each other on the stage in the eighteenth century, for a total of 363 performances of *1 Henry IV*, as against 336 of *Merry Wives*, but the comedy was staged in more seasons than the history.[6] From the 1772–3 season it was constantly played in John Bell's acting version, first presented by the leading actor Charles Kemble, which omitted not only 'that ridiculous excrescence of a scene in the original, which begins the fourth Act with an examination of Young Page in Grammar' (4.1), but also the parts concerning the planning of the hoax at Herne's oak and 4.6, between Fenton and the Host, as well as

[1] Corbyn Morris, *An Essay Towards Fixing the True Standard of Wit, Humour, Raillery, Satire, and Ridicule. To Which Is Added, an Analysis of the Characters of an Humourist, Sir John Falstaff, Sir Roger De Coverly, and Don Quixote* (1744), quoted in Mace, 60.

[2] Maurice Morgann, *Essay on the Dramatic Character of Sir John Falstaff* (1777).

[3] William Richardson, *Essays on Shakespeare's Dramatic Character of Sir John Falstaff and on His Imitation of Female Characters* (1789).

[4] '*The Merry Wives of Windsor* may be left out of account', as it is a play 'the hero of which is made to bear the name of Falstaff primarily for reasons of theatrical expediency, not of dramatic art' (4–5).

[5] William Kenrick, *Falstaff's Wedding: A Comedy. Being a Sequel to the Second Part of the Play of King Henry the Fourth* (1760, but the preface is dated 1 January 1766. Cornmarket Press facsimile, 1969). See note 2, p. 29.

[6] Mace, 62–3.

Mistress Quickly's verse, including the Garter speech, in the last scene.[1] In other words, the comedy seen by audiences in the last quarter of the eighteenth century and in the early nineteenth was much closer to the Quarto than to the Folio version.[2]

The emergence of Falstaff's music

But this was the great age of *opera buffa*, and composers, libretto writers and impresarios soon discovered that the comedy and its characters offered unrivalled opportunities for comic representations, at first in France, then on the rest of the Continent. Little is known of the two French operas with the enticing titles *Les Deux Amies, ou le Vieux Garçon*,[3] music by Louis August Papavoine, performed in Paris in 1761, and *Herne le Chasseur*, set by P.A.D. Philidor in 1773, or of the two *Die Lustigen Weiber von Windsor*, set to music from the same German libretto (Georg Christian Romer) by Peter Ritter in 1794 and by Karl Ditter von Dittersdorf in 1796, but the remarkable fact is that, out of the ten major operatic versions of the play between 1761 and 1929,[4] four are still alive on the stage today, and their merits deserve closer attention. Curiously only the last of these ten adaptations of Shakespeare's most lively comedy of languages has an English libretto.[5] Three of

---

[1] Odell, 2.27.

[2] John Philip Kemble, who became manager of the Covent Garden in the 1803–4 season, provided acting versions of twenty-seven Shakespearean plays, but his adaptation of *Merry Wives*, performed in the first year of his management, differs very little from Bell's edition. In turn, William Oxberry, who some twenty years later edited for the stage twenty-three plays (*The New English Drama, with Prefatory Remarks etc. by W. Oxberry*, 1818–23), adopted in the case of *Merry Wives* the Bell/Kemble version with few minor changes.

[3] Mentioned as *Le vieux Coquet, ou les deux amies* by Winton Dean, 'Shakespeare and Opera', in Phyllis Hartnoll, *Shakespeare and Music: A Collection of Essays* (1964), 120. Dean comments that the opera, by a French violinist, 'is said to have been killed by its libretto after one performance'.

[4] Both the 'Catalogue of musical works based on the plays and poetry of Shakespeare', compiled by Winton Dean, Dorothy Moore and P. Hartnoll, appended to Hartnoll (ed.), *Shakespeare and Music*, 263–4, and B.N.S. Gooch and D. Thatcher, *A Shakespeare Music Catalogue* (Oxford, 1991), 2.345–8 and 925–68, agree on the number of *Merry Wives* operas.

[5] I am not taking into account the American and English musicals or operettas: *Falstaff* by J.P. Webber (New York, 1928), *When the Cat's Away* by C.S. Swier (Philadelphia, 1941) and *Good Time Johnny* by James Gilbert (Birmingham, England, 1971).

the others have French librettos (besides the two already mentioned, there was a *Falstaff* by Adolphe Adam performed in Paris in 1856), three German librettos, and three Italian, even though, of these, Salieri's opera (see below) was destined for the court in Vienna, and the *Falstaff* set to music by Michael Balfe in 1838 was conceived for the greatest singers of the time at His Majesty's Theatre in London. If the latter turned out to be a failure, the fault was with the music rather than with the libretto by S.M. Maggioni, which, though retaining all three tricks played by the women on Falstaff, had ingeniously got rid of Caius, Slender and other minor characters by making Fenton jealous of Falstaff, who had addressed to Anne a third copy of his love letter to the two Windsor wives.[1] Possibly Maggioni, in writing his libretto, had in mind that of the earlier and much better *opera buffa* set to music in 1799 by Antonio Salieri, the court composer for the Austro-Hungarian emperor in Vienna; its very title, *Falstaff, o le tre burle*, underlines the theme of the triple mockery, and the brilliant libretto by Carlo Prospero De Franceschi, modelled on Da Ponte's admirably suited texts for Mozart's music, concentrates on those three leading episodes and Ford's jealousy, ignoring completely the love plot of Anne, Fenton and her other suitors, as well as Shallow and the Host. Of Falstaff's retinue only Bardolph survives and Mistress Quickly is transformed into Betty, a lively chambermaid typical of comic opera. Though the Pages are unaccountably renamed 'Slender', the Viennese destination of the opera suggested Mistress Ford's disguise at one point as a German maid who engages in an uproarious bilingual exchange with Falstaff. The latter's cavatina in the first act, '*Nell'impero di Cupido / Sono un Cesare, un Achille*', is surely one of the best musical portraits of Falstaff ever achieved in an opera. Salieri's is by no means 'a

---

[1] This coincides in part with the fanciful 'reconstruction' of the 1597 Garter entertainment, if it ever existed, that I suggested elsewhere (*Garter*, 103–6): there were possibly *not* two Windsor wives whom the unworthy knight wanted to seduce, but only one, with an unmarried daughter, who in turn is in love with a young gentleman and wooed by another suitor favoured by her father.

7 Soprano Cecilia Gasdia (Mistress Ford) and mezzo-soprano Raquel Perotti
(Mistress Slender alias Page) induce bass Domenico Trimarchi (Falstaff) to
enter the basket in Göran Järvefelt's production of Salieri's *Falstaff* at the
Teatro Regio, Parma, June 1987

superficial work in the flimsy Neapolitan style that Mozart's
genius has now rendered intolerable';[1] after nearly two centuries of oblivion, it has acquired the position it deserves in
the repertory of a number of opera houses, especially in Italy.
(Fig. 7).[2]

In the first half of the nineteenth century the version of the
play current and successful on the English and American stages

[1] Dean, 120, echoed by Schmidgall, 322.
[2] First revived by composer and director Vito Frazzi in Siena in 1961, it is frequently
performed, at times alternating with Verdi's opera and sharing its musical cast, as was
done at Teatro Regio, Parma, in the 1986–7 season. An excellent rendering by
Hungarian singers, with the Salieri Chamber Orchestra and Chorus, was recorded in
1985 (Hungarton CD 1289–91) and in 1986 the opera was broadcast by the BBC.

was already in a way operatic, or rather 'operatized',[1] because between 1816 and 1828 Frederick Reynolds provided adaptations of several Shakespeare comedies, introducing into them songs, arias and other musical pieces arranged by Henry Bishop.[2] The resounding success of their version of *Merry Wives*, presented at the Haymarket on 12 October 1824, was partly due to the celebrated Madame Vestris as Mistress Page, singing lyrics from *A Midsummer Night's Dream*, while traditional songs, as well as some from other Shakespeare plays and poems, were entrusted to the actors/singers impersonating Fenton, Anne, Mistress Ford, etc. The play in this form had a very good run, and when in 1839 Madame Vestris joined Charles Mathews in the management of Covent Garden, *Merry Wives* in its 'operatic' version was the second Shakespearean comedy they played very successfully, with Vestris as Mistress Page, Mrs Nisbett as Mistress Ford, Mathews as Slender and George Bartley as Falstaff.[3] This version enjoyed its longest run (more than a month) in 1844 at the Haymarket, with the same cast, while the manager of the theatre, Benjamin West, who had appeared since 1830 as Falstaff in other productions, reserved for himself the role of Parson Evans.

The later nineteenth century

Charles Kean, when he became sole manager of the Princess's Theatre, decided to eliminate all the musical parts from the text when presenting the play as the first production of the 1851–2 season, reserving for himself and his wife the roles of the Fords playing against George Bartley's Falstaff. In the words of a contemporary reviewer, in his production 'the fine, racy dialogue

---

[1] The definition is Odell's (2.140–42), who remarks that *Merry Wives* was the 'longest-lived of Bishop and Reynolds's re-workings of Shakespeare into the operatic mould', and that he saw their version of the play acted in New York in the 1890s.

[2] Henry Rowley Bishop, knighted in 1842, is now remembered as the author of 'Home, sweet home'.

[3] This production may well have inspired David Scott's historical painting, *Queen Elizabeth Viewing the Performance of the* Merry Wives of Windsor *at the Globe Theatre*, the centrepiece of the Royal Academy summer exhibition of 1840.

8 David Scott, *Queen Elizabeth Viewing the Performance of* The Merry Wives of Windsor *at the Globe Theatre* (1840)

was no longer impeded by the introduction of bravuras, interminable duets, and flourishes'.[1] We may wonder if Kean's decision to return to the original text was partly prompted by a wish to rediscover the native qualities of Shakespeare's language, as against foreign operatic adaptations, especially after the resounding success of Otto Nicolai's 'komisch-phantastische Oper' *Die Lustigen Weiber von Windsor*, first performed in Berlin on 9 March 1849, just two months before the 39-year-old composer's death. Nicolai's aim had been, in his own words, to fuse together 'German operatic music [which] contains enough thought [*Philosophie*] but not enough music' and 'Italian operatic music [which] contains enough music but not enough thought'.[2]. This end is achieved in his last opera where the music is a pleasant mixture of echoes of Italian *bel canto* and the suggestions of German romantic composers. The libretto by H.S. Mosenthal germanizes the English names, except for those of Falstaff, Fenton and Caius, to underline their allusive qualities: Ford becomes Fluth (Bach when in disguise), Page becomes Reich, and Slender, Spärlich. Shallow, Evans, Mistress Quickly and Falstaff's followers are eliminated, together with the side-plots in which they are involved, so that the story line is neatly developed through the three tricks played on Falstaff (one in each of the three acts), the cure of Master Fluth's unjustified jealousy, and Fenton's and Anna's honourable deception of her parents. The opera opens with the reading of Falstaff's letters by the two wives and ends with a sequence of dances and choruses by a troupe of children and all the other characters in fantastic disguises: Anna is Titania and Fenton, Oberon; Master Reich (Page), disguised as Herne the Hunter, takes Falstaff to task; while, because of their costumes, Spärlich (Slender) and Caius – as in Dennis's *Comical Gallant* – mistake each other for Anna.

---

[1] Odell, 2.285–6.
[2] Quoted from his essay *Einiger Betrachtungen über die italienische Oper, im Vergleich zur deutschen*, reported in the introduction to the excellent recording of *Die lustigen Weiber von Windsor* performed in 1963 by the Bayerische Staatsorchester and Staatsoper singers in Munich, remastered on compact discs in 1988 (EMI CMS 7 69348 2).

Anna's and Fenton's disguises are symptomatic of the tendency in the eighteenth and nineteenth centuries to associate *Merry Wives* with *A Midsummer Night's Dream* as Shakespeare's two most fanciful comedies. This tendency culminated in Ambroise Thomas's *opéra comique*, which was successfully presented in Paris in 1850 and was still on the stage in 1886, under the title *Le Songe d'une nuit d'été*. It had nothing to do with that comedy, but included the character of Sir John Falstaff as well as those of Queen Elizabeth and of William Shakespeare himself.[1]

Kean's 1851 production marks the parting of the ways between two forms of stage presentation: as prose comedy or as *opera buffa*. While on the one hand the musicians (or at least some of them) more or less consciously realized the musical potentialities of the play's linguistic texture, on the other hand professional theatre people either exploited its inventive language for merely comic effects, and saw the play as a vehicle for situational farce, or presented it as a lively picture of English bourgeois life. The opportunities offered by the number and variety of characters have made *Merry Wives* a great favourite with amateur and student companies both in England and in the United States, and in both continents the play has never been absent from the stage for more than one or two consecutive seasons, in spite of some curious moral objections, such as that of George Pope Morris when he saw the play in New York in 1824: 'there is no play in the English language of so exceptionable a character as this indelicate production of Shakespeare'.[2] Indeed, at least in the later part of the nineteenth century, all 'indelicacies' were expurgated from the text, a trend which was completely reversed in the following century, especially in the last fifty years, when actors drew attention on the stage to all possible allusive expressions, adding some extra ones for good measure, and annotators pointed out even the

---

[1] Gooch and Thatcher, 2.966, entry 9256.

[2] Quoted in Oliver, Ard², xii. The first recorded performance of *Merry Wives* in the United States dates to 1770 in Philadelphia, followed by one in New York three years later. In the nineteenth century it was frequently taken there by English companies.

vaguest sexual innuendos. Among the innumerable productions since 1851, one of the most memorable was that at the Gaiety Theatre in 1874–5, with the great Samuel Phelps as Falstaff and an all-star cast; apart from the care taken in the matter of costumes and scenery, Arthur Sullivan (not yet famous as the partner of W.S. Gilbert) was commissioned to provide the incidental music, and the famous poet and critic Algernon Charles Swinburne wrote a song for Anne Page which, set to music by Sullivan, the theatre manager John Hollingshed 'took the liberty to insert in the text of Shakespeare'.[1]

The first Shakespearean role played by Herbert Beerbohm Tree, later knighted for being the greatest interpreter of Shakespeare in his time, was that of Falstaff in a production of *Merry Wives* at the Haymarket in 1889, into which he introduced a song for his wife who played Anne Page.[2] Tree, according to some 'the finest Falstaff of them all'[3] (he was still playing the part in 1912 (Fig. 9)), chose *Merry Wives* as his offering at the Lyceum on the occasion of the coronation of Edward VII in 1902, a performance also remembered for the admirable impersonation of the two wives by the leading actresses Ellen Terry and Madge Kendall, no longer 'in the holiday time of [their] beauty', both being in their fifties. Though there was no lack of comic business, the play was given historical dignity by being staged in fifteenth-century costumes, recalling the times of Henry V rather than, as is more usual, those of Elizabeth I. This was in a way an attempt at narrowing the widening gap, both in critical opinion and on the stage, between the Falstaff of *Merry Wives* and that of the two parts of *Henry IV*.

The merit of having realized the importance of narrowing that gap – actually, in his case, of closing it altogether – belongs to a libretto-writer of genius, a musician himself, Arrigo Boito. After

---

[1] Odell, 2.365–6. In fact *Merry Wives*, apart from the lost fairy song, has less music than any other later comedy; see Long, *Music*, 1–13.
[2] Odell, 2.385, 410.
[3] W. Macqueen Pope, reported by David Crane, Cam², 24–5.

9 Beerbohm Tree as Falstaff, with Ellen Terry and Maud Holt (Lady Tree) as
the wives, *c*. 1890

having provided Giuseppe Verdi with an admirable libretto for his opera *Otello* (first performed in 1887), Boito agreed with the composer that Verdi, already in his late seventies, should enter the unexplored territory of comic opera: 'There's only one way to finish better than with *Otello*, and that's to finish triumphantly with *Falstaff*.'[1] Before submitting his libretto, Boito induced the composer to read not only *Merry Wives*, but also the two parts of *Henry IV* and even *Henry V*, to get a full picture of the character of the hero. The text of the play was pruned so as to create a sequence of arias, recitativos and especially vocal ensembles, which gave Verdi's musical inventiveness a free hand to play with six male and four female voices. Not only the Latin lesson and the 'old woman of Brentford' trick, but also Evans, Shallow, Slender, Nim and, more surprisingly, Master Page, disappeared from the revised plot: Doctor Caius is the only rival of Fenton for Anne's hand, and in the final scene he finds himself mated with Bardolfo, 'a great lubberly boy' indeed. Anne herself is italianized into Nannetta, not Page's but Ford's daughter, seconded in her love by her mother, Alice, and most appropriately cast (instead of Quickly, who is disguised as a witch) for the role of the Fairy Queen in the Windsor Forest revels. The quartet of Windsor men, balancing that of the women (Alice Ford, Meg Page, Quickly and Nannetta), includes, to compensate for the loss of Page, Bardolfo and Pistola besides Ford and Caius. Falstaff's companions come much more alive, thanks to Boito's interpolation in the opera of those passages in Shakespeare's previous Histories that most vividly present their physical and mental peculiarities. Even better, the characterization of their master is enhanced by the introduction at the close of the first scene of his magnificent outburst '*L'onore! Ladri . . .*', a vigorous musical rendering of Falstaff's catechism on honour in *1H4* 5.1.121–41. Shallow's brief evocation of Falstaff as 'a boy, and page to Thomas Mowbray, Duke of Norfolk' in *2H4* 3.2.25–6 suggests

---

[1] Boito to Verdi, 9 July 1889.

Falstaff's haunting aria in the second scene of Act II, '*Quand'ero paggio del Duca di Norfolk / ero sottile, sottile, sottile . . .*'. At the same time a new emphasis is placed on the Fenton/Nannetta love story, with a sequence of duets – one behind a screen during the buck-basket scene – and the marvellous musical refrain at the end of each of their meetings, '*Bocca baciata non perde ventura / anzi rinnova come fa la luna*', which is not Shakespearean, but a quotation from one of Boccaccio's novelle in his *Decameron*. Boito, a very competent man of letters, was fully aware that the main source at least of the jealous husband plot was Italian,[1] as was Verdi's musical genius. So he could speak to a French critic after the first triumphant performance of *Falstaff* at La Scala in Milan on 9 February 1893 of 'Latin lyric comedy . . . Shakespeare's sparkling farce is led back by the miracle of sound to its clear Tuscan source, to Ser Giovanni Fiorentino.'[2] Paradoxically, the work that had most successfully reintegrated the Falstaff of *Merry Wives* into the context of the English Histories – the sudden shock of self-recognition at the end of the opera, '*Son io che vi fo scaltri. L'arguzia mia crea l'arguzia degli altri*', is a perfect musical rendering of Falstaff's speech on first appearing in *2H4* 1.2.5–9, 'I am not only witty in myself, but the cause of wit in other men'– had on the other hand created for him a thoroughly Italian background.[3]

---

[1] See pp. 13–18 above.

[2] Quoted by Dean, 125. Much of the material for the above is from G. Melchiori's contribution 'The Fat Knight in Love' to the programme of the English version by Amanda Holden of *Falstaff* produced by the English National Opera at the London Coliseum in the 1988–9 season. An excellent recording of the original is that conducted by Herbert von Karajan with the Philarmonia Orchestra and Chorus at Kingsway Hall in 1956: Tito Gobbi as Falstaff, Elizabeth Schwarzkopf as Mistress Ford, Nan Merriman as Mistress Page, Fedora Barbieri as Quickly, Anna Moffo as Nannetta, Luigi Alva as Fenton, and Rolando Panerai as Ford.

[3] In the 1980 production at La Scala in Milan, frequently revived, director Giorgio Strehler set the opera in the countryside of the Po valley (Verdi's native land), and several other productions followed his example, stressing the atmosphere of small village life – this is the case in Peter Stein's production for the Welsh National Opera in 1989, and in Luca Ronconi's for the Salzburg Festival of 1993. But there were exceptions, such as the disastrous production at Florence in 1998, when director Willy Decker adopted as a permanent setting the refreshments room of Windsor railway station in the 1940s.

Falstaff in the twentieth century

The historical correctness of Beerbohm Tree's 1902 staging was deliberately rejected after the first world war, when a number of productions throughout the world presented the action of this eminently adaptable text as taking place in the most various times and locations. How much of the freedom taken with these essential elements of the script was due to the influence of the operatic adaptation, which had become a constant presence in opera houses, staged by the greatest directors, who would not have anything to do with Shakespeare's original comedy? In the twentieth century Falstaff was increasingly recognized as a universal figure, an archetypal myth belonging to all ages and nations; his ancestry was traced back to the Greek Silenos as well as to Santa Claus, to the folklore of ancient Egypt as well as of Islam, Mesopotamia, India, China and Russia, and the 'magnificent relevance of Falstaff' in all stages of Western and Eastern culture was finally acknowledged.[1] But the relevance of Shakespeare's unique creation was mainly discussed in terms of the Falstaff appearing in the context of the Histories as a father figure, and it was only after the advent of the Verdi/Boito opera that the fat knight of *Merry Wives* established in the general consciousness the Falstaff icon (Fig 10).[2] The new attention paid to the comedy by a number of critics in recent years has been moving away from the endless discussions on the occasion of its creation, and from the debate on its Englishness versus its Italianate sources, to a consideration of its cultural and anthropological significance, its association with traditional folk rituals on the one hand and with the social implications of 'citizen comedy' on the other.[3] Inevitably, and quite rightly, the prominence given in

---

[1] See especially the ample study by Roderick Marshall, *Falstaff: The Archetypal Myth* (Longmead, England, 1989).

[2] While, following in the steps of Campbell, *Histories* (1947), 245–54, Empson (1986), Hillman (1989), 115–29, and Everett (1990) establish the Falstaff icon on the basis of the Histories, Barton (1985) and Carroll (1985), 183–202, focus more specifically on the comedy.

[3] See the first two sections of this introduction for references to these approaches.

For Giorgia Melchiori
from
Walter Hodges.
8 Aug 85.

10 The Falstaff icon, drawn by C. Walter Hodges

the Folio title to the 'merry wives', at the expense of Falstaff himself, has stimulated lively and thoughtful discussions in the field of feminist studies.[1]

---

[1] See for instance Coppelia Kahn (1981); Marilyn French (1981), 100–10; Linda Woodbridge (1984); Anne Parten (1985); Sandra Clark (1987); Elizabeth Pittenger (1991); Grace Tiffany, 'False Staff' (1992–3) and *Monsters* (1995).

On the British stage, the first attempts at presenting the play outside its traditional merry England setting were not well received. Oscar Asche, who had already displeased audiences when in 1911 he had given the play a winter background, shocked them with his 1929 modern-dress production at the Haymarket, in which, according to horrified reports, Anne 'rode pillion on Fenton's motor-bicycle'.[1] It was in that year that at last a British composer, Ralph Vaughan Williams, who sixteen years earlier had contributed the incidental music to a stage production of the *Merry Wives*, decided to turn the original play, with Shakespeare's own language, into a full-blown opera, under the title *Sir John in Love*, privately performed in 1929, and publicly, with a number of additions, in Bristol in 1933. His aim was to vindicate the native English spirit of the comedy: he retained all its original characters, omitting only the wives' second trick – the witch of Brentford episode – and introduced into it for good measure no fewer than twenty traditional folk tunes, as well as lyrics by Shakespeare's contemporaries such as Campion, Jonson and Middleton. Though music critics could not help comparing it unfavourably with Verdi's *Falstaff*, *Sir John in Love* is a more faithful and genuine musical evocation of Shakespeare's Elizabethan England.[2] It was in this spirit of celebration of the national heritage that the most individualistic of tragic actors, Donald Wolfit, chose to face London's darkest hours during the second world war by appearing as Falstaff in 'Shakespeare's only English comedy' at the Strand in 1940 and 1942.[3]

Performances and adaptations of *Merry Wives* since 1946 are numberless. From Russia to China, from Africa to India, Falstaff underwent all kinds of transformations and reinterpretations according to local theatrical and ethnical traditions. For

---

[1] See Oliver, Ard[2], xii. Komisarjevsky's colourful production at Stratford-upon-Avon in 1935, presenting the play in the style of Viennese operetta, got a more favourable reception.

[2] See especially White, 83–5, but compare Dean, 126–7.

[3] David Crane, Cam[2], 26.

instance, in Russia in 1957 the play was acted with a strong sense of audience participation, even during the intervals between the acts;[1] in 1980 in Rome the Checco Durante Roman dialect company presented it as *Le allegre comari di Trastevere*;[2] and on the occasion of the Shakespeare World Conference in Tokyo in 1991, Shakespeare scholar Yasunari Takahashi presented as *The Braggart Samurai* his splendid adaptation to traditional Japanese theatre.[3] In England *Merry Wives* was played straight, offering extraordinary opportunities for the actors, not only Falstaff but the wives (Peggy Ashcroft and Ursula Jeans appeared in Hugh Hunt's Old Vic production of 1951) and Ford. Anthony Quayle was a magnificent fat knight with a touch of melancholy in the Shakespeare Memorial Theatre production by Glen Byam Shaw in 1955 (Fig. 11), and the play was never long absent from Stratford-upon-Avon. It was presented more and more frequently as a choral play, evoking life in an English market town, by no means a royal seat but little more than a village with its church school, its friendly inn and its gossiping inhabitants. The Latin lesson was restored to the text, and other schoolboys invaded the stage; they were present from the very beginning of the play in Trevor Nunn's and John Caird's 1979 production at the Royal Shakespeare Theatre, where Ben Kingsley was Master Ford[4] and John Woodvine took the role of Falstaff, which he was to make memorably his own some eight years later in Michael Bogdanov's brilliant and controversial London production of the *Henry* plays. Attempts at integrating the comedy within the sequence of the Falstaff

---

[1] Y. Shvedov, 'International notes', *SS12* (1959), 118, quoted by Oliver, Ard², xii–xiii.

[2] At about the same time a full version, including even the Latin lesson, by director Orazio Costa Giovangigli for the actor Tino Buazzelli, translated Windsor into an Italian village, inhabited by Don Giovanni Falzastaffa, the Paggi and Gualdi families, the busybody Monna Prescia and other enjoyable local characters. This version is included in *Teatro Completo di William Shakespeare*, ed. G. Melchiori, vol. 2 (1982), 839–1057.

[3] Videocassette (playing time about 70 minutes) available from the editor.

[4] Ben Kingsley was also a capital Ford in the Time Life/BBC television production of 1982, dominated by the Falstaff of Richard Griffiths, also an old hand in that role in the two parts of *Henry IV*.

11 Anthony Quayle as Falstaff before Herne's oak, in the Shakespeare
Memorial Theatre production directed by Glen Byam Shaw at Stratford-
upon-Avon, 1955

plays were rare. Terry Hands, who in 1968 had first revealed his
directorial talent by recreating the bustling town life of

12 The RSC production directed by Terry Hands, with Brenda Bruce and
Elizabeth Spriggs as the two wives and Ian Richardson as Ford, at
Stratford-upon-Avon, 1968

Elizabethan Windsor in his production of *Merry Wives* for the
Royal Shakespeare Company, with Brewster Mason as Falstaff,
Brenda Bruce and Elizabeth Spriggs as the two wives and Ian
Richardson as Ford (Fig. 12), revived it seven years later with
the same cast (Barbara Leigh-Hunt replacing Elizabeth
Spriggs) as part of his impressive cycle of 'Falstaff plays',
including the two parts of *Henry IV* and *Henry V*. Hands's final
staging of the comedy, for the National Theatre in the 1994–5
season, though using the same designer, Timothy O'Brien,
adopted a much more rural setting that stressed a new sense of
nostalgia for the happy times of merry England.[1] Another sort
of nostalgia for much more recent times, the 1950s, inspired
director Bill Alexander when, in the 1985 Stratford season, he

[1] On the three productions by Terry Hands see Peter Holland, 'Shakespeare
Performances in England', *SS49* (1996), 260–3.

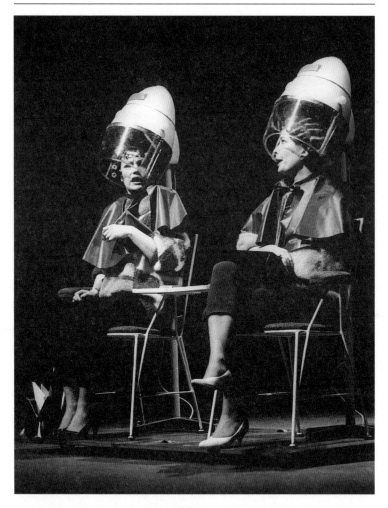

13 Janet Dale as Mistress Page and Lindsay Duncan as Mistress Ford in the
    RSC production directed by Bill Alexander at Stratford-upon-Avon, 1985

made Shallow and Slender arrive in a Morris Minor, and the
two wives read Falstaff's letters under the local hairdresser's
driers (Fig. 13). More adventurously, the provincial company
Northern Broadsides took to London, to the Lyric Theatre in

14 Barrie Rutter as Falstaff, disguised as the wise woman of Bradford (instead of Brentford), in the Northern Broadsides production at the Lyric Theatre, Hammersmith, 1993

the 1993–4 season (and later to India), their modern-dress version of *Merry Wives*, in which the action had moved from Windsor to Bradford, and the result was exhilarating (Fig. 14). As Peter Holland reports,

> Even the catechism of young William Page (4.1) worked, especially when I saw the production in Bangalore. As the legacy of colonialism ensures that Latin continues to be taught in all English-language schools attended by middle-class Indians, the scene could, for the first time in my experience, be properly laughed at for Mrs Quickly's mistakings. Even – or, perhaps, especially – in a production where Herne's Oak was a ladder and Falstaff's horns bicycle handlebars mounted on a colander, the production's energies were all generated by the company's pleasure in the text.[1]

[1] Peter Holland, 'Shakespeare performances in England', *SS48* (1995), 197–9.

Indeed, the key to the extraordinary vitality of the 'most pleasant and excellent conceited comedy of Sir John Falstaff and the merry wives of Windsor' is due to the endless pleasure that its language, its text and its texture, however translated and manipulated, can give at all times and under whatever sky.

THIS TEXT: EDITORIAL PROCEDURES AND CONVENTIONS

Editors of *The Merry Wives of Windsor* are given no alternative in the choice of their copy-text: the fullness of the version of the play in the 1623 Folio, in respect of the much shorter text printed in the 1602 Quarto, inclines the balance in favour of F, whether the editor believes that Q is an early Shakespearean version or rather, as I have tried to demonstrate, a memorial reconstruction of an authorial acting version of the play. The relationship between the two texts has been extensively discussed in several sections of this introduction, and it appears that a number of inconsistencies in F can be at least in part explained by recourse to the earlier Q.

The Folio text is one of the four in the section *Comedies* prepared for the press by the scribe Ralph Crane at a time fairly close to the publication of the volume in 1623, seven years after the author's death. It has therefore no intrinsic authority, there being no definite evidence of the sort of copy that came into Crane's hands. *The Merry Wives of Windsor* is a comedy so loosely constructed that it must have undergone, more than most of the other plays produced at the time, constant changes, omissions or additions during its stage career. It is unlikely that the original foul papers were still extant when Crane made his transcript after so many years. Possibly he based it on one or more working documents in possession of the company, such as a prompt-book prepared perhaps for a particular occasion, for instance an early court performance (as suggested by the implicit homage to the Queen in the last act), roughly adapted (by him or

by other members of the company) and integrated with papers of a later date connected with stage performances of the play, whether at court or elsewhere. The absence of profanities from F is not imputable to Crane's personal scruple not to offend the censor; it is evidence that he had at his disposal material datable from after the promulgation of the 1606 Act to Restrain Abuses of Players, an act against the use of profanities on stage, which did not apply to printed texts. Expurgation in the text of *Merry Wives* deserves a separate discussion.

What matters is that Crane, a methodical worker for the press rather than for the stage, applied to the transcript of *Merry Wives* his personal scribal habits and conventions. The best known (and irritating for the modern editor) is his regular use of the so-called 'massed entries': at the beginning of each scene the entrance stage direction lists all the characters that are going to figure in it, though their separate entrances take place later in the course of the scene (Fig. 15). This convention, presumably intended to inform the stage manager (book-keeper or prompter in Shakespeare's time) of how many and which actors are required for a particular scene, exempts from marking not only the entrances but also the exits of single characters during the performance of that scene, as well as from introducing stage directions indicating actions. In the Folio text of *Merry Wives* only once is a new entrance indicated in the course of a scene: *Enter Fairies* at the equivalent of 5.5.16.1. As for exits, besides there being no indication of actors individually leaving the stage in the course of the action, general exits are unrecorded at the

---

15 (opposite) Folio sig. E5v, showing clearly marked scene divisions and massed entry. The stage direction for 'Scena Quinta' (5.5) is an example of 'massed entry': of the characters listed in it only Falstaff is present from the beginning. Mistress Page and Mistress Ford enter at 15.1, Evans, Anne and Fairies at 36.1–3, Page and Ford at 102.7, Quickly at 36.1–3, Slender at 173.1, Fenton at 207.1, Caius at 200.1, and Pistol at 36.1–3 (Anne exits at 102.1–6 and re-enters with Fenton at 207.1; Slender, Fenton and Caius put in brief silent appearances at 102.1–6).

That quaint in greene, she shall be loose en-roab'd,
With Ribonds-pendant, flaring 'bout her head;
And when the Doctor spies his vantage ripe,
To pinch her by the hand, and on that token,
The maid hath giuen consent to go with him.

Host. Which meanes she to deceiue? Father, or Mother.

Fen. Both (my good Host) to go along with me:
And heere it rests, that you'l procure the Vicar
To stay for me at Church, 'twixt twelue, and one,'
And in the lawfull name of marrying,
To giue our hearts vnited ceremony.

Host. Well, husband your deuice; Ile to the Vicar,
Bring you the Maid, you shall not lacke a Priest.

Fen. So shall I euermore be bound to thee;
Besides, Ile make a present recompence.   *Exeunt*

Actus Quintus. Scœna Prima.

Enter Falstoffe, Quickly, and Ford.

Fal. Pre'thee no more pratling: go, Ile hold, this is the third time: I hope good lucke lies in odde numbers: Away, go, they say there is Diuinity in odde Numbers, either in natiuity, chance, or death: away.

Qui. Ile prouide you a chaine, and Ile do what I can to get you a paire of hornes.

Fall. Away I say, time weares, hold vp your head & mince. How now M. *Broome?* Master *Broome,* the matter will be knowne to night, or neuer. Bee you in the Parke about midnight, at Hernes-Oake, and you shall see wonders.

Ford. Went you not to her yesterday (Sir) as you told me you had appointed?

Fal. I went to her (Master *Broome*) as you see, like a poore-old-man, but I came from her (Master *Broome*) like a poore-old-woman; that same knaue (Ford hir husband) hath the finest mad diuell of iealousie in him (Master *Broome*) that euer gouern'd Frensie. I will tell you, he beate me greeuously, in the shape of a woman; (for in the shape of Man (Master *Broome*) I feare not Goliah with a Weauers beame, because I know also, life is a Shuttle) I am in hast, go along with mee, Ile tell you all (Master *Broome*:) since I pluckt Geese, plaide Trewant, and whipt Top, I knew not what 'twas to be beaten, till lately. Follow mee, Ile tell you strange things of this knaue Ford, on whom to night I will be reuenged, and I will deliuer his wife into your hand. Follow, straunge things in hand (M. *Broome*) follow.   *Exeunt.*

Scena Secunda.

Enter Page, Shallow, Slender.

Page. Come, come: wee'll couch i'th Castle-ditch, till we see the light of our Fairies. Remember son *Slender,* my

Slen. I forsooth, I haue spoke with her, & we haue a nay-word, how to know one another. I come to her in white, and cry Mum; she cries Budget, and by that

we know one another.

Shal. That's good too: But what needes either your Mum, or her Budget? The white will decipher her well enough. It hath strooke ten a'clocke.

Page. The night is darke, Light and Spirits will become it wel: Heauen prosper our sport. No man meanes euill but the deuill, and we shal know him by his hornes, Lets away: follow me.   *Exeunt.*

Scena Tertia.

Enter Mist. Page, Mist. Ford, Caius.

Mist. Page. Mr Doctor, my daughter is in greene, when you see your time, take her by the hand, away with her to the Deanerie, and dispatch it quickly: go before into the Parke: we two must go together.

Cai. I know vat I haue to do, adieu.

Mist Page. Fare you well (Sir:) my husband will not reioyce so much at the abuse of *Falstaffe,* as he will chafe at the Doctors marrying my daughter: But 'tis no matter; better a little chiding, then a great deale of heart-breake.

Mist. Ford. Where is Nan now? and her troop of Fairies? and the Welch-deuill Herne?

Mist. Page. They are all couch'd in a pit hard by Hernes Oake, with obscur'd Lights; which at the very instant of *Falstaffes* and our meeting, they will at once display to the night.

Mist. Ford. That cannot choose but amaze him.

Mist. Page. If he be not amaz'd he will be mock'd: If he be amaz'd, he will euery way be mock'd.

Mist. Ford. Wee'll betray him finely.

Mist. Page. Against such Lewdsters, and their lechery, Those that betray them, do no treachery.

Mist. Ford. The houre drawes-on: to the Oake, to the Oake.   *Exeunt.*

Scena Quarta.

Enter Euans and Fairies.

Euans. Trib, trib Fairies: Come, and remember your parts: be pold (I pray you) follow me into the pit, and when I giue the watch-'ords, do as I pid you: Come, come, trib, trib.   *Exeunt*

Scena Quinta.

Enter Falstaffe, Mistris Page, Mistris Ford, Euans, Anne Page, Fairies, Page, Ford, Quickly, Slender, Fenton, Caius, Pistoll.

Fal. The Windsor-bell hath stroke twelue: the Minute drawes-on: Now the hot-bloodied-Gods assist mee: Remember loue, thou was't a Bull for thy *Europa,* Loue set on thy hornes. O powerfull Loue, that in some respects makes a Beast a Man: in som other, a Man a beast. You were also (Iupiter) a Swan, for the loue of *Leda:* O omnipotent

end of 3.1 and 4.4, and the plural form *Exeunt* appears at the conclusion of 2.1, 3.4 and 3.5, in spite of the fact that only one character is present on stage at the time. More correctly, *Exit* marks the end of 1.4, when Quickly is alone on the stage, and, misprinted *Exti.*, after Ford's second soliloquy at the end of 2.2.

Q, in turn, tries to compensate for the very imperfect reproduction of the dialogue by providing not only indications of new entrances and exits in the course of the action, but also fairly numerous descriptive directions for the action itself, for instance the business of Simple hiding in Caius's closet (called in Q 'Counting-house') at 1.4, that with the buck-basket at 3.3, the beating of Falstaff disguised as a woman at 4.2, as well as, in 5.5, those connected with the Herne's oak hoax.

In the present edition, while all such indications provided by Q have been taken into account, with the necessary modifications, an effort has been made to avoid as far as possible additional editorial directions. The management of the stage action is not the editor's but the director's and the actors' business, and the text with which they are provided should allow them freedom of deciding how a particular action is to be conducted. Therefore asides are marked only when there is a possibility that a speech may be mistaken as being addressed to all those on stage, instead of being meant for only one of them or as a remark by the speaker to himself or herself (and the audience). At times substantial differences between the action represented in the two texts render inappropriate the directions contained in Q. A case in point is 4.2, where Q makes it clear that the buck-basket is on stage from the beginning, carried by Ford's two servants; in F by contrast there is no mention of them until 103, when Mistress Ford (who had gone out at 98 to 'direct my men what they shall do') suddenly calls on them to 'take the basket again on your shoulders' and one of them wonders 'Pray heaven it be not full of knight again' (107). This renders it indispensable to mark an additional entrance direction for Mistress Ford with the servants at 102.1, but it is obviously inadequate a few lines later to

borrow from Q the entrance direction at the equivalent of 108.1 for Ford, Page, Evans and Shallow, ending with the words '*the two men carries the basket, and Ford meets it*'. In devising in its place a fuller description of the action for the reader it must be made clear, in a commentary note, that what is offered is merely one of several possible ways of staging the situation and that the ultimate decision rests with the director and the actors involved in it. The note in the commentary is a last resort; it is preferable not to tamper with the essential indications found in the original texts. For instance, Q ends each scene with the formula *Exit omnes* (they all go out). Obviously these general exits do not mean that all the characters on stage in the last part of the scene crowd to the doors at exactly the same time. Separate exits for early leavers have been introduced when the text makes it quite clear that one or two characters remain on the stage commenting on those that have just left, but when in the course of, or at the end of, a scene (as for instance at 1.1.182 and at the end of 1.2) separate exits by individual actors in close sequence are merely implied, no additional directions have been supplied to indicate who goes out first.

In this edition only editorial additions or substantial changes to the original stage directions, whether in both F and Q or – as in most cases – only in Q, are enclosed in square brackets. See, for instance, the final exit at 1.1.294, present in both texts, where only the words *Slender leading* are marked as editorial additions. An example of direction peculiar to Q is 5.5.102.1–6, where the additions *During the song* (1.1) and *comes in and* (1.3), as well as the change from *the Doctor* to CAIUS (1.1) are editorial, while the changes in the colour of costumes (from *red* to *green* in 1.2 and from *greene* to *white* in 1.3) go unmarked as conforming to the 'colour policy' (see pp. 53–4) adopted in the text of previous scenes. Textual notes record the sources of all alterations in text and directions.

A major point is the treatment of profanity, or rather how far to restore to the text oaths or blasphemous expressions sup-

pressed or replaced in accordance with the 1606 Act.[1] A comparison between F and Q may provide some guidance. The question to be asked is: how far is the abundance of oaths and the like in Q due to the reporter of the text who, not remembering the exact original wording, tried to fill the memory gaps by inserting current profanities in places where there were none?

In Q the name of the Lord is abused fifteen times in such expressions as 'O Lord', 'By the Lord' and the like. None of them is present in F, except for Mistress Quickly's mild oath 'Lord, Lord' at 2.2.53, which may even sound like a flattering allusion to Falstaff's social status. 'Ieshu' or 'O Ieshu', Hostess Quickly's favourite exclamation in *1 Henry IV*, does not appear in Folio *Merry Wives*, but is peppered throughout the Quarto version (eleven times), on the lips of a variety of characters, though mainly on those of Parson Evans.

It is revealing that while in Q the word 'God' (or 'Gode' and genitive 'Gods', 'Godes') figures no fewer than fifty-seven times, there are only two instances of it in F: Slender mentions the 'feare of God' at 1.1.169-70, and Quickly foresees 'an old abusing of Gods patience, and the Kings English' by Doctor Caius at 1.4.5. By contrast 'Heauen' (or 'Heauens'), totally absent from Q, appears twenty-six times in F. The expletive 'Godso' – only apparently an abuse of God's name, because in fact it adapts the Italian obscene oath *Cazzo*, meaning 'penis' – is used twice, as 'Godeso', in Q, by Slender at the equivalent of 3.4.56, and by Ford soliloquizing at the end of 3.5 in a passage that corresponds to 2.2.278-84 in the present edition. In the second case, where Q has 'cuckold, wittold, godeso / The diuel himself hath not such a name' F simply omits the offending word, though keeping the

---

[1] The following pages integrate Gary Taylor's outstanding treatment of the problem, implementing its conclusions (Taylor, 'Expurgation', 105-6): 'A few editors . . . have added profanity whenever they could find any contemporary warrant, drawing routinely upon memorial reconstructions to increase the amount of profanities in Folio texts . . . . On the other hand, most editors have made no attempt at all to restore profanities, even in texts which they believe to have been expurgated. Neither of these editorial habits is defensible. Editors should instead identify where the problem exists, and then do something to solve it.'

114

rest of the phrase unchanged (see 2.2.283-4). In the case of Slender, the variation in the two texts is interesting: in Q he replies to Anne Page's question 'whats your will?' with the words 'Godeso theres a Iest indeed', an unsuitable remark from a would-be courtier, however stupid, to a lady; the remark in the Folio version is a much more appropriate exposure of Slender's foolishness: 'My will? Odd's-hart-lings, that's a prettie iest indeede'. As in a number of other cases, the Q reporter remembered the meaning and tone of Slender's reply but not its precise wording, and used the vulgar expletive 'Godso' in place of the affected ''Od's heartlings', a euphemistic form that was not considered blasphemous. In fact the elided form ''Od's', totally absent from Q, is found three more times in F: in 4.1, the Latin-lesson scene missing from Q, Quickly equivocates between an innocent grammatical definition and the strong oath ''Od's nouns' (God's wounds); at 1.1.246 Parson Evans invokes ''Od's plessed will' in a phrase which, in Q, is found at the equivalent of 1.2, with no mention of God; finally Caius at 1.4.57 exclaims ''Od's me' where in the equivalent phrase in Q he uses the expression 'begar', an obvious euphemism for 'by God'.

'Begar', or 'by-gar', is Caius's pet interjection, occurring twenty times in Q and becoming his obsessive verbal tic repeated thirty-one times in F. Evidently 'begar', like the elided ''Od's', was not considered a swear word, but a peculiar mannerism of the Frenchman Caius, and, working on this assumption, whoever expurgated the play in conformity with the 1606 Profanity Act (see p. 110) replaced some of the offending oaths with 'begar', adding a few more for good measure. In the same way, Parson Evans's Welsh accent was considered another extenuating factor in the matter of oaths: apart from his injunction to Falstaff at 5.5.128, 'serue Got', that would have been acceptable (like the expression 'the fear of God') even in normal spelling, in the F first scene, and only there, Evans is allowed to mention 'Got' six times: twice (at 33 and 34) as the innocent 'feare of Got', and then in the current expressions 'Got deliuer' (48),

'Got-plesse' (66), 'go't's plessing' (69), whose English equivalents are systematically omitted or modified in the rest of the play, and finally in the variant 'So got-udge me' (171). This is particularly interesting because, though the expression has no counterpart in Q in this scene, in its rougher form 'So kad vdge me' it appears five times in the rest of Q as a kind of tag line characterizing Parson Evans, at the equivalent of 3.1.21 (where F has instead 'Mercy on me'), 3.1.84 (F: 'As I am a Christians soul'), 3.3.225-6 (in Q Evans comments on Ford's behaviour, in F he vents his resentment against the Host, 'A lousy knave'), 4.2.133 (F: ''Tis unreasonable!'), 4.4.65 (Q: 'So kad vdge me the deuises are excellent'; F: 'I will teach the children their behaviours'). As in the case of Nim's phrase 'there's the humour of it' replacing in Q the various mentions of 'humour' in his speeches in F, the compiler of Q, remembering out of context Evans's asseveration in the first scene, turned it into a recurrent tag to fill up memory gaps in reporting the Parson's later speeches.

It is obvious that in this case there is no reason to restore to the play-text such recurring tags; neither should 'Godso' be reintroduced at 2.2.284, given also that the expression is found nowhere else in Shakespeare. On the contrary, the strong oath ''Sblood' which, like 'By the Lord', was among Falstaff's favourites in the uncensored Quarto of *1 Henry IV*, is not found in F but figures twice in Falstaff's speeches in Q, at the equivalent of 3.5.8 and in a passage in the last scene that has no counterpart in F. It seems appropriate to restore it to the text in the first case and to ignore it in the second. As for 'By the Lord', the only two speeches of Falstaff in which it seems required by the context are at 3.3.55 (see 3.3.55n.) and at 3.5.82, where a stronger oath is required than 'Yes' in F. Similarly, Q's 'Afore God', an expression repeatedly found in Shakespeare, for instance in *Richard II* and *Romeo and Juliet*, has been preferred to F's insignificant 'Trust me' in Shallow's speech at 3.1.101.

While Caius's repetitions of 'by gar' or 'begar' require no comment, the numerous mentions of the name of God in Q

which have disappeared from F invite much greater attention in deciding when they merely reflect the Q reporter's lack of imagination and when their disappearance is more probably the result of expurgation. The latter is evident when the context is identical in the two texts and the only variant is 'Heaven' or a mark of omission (for example ''bless' or ''save') in F in place of 'God' in Q. But there is no reason to change 'heaven' into 'God' in the expression 'Heaven forgive my (our) sins' at 3.3.197 and 5.5.31, where Q gives no warrant for it. Finally, in a few instances, F 'Heaven' has been replaced with 'God' in this edition in expressions without exact equivalents in the Q wording (for example 3.4.57, 58 and 5.5.230, 234), when Q mentioned the name of God in similar contexts close by. In the textual notes such emendations are signalled by the words *after Q* or *suggested by Q* (i.e. 'by analogy with Q's usual variant') after the indication of the edition that adopted them first.

Merry Wives has only four scenes partly in verse. All the rest are in prose except for Pistol's doggerel. But while Pistol's speeches in the early editions are frequently printed as prose, a number of prose passages are lined as verse. The textual notes record the names of the editors who first relined prose passages as verse, but no indication is given when passages printed as verse lines in F are so recognizably prose as to leave no doubt even in the earliest modern editions. Relineation of verse is always recorded in the textual notes, and at times discussed in the commentary, especially in the case of verse alternating with prose speeches or of consecutive half-line speeches that offer more than one possibility of line divisions, as at 3.4.71-2.

SIR JOHN FALSTAFF
AND
THE MERRY WIVES
OF
WINDSOR

LIST OF ROLES

AT THE GARTER INN

HOST	*of the Garter Inn*
Sir John FALSTAFF	*a Crown pensioner, lodging at the Inn*
ROBIN	*his page-boy*
'Corporal' BARDOLPH	*Falstaff's attendant, later a drawer* 5 *in the Inn*
'Ancient' PISTOL Corporal NIM	} *Falstaff's other attendants*
Robert SHALLOW	*a justice of the peace*
Abraham SLENDER	*a young gentleman, his relative*
Peter SIMPLE	*Slender's servant* 10
FENTON	*a gentleman, former companion of the Prince of Wales*

TOWNSPEOPLE

George PAGE	*a citizen*
MISTRESS Margaret (Meg) PAGE	*his wife*
ANNE (Nan) PAGE	*their daughter* 15
WILLIAM Page	*a schoolboy, their son*
Frank FORD	*another citizen*
MISTRESS Alice FORD	*his wife*
JOHN ROBERT	} *servants in Ford's household* 20
Sir Hugh EVANS	*a Welsh parson*
Doctor CAIUS	*a French physician*
Mistress QUICKLY	*his housekeeper*
John RUGBY	*his servant*
Children,	*disguised as Fairies, instructed by Parson Evans* 25

LIST OF ROLES So arranged this edn; first supplied by Rowe; not in Q, F

3 FALSTAFF, *a Crown pensioner* See *pensioners*, 2.2.73n. The reasons for considering Falstaff in *MW*, after his rejection by Henry V at the end of *2H4*, as one of those retired impecunious soldiers who received a Crown subsidy ('competence of life I will allow you', *2H4* 5.5.66) and who were commonly known as 'the poor knights of Windsor', are discussed on pp. 20–1.

4 ROBIN The name of Falstaff's page does not figure in *2H4*, where he is called 'page' or 'boy', nor in *H5*, where he is always 'boy'.

5 'Corporal' BARDOLPH ... *Inn* The military rank of Bardolph is never mentioned in *MW*, nor in *1H4*, but he is constantly called 'corporal' in *2H4*, while in *H5* Nim refers to him both as 'corporal' (3.2.3) and as 'lieutenant' (2.1.2). Here, as in the Histories, he is characterized by the redness of his complexion. In the original version of the play *Henry IV*, where Falstaff was called 'Oldcastle' and Peto 'Harvey', Bardolph's name was Sir John Russell (see *2H4* 2.2.0.1 in 1600 Quarto), familiarly 'Rossill' (see *1H4* 1.2.162 and SPs at 2.4.174, 176, 180 in 1598 Quarto), a slur on the Russell family name punning on Italian *rosso* meaning 'red'. For *drawer* see 1.3.10n.

6 'Ancient' PISTOL There is no mention in *MW* of the military rank of Pistol, the type of the boasting soldier fond of speaking in the bombastic blank-verse style of Marlowe and his imitators; but from his first appearance in a play, *2H4* 2.4, he is called 'ancient', i.e. 'ensign', a rank above that of corporal. Falstaff calls him 'lieutenant' in *2H4* 5.5.89, meaning second to him in command. Pistol is again 'ancient' in *H5*, except at 2.1.39 where Bardolph calls him 'lieutenant', while at 3.6.12 Fluellen speaks of him as 'an aunchient lieutenant . . . as valiant . . . as Mark Antony'. In *H5* 2.1, however, he is 'host Pistol', having married the hostess Mistress Quickly (*MW* 2.2.127–9

may hint at this development – see note), and quarrels with Nim, his defeated rival in love.

7 Corporal NIM The only attendant of Falstaff whose military rank is mentioned in *MW*. The name is spelt indifferently 'Nim' or 'Nym' in the early editions of both *MW* and *H5*, the two plays where he appears; 'Nim' is preferred because of the verb 'nim' ('take'), which acquired the meaning 'steal, filch, pilfer' (*OED* Nim *v*. 3), appropriate to Nim's sad fate in *H5*, where we learn (4.4.70–4) that he, like Bardolph, was hanged for stealing. In both plays he is characterized by his obsession with the word 'humour', an ironical reference to the fashion of presenting 'humours' in stage comedies, established by Ben Jonson's *Every Man in His Humour* in 1598 (see pp. 5, 11); but while in *H5* his tag line is nearly always 'that's the humour of it' (repeated six times in the Folio and eight in the Quarto version), the phrase is constantly varied in *MW* (though not so much in the Quarto of 1602).

8 SHALLOW, *a justice* Slender says at 1.1.4 that Shallow is a justice 'in the County of Gloucester', a phrase (omitted in Q) meant to remind the audience of Shallow's presence in the Gloucestershire scenes of *2H4*. Later in the play (see 2.3.52n.) he is addressed not as a Windsor resident but as a lodger at the Garter Inn. The mention of Gloucester makes it unlikely that he appeared first in *MW* as a satire on a living person, as Leslie Hotson argued when, in *Shakespeare versus Shallow* (1931), he suggested that Shallow and Slender represent the justice of the peace William Gardiner and his step-son William Wayte respectively, who were involved in 1596 in a legal battle with Shakespeare and the owner of the Swan theatre, Francis Langley. The family connection between Shallow and Slender is never stated in unequivocal terms (see 1.1.6n.), and in *2H4* there is no mention of Shallow's family or relations,

therefore there is no reason to believe that these two represent the litigants in the legal case.

9 **Abraham** SLENDER . . . *relative* Slender's first name, Abraham, mentioned only twice in the play (1.1.51 and 216), is perhaps an ironical allusion to his clumsiness as a wooer, in contrast with the love god Cupid, called by Mercutio, in *RJ* 2.1.13–14, 'Abraham Cupid, he that shot so trim / When King Cophetua loved the beggar maid' (the beggars who wandered round half-naked were called 'abraham men'). What makes Slender a suitable match for Anne, in Master Page's view, is not the fact that he is Justice Shallow's relative, but that he stands to inherit a large family fortune (see 1.1.256n. and 257n.). Close similarities have been noted between Slender and Sir Andrew Aguecheek in *TN* (see 1.1.271–2n.); both names seem to allude to the lean physical appearance (cf. 1.1.120n.) of the actor impersonating them, possibly John Sinklo, whose name is mentioned in *TS* Induction 1.88 and in SDs and SPs of *3H6* 3.1, as well as of *2H4* 5.4, where he is the Beadle addressed by Mistress Quickly as 'starved bloodhound' and by Doll Tearsheet as 'nuthook' (cf. *MW* 1.1.155n.), 'paper-faced villain' and 'thin man'.

11 FENTON . . . *Wales* At 3.2.65-6 Page says that Fenton 'kept company with the wild Prince and Poins'; the mention of Poins is meant to place Fenton in a separate category from Falstaff and the other companions of the Prince. Poins, who figures only in *1* and *2H4*, is presented as the Prince's confidant, setting together with him the traps in which Falstaff and the rest fall, both at Gad's Hill (*1H4* 1.2, 2.2, 2.4) and in the Eastcheap tavern (*2H4* 2.2, 2.4). Significantly, Poins's name is the only one that remained unchanged when those of the other 'irregular humourists' appearing in the early version of *Henry IV* had to be altered.

21 **Sir Hugh** EVANS 'Sir' was a current form of address to a parson, translating the Latin *dominus* (master), abbreviated to *Dom* or *Don* in romance languages, prefixed to the name of clergymen. The compiler of the title-page of the 1602 Quarto confused the two uses of 'Sir' and listed among the 'humors' of the comedy 'Syr *Hugh* the Welch Knight'. Evans's Welshness, much emphasized in the play, was probably prompted by the fact that in 1599 the Chamberlain's Men had replaced the clown Will Kemp with Robert Armin, an expert in the presentation of comic Welshmen (see Fluellen in *H5* and p. 11).

22 **Doctor** CAIUS Apparently the name does not refer to Doctor John Caius (1510–73), a famous English physician and co-founder of Gonville and Caius College, Cambridge, but was chosen because Caius is the most common Latin name – in Italian '*Tizio, Caio e Sempronio*' is the equivalent of 'Tom, Dick and Harry'; its commonness was tantamount to anonymity, hence its adoption by Kent for his disguise in *KL* 5.3.284. Dover Wilson (Cam[1]) suggested that 'the character was intended as the caricature of the Englishman in an earlier draft of the play and that he was converted into a Frenchman in a subsequent revision'. It is more likely that in the hypothetical 'early draft' Shakespeare meant to place side by side with that of a Welshman (Evans) the caricature not of an Englishman but of a Scotsman, and changed it to a Frenchman partly because of the success of the comic scenes with the Dauphin and with Princess Katherine in *H5*, and partly for the reasons given in the note to *French thrift*, 1.3.81. Court physicians came frequently from the Continent, and it is Caius's connection with the court that makes him a desirable suitor for Anne in her mother's eyes.

23 **Mistress** QUICKLY, *his housekeeper* Described as Caius's *nurse* in 1.2, Mistress Quickly had appeared in Shakespeare's histories in the role of Hostess – at first in Eastcheap as 'an honest man's wife' in *1H4*, and as a

superannuated widow with a genius for malapropisms in *2H4*. In *H5* she also keeps an inn, but outside London (see Melchiori, *Garter*, 111), and is the wife of Pistol. Audiences' appreciation of her linguistic vagaries may have persuaded Shakespeare to reintroduce her in *MW*, and the way he found for doing so was to imagine that, after the rejection of Falstaff in *2H4* and before the French campaign in *H5*, Quickly had moved with Falstaff, Bardolph and Pistol to Windsor, taking a job as private housekeeper.

SIR JOHN FALSTAFF
AND
THE MERRY WIVES
OF WINDSOR

1.1   *Enter* Justice SHALLOW, SLENDER *and*
                           Sir Hugh EVANS.

SHALLOW   Sir Hugh, persuade me not: I will make a Star
  Chamber matter of it. If he were twenty Sir John
  Falstaffs, he shall not abuse Robert Shallow esquire.
SLENDER   In the County of Gloucester, Justice of Peace
  and Coram.   5

1.1 The location is a Windsor street before
Page's house. In Q the scene is structured differently: Master Page is present
from the beginning and agrees immediately to the match between Anne and
Slender and to Evans's proposal to have
him as one of the umpires in the quarrel
between Shallow and Falstaff. This is
followed by the entrance of Falstaff and
his companions, and then of Mistress
Page, Mistress Ford and Anne. When
Slender is left alone with Anne, he uses
phrases which in F are found at 3.4.59–
63. The two versions coincide in the last
part of the scene.
1   **Sir Hugh** For *Sir* as a form of address
  to a parson see note on Evans in the
  List of Roles.
    persuade me not do not try to dis-
  suade me

1–2 **Star Chamber matter** a matter for
  the special court which took its name
  from the stars decorating the ceiling of
  the hall in Westminster Palace where it
  was held; it was authorized by Parliament to 'punish divers misdemeanours' and consisted of the members of
  the Privy Council and the two Chief
  Justices of the King's Bench and
  Common Pleas.
3   **abuse** wrong
    esquire originally a man of gentle
  birth carrying the shield of a knight in
  the field – *armiger* in Latin; later it
  designated a gentleman, one degree
  below knight, entitled to bear heraldic
  arms.
5   **Coram** a current corruption of Latin
  quorum, from the formula with which
  justices were installed: *quorum vos . . .*

Title. SIR . . . AND] *Q (subst.); not in F*   **1.1**] *Actus primus, Scena prima. F*   0.1] *Rowe; Enter*
Iustice Shallow, Slender, *Sir* Hugh Evans, *Master* Page, Falstoffe, Bardolph, Nym, Pistoll, Anne
Page, *Mistresse* Ford, *Mistresse* Page, Simple. *F; Enter Iustice* Shallow, *Syr* Hugh, *Maister* Page, *and*
Slender. *Q*

SHALLOW   Ay, cousin Slender, and Cust-a-lorum.

SLENDER   Ay, and Rato lorum too; and a gentleman born,
master parson, who writes himself *Armigero*, in any bill,
warrant, quittance, or obligation – *Armigero*.

SHALLOW   Ay, that I do, and have done any time these   10
three hundred years.

SLENDER   All his successors – gone before him – hath
done't; and all his ancestors – that come after him –
may. They may give the dozen white luces in their coat.

SHALLOW   It is an old coat.   15

---

unum esse volumus, i.e. 'of whom we
wish you to be one' (Ard¹). It implies
official recognition of the title of justice
for Shallow, while anticipating the
comedy of language equivocation
involving most characters – notably
Slender, Evans, Doctor Caius and
Mistress Quickly – which culminates
in the Latin lesson (4.1).

6   **cousin** a form of address to any kins-
man. Shallow seems to be Slender's
uncle (see 3.4.41), or, in view of his
age, his great-uncle (Oxf¹).
      Cust-a-lorum a contraction of the
Latin *custos rotulorum*, keeper of the
rolls, i.e. the records of trials, a distinction of the chief Justice of the
Peace in each county

7   **Rato lorum** Slender's emphasis on
the first two syllables, separated from
the ending *lorum*, is meant to compensate for what he considers Shallow's
omission of part of his title; but his *Rato*
for *Rotu* proves his ignorance of Latin.

8   **writes himself** *Armigero* adds to his
name, in official documents, the title of
'esquire'; see 3n. Slender gets his Latin
wrong again; he should have said
armiger instead of *armigero*, which is
Italian (or a misuse of the Latin abla-
tive form).

9   **quittance, or obligation** receipt or
bond

10–11 **any . . . years** Shallow implies that

his family's arms were granted three
centuries before the accession of
Henry V (1413), i.e. at the time of
Henry I, son of William the
Conqueror. But Shakespeare (and his
audience) might have been thinking in
contemporary terms, placing the grant
of arms at the time of Edward I
(1272–1307).

12–13 **gone . . . after** another of Slender's
ignorant blunders: successors come
after and ancestors go before.

12   **hath** have. The use of the third person
singular for the plural was current at
the time (Abbott, 334).

14   **give** heraldic: 'display in a coat of
arms' (see *coat* at end of speech)
      luces *Luce* is the heraldic designation,
from the French, of the pike, a fresh-
water fish (see 19n.). Three (not
twelve) silver luces figured, placed ver-
tically, in the coat of arms of the Lucy
family of Charlecote, near Stratford-
upon-Avon, and young Shakespeare,
according to a rumour reported a century later by Nicholas Rowe (1709),
was accused of deer-stealing from
Charlecote park. Lines 12–35 and the
exchanges with Falstaff at 102–12 have
been interpreted as satirical allusions
to the Lucy episode, but possibly the
whole deer-stealing story was invented
later to account for the puzzling allusive nature of this passage.

6 Cust-a-lorum] *this edn; Cust-alorum F;* Custalorum *mod. eds*   7 Rato lorum] *(Rato lorum);*
Rotulorum Q3; Ratolorum *mod. eds*

EVANS   The dozen white louses do become an old coat
    well. It agrees well passant. It is a familiar beast to man,
    and signifies love.

SHALLOW   The luce is the fresh fish – the salt fish is an
    old coat.   20

SLENDER   I may quarter, coz.

SHALLOW   You may, by marrying.

16–17 **The . . . well.** the first of the many
equivocations caused by Evans's
Welsh accent ('d' for 't' and vice versa,
'ou' for 'u', 'p' for 'b', 'f' for 'v', omission of initial 'w') and syntax. The
innocent statement 'A dozen white
luces are well suited for an ancient coat
of arms' is transformed into 'It is common that an old coat should have some
dozen lice (louses) in it'. There may be
a further pun in Evans's pronunciation
of 'coat' as 'coad' (Oxf), i.e. 'cod', a
salt-water fish (see 19n.), as well as a
possible allusion to 'codpiece'.

17 **well passant** passing well; but
'passant' is the heraldic term used
when the animal ('beast') in a coat of
arms is represented as walking. Such
is the case of the three lions 'passant
gardant' in the Plantagenet coat of
arms.

17–18 **a . . . love** Traditionally the fish –
the emblem of Christ – *signifies love*.
Evans seems to allude to the heraldic
luce, but the mention of *familiar beast*
lends itself to further equivocation: it
refers to 1) domestic animals; 2) the
heraldic animals displayed in family
arms; 3) the parasitical lice; 4) attendant devils ('familiars') in animal form.
Oxf[1] quotes *Doctor Faustus*, sc. 4.21–2,
'I'll turn all the lice about thee into
familiars and make them tear thee in
pieces', and the proverb (from 1586,
Dent, L471) 'A louse is a gentleman's
companion'.

19–20 **the salt . . . coat** Because this

seems to make little sense, it is
suspected that a scribe or compositor
has tampered with this sentence.
Johnson – followed by Craik (Oxf[1]) –
conjectured that 'not' had been
dropped before 'an old coat' (Shallow
jocularly contrasts the luce, a fresh-
water fish, with old stale fish, preserved by salting); Dover Wilson
(Cam[1]) sees a joke on Evans's Welsh
pronunciation of 'coat' at 16 as 'coad'
(adopted by the Oxford editors), and
emends 'coat' at 20 to 'cod', a salt-
water fish; Crane (Cam[2]) understands
Shallow remarking that what is suitable ('is' meaning 'fits') for an old
coat is not fresh but 'salt' (i.e. salted,
stale) fish. The F reading as it stands
suggests that Shallow, resenting
Evans's equivocation on 'coat', though
pronouncing the word correctly,
alludes to the Welsh mispronunciation
as 'cod', acknowledging that, in contrast with an ancient coat of arms, a
much-worn coat may well smell like
stale fish.

21 **quarter** the heraldic term designating
the division of a shield into four parts,
two bearing the original family arms
and the other two those acquired later
through marriage or other alliances.
Slender, as Shallow remarks at 22, may
quarter his coat of arms by marrying
a gentlewoman – but Anne Page is a
citizen's daughter.

coz familiar for 'cousin', in addressing
any relative; cf. 6n.

16 coat] coad *Oxf*   19–20 fresh . . . coat] *F (subst.);* fresh fish – the salt fish is an old cod *Cam[1];*
fresh fish, the salt fish – is an old coat *Sisson;* fresh fish. The salt fish is not an old coat *Oxf[1]*
(Johnson); fresh fish. The salt fish fits an old coat *(Cam[2])*   21 coz.] coz? *Steevens[3]*

EVANS   It is marring indeed, if he quarter it.

SHALLOW   Not a whit.

EVANS   Yes, py'r lady: if he has a quarter of your coat,   25
there is but three skirts for yourself, in my simple
conjectures. But that is all one: if Sir John Falstaff have
committed disparagements unto you, I am of the
Church, and will be glad to do my benevolence, to make
atonements and compremises between you.   30

SHALLOW   The Council shall hear it, it is a riot.

EVANS   It is not meet the Council hear a riot. There is no
fear of Got in a riot. The Council, look you, shall desire
to hear the fear of Got, and not to hear a riot. Take your
vizaments in that.   35

SHALLOW   Ha, o'my life, if I were young again, the sword
should end it.

EVANS   It is petter that friends is the sword, and end it; and
there is also another device in my prain, which

---

23 Evans's deliberate double equivocation. The first is based on the current
punning proverb 'Marrying is marring' (Dent, M701), the second on the
basic meaning of 'quarter', divide by
four.

24 not at all

25 *py'r lady the Welsh pronunciation
of the current oath 'By our Lady'

26 skirts the four panels forming the
lower section of a long coat

27 conjectures Evans's way of emphasizing polysyllables by making them
plural is a Welsh habit shared with
Fluellen in *H5*.

30 atonements reconciliation (Welsh
plural)
compremises possibly F's alternative spelling of 'compromise' in the
usual 'Welsh plural' (cf. F *KJ* 5.1.69,
'make comprimise'); but Evans may be
thinking in terms of 'premises' for
reconciliation.

31 **Council** the Privy Council sitting as
the Court of Star Chamber (see 1–2n.)
riot public disturbance (*OED sb.* 36)

32 **meet** proper, fitting. Evans apparently
takes *Council* to mean a church council
(Cam[1]'s suggestion) and, missing the
legal meaning of *hear* (a case in court),
finds it improper that the church
should be involved in a riot.

34–5 **Take your vizaments** Be advised.
Evans's version of the legal phrase
'take advisement'. The pretentious use
and misuse of legal terminology is
another aspect of the 'comedy of language' in this play.

36 **o'my life** on my life (as true as I am
alive)

38 **It ... sword** It is better to put the matter to arbitration (friends replacing the
sword). Cam[1] emends 'sword' to
'swort' (Evans's pronunciation) as 'a
quibble upon "sort" (= issue, upshot)',
or rather 'sorting out'.

---

25 py'r lady] *Capell;* per-lady *F*   30 compremises] compromises *mod. eds*   38 sword] swort *Cam[1]*

peradventure prings goot discretions with it. There is   40
Anne Page, which is daughter to Master George Page
– which is pretty virginity.

SLENDER   Mistress Anne Page? She has brown hair, and
speaks small like a woman?

EVANS   It is that ferry person for all the 'orld, as just as   45
you will desire, and seven hundred pounds of moneys,
and gold, and silver, is her grandsire upon his death's-
bed – Got deliver to a joyful resurrections! – give, when
she is able to overtake seventeen years old. It were a
goot motion, if we leave our pribbles and prabbles,   50
and desire a marriage between Master Abraham and
Mistress Anne Page.

SLENDER   Did her grandsire leave her seven hundred
pound?

EVANS   Ay, and her father is make her a petter penny.   55

40 **discretions** discernment (Welsh
plural)
41 ***George** 'Thomas' in F, but 'George'
in all three later mentions of Page's
name in the text. Either an authorial
slip or a misreading as 'Tho' of 'Geo'
in Shakespeare's handwriting (Oxf).
42 **virginity** Evans uses the abstract for
the concrete noun 'virgin'.
44 **small** in a soprano voice (Hibbard).
Oliver (Ard²) quotes *TN* 1.4.32–4
(Orsino to Viola/Cesario): 'thy small
pipe / Is as the maiden's organ, shrill
and sound / And all is semblative a
woman's part.'
woman? Slender asks for confirma-
tion of the correctness (*just*, 45) of his
identification of Anne.
45 **ferry** very (Welsh accent); Oxf
emends to 'fery', the form of the word
in the Folio version at 1.1.236, 3.1.48
and 3.3.156. Double 'r' in Folio, here
as well as at 133 and at 4.4.79, suggests
particular emphasis.
for . . . 'orld exactly, in every respect;

cf. *TS* 3.2.65 and *1H4* 3.2.93 (Dent,
WW27), and Caius's 'not for the varld'
at 1.4.58–9.
47–8 **is . . . give** has given (or 'did give').
In Evans's Welsh syntax 'is' replaces all
tenses and moods of the auxiliary verbs
'to do', 'to be' and 'to have' – here the
past, at 38 (*is the sword*) the infinitive, at
49 (*is able*) and 55 (*is make*) the future.
50 **pribbles and prabbles** Evans's
improvement on 'brabbles' (brawls,
quarrels), with a further suggestion of
legal 'quibbles', equivocations. Cf. the
Welshman Fluellen's 'no tittle tattle
nor pibble babble' at *H5* 4.1.70–1.
51 **Abraham** Slender's first name is
mentioned only twice in the play, here
and at 216. On its significance see note
on Slender in the List of Roles.
55 **is make** is to give (make over to), i.e.
will give. An instance of Evans's
unorthodox syntax; see 47–8n.
a petter penny 'A better penny' is
proverbial (Dent, P189) for 'much
more besides'.

41 George] *Theobald; Thomas F*   41–2 Page – . . . virginity.] *this edn; Page, . . . virginity. F; Page, . . .*
virginity – *Oxf¹*   44 woman?] *Hibbard (Lambrechts); woman. F*   53 SP] *(Slen.); Shal. / Capell*

SHALLOW   I know the young gentlewoman, she has good
   gifts.

EVANS   Seven hundred pounds, and possibilities, is goot
   gifts.

SHALLOW   Well, let us see honest Master Page. Is Falstaff   60
   there?

EVANS   Shall I tell you a lie? I do despise a liar, as I do
   despise one that is false, or as I despise one that is not
   true: the knight Sir John is there, and I beseech you be
   ruled by your well-willers. I will peat the door for   65
   Master Page. [*Knocks.*] What ho! Got pless your house
   here!

PAGE [*within*]   Who's there?

[*Enter* PAGE.]

EVANS   Here is Got's plessing and your friend, and Justice
   Shallow, and here young Master Slender, that per-   70
   adventures shall tell you another tale, if matters grow
   to your likings.

56–7 *F assigns this speech to Slender,
   improbably in view of what he said at
   43–4. Capell is right in giving it to
   Shallow, but his allotting to the latter
   also the speech at 53–4 seems unnecessary.
58 **possibilities** prospects (of future
   inheritance). Evans takes Shallow's
   mention of *gifts* at 57 (moral and physical qualities) to refer to material
   wealth.
65 **well-willers** well-wishers
68 The performers may choose between
   having Page reply from behind the
   door, which he then opens to enter the
   stage, or appearing on the upper stage,
   half-listening to Evans's words at

69–72 before coming down to greet his
   visitors (see t.n.).
69 **Got's . . . friend** Evans refers to
   himself in his double capacity as
   God's minister and as Page's private
   friend.
70–1 **peradventures** 'Peradventure' means
   'it may well be' (Welsh plural).
71 **tell . . . tale** have something to say,
   proverbial (Dent, T49). Oxf suggests
   that the last part of the speech, from
   'that peradventures', is spoken aside to
   Shallow and Slender.
72 **likings** probably the usual 'Welsh
   plural'; but if this is an aside, it refers
   to Shallow's and Slender's wishes.

---

56 SP] *Capell; Slen. F*   66 SD] *Rowe (subst.)*   68 SP] *Q (Page, Pa. or Pag. throughout play); M^r*
Page, M. Page, M.Pa. or Ma. Pa, F (throughout play)   68 SD] *Dyce; Above, at the window / Collier²*
68.1] *Rowe (before 68); after 72 Collier²*   69 Got's] *(go't's)*   70 here] here's *F2*   that] [*aside*] that
Oxf

PAGE I am glad to see your worships well. I thank you for
my venison, Master Shallow.

SHALLOW Master Page, I am glad to see you, much good   75
do it your good heart. I wished your venison better, it
was ill killed. How doth good Mistress Page? And I
thank you always with my heart, la – with my heart.

PAGE Sir, I thank you.

SHALLOW Sir, I thank you; by yea and no I do.   80

PAGE I am glad to see you, good Master Slender.

SLENDER How does your fallow greyhound, sir? I heard
say he was outrun on Cotsall.

PAGE It could not be judged, sir.

SLENDER You'll not confess, you'll not confess!   85

SHALLOW That he will not 'tis your fault, 'tis your fault.
'Tis a good dog.

PAGE A cur, sir.

---

73 **worships** perhaps 'worship's' for 'worship is', if Page is addressing only Shallow

75–6 **much . . . heart** a common good wish (Dent, MM23)

77 **ill killed** damaged by not having been killed in the proper way. Shallow seems to refer to his deer, which he accuses Falstaff of having killed (104–5); but it is not clear why he should have regaled Page with it, unless he wished to secure the latter's sympathy in his case against Falstaff (see 1–3) by offering Page material evidence of the suffered 'abuse'.

78 **la** a common interjection intended to confirm a statement

80 **by . . . no** a mild oath, reputedly typical of Puritans, from Matthew, 5.37: 'Let your communication be, Yea, yea: Nay, nay. For whatsoeuer is more then these, commeth of euill.' Shallow uses it also in *2H4* 3.2.9, and Falstaff in his letter to Prince Hal (*2H4* 2.2.131). See Mistress Quickly's personal variant of it at 1.4.87–8.

82 **fallow** fawn-coloured

83 **Cotsall** a phonetic spelling of 'Cotswold', the hills where competitions of hunting dogs took place

84 **It . . . judged** The dog's defeat is still an open matter.

85 Slender is teasing Page for not acknowledging his dog's fault.

86 **That . . . fault** an ambiguous statement. 1) 'You are mistaken in thinking that the dog will not be judged positively' (*he* refers to the dog). 2) The hunting term *fault* being used for the dog losing the scent or the sight of the hare, Shallow maintains that Page (*he*) is right not to confess defeat, because it was a case of accidental *fault – your* is not used as a possessive but in a general sense, as in *Ham* 4.3.22: 'your worm is your only emperor for diet' (Cam[1]). 3) Less probably, *'tis your fault* is Shallow's aside to Slender, reproaching him for teasing Page (Oxf[1]).

88 **cur** self-deprecatory: Page acknowledges the inferiority of his dog.

---

73 worships] Worship's *Rowe*   83 Cotsall] Cotswold *Oxf*   86 not 'tis] *this edn;* not, 'tis *F;* not. [*Aside to Slender*] 'Tis *Oxf*[1]   86–7 fault. 'Tis] *(*fault: 'tis*);* fault. [*To Page*] 'Tis *Oxf*

SHALLOW   Sir, he's a good dog, and a fair dog, can there
   be more said? He is good, and fair. – Is Sir John Falstaff   90
   here?

PAGE   Sir, he is within; and I would I could do a good
   office between you.

EVANS   It is spoke as a Christians ought to speak.

SHALLOW   He hath wronged me, Master Page.   95

PAGE   Sir, he doth in some sort confess it.

SHALLOW   If it be confessed, it is not redressed. Is not that
   so, Master Page? He hath wronged me, indeed he hath,
   at a word he hath. Believe me: Robert Shallow esquire
   saith he is wronged.   100

PAGE   Here comes Sir John.

   Enter Sir John FALSTAFF, PISTOL, BARDOLPH
   and NIM.

FALSTAFF   Now, Master Shallow, you'll complain of me
   to the King?

SHALLOW   Knight, you have beaten my men, killed my
   deer and broke open my lodge.   105

FALSTAFF   But not kissed your keeper's daughter!

92–3 **I would . . . you** It would give me
pleasure to mediate between you.

96 **in some sort** to some extent

97 **If . . . redressed.** Shallow questions
such proverbs as 'A fault confessed is
half redressed' or 'Confession of a fault
is half amends' (Dent, C589).

99 **at a word** in short (*OED* Word *sb.* I
3a); but see 1.3.14n.

101.2 NIM For the spelling of the name
see note on the List of Roles.

103 **King** Henry IV or Henry V? See the
discussion of the placing of *MW* in the
sequence of the 'Falstaff plays', pp.
20–1. More likely this is a reference to

the Court of Star Chamber, which was
formed by the King's Privy Council;
see 1–2n. Significantly, Q has
'Councell' instead of *King*.

104–5 **killed my deer** Q has instead
'Kild my dogs, stolne my deere',
linking up with the Charlecote deer-
stealing legend (see 14n.). But dogs
are not 'venison', and see *ill killed*, said
of the venison given to Page (77n.).

105 **lodge** the keeper's house at a park
gate. At 104, instead of *beaten my men*
Q has 'hurt my keeper'.

106 **kissed . . . daughter** Craik (Oxf[1])
sees here an allusion to Robert Greene,

99 hath. Believe me:] *(*hath: beleeue me,*) F;* hath, believe me. *Dyce*[2]   101] Here is sir *Iohn*
himselfe now, looke you. *Q*   101.1–2] *Q; not in F*   103 King?] Councell, I heare? *Q*   104–5] Sir
Iohn, sir *Iohn*, you haue hurt my keeper, / Kild my dogs, stolne my deere. *Q*   106 daughter!]
*(*daughter?*)*; daughter. *Q*

SHALLOW   Tut, a pin! This shall be answered.

FALSTAFF   I will answer it straight: I have done all this.
That is now answered.

SHALLOW   The Council shall know this.   110

FALSTAFF   'Twere better for you if it were known in
counsel: you'll be laughed at.

EVANS   *Pauca verba*, Sir John, good worts.

FALSTAFF   Good worts? Good cabbage! – Slender, I
broke your head: what matter have you against me?   115

SLENDER   Marry, sir, I have matter in my head against
you, and against your cony-catching rascals, Bardolph,
Nim and Pistol. They carried me to the tavern and
made me drunk, and afterward picked my pocket.

BARDOLPH   You Banbury cheese!   120

Friar Bacon and Friar Bungay, where
Prince Edward, hunting at Fressing-
field, falls in love with the keeper's
daughter.

107 **a pin** a trifle (*OED sb.* 3b); cf. Dent,
P333, P334, 'Not to care (not worth) a
pin'

107–9 **answered . . . answered** Shallow
means 'answered in law', but Falstaff
shifts the meaning to the merely verbal
sense.

111–12 **in counsel** in confidence (*OED*
Counsel *sb.* 5c), punning on *Council*

113 *Pauca verba* few words, a current
Latin expression used correctly by
Holofernes in *LLL* 4.2.165; Evans (a
less learned pedant) translates *pauca* as
good, but Nim at 124 seems to understand its meaning, as does Pistol, who,
in *H5* 2.1.79, renders it with 'there's
enough'. Cf. the expressions 'Few
words are best' or 'Few words show
men wise' (Dent, W798, W799).

114 **Good cabbage** Falstaff sneers at
Evans's pronunciation of 'words':
worts designated vegetables of the

cabbage family.

115 **broke** wounded, grazed the skin of;
see 264–5n.

116 **matter** cause of complaint, argument
against (as at 115); pus from the wound
in the head

117 **cony-catching** cheating (literally
'rabbit-catching'), an expression made
current by Robert Greene's 'cony-
catching' pamphlets of 1591, describing the devices of the London
underworld. Q has 'cogging companions', a phrase found in F at 3.1.109;
but see Falstaff: 'I must cony-catch, I
must shift' at 1.3.30–1.

118–19 *They . . . pocket This sentence
is borrowed from Q (however corrupt
in its wording) to account for the
exchanges at 140–6. Its equivalent was
probably accidentally omitted by the F
compositor.

120 **Banbury cheese** As his name
implies, Slender is a thin man, in the
same way as cheeses made at Banbury
were proverbially thin ('As thin as
Banbury cheese', Dent, C268).

---

107 Tut, a pin!] Well *Q*   108 I will] Ile *Q*   110 The Council] *(*The Councell*)*; Well, the Councell
Q   112 counsel] *Q (*counsell*);* coun-/cell *F*   113] Good vrdes sir *Iohn*, good vrdes. *Q*   114
worts?] vrdes, *Q*   cabbage] *Q, F (*Cabidge*)*   117 cony-catching rascals] cogging companions *Q*
117–18 Bardolph . . . Pistol] *Pistoll* and *Nym Q*   118–19 They . . . pocket.] *Q; not in F*

SLENDER   Ay, it is no matter.

PISTOL   How now, Mephostophilus?

SLENDER   Ay, it is no matter.

NIM   Slice, I say! *Pauca, pauca*, slice, that's my humour.

SLENDER   Where's Simple, my man? Can you tell,   125
cousin?

EVANS   Peace, I pray you! Now let us understand: there is
three umpires in this matter, as I understand. That is,
Master Page, *fidelicet* Master Page; and there is myself,
fidelicet myself; and the three party is, lastly and finally,   130
mine host of the Garter.

PAGE   We three to hear it, and end it between them.

EVANS   Ferry goot, I will make a prief of it in my notebook, and we will afterwards 'ork upon the cause with
as great discreetly as we can.   135

121, 123 **no matter** no valid argument. It can be taken as a clumsy dismissal of Bardolph's and Nim's ironies as beneath Slender's dignity (as at 166–7), or as revealing how far he is intimidated – a decision left to the actor's general conception of the character he impersonates.

122 **Mephostophilus** As in *2H4* and *H5*, Pistol is characterized by his fondness for alluding to and misquoting from popular Elizabethan tragedies, in the present case *Doctor Faustus*. In the early editions of this play the name is spelt 'Mephostophilus', 'Mephostophilis' or 'Mephastophilus', never 'Mephistophilis' as in more recent versions.

124 **Slice . . . slice** cut it, make it short (*pauca*); with an allusion to the slicing of the Banbury cheese, the definition that Bardolph had given of Slender (Nim may be brandishing a weapon in a threatening attitude)
   that's my humour a variant of Nim's characteristic tag (see note on the List of Roles)

125 **man** Slender seeks the help of his servant to defend him.

127 **understand** come to an understanding, or agreement

127–31 **there . . . Garter** The *matter*, i.e. the dispute between Falstaff and Shallow, is never mentioned again in the rest of the play. The naming of the *umpires* serves only to introduce indirectly the Host of the Garter Inn, who in fact is to have such a role in another quarrel, that between Doctor Caius and Parson Evans (2.1–3.1).

130 *fidelicet* videlicet, Latin for 'namely'
   three . . . finally reminiscent of Dogberry's pompous enumeration in *MA* 5.1.215–19

131 **Garter** There is no positive evidence of the existence of a Garter Inn in Windsor either in Henry V's or in Shakespeare's time. The name was probably chosen to equivocate on Falstaff's status; see p. 26.

133 **prief** brief, abstract, entry in a document

135 **discreetly** The interchange of the parts of speech is a feature of Evans's 'Welshness': here he prefers an adverb to the noun 'discretion'.

131 Garter] *Q3;* Gater *F*   133 goot] *(*goo't*)*

FALSTAFF Pistol!

PISTOL He hears with ears.

EVANS The tevil and his tam, what phrase is this? He
hears with ears! Why, it is affectations!

FALSTAFF Pistol, did you pick Master Slender's purse? 140

SLENDER Ay, by these gloves did he, or I would I might
never come in mine own great chamber again else! Of
seven groats in mill-sixpences, and two Edward shovel-
boards, that cost me two shilling and two pence a-piece
of Ed miller – by these gloves! 145

FALSTAFF Is it true, Pistol?

EVANS No, it is false, if it is a pick-purse.

PISTOL Ha, thou mountain-foreigner! –

---

138 **The . . . tam** 'The devil and his dam
[his mother]' was a current intensive of
oaths mentioning the devil (Dent,
D225). See Falstaff at 4.5.99–100:
'The devil take one party and his dam
the other.'

139 ***hears with ears** Evans does not recognize Pistol's allusion to the Litany
(from Psalms, 44.1: 'Wee haue heard
with our eares').

141 **by these gloves** Slender mimics the
gallants' habit of swearing by their articles of clothing; again at 145, 153 and 157
(*By this hat*). Q has 'by this handkercher'.

142 **great chamber** main living room
(implying ownership of a mansion)

143 **seven . . . mill-sixpences** the sum of
two shillings and four pence (a groat
was worth four pence, and there were
twelve pence in a shilling) in newly
minted sixpence coins. Either this is a
miscalculation (two shillings and four
pence cannot be divided into sixpence
pieces: four of them would add up to
two shillings, five to two shillings and
sixpence), or Slender means that,
newly-minted coins being worth more
than their face value (see 144–5n.),
four sixpenny pieces (i.e. two shillings)

had cost him four extra pence.

144–5 **two . . . miller** Apparently Slender
had acquired two new machine-made
shilling pieces from the manufacturer
('miller'; see 'mill-sixpences', 143n.),
paying two shillings and twopence
(more than twice their face value) for
each in view of their superior quality in
comparison with handmade coins.
Edward shovel-board designates a large
shilling piece first minted in Edward
VI's reign (1547–53, well after Henry
V's time), which could be used as a
counter for sliding along a shovel-board
in a popular table game. Cf. 'shove-
groat shilling' in *2H4* 2.4.192–3.

145 ***Ed** like 'Ned', a diminutive of
Edward: in F 'Yead', suggesting a variant pronunciation

147 Evans pretends to have understood
Falstaff to say that Pistol is *true*, i.e.
'honest'. Pistol's retort at 148 shows
that this is no aside.

148 **mountain-foreigner** addressed to
Evans, referring to the Welsh as
strangers from a wild mountainous
country. In *H5* 5.1.35 Fluellen resents
Pistol's insulting language: 'You called
me yesterday mountain-squire.'

---

139 ears!] *this edn after Daly (*ears?*)*; eare? *F*   141 these gloves] this handkercher *Q*   145 Ed] *Oxf*;
Yead *F*   148 mountain-foreigner! –] *Hamner (subst.)*; mountaine Forreyner: *F*; mountain-
foreigner? – *Oxf¹*

Sir John and master mine,
I combat challenge of this latten bilbo. –   150
Word of denial in thy *labras* here!
Word of denial! Froth and scum, thou liest!

SLENDER [*Points at Nim.*]   By these gloves, then 'twas he.

NIM   Be advised, sir, and pass good humours. I will say
'marry trap with you', if you run the nuthook's humour   155
on me – that is the very note of it.

SLENDER   By this hat, then he in the red face had it. For,
though I cannot remember what I did when you made
me drunk, yet I am not altogether an ass.

FALSTAFF   What say you, Scarlet and John?   160

150 **combat challenge of** challenge to a
duel; a 'poetic' inversion
*latten bilbo a mocking reference to
Slender, suggesting that his sword is as
useless as a stage sword made of lath (a
thin strip of wood) or tin-sheet (*OED*
Latten *a.* 3). 'Bilbo', from Bilboa
(Bilbao in Spain, an armourers' centre), designated any kind of sword.
The Clown in *TN* 4.2.124–8 satirizes
the Vice in old morality plays 'Who
with dagger of lath, / In his rage and
his wrath, / Cries ah, ha to the devil'.

151 '[I want to hear] a recantation from
your own lips.' Pistol (who flaunts his
knowledge of Italian in *2H4* 2.4.181
and 5.5.96) does not know that the
Latin *labra* – or rather Italian *labbra* –
for lips is plural, and adds an 's'. Craik
(Oxf[1]) suggests a confusion with
Spanish *palabras* ('words').

154–6 *The Q version of this speech (see
t.n.) largely clarifies its meaning, which
could be rendered with: 'You would do
well [*Be advised* in a threatening tone]
to speak fair of me [*pass good humours*;
cf. 'My honor is not for many words' in
Q, where 'honor' is perhaps an error for
'humor']; if you mean to act as a constable [*nuthook*, 155n.] with me, I say

shut up [*marry* (192n.) is a common
oath, and *trap* is vulgar for 'mouth'
(*OED Suppl.* Trap *sb.*[1] 2b)]; this is the
gist of the matter [*very note of it*, with a
possible pun *note/nut*, corresponds to
'humor of it' in Q].'

155 **nuthook** a hooked pole used to
pull down the branches of nut trees;
in the language of the London
underworld it designated any officer
empowered to arrest (hook) male-
factors. Doll Tearsheet addresses it as
an insult to the Beadle in *2H4* 5.4.7.
Nuthook's humour corresponds to 'bace
[base, i.e. villainous] humors' in Q.

157 **he ... face** Throughout the two Parts
of *H4* and *H5* Bardolph is characterized by the redness of his complexion:
in may suggest that coloured make-up
was considered as a kind of mask covering the face (RP).

159 **I ... ass** recorded by Dent (A231.1)
as a current phrase since 1561

160 **Scarlet and John** Falstaff addresses
Bardolph as summing up in his person
two of the legendary companions of
Robin Hood: Will Scarlet (another
allusion to his complexion) and Little
John in view of his bulk. 'Little' John
was in fact the largest of the 'merry

149–52] *prose F; as verse Q (*Sir *Iohn,* and Maister mine, I combat craue / Of this same laten bilbo. I
do retort the lie / Euen in thy gorge, thy gorge, thy gorge.*)*   150 latten] *Q (*laten*);* Latine *F*   153
SD] *Cam*[1] *(subst.)*   154–6] *as verse Q (*Syr my honor is not for many words, / But if you run bace
humors of me, / I will say mary trap. And there's the humor of it.*)*

BARDOLPH   Why, sir, for my part, I say the gentleman had
drunk himself out of his five sentences.

EVANS   It is 'his five senses'. Fie, what the ignorance is!

BARDOLPH   And being fap, sir, was, as they say,
cashiered; and so conclusions passed the careers.   165

SLENDER   Ay, you spake in Latin then too; but 'tis no
matter. I'll ne'er be drunk whilst I live again, but in
honest, civil, godly company, for this trick. If I be
drunk, I'll be drunk with those that have the fear of
God, and not with drunken knaves.   170

EVANS   So Got 'udge me, that is a virtuous mind.

FALSTAFF   You hear all these matters denied, gentlemen;
you hear it.

Enter MISTRESS FORD, MISTRESS PAGE *and her*
daughter ANNE [*with wine*].

PAGE   Nay, daughter, carry the wine in, we'll drink
within.   [*Exit Anne Page.*]

men' in the ballad 'Robin Hood and the Pinder of Wakefield', sung by Justice Silence in *2H4* 5.3.103 ('And Robin Hood, Scarlet, and John').

162 **sentences** Bardolph's error, promptly corrected by Evans, is perhaps deliberate, alluding to Slender's limited range of expression.

164 **fap** drunk – a nonce usage, or a misreading of 'sap' (Cam¹), a word found in the sense of 'fool' only in the nineteenth century (*OED* Sap *sb.* 5)

165 **cashiered** normally in Shakespeare 'dismissed from service' (cf. 1.3.6), but here 'deprived of' (*OED* Cashier *v.* 5) his wits (161–3) – and his cash: Hibbard detects a pun on 'cash-sheared', i.e. 'fleeced', 'robbed' (supported by F spelling 'casheerd'). In *Oth* 2.3.275 Cassio is 'cashiered' for being drunk.

conclusions . . . careers 'matters got

out of hand' (Hibbard); 'career' is the set course of a horse-race (*OED sb.* 1). In *H5* 2.1.125–6 Nim says of the King's changes of mood: 'he passes some humours and careers'.

166 **in Latin** incomprehensibly; Slender is unaware of what is Latin and what is not (GWW).

171 **'udge** judge, in Evans's Welsh pronunciation throughout the play
mind intention

173 Daly places here the exit for Bardolph, Pistol and Nim. This seems unnecessary: they may stay, commenting apart during the next four speeches, and leave at 182 through a different door from that which in this scene is identified as leading into Page's house, to which the rest are invited.

173.2 The brief appearance of Anne Page, eliciting Slender's comment at 176, is

165 careers] *(Car-eires)*   171 Got 'udge] *(got-udge)*   172 all] *not in Q*   173.1–2] *Q (subst.); not in F; Enter Mistress* Anne Page, *with wine.* / *Rowe; Enter Mistress Ford and Mistress Page.* / *Rowe after 176*
175 SD] *Theobald*

136

SLENDER　O heaven, this is Mistress Anne Page.　　176

PAGE　How now, Mistress Ford?

FALSTAFF　Mistress Ford, by my troth you are very well
met. By your leave, good mistress. *Kisses her.*

PAGE　Wife, bid these gentlemen welcome. – Come, we　180
have a hot venison pasty to dinner. Come, gentlemen,
I hope we shall drink down all unkindness.

[Exeunt all except Slender.]

SLENDER　I had rather than forty shillings I had my book
of *Songs and Sonnets* here.

[Enter SIMPLE.]

How now, Simple, where have you been? I must wait　185
on myself, must I? You have not the *Book of Riddles*
about you?

SIMPLE　*Book of Riddles?* Why, did you not lend it to Alice
Shortcake upon Allhallowmas last, a fortnight before
Michaelmas?　　190

possibly a survival from a reduced
stage version (reflected in Q) where
Anne was left alone on the stage with
Slender, who began his courting. But
'the important point is that the audience gets a glimpse of Anne, thus
heightening comic expectation of the
scene with Slender' (RP).

179 SD *a direction in Q implicit in
Falstaff's *By your leave*

181 **to dinner** for dinner – not an evening
but a midday meal

182 **drink . . . unkindness** Oxf[1] compares *JC* 4.3.159: 'In this [a bowl of
wine] I bury all unkindness, Cassius.'

183 **I . . . shillings** a typical gallant's
asseveration, used in identical form by
Sir Andrew Aguecheek, *TN* 2.3.20

183–4 **book . . . Sonnets** a specific reference to the collection of poems

entitled *Songs and Sonets written by
the . . . Earle of Surrey, and other*
(1557), known as *Tottell's Miscellany*
from the name of its publisher Richard
Tottell, which was very popular and
frequently reprinted in Elizabeth's
time. Such books were considered
handbooks of courtship.

186 *Book of Riddles* another, unidenti-
fied, collection, presumably of witty
jokes used by dull people like Slender
to enliven their conversation

189–90 **Allhallowmas . . . Michaelmas**
Allhallowmas (All Saints' Day, 1
November) is not a fortnight before
Michaelmas (St Michael's, 29
September) but a month *after*. Perhaps
Simple confuses this with Martlemas
(St Martin's, 11 November), which
comes ten days after All Saints.

179 SD] *Q (Syr* Iohn kisses her.*)　　182 SD] *Cam[1]; Exit all, but* Slender *and mistresse* Anne *Q; Ex.*
Fal. Page, *&c. Manent* Shallow, Evans *and* Slender. *Rowe*　184.1] *Rowe*　190 Michaelmas]
Martlemas *Theobald*

[*Enter* SHALLOW *and* EVANS.]

SHALLOW   Come, coz, come, coz, we stay for you. A word
with you, coz. Marry, this, coz: there is, as 'twere, a
tender, a kind of tender, made afar off by Sir Hugh
here. Do you understand me?

SLENDER   Ay, sir, you shall find me reasonable. If it be so,   195
I shall do that that is reason.

SHALLOW   Nay, but understand me.

SLENDER   So I do, sir.

EVANS   Give ear to his motions. Master Slender, I will
description the matter to you, if you be capacity of it.   200

SLENDER   Nay, I will do as my cousin Shallow says. I pray
you pardon me, he's a Justice of Peace in his country,
simple though I stand here.

EVANS   But that is not the question. The question is concerning your marriage.   205

SHALLOW   Ay, there's the point, sir.

---

191 **stay** are waiting
192 **Marry** a common asseverative mild
oath (see 154–6n.), replacing the habit
of swearing 'by the Virgin Mary'
193 **tender** offer
   afar off 'in a roundabout manner'
   (Hibbard)
196 **that that is reason** what is right (in
your opinion). Cf. *find me reasonable*
(195), *upon any reasonable demands*
(209–10), *would do reason* (218), *in any
reason* (225), more or less involuntary
quibbles on the meanings of
reason/reasonable, as 'rational', 'right',
'convenient'.
199 **motions** proposal (Welsh plural).
Evans uses the word in its legal meaning, unaware of its comic overtones
due to the fact that 'motions' are vul-
garly the result of taking a purge; see
the Host at 3.1.92.

200 **description . . . capacity** more
substitutions of parts of speech
(see 135n.): noun for verb ('describe')
and adjective ('capable') respectively
202 **country** district, possibly a misreading of 'county'
203 **simple . . . stand** a common modest
disclaimer: 'though I am not as important a person (as Shallow)'; see *OED*
Simple *a.* 4c, and Dent, S462.1.
204–5 Evans realizes that Slender had
understood his proposal to be one concerned with the dispute with Falstaff
and his followers; *question* signifies
'matter at issue'.
206 **point** a synonym of *question*; in *Ham*
3.1.55 'that is the question' is the Q2
and F reading where Q1 has 'there's
the point'.

190.1] *Cam¹*   199 motions. Master Slender, I] *(*motions; (Mʳ *Slender*) I*); motions, Mr. *Slender*: I
Rowe   202 country] county *(this edn)*

EVANS   Marry, is it, the very point of it – to Mistress Anne
   Page.

SLENDER   Why, if it be so, I will marry her upon any
   reasonable demands.   210

EVANS   But can you affection the 'oman? Let us command
   to know that of your mouth, or of your lips – for diverse
   philosophers hold that the lips is parcel of the mouth.
   Therefore precisely, can you carry your good will to the
   maid?   215

SHALLOW   Cousin Abraham Slender, can you love her?

SLENDER   I hope, sir, I will do as it shall become one that
   would do reason.

EVANS   Nay, Got's lords, and his ladies, you must speak
   possitable if you can carry-her your desires towards   220
   her.

SHALLOW   That you must: will you, upon good dowry,
   marry her?

SLENDER   I will do a greater thing than that, upon your
   request, cousin, in any reason.   225

SHALLOW   Nay, conceive me, conceive me, sweet coz.

---

207 **the very point** Evans's repetition of
   point is the first of several (involuntary?) sexual innuendos in his speeches.
   It is surprising to find here *very* instead
   of the emphatic *ferry*, as at 45 and 133.
210 **reasonable demands** acceptable
   conditions: the wooer is behaving as if
   he were the wooed (RP).
212 **diverse** several, some
213 **parcel** part (from the standard formula 'part and parcel')
214–15 **carry ... maid** feel affection for
   her; equivalent to his 'Evansism' (211)
   affection the 'oman, but with a further
   innuendo in *will*, a term frequently
   alluding to the penis
216 Shallow translates into plain language
   Evans's involuted question, and
   repeats it at 227–8.
219 **Got's ... ladies** Evans's peculiar

amplification of such ejaculations as
'Good Lord' or 'God Lord'. Craik
(Oxf[1]) sees another innuendo in that
'lord and ladies' was the popular name
of a flower known also as 'cuckoo-
pint', '"pint" being an abbreviation of
"pintle", i.e. penis'.
220 **possitable** positively (in Evans's
   pompous parlance)
220–1 **carry-her ... her** Evans's third
   formulation of the question 'can you
   feel affection for her?' (see 211 and
   214–15n.), punning on 'carry-her': 1)
   a way of emphasizing *carry* (your
   desires towards her) by adding a superfluous *her*; 2) career, meaning 'direct'
   (implying violent motion)
225 **in any reason** within reason; see
   196n.
226 **conceive me** understand my meaning

222–3] *Pope; F lines* must: / her?

139

What I do is to pleasure you, coz. Can you love the
maid?

SLENDER   I will marry her, sir, at your request. But if
there be no great love in the beginning, yet heaven may   230
decrease it upon better acquaintance, when we are
married, and have more occasion to know one another.
I hope upon familiarity will grow more contempt. But
if you say marry her, I will marry her – that I am freely
dissolved, and dissolutely.   235

EVANS   It is a fery discretion answer. Save the faul' is in
the 'ord 'dissolutely' – the 'ort is, according to our
meaning, 'resolutely' – his meaning is good.

SHALLOW   Ay, I think my cousin meant well.

SLENDER   Ay, or else I would I might be hanged, la!   240

[*Enter* ANNE PAGE.]

SHALLOW   Here comes fair Mistress Anne. – Would I
were young for your sake, Mistress Anne.

231 **decrease** Slender's blunder for
  'increase'
232 **know one another** possibly referring
  to carnal knowledge
233 ***contempt** Theobald's emendation
  of F's 'content' ('contentment') has
  been generally accepted because of
  Slender's genius for using wrong com-
  monplaces ('familiarity breeds contempt' was known since 1576; see
  Dent, F47). A possible alternative is
  'consent', in view of such phrases as
  'marry first and love will come after'
  (Dent, L534).
235 **dissolved** Slender means 'resolved'.
  Cf. Shakespeare's word-play in *E3*
  2.2.167, 'Resolved to be dissolved'
  (1596 Q: 'Resolute to be dissolude').
  dissolutely This is Slender's only
  blunder corrected by Evans – at 236–8:

  'resolutely'.
236 **discretion answer** answer showing
  discernment. As usual, Evans prefers a
  noun to an adjective or a verb.
  ***faul'** Though F's 'fall' is defensible
  as the result of *dissolute* behaviour, it is
  more likely that this is an attempt to
  reproduce Evans's pronunciation of
  'fault' without the final 't'.
237–8 **our meaning** currently accepted
  semantic meaning. There is no need to
  suspect a misprint of 'your', especially
  since Evans is not addressing Slender
  directly.
238 **his meaning** his (Slender's) intention; cf. Shallow's *meant well* at 239.
240 perhaps recalling the proverb 'Wedding and hanging go by destiny' (RP)
241–2 **Would . . . sake** a current compli-
  mentary phrase (Dent, S68)

233 contempt] *Theobald;* content *F;* consent *(RP)*   236 discretion answer] *mod. eds;* discetion-
answere *F*   faul'] *Hanmer;* fall *F;* fault *Collier*   237 our] your *(Oxf¹)*   240.1] *Rowe*

ANNE   The dinner is on the table, my father desires your
worships' company.

SHALLOW   I will wait on him, fair Mistress Anne.   245

EVANS   'Od's plessed will! I will not be absence at the
grace.   [*Exeunt Shallow and Evans.*]

ANNE   Will't please your worship to come in, sir?

SLENDER   No, I thank you, forsooth, heartily; I am very
well.   250

ANNE   The dinner attends you, sir.

SLENDER   I am not a-hungry, I thank you, forsooth. [*to
Simple*] Go, sirrah, for all you are my man, go wait
upon my cousin Shallow.   [*Exit Simple.*]
A justice of peace sometime may be beholding to his   255
friend for a man. I keep but three men and a boy yet,
till my mother be dead. But what though, yet I live like
a poor gentleman born.

ANNE   I may not go in without your worship: they will not
sit till you come.   260

243–4 **your worships' company** Shallow
is the only person present entitled to this
form of address, and he replies as if he
understood Anne as saying 'your worship's company'. But Anne uses the
same title for Slender at 248.

245 **wait on** join

246–7 **I . . . grace** A slightly modified version of this sentence is found in Q after the
words 'be gone' at 1.2.11; but it is more
appropriate here, since grace is said at the
beginning and not at the end of dinner.

248–80 In Q the conversation between
Slender and Anne begins with a passage found in F at 3.4.59–63, followed
by the equivalent of 269–89 in the present scene, and finally by a speech
echoing 261–8.

249 **forsooth** truly; an interjection (see
also 252) derived from the obsolete
word 'sooth', meaning 'truth' or
'troth'. Cf. 'by my troth' at 267.

249–50 **I am very well** I'm fine. Slender

gives the reason for refusing meat at
264–8.

251 **attends you** awaits, is ready for you

252 **a-hungry** hungry. The emphatic 'a'
before an adjective is a typical affectation.

253 **sirrah** sir, fellow, addressed to social
inferiors
for all although

253–4 **wait upon** attend on, serve

255–6 **beholding . . . man** beholden,
under obligation to a relative (*friend*)
for the use of one of his servants

256 **I . . . boy** As in the allusion to his *great
chamber* (see 142n.), Slender implies
that his family wealth could afford a
larger number of servants, though for
the time being he must figure *a poor
gentleman*, 258.

257 **till . . . dead** a candid rather than cyn-
ical statement: only after his mother's
death will Slender come into his own.
what though never mind

260 **sit** sit down, start (dinner)

247 SD] *Rowe*   252–3 SD] *Steevens² (subst.)*   254 SD] *Rowe*

SLENDER   I'faith, I'll eat nothing. I thank you as much as
   though I did.

ANNE   I pray you, sir, walk in.

SLENDER   I had rather walk here, I thank you. I bruised
   my shin th'other day with playing at sword and dagger   265
   with a master of fence – three venues for a dish of
   stewed prunes – and, by my troth, I cannot abide the
   smell of hot meat since. – Why do your dogs bark so?
   Be there bears i'the town?

ANNE   I think there are, sir; I heard them talked of.   270

SLENDER   I love the sport well, but I shall as soon quarrel
   at it, as any man in England. You are afraid if you see
   the bear loose, are you not?

ANNE   Ay indeed, sir.

SLENDER   That's meat and drink to me now. I have seen   275
   Sackerson loose twenty times, and have taken him by
   the chain; but, I warrant you, the women have so cried

263 **walk in** come in; but Slender takes
   walk too literally (RP)
264–5 **bruised my shin** in Q 'broke
   [grazed] my shin', and Slender
   explains: 'I with my ward / Defending
   my head, he [a fencer] hot [hit] my
   shin'. The expression 'to break one's
   shins' was current in cautionary
   phrases since 1553 (Dent, S342.1).
265 **playing . . . dagger** having a fencing
   match
266 **venues** *Venue* is the French term for
   each assault in a fencing match.
267 **stewed prunes** In all other Shakespearean contexts (*1H4* 3.3.112–13,
   2H4 2.4.146–7, *MM* 2.1.89–107)
   stewed prunes (here the stakes of the
   fencing match) are the 'delicacies'
   offered in brothels (stews).
268 **hot meat** a complex equivocation: 1)
   cooked food; 2) the wounded shin (*hot*
   meaning 'hit'; see 264–5n.); 3) hot
   stuff, prostitutes (see *stewed prunes*,
   267n.). The notion of courting seems

indissolubly linked in Slender's mind
with his only previous sexual experiences in town brothels.
268–9 **dogs . . . bears** Bear-baiting,
unleashing dogs against a chained
bear, was a favourite sport at the time.
Off-stage barking noises at this point
are optional for the director.
271–2 **quarrel at** it start quarrelling when
I watch it. Spectators in bear pits bet on
the dogs, causing frequent quarrels. Craik
(Oxf1) is right in discounting Hibbard's
gloss 'take exception to it', and in noting
the affinity between Slender and Sir
Andrew Aguecheek in *TN*: both of them
are quarrelsome, cowardly, ignorantly
affected (see 183n.); the two roles seem to
have been written for the same actor (see
note on Slender in the List of Roles).
275 **That's . . . me** proverbial (Dent,
M842); see *AYL* 5.1.10.
276 **Sackerson** a celebrated performing
bear in the Paris Garden, a bear ring
close to the Globe theatre

266 venues] *(veneys)*

and shrieked at it that it passed. But women, indeed,
cannot abide 'em: they are very ill-favoured rough
things.   280

Enter PAGE.

PAGE   Come, gentle Master Slender, come: we stay for
    you.
SLENDER   I'll eat nothing, I thank you, sir.
PAGE   By cock and pie, you shall not choose, sir. Come,
    come.   285
SLENDER   Nay, pray you, lead the way.
PAGE   Come on, sir.
SLENDER   Mistress Anne, yourself shall go first.
ANNE   Not I, sir; pray you, keep on.
SLENDER   Truly, I will not go first; truly – la! I will not do   290
    you that wrong.
ANNE   I pray you, sir.
SLENDER   I'll rather be unmannerly than troublesome.
    You do yourself wrong, indeed – la!

Exeunt [, *Slender leading*].

278 **it passed** surpassed belief, was
incredible. The expression is used by
Page at 4.2.116 and 129 (*This passes*),
and cf. *TC* 1.2.167.

279–80 **ill-favoured . . . things** ugly sav-
age beasts. Cf. *MND* 5.1.222, 'The
lion rough in wildest rage doth roar'.
But *they* could be understood as referring to *women* in the previous sentence
– a further example of Slender's clumsiness and of the misogyny of his wooing technique (RP).

281 **gentle** of gentle birth. Page, who sees
Slender as his future son-in-law, uses
a courteous form of address, in contrast with Anne's too deferential *your
worship* at 248, mocking in its excess.

284 **By . . . pie** a jocular oath (Dent,
CC15) used also by Shallow in *2H4*
5.1.1. 'Cock' is a euphemism for 'God'
and 'pie' a slighting reference to the
Roman Catholic rule book for church
services (*OED* Pie *sb.*³ 1).
  you . . . choose I give you no alternative – a courteous way of insisting

293 **I'll . . . troublesome** proverbial
(Dent, U15). Slender reluctantly
agrees to go in first; but in Q (see t.n.)
Anne Page takes precedence.

294 **You . . . wrong** another conventional
phrase (see 3.3.152–3 and 192). In *2H4*
3.2.254 Shallow addresses Falstaff: 'Sir
John, Sir John, do not yourself wrong.'

280.1] *Q (Enter Maister* Page.*); not in F*   288–94] Nay be God misteris *Anne*, you shall goe first, / I
haue more manners then so, I hope. / *An.* Well sir, I will not be troublesome. *Q*   294 SD] *Exit
omnes. Q; Exeunt Slender first, the others following. Oxf*

1.2 *Enter* Sir Hugh EVANS *and* SIMPLE, *from dinner.*

EVANS   Go your ways, and ask of Doctor Caius' house,
which is the way. And there dwells one Mistress
Quickly, which is in the manner of his nurse, or his dry
nurse, or his cook, or his laundry, his washer and his
wringer.   5

SIMPLE   Well, sir.

EVANS   Nay, it is petter yet: give her this letter. For it is a
'oman that altogether's acquaintance with Mistress
Anne Page, and the letter is to desire, and require her,
to solicit your master's desires to Mistress Anne Page.   10
I pray you be gone; I will make an end of my dinner,
there's pippins and cheese to come.   *Exeunt.*

1.2 The location is the same as in 1.1, a
short time later. The words *from dinner*
(only in Q entrance direction) do not
mean that the dinner at Page's is over,
but that Evans has left it briefly in
order to give instructions to Slender's
man, Simple, who had been sent in
(1.1.253–4) to attend on Shallow.

0.1 *from dinner* a visual notation suggesting that Evans enters carrying some sign,
such as a napkin tucked under his chin,
of his coming from the dinner table. Cf.
Capulet's servingmen who 'come forth
with napkins' at the end of *RJ* 1.4.

1–2 **ask ... way** Evans's convoluted syntax makes it seem that the *house* is to be
asked (RP).

1 **Doctor Caius** See note on the List of
Roles for the choice of this name.

3 **nurse** housekeeper (Caius calls
Quickly *my nursh-a* at 3.2.58), but the
addition of *dry nurse* suggests a comic
preoccupation with distinguishing her
from a child's 'wet' nurse. The Oxford
editors argue, in view of the Q version
(see t.n.), that the first 'nurse' is a misreading of ''oman'; but surely the rep-

etition of 'nurse' is more effective. Q's
'try' for F's 'dry' is a more convincing
emendation, but it risks obscuring the
implicit contrast 'dry'/'wet' nurse.

4–5 **his laundry ... wringer** Evans uses
the abstract *laundry* for 'laundress', per-
sonifying the action of washing and
wringing associated with the profession.

7 **it ... yet** There's more to come, I have
not finished yet. Evans holds back
Simple, who is about to leave (*Well,
sir*), thinking that the parson has com-
pleted his instructions.

8 ***altogether's acquaintance** is well
acquainted. A transposition of auxiliary (*'s*) and adverb (*altogether* meaning
'thoroughly'); *acquaintance* is Evans's
noun for adjective or verb; but F's
reading 'altogeathers' may be a 'Welsh
plural', with the accidental omission of
'is' before it (Oxf[1]).

9 **require** request

10 **solicit** a transitive use of the verb; normally 'solicit for'

11–12 **I will ... come** Oxf and Oxf[1] treat
this as an aside after Simple's exit;
perhaps it is spoken while Simple is

1.2] *Scena Secunda.* F   0.1] *Q (subst.); Enter Euans, and Simple.* F   3–5 which ... wringer] his
woman, or his try nurse *Q*   3 his nurse] his 'oman *Oxf*   5 wringer] *Theobald;* Ringer F   8
altogether's] *Steevens³ (Tyrwhitt);* altogeathers F; is altogether *Oxf¹*   11 you be gone;] you do, I
must not be absent at the grace. *Q;* you be gone. [*Exit Simple*] *Oxf*   11–12 I will ... come] I will goe
make an end of my dinner, / There is pepions and cheese behinde. *Q*   12 SD] F; *Exit omnes. Q*

1.3   *Enter* FALSTAFF, HOST, BARDOLPH, NIM,
                    PISTOL *and* ROBIN.

FALSTAFF   Mine host of the Garter –
HOST   What says my bully rook? Speak scholarly and
wisely.
FALSTAFF   Truly, mine host, I must turn away some of
my followers.   5
HOST   Discard, bully Hercules, cashier! Let them wag;
trot, trot!
FALSTAFF   I sit at ten pounds a week.
HOST   Thou'rt an emperor – Caesar, Kaiser and Vizier. I

---

leaving at a separate door from Evans, who is supposed to re-enter Page's house (*pippins* are apples, and the Welsh fondness for cheese was proverbial).

1.3 The change of location is announced by Falstaff's first words and by the presence on stage of the Host of the Garter Inn.

1   **Garter** – Falstaff is speaking to the Host, not calling for him.

2   **bully rook** The Host addresses Page, Shallow and Ford in the same form at 2.1.175, 180 and 184 respectively, so that *rook* cannot mean, as has been suggested, 'castle', with reference either to Falstaff's bulk or to the name of Oldcastle that he bore in the first version of *Henry IV*; more likely, it is a term of disparagement (*OED* Rook *sb.* 2b 'cheat', 2c 'gull'), used playfully as a term of endearment, like 'rogue' (phonetically similar) in *2H4* 2.4.216 and 218 (Doll to Falstaff), quoted by *OED* Rogue *sb.* 3. The same is certainly true of *bully*, an affectionate form of address that the Host uses eight more times, also in association

with other words (Hercules, Hector, etc.). Cf. 'bully Bottom' in *MND* 3.1.8, 4.2.19.

4   **turn away** dismiss

6   **bully Hercules** See 2n. and cf. 11n.
     cashier dismiss (see 1.1.165n.), synonymous with *turn away* and *discard*. A feature of the Host's verbal habit is his fondness for synonyms.
     wag depart (*OED v.* 7)

8   **sit** lodge here. (Ten pounds – a large sum for the time – is Falstaff's weekly rate at the Garter Inn, inclusive of food and lodging for his retinue; it could be reduced if he dismissed some of them.)

9   **Kaiser** German for Caesar, it came to mean 'monarch'.
     *Vizier This emendation of 'Phesser', Q, or 'Pheazar', F, adopted by Ard[1], being the title of Eastern potentates, agrees better with Caesar and Kaiser than does 'feezer' (Oxf[1]) for 'pheezer' suggested by Malone as coined by the Host from the verb 'pheeze' (fix, do for). See also *TS* Induction 1.1 ('I'll pheeze you'). It may well be that the Host means 'vizier' but says 'the comically inappropriate *pheezer*' (Oxf).

1.3] *Scena Tertia. F*   0.1–2 *Enter . . .*PISTOL] *Enter sir* Iohn Falstaffes *Host of the Garter,* Nym, Bardolfe, Pistoll, *Q; Enter Sir John Falstaff, Bardolph, Nim, Pistol, Oxf   and* ROBIN] *Rowe, Oxf; Page F; and the boy Q*   1   Garter –] *Hibbard;* Garter. *Q;* Garter? *F;* Garter! *Enter the Host of the Garter Oxf*   9   Kaiser and] *(Keiser and); and Kesar Q (after Phesser);* Keisar and *F2*   Vizier] *(Ard[1]); Phesser Q; Pheazar F;* pheezer *Oxf;* Feezer *Oxf[1]*

> will entertain Bardolph: he shall draw, he shall tap.   10
> Said I well, bully Hector?

FALSTAFF   Do so, good mine host.

HOST   I have spoke, let him follow. – Let me see thee
froth and lime. I am at a word, follow.   *Exit.*

FALSTAFF   Bardolph, follow him. A tapster is a good   15
trade: an old cloak makes a new jerkin; a withered
servingman, a fresh tapster. Go, adieu.

BARDOLPH   It is a life that I have desired. I will thrive.   *Exit.*

PISTOL

> O base Hungarian wight, wilt thou the spigot wield?

NIM   He was gotten in drink. Is not the humour   20
conceited?

FALSTAFF   I am glad I am so acquit of this tinderbox.

---

10 **entertain . . . tap** employ (*entertain*)
Bardolph as drawer or tapster – synonymous designations of tavern atten-
dants; both the verbs *draw* and *tap*
mean 'draw beer out of a barrel'.

11 **Hector** The Trojan hero was the first
of the Nine Worthies, i.e. the greatest
men in the world. The pedant
Holofernes in *LLL* 5.1.117–55 and
5.2.588–94 includes among them also
Hercules – see here *bully Hercules* at 6.
The Host is jocularly treating Falstaff
as one of the Worthies.

13–14 **Let . . . *lime** Addressed to
Bardolph. 'Froth' and 'lime' are used as
verbs, the first meaning to draw beer so
that it produces a lot of froth – an econ-
omy on the amount served – the second
to adulterate drinks with lime (calcium
carbonate), a practice against which
Falstaff protests in *1H4* 2.4.124: 'You
rogue, here's lime in this sack too'.

14 **I . . . word** I mean what I say. Cf. 1.1.99n.
and *2H4* 3.2.279: 'I spoke at a word'.

16 **an . . . jerkin** proverbial (Dent, B607);
a jerkin was a close-fitting jacket need-
ing less cloth than a coat.

16–17 **a withered . . . tapster** a reversal,
in line with the previous proverb, of
the saying 'An old servingman, a
young beggar' (Dent, S255)

19 Pistol's speech, given while Bardolph
is leaving the stage, is couched in the
outdated language and metre – hexam-
eters (twelve-syllable lines) instead of
the iambic pentameters of Elizabethan
plays – of the verse drama of the 1580s
and before. *Hungarian* is 'beggarly',
punning on 'hungry', *wight* is obsolete
for 'man', 'fellow' (see 34), *spigot* is the
tap of a barrel, treated as the weapon of
Bardolph's new trade.

20 **gotten in drink** begotten while his
parents were drunk – hence unmanly;
see *2H4* 4.3.93–4. From the proverb
'Who goes drunk to bed begets but a
girl' (Tilley, B195). Q has instead 'His
minde is not heroick', accepted by Oxf.

20–1 **Is . . . conceited?** Isn't this saying
(*humour*) witty (*conceited*)?

22 **acquit** rid
tinderbox easily kindled – alluding to
Bardolph's fiery complexion (see
1.1.157n.)

---

14 lime] *Q (*lyme*);* liue *F*   14 SD] *Q (Exit Host.); not in F*   18 SD] *Q (Exit Bardolfe.); opp.* 19
Dyce; not in F   19 Hungarian] gongarian *Q*   20–1] His minde is not heroick. And theres the
humor of it. *Q*   22 tinderbox] tinder Boy *Q*

His thefts were too open: his filching was like an
unskilful singer, he kept not time.

NIM   The good humour is to steal at a minute's rest.   25

PISTOL

'Convey', the wise it call. 'Steal'? Foh!
A fico for the phrase!

FALSTAFF   Well, sirs, I am almost out at heels.

PISTOL   Why then, let kibes ensue.

FALSTAFF   There is no remedy, I must cony-catch, I   30
must shift.

PISTOL   Young ravens must have food.

FALSTAFF   Which of you know Ford of this town?

PISTOL

I ken the wight, he is of substance good.

---

23 **filching** petty thefts
24 **kept not time** stole at the wrong
   moment (playing on the musical term)
25 **good humour** right way
   at . . . rest within a minute's space
   (*rest*, in music, interval between notes).
   Collier's emendation ('minim's', a
   musical term, for *minute's*), though
   unnecessary, is supported by *RJ*
   2.4.22, 'he rests his minim rests'.
26 **Convey** a cant use recorded in *OED*
   Convey *v.* 6b, played upon in *R2* 4.1.317:
   Richard reacts to Bolingbroke's order
   ('Convey him to the Tower') with 'O,
   good! convey! Conveyors are you all /
   That rise so nimbly by a true king's fall'.
27 **fico** fig (Italian). 'A fig for it' was a
   phrase of contempt (Dent, F210)
   accompanied by an obscene gesture
   (thumb thrust between index and middle fingers; the feminine form of *fico*
   designates the female genitals). Pistol
   varies it in *H5* 3.6.57 using Spanish
   figo for Italian *fico*.
28 **sirs** not a courtesy form but the plural
   of 'sirrah'; see 1.1.253n. Q has 'my
   Laddes', anticipating 35.

out at heels destitute (with bare heels
showing through the back of the stockings); proverbial (Dent, H389)
29 **let kibes ensue** let chilblains, or blis-
   ters on the heels, follow
30 **There . . . remedy** a current catch-
   phrase (Dent, RR3) made frequently
   to rhyme with 'die'
30–1 **cony-catch . . . shift** For *cony-catch*
   (cheat) see 1.1.117n.; *shift* means 'manage as best I can' (but Q replaces it with
   'cheat').
32 **Young . . . food.** Pistol combines a
   proverb, 'Small birds must have meat'
   (Dent, B397), with an allusion to
   Psalms 147.9, 'He feedeth the yong
   rauens that call vpon him' – a verse
   recalled also in *AYL* 2.3.43–4, 'He that
   doth the ravens feed, / Yea, provi-
   dently caters for the sparrow'. An
   ironic reference to Falstaff's pretence
   at youth, exposed by the Lord Chief
   Justice in *2H4* 1.2.173–86.
34 a line of mock-dramatic blank verse: 'I
   ken the wight' is a deliberate archaism
   for 'I know the fellow', and *of substance
   good* is a 'poetic' inversion.

25 minute's] *Q*, *F* (minutes*); minim's Collier² (Langton)   26–7] *Hibbard; prose F; 'Tis so indeed
Nym, thou hast hit it right. Q   28 sirs] my Laddes Q   30–1] Well, afore God, I must cheat, I must
cony-/catch. Q*

FALSTAFF My honest lads, I will tell you what I am 35
about.

PISTOL Two yards, and more.

FALSTAFF No quips now, Pistol. – Indeed I am in the
waist two yards about, but I am now about no waste: I
am about thrift. Briefly, I do mean to make love to 40
Ford's wife. I spy entertainment in her: she discourses,
she carves, she gives the leer of invitation. I can construe the action of her familiar style, and the hardest
voice of her behaviour – to be Englished rightly – is:
'I am Sir John Falstaff's'. 45

PISTOL He hath studied her well, and translated her will
– out of honesty into English.

35–6 **what . . . about** what I intend to do.
But Pistol pretends to understand
'what I measure round the waist'.

39 **waste** There is the same play on
'waist'/'waste' in *2H4* 1.2.140–3.

41 **entertainment** welcome; financial
support (*OED sb.* 2b)

42 **she carves** either 'she is generous in
her welcome' (carving at table was the
task of the host or hostess); or 'in discoursing affably she minces her words'
(Hibbard); see also Boyet described by
Biron in *LLL* 5.2.323: ''A can carve
too, and lisp'
leer look (without the modern derogatory implication)

42–3 **construe . . . style** interpret her
friendly behaviour. Falstaff uses the
terminology of syntactical analysis,
'construe the working of words in a
passage couched in plain style'.

43–4 **the hardest . . . is** 'the most difficult
passage, correctly translated into
English, means'. (In grammar 'voice'
signifies 'verbal form', suggesting a
schoolboy parsing a Latin sentence, as
Pistol remarks in his rejoinder.)

46 *****well . . . will** F has 'will' in both cases,
while Q has only the first part of the
sentence, using 'well'. Of the many
emendations proposed (see t.n.) and
suggested explanations, Grant White's
underlines the undoubted pun
well/*will*, playing on the various meanings of the latter: intention; sexual
desire; sexual organ; last will and testament. Accepting 'He hath studied
her will', Craik (Oxf[1]) glosses 'He has
had his eye on her sexual parts (figuratively)', which sounds rather far-
fetched.

47 **out . . . English** 1) pursuing the school
parsing imagery: Falstaff has translated her *will* from *honesty*, which is the
language of appearances, into plain
English ('I am Sir John Falstaff's'); 2)
Falstaff, in interpreting her *will*,
induces her to leave honesty in order to
fulfil her desires. Hibbard sees a possible pun on *English* and the verb 'ingle'
meaning 'to cuddle': Falstaff has transformed Mistress Ford from an honest
woman into one who is 'ingle-ish', i.e.
responsive to his advances.

38 quips] gibes *Q* 40 mean] intend *Q* 42 leer] *(*leere*)*; lyre *Q* 42–4 I . . . is] And euery part to
be construed rightly is *Q* 46 studied . . . will] *White;* studied her well, *Q;* studied her will; and
translated her will: *F;* study'd her well, and translated her well, *Pope;* studied her will, and translated
her well *Collier[2];* studied her well and translated her ill *(Cam[1])*

NIM   The anchor is deep: will that humour pass?

FALSTAFF   Now, the report goes she has all the rule of
her husband's purse: he hath a legion of angels.   50

PISTOL   As many devils attend her!
And 'To her, boy!' say I.

NIM   The humour rises: it is good. Humour me the
angels.

FALSTAFF   I have writ me here a letter to her; and here   55
another to Page's wife, who even now gave me good
eyes too, examined my parts with most judicious oeillades. Sometimes the beam of her view gilded my foot,
sometimes my portly belly.

48 **The . . . deep** Though sounding like a
current saying (a 'humour' in Nim's
parlance), no parallel has been found
for it. Suggested glosses: 'Falstaff's
ideas are firm' (Ard²); 'This is a deep
plot' (Hibbard); Falstaff has got a firm
hold there (with a sexual innuendo).
    will . . . pass Either Nim asks for
approval (pass muster) of his newly
coined phrase (*humour*), or he wonders
whether that of Falstaff (and of
Mistress Ford) is only a passing inclination (*humour*).

50 ***legion of angels** playing on the biblical expression 'legions of angels'
(Matthew, 26.53). *Legion* is 'a great
number' (*OED sb.* 3) and an *angel* (the
object of many puns) was a gold coin
worth ten shillings (so called from the
figure of the archangel Michael stamped
on it; see *MV* 2.7.55–6: 'They have in
England / A coin that bears the figure of
an angel'). The allusion is to Ford's
wealth. 'Legion' is Rowe's emendation
of F reading 'legend', a confusing alternative spelling of the word.

51 ***attend her** This is the Q reading,
implying that Mistress Ford should yield
to as many temptations of the devil as her
husband has coins. Most editors accept
the F reading 'entertaine', glossing either

'let as many devils do battle with them
["angels"]', or 'you must enrol ["entertain") as many devils [as Ford has
angels]'. Cf. Luke, 8.30: 'What is thy
name? And he said, Legion, because
many deuils were entred into him.'

52 **To her** a current expression of encouragement (see 3.4.36), normally
addressed to hunting dogs, but see *TS*
5.2.33–4, where two competing
women are encouraged with 'To her,
Kate!' and 'To her, widow!'

53–4 As usual, plays with *humour*,
using the word first as noun ('the wit is
improving' or 'the plot is thickening'),
then as verb ('I enjoy the joke about
angels' as well as 'spirit away the cash').

55 **writ me** Here (as in *Humour me*, 53)
me is an ethic dative, i.e. a superfluous
pronoun to reinforce the meaning of
the verb (Abbott, 220).

56–7 **good eyes** significant glances,
'speaking looks'; the same as *oeillades*,
57–8, a French expression found also
in *KL* 4.5.25–6: 'She gave strange oeillades and most speaking looks / To
noble Edmund.'

57 **parts** physical attributes

58 **gilded** shone upon (like sun rays)

59 **portly belly** impressive paunch (said
with more pride than self-mockery)

48] *not in Q (Nim's speeches omitted also at 53–4, 61)*   50 he] She *Q*   a legion] *Rowe³;* legians *Q;* a
legend *F*   51–2] *Q; prose F*   51 attend her!] *Q (her.);* entertaine: *F*   57–62 my . . . course o'er]
not in Q   57–8 oeillades] *Hanmer (Pope);* illiads *F*

PISTOL   Then did the sun on dunghill shine.   60
NIM   I thank thee for that humour.
FALSTAFF   O, she did so course o'er my exteriors, with
such a greedy intention, that the appetite of her eye did
seem to scorch me up like a burning glass. Here's
another letter to her. She bears the purse too: she is a   65
region in Guiana, all gold and bounty. I will be cheaters
to them both, and they shall be exchequers to me. They
shall be my East and West Indies, and I will trade to
them both. [*to Nim*] Go, bear thou this letter to
Mistress Page; [*to Pistol*] and thou this to Mistress   70
Ford. – We will thrive, lads, we will thrive.
PISTOL
    Shall I Sir Pandarus of Troy become,
    And by my side wear steel? Then Lucifer take all!
NIM   I will run no base humour. Here, take the humour-

---

60 a reference to the proverb 'The sun is never the worse for shining on a dunghill' (Dent, S982)
62 **course o'er** run through one by one (*OED* Course *v.* 5c)
63 **intention** attention; purpose; inclination (*OED sb.* 1, 6, 9)
64 **burning glass** lens through which the sun's rays can be concentrated on an object so as to burn it
66 **Guiana** In 1596 Sir Walter Ralegh published *The Discovery of Guiana*, describing his expedition to the South American colony in search of El Dorado.
cheaters 1) escheators, officials of the Exchequer supervising estates forfeited to the Crown (escheats); 2) swindlers, cheats. Cf. *Tit* 5.1.111.
68 **East . . . Indies** The richest resources of English trade were spices from the East Indies and precious ore from the West Indies.
69, 70 SD *Neither Q nor F specifies to which of the two messengers Falstaff wants to entrust each letter. See 89–90n.

72 **Sir . . . Troy** The word 'pander' derives from the name of Cressida's uncle in Chaucer's *Troilus and Criseyde*, Pandarus (*Sir* is Pistol's addition), acting as go-between. Before writing his *Troilus and Cressida* (based on an earlier play on the subject), Shakespeare had the Clown in *TN* 3.1.51–2 say 'I would play Lord Pandarus of Phrygia, to bring a Cressida to this Troilus', and in *AW* 2.1.97–8 Lafeu says 'I am Cressid's uncle, / That dare leave two together'. Pistol's protest against acting as pander shows that he considers himself an esquire ('by my side wear steel', i.e. 'carry a sword'; see 1.1.3n.).
73 **Lucifer take all** 'I'll be damned if I will.' Cf. 'the devil take all' (Dent, D266.1), but Pistol is again recalling *Doctor Faustus*; see 1.1.122n.
74 **run . . . humour** not act as a menial. 'Base humour' is found in Q; see 1.1.155n.
74–5 **humour-letter** Cf. 'humoured

---

69 SD] *Furnivall*   70 SD] *Cam¹*   72–3] *Q lines* become? / steele. / all. /   72 Pandarus]
Panderowes *Q*   73 side] sword *Q*   74 I . . . base humour] *not in Q*

letter – I will keep the 'haviour of reputation.   75

FALSTAFF [*to Robin*]

Hold, sirrah, bear you these letters titely,

Sail like my pinnace to these golden shores. –

Rogues, hence, avaunt! Vanish like hailstones, go!

Trudge, plod away o'th' hoof, seek shelter, pack!

Falstaff will learn the humour of this age: 80

French thrift, you rogues – myself and skirted page!

Exit with Robin.

PISTOL

Let vultures gripe thy guts! For gourd and fullam
     holds,

And high and low beguiles the rich and poor.

letter' at 2.1.118; in both cases *humour* is used as a term of contempt.

75 **'haviour of reputation** appearance of respectability (Hibbard)

76 ***titely** quickly, speedily (*OED adv.*); a word (so spelt in Q) already obsolete in the sixteenth century, but still found in *E3* 3.1.77. 'Tightly' in F is an accepted alternative spelling, but it misleads the modern reader by suggesting other meanings.

77 **pinnace** a small and fast ship

78 **avaunt!** be gone – used in exorcising evil spirits

79 ***o'th' hoof** on the hoof, on foot. Tilley (H587) records the expression 'to beat it on the hoof' for 'travel the hard way' (Ard²).
    pack be off

80 ***humour** mood, fashion. This is the Q reading; F has instead 'honor'. Though 'the honour of the age' would agree with Falstaff's sceptical view of honour in his 'catechism' in *1H4* 5.1.128–41 ('I'll none of it, honour is a mere scutcheon'), his appropriation in this case of Nim's pet word, *humour*, seems more suited to an age intent on keeping up appearances

with a minimum of expense.

81 **French thrift** Possibly *French* replaces 'Scottish' (the reputation of Scotsmen for thrift was proverbial), at a time when there had been official protests against the abuse of the Scottish nation on the English stage (see Melchiori, *Garter*, 117–18).
    myself . . . page Falstaff's thrift consists in dismissing all his attendants except the page (pages did not receive a salary beyond their keep), dressing him up in the long coat (*skirted*; see 1.1.26) of a servant.

82 **Let . . . guts!** Pistol uses a similar mock-dramatic invective in *2H4* 5.3.139: 'Let vultures vile seize on his lungs also.'
    gourd . . . holds Gaming tricks prevail: *gourd* (*OED* Gourd³ *sb.*) and *fullam* or 'fulham' (*OED* Fulham *sb.*) are false dice loaded to throw high or low numbers (see 83). *Holds*, like *beguiles*, 83, is a singular form for the plural; see 1.1.12n.

83 **high . . . poor** Pistol perverts to a cant use ('all are deceived by gaming tricks') a quotation from Psalms, 49.2: 'High and lowe, rich and poore: one with another'.

75 reputation.] reputation. And theres the humor of it. *Q*   76 SD] *Theobald*   76 titely] *Q;* tightly *F;* rightly *Q3*   77 shores.] *Q, F;* shores. *Exit Robin / Oxberry*   78 Rogues, . . . avaunt!] *(auaunt,);* Hence slaues, avant. *Q*   79] *not in Q*   o'th'] *F2* (oth'); ith' *F*   80 humour of this] *Q;* honor of the *F*   81 SD] *Q (Exit Falstaffe, and the Boy.); not in F*   82–3] *as verse Pope; prose F; not in Q*

Tester I'll have in pouch when thou shalt lack,
Base Phrygian Turk!

NIM   I have operations   85
In my head, which be humours of revenge.

PISTOL
Wilt thou revenge?

NIM   By welkin and her stars!

PISTOL
With wit, or steel?

NIM   With both the humours, I.
I will discuss the humour of this love to Ford.

PISTOL   And I to Page shall eke unfold   90
How Falstaff, varlet vile,
His dove will prove, his gold will hold,

---

84 **Tester** a coin worth sixpence (for 'money' in general)
pouch purse or pocket outside the dress for carrying money
85 **Phrygian Turk** 'Turk', i.e. 'infidel', was a common term of abuse. Phrygia was a western region of Turkey, but *Phrygian*, as a high-sounding national attribute, was probably suggested to Pistol by his previous mention of Sir Pandarus ('Lord Pandarus of Phrygia' in *TN*); see 72n.
85–6 *****operations ... head** mental plans. The omission of 'in my head' in F looks like a printing-house accident (the line is defective).
87 **welkin** sky or heaven, personified in the feminine
*****stars** 'Fairies' in Q is probably a misreading of manuscript 'starres' (Oxf[1]). 'Star', capitalized, in F may allude to Sirius, the queen of stars.
88 **With both the humours** '[I will take revenge] both by ingenuity [*wit*] and by action' (*steel* signifies 'sword' as at

73; 'sword' in Q).
89–90 There is some confusion: Nim states that he will report to Ford, and Pistol to Page, but in 2.1 Nim goes to Page and Pistol to Ford. Q makes good this apparent authorial inconsistency by replacing Nim's whole speech at 94–7 with 'Let vs about it then', and having him say at 89 'I will disclose this loue to *Page*' and Pistol at 90 'to *Foord* will likewise tell'. Several modern editors replace *Ford* with 'Page' at 89 and 94, and *Page* with 'Ford' at 90.
89 **discuss** disclose (*OED v.* 5). Cf. Pistol at *H5* 4.1.37, 'Discuss unto me, art thou officer . . .?'
90 **eke** Pistol's deliberate archaism, transferred in Q to 93
91 **varlet** a common term of abuse
92 The two forced internal rhymes *dove/prove*, *gold/hold* are for comic effect.
prove test (the fidelity of)
hold get hold of

84 Tester] And art thou gone? Teaster *Q*   lack] want *Q*   84–5 Tester . . . Turk.] *Q lines* pouch / Turke.   85–6 I . . . revenge] *prose Q*   86 in my head] *Q; not in F*   be] are *Q*   87 stars] *Collier[2];* Star *F;* Fairies *Q*   88 steel] sword *Q*   88–9 humours, . . . Ford.] humors I will disclose this / loue to *Page.* Ile poses him with Iallowes, / And theres the humor of it. *Q*   90 to . . . unfold] *F;* to *Foord* will likewise tell *Q*   92] Would haue her loue, his doue would proue, *Q*

And his soft couch defile.

NIM   My humour shall not cool: I will incense Ford to
deal with poison, I will possess him with yellowness, for   95
this revolt of mine is dangerous. That is my true
humour.

PISTOL   Thou art the Mars of malcontents. I second thee
– troop on.   *Exeunt.*

1.4   *Enter* Mistress QUICKLY *and* SIMPLE.

QUICKLY   What, John Rugby!

[*Enter* RUGBY.]

I pray thee go to the casement, and see if you can see
my master, Master Doctor Caius, coming. If he do,
i'faith, and find anybody in the house, here will be an
old abusing of God's patience and the King's English.   5

95 **deal with** use
   possess . . . yellowness make him
   jealous (*OED* Yellowness *sb.* 2). Dent
   (Y29.1) compares 'Iallowes' in Q (see
   88–9 t.n.) with the phrase 'to be sick of
   the yellows'.
96 ***this . . . mine** my rebellion (against
   Falstaff). F's reading 'the' for *this* (see
   t.n.) suggests a generalized sense inappropriate to the context.
98 **Mars of malcontents** the war god of
   disaffected people. Pistol flatters Nim,
   calling on him as a godlike military
   leader (in Q 'sir Corporall *Nym*'). The
   'malcontent' was the most sophisti-
   cated of stage 'humours', as John
   Marston's *The Malcontent* (*c.* 1603)
   was to prove.
1.4 Mistress Quickly's first speech makes
   it clear that the location is the house of
   Doctor Caius. The habit of the scribe

Ralph Crane of confining the directions in this text to 'massed entries'
(see pp. 31, 110–11) makes it necessary
to rely on the 1602 Quarto for some
indications of stage business, which in
this case implies also the use of a 'discovery place' – see *closet*, 35n.
2 **casement** window. 'At the window' in
   Elizabethan stage directions usually
   means 'above', in the gallery overlook-
   ing the stage. Either Rugby goes up and
   remains on the look-out in view of the
   audience until he calls out from above at
   33 and then retires, or he simply walks
   out at 8 and rushes in again after 32.
5 **old** great, plentiful (*OED a.*[1] 6), a common intensive. Cf. *2H4* 2.4.19, 'here
   will be old utis [ado, outcry]'.
   King's English an emphatic expression (Dent, K80) current also in the
   reign of Queen Elizabeth

93 his soft couch] eke his bed *Q*   94–7] Let vs about it then. *Q*   94 Ford] Page *Rann*   96 this]
Pope; the *F*   mine] mien *Theobald;* men *(Johnson);* mind *(Jackson);* mine anger *Cam¹*   98–9] Ile
seconde thee: sir Corporall *Nym* troope on. *Q*   99 SD] *Exit omnes. Q*   1.4] *Scoena Quarta. F*   0.1]
Q; Enter Mistris Quickly, Simple, Iohn Rugby, Doctor, Caius, Fenton. F   1 SP] *Q (Quic. throughout
play); Qu. (or Qui. throughout scene) F*   1.1] *Wheatley*

RUGBY   I'll go watch.

QUICKLY   Go; and we'll have a posset for't soon at night, in faith, at the latter end of a sea-coal fire.   [*Exit Rugby.*] An honest, willing, kind fellow, as ever servant shall come in house withal; and I warrant you, no tell-tale,   10 nor no breed-bate. His worst fault is that he is given to prayer; he is something peevish that way, but nobody but has his fault. But let that pass. – Peter Simple, you say your name is?

SIMPLE   Ay, for fault of a better.   15

QUICKLY   And Master Slender's your master?

SIMPLE   Ay, forsooth.

QUICKLY   Does he not wear a great round beard, like a glover's paring-knife?

SIMPLE   No, forsooth, he hath but a little wee face, with   20 a little yellow beard: a Cain-coloured beard.

---

7   **posset** a drink of hot curdled milk laced with wine or beer
for't for it, i.e. as a reward
soon at night in the evening; see Dent, S639.1

8   **at . . . end** (sitting) by the side
sea-coal best-quality coal mined in the North and brought by sea to London

9–10 **as . . . withal** an idiomatic construction: '[the best] servant that shall ever come into a house'

11 **breed-bate** trouble-maker. In *2H4* 2.4.249–50 Falstaff says that Poins 'breeds no bate with telling of discreet stories', meaning 'he raises no quarrel by reporting gossip'.

12 **something peevish** somewhat silly

12–13 **nobody . . . fault** There is nobody who does not have a fault; proverbial (Dent, M116)

15 **for . . . better** proverbial (Dent, F106)

17, 20, 23 **forsooth** The repetition of this interjection (meaning 'truly'; see 1.1.249n.) shows Simple's embarrass-

ment.

19 **glover's paring-knife** a flat round-bladed knife for smoothing leather. Shakespeare's father was a glover, i.e. a leather worker.

20 **wee face** small face, like a child's. Capell's emendation 'whey-face' (pale face, the colour of whey) was suggested by Quickly's previous speech in Q describing Slender as 'a weakly man' with 'a whay coloured beard' and by the use of the expression 'Whay-face' in F *Mac* 5.3.17.

21 **Cain-coloured** reddish-yellow, the colour of Cain's or Judas's hair in paintings (*OED* Cain *sb.*[2] 2; also Judas *sb.* 4). Q spells 'kane colored', taken by Rowe to mean the colour of cane (light yellow). Dover Wilson (Cam[1]), noting that 'cane' is dialectal for 'weasel', commented: 'a whey-face, with a weasel beard, makes a perfect vignette of Slender'; but this meaning of 'cane' is not recorded before 1789.

---

7 Go;] *(Goe,); Do; (Oxf¹)*   8 SD] *Rowe opp. 6; Rugby goes to the window. Cam¹*   20 wee face] *(wee-face);* whey-face *Capell (after Q* whay coloured beard *at 21)*   21 little yellow] whay coloured *Q*   Cain-coloured] *(Caine colourd);* kane colored *Q;* cane-colour'd *Rowe³*

QUICKLY   A softly-sprighted man, is he not?

SIMPLE   Ay, forsooth. But he is as tall a man of his hands,
as any is between this and his head. He hath fought with
a warrener.   25

QUICKLY   How, say you? – O, I should remember him:
does he not hold up his head, as it were, and strut in his
gait?

SIMPLE   Yes, indeed, does he.

QUICKLY   Well, heaven send Anne Page no worse for-   30
tune. Tell Master Parson Evans I will do what I can for
your master. Anne is a good girl, and I wish –

[*Enter* RUGBY.]

RUGBY   Out, alas! Here comes my master!   [*Exit.*]

QUICKLY   We shall all be shent. Run in here, good young
man, go into this closet – he will not stay long.   35

22 **softly-sprighted** soft-spirited, mild
tempered. An ambiguous praise: 1) of a
gentle disposition; 2) 'soft in the brain'
23 **as . . . hands** as valiant a fighter; a current expression (Dent, M163). Cf. *WT*
5.2.167–8: 'a tall fellow of thy hands'.
24 **between . . . head** a common expression
with many variations (Dent, H237.1,
Tilley H429) meaning 'in these parts'
25 **warrener** keeper of a warren (where
rabbits are bred). Warreners were not
particularly noted for courage –
Simple's praise of Slender's prowess
('tall . . . of his hands . . . between this
and his head') is comically inadequate.
26 **How, say you?** Is it so?
   I . . . him 'Now I can call him to mind'
   (Oxf[1]).
28 **gait** way of walking; Quickly may be
mimicking Slender's 'gait'.
32.1 For Rugby's movements see 2n. If he
comes on stage, he may remain till
immediately before the entrance of
Caius; see 36–8n.

33 **Out, alas!** an exclamation of distress:
'we are caught'; see 4.5.61.
34 **shent** disgraced, ruined (*OED ppl.*)
35 **closet** study. In Q 'counting house', a
private office, and therefore not a cupboard (which is the other meaning of
'closet'). Here it is used as a 'discovery
place', the same function as the 'counting house' mentioned (sc. 14) as the
hiding place of the assassins in the earlier anonymous play *Arden of Faver-
sham* (1589–91). It seems unlikely that
it is a structure brought in at the beginning and removed at the end of the
scene, or a space obtained by drawing a
curtain between the pillars supporting
the stage 'heaven'; more probably it is a
permanent curtained opening or recess
in the back wall of the stage, which
must have existed at the Globe, though
it does not figure in Aernout van
Buchell's drawing of the Swan theatre
in 1596. Q's 'For Gods sake step into
the Counting-house' may preserve

26 How, say you?] *Oxf[1]*; How say you: *F*   32.1] *Rowe;* RUGBY *(calls from the window) Cam[1] opp.
33;* RUGBY *(within) Oxf[1] opp. 33*   33] *not in Q*   33 SD] *Rowe*   34 We . . . shent] Lord blesse me,
who knocks there? *Q*   34–5 Run . . . closet] For Gods sake step into the Counting-house *Q*

Simple steps into the closet.

What, John Rugby! John! What, John, I say! Go, John,
go inquire for my master. I doubt he be not well, that
he comes not home.

[*Sings.*]   And down, down, adown-a (etc.)

[*Enter* Doctor CAIUS.]

CAIUS   Vat is you sing? I do not like dese toys. Pray you   40
go and vetch me in my closet *une boîtine verte* – a box,
a green-a-box. Do intend vat I speak? A green-a-box.

QUICKLY   Ay, forsooth, I'll fetch it you. – [*aside*] I am
glad he went not in himself: if he had found the young
man he would have been horn-mad.   45

CAIUS   *Fe, fe, fe, fe, ma foi, il fait fort chaud. Je m'en vais
voir à la cour la grande affaire.*

Quickly's interjection omitted after the
1606 Profanity Act.

36–8 Mistress Quickly pretends to be calling loudly for Rugby, whether he is on
the stage or not, only in order to be
heard by Doctor Caius. There is no
need to suppose, with the Oxford editors, that Rugby enters after 'I say' and
exits at the end of her speech.

39 And...(etc.) The refrain of a song (cf.
Ham 4.5.171–2, 'You must sing "A-
down, a-down" and you call him a-
down-a') which Quickly goes on
singing till interrupted by the arrival of
Caius. Q, which omits all the business
with Rugby, has Quickly saying at the
equivalent of 33 'Lord blesse me, who
knocks there?', adding the stage direction '*And she opens the doore*'.

40 dese toys these whims. Caius's
French pronunciation is represented

by the use of 'd' or 't' for 'th', of 'v' for
'w', 'wh' and 'f', and of 'sh' for 'ch'.

41 *une boîtine verte* a little green box.
French words and expressions are
hopelessly confused in F's attempt at
phonetic rendering.

42 intend understand, or hear (French
entendre); the absence of 'you' before
intend is either more of Caius's bad
English or F's accidental omission.

45 horn-mad fighting mad like a raging
bull; a common expression (Dent,
H628) frequently associated with cuck-
oldry, but see *CE* 2.1.57–9: '*E. Dromio
. . .* sure my master is horn-mad. /
Adriana Horn-mad, thou villain! / *E.
Dromio* I mean not cuckold-mad – /
But sure he is stark mad.'

46–7 *Fie, fie, fie, fie, faith, it's very hot.
I am going to watch the great ado at
Court' (a possible allusion to the

35 SD] *Q* (*He steps into the Counting-house.*); not in *F*; *Shuts Simple in the closet.* / *Rowe, after* closet
36 say!] say! *Enter Rugby. Oxf*   38 home.] home. *Exit Rugby. Oxf*   39 SD] *Theobald (subst.)*
39.1] *Rowe; And she opens the doore. Q*   40 dese toys] *(des-toyes)*   41 *une boîtine verte*] *Craig (une
boitine verde)*; vnboyteene verd *F*; *un boitier verd / Rowe*; un boitier vert *Cam*; une boite en verde
Ard¹; *une boite, une vert / Oxf (RP)*   43 SD] *Pope; to Rugby Cam¹*   46 *ma foi*] mai foy *F*
46–7 *fort . . . affaire*] *Ard²; for ehando, Ie man voi a le Court la grand affaires F; fort chaud. Je m'en va à
la Cour – la grande Affaire / Rowe (vais / Rowe³)*

QUICKLY   Is it this, sir?

CAIUS   *Oui, mette-le au mon* pocket. *Dépêche* quickly. Vere
    is dat knave Rugby?   50

QUICKLY   What, John Rugby! John!

[*Enter* RUGBY.]

RUGBY   Here, sir.

CAIUS   You are John Rugby, and you are Jack Rugby.
    Come take-a your rapier, and come after my heel to the
    court.   55

RUGBY   'Tis ready, sir, here in the porch.

CAIUS   By my trot, I tarry too long. 'Od's me, *qu'ai-je*
    oublié! Dere is some simples in my closet dat I will not
    for the varld I shall leave behind.

QUICKLY   Ay me, he'll find the young man there, and be   60
    mad!

preparation for the Garter ceremonies
announced at 5.5.56–73). This seems
the most likely interpretation of the
garbled transcription of the French
sentences in F, entailing only two
major emendations: *fort chaud* generally adopted for '*for ehando*', and *m'en
vais voir* for '*man voi*'.

49 *Oui . . . pocket* 'Yes, put it in my bag.'
Caius takes *pocket* to be masculine
English for feminine French *pochette*,
small bag.
    Dépêche quickly Since *dépêche* (the
only possible interpretation of F's '*de-
peech*') is the exact equivalent of
'quickly', Dover Wilson (Cam¹) thinks
that this should be capitalized as a personal name: 'Hurry up, [Mistress]
Quickly'.

53 Jack used instead of 'John' as a term of
abuse (*knave*, 50). Cf. *Jack-priest* at
109. Cam² prints lower case 'jack' and
'jack priest'.

54 **your rapier** Caius means his own
rapier (*my rapier*, 63), that Rugby, acting as his escort on courtly occasions,
had the task of carrying after him (*after
my heel*; cf. *Follow my heels*, 116).

57 **By my trot** truly; *trot* = troth (truth),
an involuntary pun on 'trot'
    'Od's me God save me; the euphe-
mistic form of a common ejaculation

57–8 **qu'ai-je oublié!** Now I remember!
Caius is not wondering, like Mistress
Quickly at 154, and as most editors
think, 'What have I forgot?', but realizing that he *has* forgotten a particular
object.

58 **simples** herbal medicines (Caius is
unaware that there is a [Peter] Simple
in his closet)

58–9 **not . . . varld** not for the world, i.e.
'by no means', very common in
Shakespeare (Dent, WW28)

60–1 not a real aside. Quickly speaks to
Rugby while Caius looks into the closet.

49 *Oui, mette-le*] *(Ouy mette le)   au mon* pocket.] *(au mon pocket,); à ma pochette.* Oxf   *Dépêche . . .*
Vere] *(de-peech quickly: / Vere); dépêche* Quickly. Vere *Cam¹*   51.1] *Wheatley*   53 Jack] *(Iacke)*;
jack *Cam²*   57 *qu'ai] (que ai)*   58 *oublié*!] *(oublie:); oublié?* mod. eds *(subst.)*   58, 63   closet]
Counting-house *Q*

157

CAIUS [*Pulls Simple out.*]   O *diable, diable,* vat is in my
  closet? Villainy, *larron!* – Rugby, my rapier!

QUICKLY   Good master, be content.

CAIUS   Wherefore shall I be content-a?   65

QUICKLY   The young man is an honest man.

CAIUS   What shall de honest man do in my closet? Dere
  is no honest man dat shall come in my closet.

QUICKLY   I beseech you, be not so phlegmatic, hear the
  truth of it. He came of an errand to me, from Parson   70
  Hugh.

CAIUS   Vell?

SIMPLE   Ay, forsooth, to desire her to –

QUICKLY   Peace, I pray you.

CAIUS   Peace-a your tongue! [*to Simple*] Speak-a your   75
  tale.

SIMPLE   To desire this honest gentlewoman, your maid,
  to speak a good word to Mistress Anne Page for my
  master in the way of marriage.

---

62 **O *diable, diable*** In Q Caius calls
Simple 'a deuella, a deuella' (for 'a
devil-a') and his exclamation of surprise is not 'O *diable*' but the mildly
blasphemous 'O Ieshu'.

63 ***Villainy, *larron!*** Caius lapses into
French in calling Simple 'thief', but he
uses first what he takes to be a more
general English expression. The F
spelling 'Villanie' may stand for
'Villainy', but is possibly meant to suggest his usual tendency to add a final 'a'
to the words he wants to emphasize:
'villain-a' – cf. *green-a-box*, 42, *take-a*,
54, *content-a*, 65, *Peace-a*, *Speak-a*, 75,
and so on.

  rapier The Oxford editors suggest
that Caius takes his rapier from Rugby,
a piece of business that must be left to
the actor's discretion; but at 53–6

Rugby had not yet fetched the rapier
from the *porch*.

64 **content** calm

67–8 **Dere . . . closet.** Caius means 'if the
man is honest he would not hide in my
closet', but his erratic grammar makes
it seem to read 'all persons coming into
the closet [Caius himself included] are
dishonest'.

69 **phlegmatic** Quickly means the opposite, i.e. 'choleric', a hot and dry
humour, while phlegm was considered
cold and moist.

70 **of an** on an

75–6 Craik (Oxf[1]) detects two unconscious obscenities. The words to
Quickly sound like 'Piss o' your
tongue', and those to Simple could be
construed as 'Let your tail [bottom or
penis] speak'.

---

62 SD] *Theobald (subst.)*   62–3 O . . . closet] O Ieshu vat be here, a deuella, a deuella *Q*   63
Villainy] *(Villanie); Villaine Q3;* Villain-a *(this edn)*   larron] *Rowe;* La-roone *F*   72 Vell?] *Neilson;*
Vell. *F*   75 SD] *Ard²*

QUICKLY   This is all indeed, la! But I'll ne'er put my   80
    finger in the fire, an't need not.

CAIUS   Sir Hugh send-a you? – Rugby, *baille* me some
    paper. – Tarry you a little-a-while. *Writes.*

QUICKLY [*aside to Simple*]   I am glad he is so quiet. If he
    had been throughly moved, you should have heard him   85
    so loud and so melancholy. But notwithstanding, man,
    I'll do you your master what good I can; and the very
    yea and the no is, the French doctor my master – I may
    call him my master, look you, for I keep his house, and
    I wash, wring, brew, bake, scour, dress meat and drink,   90
    make the beds and do all myself –

80–1 **I'll . . . not** proverbial (Dent, F230): 'I'll not meddle where I need not'; *an't* ('and', F) means 'if it'.

82 ***baille*** bring (French). Theobald's emendation of F 'ballow' (see t.n.) is based on the fact that in Q, at the equivalent of 2.3.12, Caius orders 'Bully moy, mon rapier *Iohn Rugbie*', where F has 'take your Rapier, (*Iacke*)'.

83 SD Instead of '*baille* me some paper' at 82–3 Q has 'giue a ma pen An Inck' ('give-a me pen and ink'). The absence of this last order in F implies that Caius either carries pen and ink on his person or finds them ready on the desk at which he sits down to write in the *closet* – Simple's hiding place now 'discovered' to the view of the audience; while Caius is busy writing, Quickly and Simple talk aside (84–99) frontstage.

84–99 In Q the substance of this dialogue between Mistress Quickly and Simple is found at the beginning of the scene, before Doctor Caius's entrance, with a much greater stress on sexual innuendos.

85 **throughly moved** thoroughly or truly angered

86 **melancholy** As at 69 Quickly means 'choleric'; melancholy was a cold and dry humour.

87 **do . . . master** In direct speech, 'you' after a verb is a common 'ethic dative' (see 1.3.55n.). F has 'yoe' for 'you', which the Oxford editors argue is not a misprint, but a miscorrection of a superfluous 'doe' for 'do'. Otherwise 'yoe' could be an erroneous first shot at 'your' (RP).

87–8 **the very . . . no** an adaptation of the formula used by Shallow at 1.1.80; see note.

89 **look you** mind you; an emphatic phrase particularly favoured (over twenty occurrences) by Fluellen in *H5*, but used also by Hostess Quickly in *2H4*

89–91 **I keep . . . all** Cf. Evans's description of Mistress Quickly's job as Caius's *nurse* at 1.2.3–5. The equivalent passage in Q (see 84–99n.) is heavily charged with sexual equivocations ('he puts all his priuities in me . . . all goes through my hands').

90 **dress meat** prepare, cook food

---

81 an't] *Oxf¹;* and *F*   82–3 *baille . . . paper] this edn after Theobald (baillez);* ballow mee some paper *F;* giue a ma pen / An Inck *Q (cf. 2.3.12* Bully moy, mon rapier*)*   83 Tarry . . . -while] tarche vn pettit tarche a little *Q*   83 SD] *Q (The Doctor writes.); not in F*   84 SD] *Cam*   87 you your] *(yoe your);* for your *F2;* your *Capell*   90 wring] *(ring)*

SIMPLE [*aside to Mistress Quickly*]　'Tis a great charge to come under one body's hand.

QUICKLY [*aside to Simple*]　Are you avised o'that? You shall find it a great charge, and to be up early and down　95
late; but notwithstanding – to tell you in your ear, I would have no words of it – my master himself is in love with Mistress Anne Page; but notwithstanding that, I know Anne's mind – that's neither here nor there.

CAIUS　You, Jack'nape: give-a this letter to Sir Hugh. By　100
gar, it is a shallenge: I will cut his troat in de park, and I will teach a scurvy jackanape priest to meddle or make. – You may be gone, it is not good you tarry here.
– By gar, I will cut all his two stones. By gar, he shall not have a stone to throw at his dog.　　*[Exit Simple.]*

QUICKLY　Alas, he speaks but for his friend.　　106

CAIUS　It is no matter-a ver dat. Do not you tell-a-me dat I shall have Anne Page for myself? By gar, I vill kill de Jack-priest; and I have appointed mine host of the

---

92, 95　**a great charge** a big task (for a single person); a great responsibility; a heavy burden (being under somebody else – with a sexual innuendo)

94　**Are . . . that?** So you are aware of it (how heavy a burden it is).

98–9　**but . . . mind** There is no comma after 'that' in F, so Quickly's unfinished sentence would mean 'but though I know what Anne thinks –'.

99　**that's . . . there** no matter for that; a common phrase (Dent, H438)

100　**Jack'nape** jackanapes, meaning 'tame monkey', hence 'idiot'. Caius is playing on John Rugby's name; see 53n. (cf. 102 *jackanape priest*).

100–1　**By gar** Caius's favourite euphemistic version of the strong oath 'By God', found also at 104 (twice), 108, 110, 115 and later in the play

101　**shallenge** challenge (indicating French pronunciation)
　　troat for 'throat' – but Q has instead 'nase' for 'nose'; cf. 'to cut off one's nose', meaning 'to ruin' (*OED* Nose *sb.* 8d).

102–3　**meddle or make** interfere, a current expression (Dent, M852)

105　**stone . . . dog** Playing on 'stones', meaning 'testicles', and a proverb about not having a stone to throw to a dog (Dent, S880, cf. *AYL* 1.3.2–3: '*Celia* . . . not a word? / *Rosalind* Not one to throw to a dog'). Here used by Caius to express a threat to castrate Evans (GWW).

106　**friend** colloquial for any acquaintance, here his master

109　**Jack-priest** knavish priest; see 53n.

---

92 SD] *Cam*　94 SD] *Cam*　98 that,] *Rowe;* that *F*　101 shallenge] chalége *Q*　troat] nase *Q*
105 SD] *Rowe; after* here. *at 103 Cam¹*　107 matter-a ver] *(*matter'a ver*)*; matter a ver *(Lambrechts)*
109 Jack-priest] *(*Iack-Priest*)*; jack priest *Cam²*

Jarteer to measure our weapon. By gar, I will myself   110
have Anne Page.
QUICKLY   Sir, the maid loves you, and all shall be well.
We must give folks leave to prate, what the good-year!
CAIUS   Rugby, come to the court with me. [*to Mistress
Quickly*] By gar, if I have not Anne Page, I shall turn   115
your head out of my door. – Follow my heels, Rugby.
                                      [*Exit with Rugby.*]
QUICKLY   You shall have An – fool's head of your own.
No, I know Anne's mind for that. Never a woman in
Windsor knows more of Anne's mind than I do, nor can
do more than I do with her, I thank heaven.   120
FENTON [*within*]   Who's within there, ho?
QUICKLY   Who's there, I trow? Come near the house, I
pray you.

[*Enter* FENTON.]

FENTON   How now, good woman, how dost thou?

110 **Jarteer** Garter (French *jarretière*)
measure our weapon act as umpire in a
duel (with the task of checking the equal-
ity of the weapons). Actually the Host
of the Garter had been chosen by Evans
as an umpire in the quarrel between
Shallow and Falstaff (see 1.1.127–31),
not between Evans and Caius.
112 **all . . . well** proverbial: 'All shall be
well and Jack shall have his Jill' (Dent,
A164)
113 **give . . . prate** proverbial: 'Give
lovers leave to talk' (Dent, L458)
what the good-year a common
exclamation of impatience, used twice
by Mistress Quickly in *2H4* 2.4.58–9
and 177, possibly derived from the
expression 'as I hope to have a good
year' (*OED* Goodyear *Obs.* a)
117 **You . . . An** – Quickly pretends to
reassure Caius about Anne, but as soon

as he is out of hearing she turns the girl's
name – *An* is an alternative spelling of
'Anne' – into an article (though 'a'
would be more appropriate than 'an') in
the proverbial phrase 'to have a fool's
head of one's own' (Dent, F519). Daniel
suggested that Caius's and Rugby's exit
should be placed after *An* –, but they are
probably already out of the audience's
view when Quickly speaks.
121–54 There is no counterpart to this
section of the scene in Q, where
Fenton appears for the first time only
in the equivalent of 3.4.
122 **I trow** I ask, I wonder (see 2.1.56).
When used in the affirmative the
expression means 'I believe'.
Come near Come into, enter. Cf.
3.3.138.
124–6 Fenton's condescending tone
(*good woman*) and Mistress Quickly's

110 Jarteer] *(Iarteer); Garter F4; Jartere / Rowe; Jarretière / Collier*   113 good-year] *(good-ier)*
114–15 SD] *Wheatley*   116 SD] *Rowe; after An – at 117 (Daniel)*   117 An – fool's head] *(An-
fooles head); An – ass-head Oxf*   121 SD] *Rowe*   123.1] *Rowe*

QUICKLY   The better that it pleases your good worship to   125
ask.

FENTON   What news? How does pretty Mistress Anne?

QUICKLY   In truth, sir, and she is pretty, and honest, and
gentle, and one that is your friend – I can tell you that
by the way, I praise heaven for it.   130

FENTON   Shall I do any good, thinkst thou? Shall I not
lose my suit?

QUICKLY   Troth, sir, all is in His hands above. But
notwithstanding, Master Fenton, I'll be sworn on a
book she loves you. Have not your worship a wart   135
above your eye?

FENTON   Yes, marry, have I; what of that?

QUICKLY   Well, thereby hangs a tale. Good faith, it is
such another Nan – but, I detest, an honest maid as ever
broke bread. We had an hour's talk of that wart. I shall   140
never laugh but in that maid's company. But, indeed,
she is given too much to allicholy and musing. But for
you – well – go to –

FENTON   Well, I shall see her today. Hold, there's money

---

conventional unctuous reply (*The better. . .*'; see Dent, B332.1) establish the
social difference between a gentleman
and a menial.

128–9 **and she . . . friend** The initial
superfluous *and* is meant to emphasize
the catalogue of Anne's qualities: *honest* meaning 'virtuous', *gentle* 'kindly',
your friend 'well disposed towards
you'.

134–5 **sworn . . . book** The *book* to swear
on is of course the Bible, but for
Quickly one book is as good as another.

135 **Have . . . worship** 'Your worship'
would require 'has', but Quickly is
thinking in terms of the more familiar
'Have not you'.

138 **thereby . . . tale** a common phrase
(Dent, T48), at times with a sexual pun
on 'tale'/'tail'; see *Oth* 3.1.8.

138–9 **it . . . Nan** Nan (familiar for Anne)

is such a remarkable person. A colloquial construction (Dent, A250).

139 **detest** a blunder for 'protest', the
opposite meaning; see 69n. The misuse of 'detest' by the constable Elbow
is played upon at length in *MM*
2.1.69ff.

139–40 **as . . . bread** as ever lived; another
commonplace (Dent, M68)

140–1 **I . . . company** No one can make
me laugh as she can. Fenton's wart is a
laughing matter; it reveals Anne's
interest in her wooer.

142 **allicholy** An error for 'melancholy',
which Quickly shares with the Host in
TGV 4.2.27. At 86 she uses *melancholy*
in the proper form but with the wrong
meaning. Anne's moods are further signs of her involvement with
Fenton.

143 **go to** enough said

for thee: let me have thy voice in my behalf. If thou   145
seest her before me, commend me –

QUICKLY   Will I? I'faith, that we will! And I will tell your
worship more of the wart the next time we have confidence, and of other wooers.

FENTON   Well, farewell, I am in great haste now.   150

QUICKLY   Farewell to your worship.   *[Exit Fenton.]*
Truly an honest gentleman – but Anne loves him not.
For I know Anne's mind as well as another does. – Out
upon't, what have I forgot?   *Exit.*

2.1   *Enter* MISTRESS PAGE *reading of a letter.*

MISTRESS PAGE   What, have I scaped love-letters in the
holiday-time of my beauty, and am I now a subject for
them? Let me see:

*[Reads.] Ask me no reason why I love you, for, though
Love use Reason for his precisian, he admits him not for his*   5

145 **voice** vote, support
147 **we will** not a misreading of 'I will':
Quickly uses half-jocularly the 'royal
plural' to create confidence in her
promise
148–9 **we have confidence** either a
Quicklyism for 'we have conference'
(we talk with each other), or 'we have
the opportunity of talking in private,
confidentially'
153 **as well . . . does** better than any other
(Dent, A249.1, first example from Ben
Jonson, *Every Man in His Humour*,
1598)
153–4 **Out . . . forgot?** 'O dear, I am sure
I have forgotten something.' *Out
upon't*, a very common exclamation
(Dent, OO1), expresses impatience at
herself for not remembering. Cf.
Caius's *qu'ai-je oublié*, 57–8n.
2.1 The absence of visual indication of
locality on the Elizabethan stage allows

for the unmarked transition from the
interior setting of Mistress Page's initial
soliloquy (1–26) to a location in the
street outside Page's house, as in 1.1,
where the rest of the scene takes place.
Otherwise it can be imagined that
Mistress Page, not believing her own
eyes, reads once again the letter while on
her way to see Mistress Ford (GWW).
1   **scaped** escaped; not an aphetic but an
accepted alternative form of the verb
2   **holiday-time** hey-day, best time. An
uncommon use of 'holiday', which
induced the Q reporter to insert the
word in a new context: 'if then I
thought I gaue such assurance
[encouragement to him] with my eies,
Ide pul them out, they should neuer
see more holie daies'.
4–6 *though . . . counsellor* proverbially
'love is without reason' (Dent, L517).
Falstaff presents Love as a monarch

147 we] *(wee); I Hanmer*   151 SD] *Rowe (opp. 150)*   2.1] *Actus Secundus. Scoena Prima. F*   0.1]
*Q; Enter Mistris Page, Mistris Ford, Master Page, Master Ford, Pistoll, Nim, Quickly, Host, Shallow.
F*   1 I] *Q3; not in F*   4 SD] *Capell*   5 *precisian*] physician *Collier² (Johnson)*

counsellor. You are not young, no more am I: go to, then,
there's sympathy; you are merry, so am I: ha, ha, then
there's more sympathy; you love sack, and so do I: would
you desire better sympathy? Let it suffice thee, Mistress
Page, at the least if the love of soldier can suffice, that I   10
love thee. I will not say 'pity me' – 'tis not a soldier-like
phrase – but I say 'love me'.

> *By me, thine own true knight, by day or night,*
> *Or any kind of light, with all his might,*
> *For thee to fight.*   *John Falstaff.*   15

What a Herod of Jewry is this? O wicked, wicked world!
One that is well-nigh worn to pieces with age, to show
himself a young gallant? What an unweighed behaviour
hath this Flemish drunkard picked – with the devil's

who, though recognizing Reason as his court chaplain, i.e. strict spiritual adviser (a *precisian* is a Puritan minister), does not act on his advice (*counsellor*, i.e. adviser).

6   *go to* come, come! (*OED* Go *v.* 91b); cf. 1.4.143n.

7, 8, 9   *sympathy* shared disposition

8   *sack* wine from Spain or the Canaries, like sherry. See Falstaff's soliloquy in praise of 'sherris-sack' in *2H4* 4.3.90–135.

10–11   *soldier . . . soldier-like* Falstaff insists on the military exploits (he never asked for pity from an enemy) that have gained him a knighthood.

13–15   The five-fold repetition of the internal rhyme is meant to emphasize Falstaff's status as of 'knight', while the omission of 'Sir' before his signature suggests the lover's familiarity.

16   **Herod of Jewry** ranting villain (Oxf[1]), as the character was presented in mystery plays. Herod the Great, responsible for the slaughter of the innocents, and his son Herod the Tetrarch, who

beheaded John the Baptist, were often confused and were both referred to as 'Herod of Jewry'. Hamlet warns against the actor who 'out-Herods Herod' (*Ham* 3.2.14).

17–18   **One . . . gallant** cf. the Lord Chief Justice's reproach to Falstaff in *2H4* 1.2.178–86: 'Do you set down your name in the scroll of youth, that are written down with all the characters of age? . . . Fie, fie, fie, Sir John!'

18   **unweighed** inconsiderate (*OED ppl.a.* 2), thoughtless, possibly with a glance at Falstaff's weight (GWW). Cf. *MM* 3.2.140: 'A very superficial, ignorant, unweighing fellow'.

19   **Flemish drunkard** Flemings had a reputation for heavy drinking, as well as for being overfond of fat food; see 2.2.286–8n.

19–20   **with . . . name** an interjection, possibly replacing, because of the 1606 Profanity Act, the blasphemous 'a Gods name' found in Q; but implying 'with the help of the devil' or 'acting in the name of the devil' (Ard[2])

10   *soldier*] a soldier *F3*   13–15] *Johnson lines* knight, / night, / light, / might, / fight. / Falstaff. / 16-24 What . . . down] *Pope; F lines* world: / age / vnwaied / with / dares / thrice / then / Ile / downe /   18 an unweighed] *(*an vnwaied*)*; unwayd *F3;* one unweigh'd *Capell*   19   with the devil's] ith Deuills *F3;* a Gods *Q*

name! – out of my conversation, that he dares in this   20
manner assay me? Why, he hath not been thrice in my
company! What should I say to him? I was then frugal
of my mirth – heaven forgive me! – Why, I'll exhibit a
bill in the parliament for the putting down of men.
How shall I be revenged on him? For revenged I will   25
be, as sure as his guts are made of puddings.

Enter MISTRESS FORD.

MISTRESS FORD   Mistress Page, trust me, I was going to
your house.

MISTRESS PAGE   And trust me, I was coming to you. You
look very ill.   30

MISTRESS FORD   Nay, I'll ne'er believe that. I have to
show to the contrary.

MISTRESS PAGE   'Faith, but you do, in my mind.

MISTRESS FORD   Well, I do, then. Yet I say I could show
you to the contrary. O, Mistress Page, give me some   35
counsel!

20 **conversation** behaviour, social intercourse
21 **assay** make advances to
21–2 **he . . . company** I've only met him
twice.
22 **should I say** can I have said
22–3 **frugal of** restrained in
23 **heaven forgive me!** Possibly the
exclamation does not refer to the previous sentence, but anticipates the
next, where Mistress Page invokes the
annihilation of all men.
23–4 **Why . . . men** In place of this Q has
'Well, I shall trust fat men the worse
while I liue for his sake', anticipating
Mistress Ford's 'I shall think the worse
of fat men' etc. at 48–9. This made
Theobald suspect that in the F version
'fat' had been accidentally omitted
before 'men' (see t.n. 24).

23 **exhibit** introduce, submit
24 **putting . . . men** suppression of
males, so that they could not put down
(sexually) women, but see 23–4n.
25–6 **How . . . be** The Oxford editors
replace with the Q reading (see t.n.) 'O
God that I knew how to be'.
26 **puddings** the entrails of a pig or sheep
stuffed with minced meat or the like
(*OED* Pudding *sb*. 1.1)
27, 29 **trust me** believe me. Finding it an
uncharacteristic interjection in Shakespeare, the Oxford editors replace it
with 'by my faith' (cf. '*Faith* at 33).
30 **ill** upset. But Mistress Ford takes it to
mean 'ugly, unattractive'.
31–2 **have . . . contrary** have evidence to
prove the opposite; cf. 34–5.
33 **mind** opinion

20–1 that . . . me] that thus he shootes at my honestie *Q*   21 thrice] twice *Q*   24 men] fat men
Theobald   25–6 How . . . puddings] O God that I knew how to be reuenged of him. But in good
time, heeres mistresse Foord *Q*   26.1] *Q; not in F*

MISTRESS PAGE   What's the matter, woman?

MISTRESS FORD   O, woman, if it were not for one trifling
respect, I could come to such honour!

MISTRESS PAGE   Hang the trifle, woman, take the   40
honour! What is it? Dispense with trifles: what is it?

MISTRESS FORD   If I would but go to hell for an eternal
moment or so, I could be knighted.

MISTRESS PAGE   What? Thou liest! Sir Alice Ford?
These knights will hack, and so thou shouldst not alter   45
the article of thy gentry.

MISTRESS FORD   We burn daylight. Here, read, read:
perceive how I might be knighted. I shall think the
worse of fat men as long as I have an eye to make
difference of men's liking. And yet he would not swear,   50
praised women's modesty, and gave such orderly and

---

39 **respect** consideration
honour social distinction
42–3 **for ... so** for a moment, more or less
(but the sin committed in that moment
would entail eternal punishment)
43 **knighted** The use of the word, like the
rest of both women's speeches from 34
on, is sarcastic, since the rank of knight
and the title of *Sir* (44) were not conferred upon women. At 48 *knighted*
quibbles on 'nighted' or 'benighted',
with reference to the 'night-work' (the
consummation of adultery) hinted at
in Falstaff's letter.
45 **These ... hack** 'knights are prone to
being promiscuous' (a behaviour that
would dishonour them, thus negating
their rank, i.e. 'alter the article of their
gentry'; see 45–6n.). Possibly playing on
two meanings of 'hack': to deal cutting
blows (*OED v.*[1] 8) – with a sexual innuendo; to hackney (*OED v.*[3] 1), in the
sense of 'practising prostitution', i.e.
being promiscuous – a meaning unrecorded for 'hack' before the eighteenth
century, but current for 'hackney', verb

and noun, in Shakespeare's time.
45–6 **alter ... gentry** change the desig-
nation of your social rank (have the
title of 'Sir' conferred upon you)
47 **burn daylight** waste time; proverbial
(Dent, D123). Mistress Ford's words
accompany her action: she hands
Falstaff's letter over to Mistress Page.
The stage business with the letters is
left to the actors' discretion, and there
is no need for additional directions.
48–50 **I shall ... liking.** Cf. 23–4n.
49–50 **make ... liking** distinguish
between men's bodily conditions
(*OED Liking sb.* 6). In *1H4* 3.3.1–10
Falstaff, commenting on the physical
decay brought on by his misconduct,
exclaims: 'I'll repent, and that suddenly, while I am in some liking.'
51 ***praised** 'praise' in F is a common
compositorial misreading of the copy,
since final 'e' and final 'd' (praisd) are
indistinguishable in secretary hand;
and the error occurs in the first line of
a new page of the Folio, so that it would
have been set out of context (RP)

---

44 What? Thou liest!] *Johnson;* What thou liest? *F*   45 will hack] will lack *Warburton;* we'll hack
(*Johnson*)   51 praised] *Theobald;* praise *F*

well-behaved reproof to all uncomeliness, that I would
have sworn his disposition would have gone to the truth
of his words. But they do no more adhere and keep
place together than the hundred psalms to the tune of   55
'Greensleeves'. What tempest, I trow, threw this
whale, with so many tuns of oil in his belly, ashore at
Windsor? How shall I be revenged on him? I think the
best way were to entertain him with hope, till the
wicked fire of lust have melted him in his own grease.   60
Did you ever hear the like?

MISTRESS PAGE   Letter for letter, but that the name of
Page and Ford differs! To thy great comfort in this
mystery of ill opinions, here's the twin brother of thy
letter. But let thine inherit first, for I protest mine never   65
shall. I warrant he hath a thousand of these letters, writ

---

52 **uncomeliness** improper behaviour
53–4 **gone . . . of** accorded, in point of
truth, with
54–6 **they . . . 'Greensleeves'** His character (disposition) agrees with his
words no better than the tune of a love
ballad would suit the singing of
psalms. ('Greensleeves' was a very
popular song dating from the 1580s.)
55 **hundred psalms** Actually there are
one hundred and fifty psalms, and the
Oxford editors emend accordingly.
But, *hundred* being a feasible spelling
of 'hundredth', most other editors
since Rowe emend also the plural
'psalms' and read 'Hundredth Psalm',
one of the best known under the title
Iubilate Deo. Shaheen (140) remarks
that 'some chose to sing it to the popular love song "Greensleeves"',
though it is unlikely that the standard
text of Psalm 100 could be set to that
tune (GWW). Mistress Ford's point is
the inappropriateness of setting any
religious text to an amorous tune; hers
is a general reference to the psalms, not
a precise figure; *hundred psalms* means

'any number of psalms'.
56 **I trow** I wonder; see 1.4.122n.
57 **tuns** barrels
58 **How . . . him?** Cf. 25–6 and note.
59 **entertain him** keep his mind busy
(*OED* Entertain *sb.* 9), lead him on
59–60 **the . . . grease** adapting the
proverb 'Frying (stewing) in one's own
grease' (Dent, G433)
62 **Letter for letter** In placing side by
side the two letters, Mistress Page
notes that they coincide 'letter by letter' – in Q 'line for line, word for
word'.
64 **mystery . . . opinions** revelation of
the low opinion (he has of us)
65 **inherit first** enjoy as the first-born
(Falstaff's offer). With twins, it was
hard to determine who had the first-
born's right of inheritance.
66–8 **a . . . edition** alluding to the practice of dedicating the same work to different personages in order to curry
their favour, and especially of changing the name of the dedicatee with each
new issue, assuming that a thousand
was the usual size of a printed edition

---

55 place] pace *Rann (Mason)*   hundred psalms] hundredth psalm *Rowe;* hundred and fifty psalms
Oxf   56 trow] *(troa)*

167

with blank space for different names – sure, more, and
these are of the second edition. He will print them, out
of doubt; for he cares not what he puts into the press,
when he would put us two. I had rather be a giantess,   70
and lie under Mount Pelion. Well, I will find you
twenty lascivious turtles ere one chaste man.

MISTRESS FORD   Why, this is the very same – the very
hand, the very words! What doth he think of us?

MISTRESS PAGE   Nay, I know not. It makes me almost   75
ready to wrangle with mine own honesty. I'll entertain
myself like one that I am not acquainted withal. For,
sure, unless he know some strain in me that I know not
myself, he would never have boarded me in this fury.

MISTRESS FORD   Boarding, call you it? I'll be sure to keep   80
him above deck.

MISTRESS PAGE   So will I. If he come under my hatches,
I'll never to sea again. Let's be revenged on him. Let's
appoint him a meeting, give him a show of comfort in

---

69 **puts . . . press** The book-publishing
metaphor continues with a pun: 1)
prints; 2) has sexual intercourse with.

70–1 **giantess . . . Pelion** In Greek
mythology the Titans were giants who
tried to scale Olympus, the seat of the
gods, by piling Mount Pelion, in
Thessaly, on top of Mount Ossa (or
vice versa), but Zeus buried them
under Pelion as punishment.

72 **turtles** Turtle-doves are emblems of
faithfulness (see Dent, T624), the
opposite of lascivious.
ere before (I find)

73–4 **very hand** same handwriting

76 **wrangle . . . honesty** quarrel with,
question my natural virtue

76–7 **I'll . . . withal.** Cf. Q 'I thinke I
knowe not my selfe'; *entertain* signifies
'treat', 'consider'.

78 **strain** disposition. No need for Pope's
emendation, 'stain'.

79 **boarded** accosted, assaulted. A nautical metaphor referring to piracy; its
sexual innuendos are underlined in the
next two speeches (see 80–1n., 82n.,
and cf. *MA* 2.1.143: 'I would he had
boarded me', as well as Iago on
Othello's secret marriage, at *Oth* 1.2.50
'he tonight hath boarded a land car-
rack').

80–1 **keep . . . deck** nautical: prevent the
assailant from entering the inside of
the ship

82 **come . . . hatches** descend under the
ship's deck; figuratively 'under the
hatches', meaning in a state of subjec-
tion (*OED* Hatch *sb.*[1] 3, 4; cf. Dent,
HH9)

83 **I'll . . . again** i.e. I will be unsea-
worthy, because leaky, or sunk under
his weight (RP).

84 **show of comfort** pretence of encouragement (*OED* Comfort *sb.* 1)

78 strain] stain *Pope*

his suit, and lead him on with a fine-baited delay, till he   85
hath pawned his horses to mine host of the Garter.
MISTRESS FORD   Nay, I will consent to act any villainy
    against him, that may not sully the chariness of our
    honesty. O, that my husband saw this letter! It would
    give eternal food to his jealousy.   90

Enter FORD *with* PISTOL *and* PAGE *with* NIM.

MISTRESS PAGE   Why, look where he comes; and my
    good man too – he's as far from jealousy as I am from
    giving him cause, and that, I hope, is an unmeasurable
    distance.
MISTRESS FORD   You are the happier woman.   95
MISTRESS PAGE   Let's consult together against this
    greasy knight. Come hither.   [*They withdraw.*]
FORD   Well, I hope it be not so.
PISTOL
    Hope is a curtal dog in some affairs.
    Sir John affects thy wife.   100
FORD   Why, sir, my wife is not young.
PISTOL
    He woos both high and low, both rich and poor,

---

85 **fine-baited delay** delaying tactics during which tempting bait will be dangled before him (Ard²)
86 **pawned . . . Garter** Falstaff's only means of getting money to pay for his courtship. Actually from his conversation with the Host at 1.3.1–13 it seems unlikely that Falstaff had any horses to pawn; possibly the allusion was introduced in view of a different development of the horse-stealing episode involving the Host in 4.3 and 4.5 (see pp. 26–7).
88–9 **that . . . honesty** provided it does not spoil the integrity (*OED* Chariness *sb.* 2) of our virtue
92 **good man** two words to emphasize

her husband's (*goodman*; see 3.2.23) goodness
97 **greasy** 1) literally, oily, fat; 2) lascivious; cf. *LLL* 4.1.137: 'Come, come, you talk greasily, your lips grow foul' (RP).
99 **curtal dog** small dog with docked tail, trained to run in a treadwheel; see *CE* 3.2.146: 'She had transformed me to a curtal dog, and made me turn i'th' wheel'. Pistol implies that Hope may turn the wheel of Fortune against those who invoke it.
100 **affects** is interested in, loves
102–3 **both high . . . another** another ironical adaptation of Psalms, 49.2; see 1.3.83n.

90.1] `Rowe (after 97); Enter Ford, Page, Pistoll and Nym Q; not in F   92 good man] goodman Bowers   97 SD] Theobald (subst.)   102–4] Pope; prose F

Both young and old, one with another, Ford.
He loves the gallimaufry, Ford: perpend.

FORD   Love my wife?

PISTOL   With liver burning hot.   105
Prevent, or go thou like Sir Actaeon he,
With Ringwood at his heels.
O, odious is the name!

FORD   What name, sir?

PISTOL   The horn, I say. Farewell.   110
Take heed, have open eye, for thieves do foot by night.
Take heed, ere summer comes, or cuckoo-birds do sing. –
Away, Sir Corporal Nim! – Believe it, Page, he speaks
sense.   *Exit.*

FORD [*aside*]   I will be patient, I will find out this.   115

NIM [*to Page*]   And this is true, I like not the humour of
lying. He hath wronged me in some humours. I should

104 **gallimaufry** mixture of all sorts.
'Gallimaufry' is a stew made with any
kind of viand available, a hotchpotch.
perpend consider, think it over; an
affected term used by Pistol also in *H5*
4.4.8, as well as by fools or foolish characters: Touchstone (*AYL*), Feste
(*TN*) and Polonius (*Ham*)

105 **liver** seen as the seat of irrational love
passion. Cf., for example, *LLL*
4.3.72–3: 'This is the liver-vein, which
makes flesh a deity, / A green goose a
goddess . . .'

106 **Sir Actaeon** The hunter Actaeon, in
punishment for spying on Diana and
her nymphs bathing, was transformed
into a stag and killed by his own hounds.
Because of his horns, he was considered
emblematic of cuckoldry; the title 'Sir'
is frequently attributed in romances to
mythological or classical characters; see
'Sir Pandarus of Troy', 1.3.72.

107 **Ringwood** a common English name
for a hound, used also by Arthur
Golding as that of one of Actaeon's
dogs in his translation of the story in
Met., 3.270

110 **The horn** Pistol implies that 'horn' is
another name for 'Actaeon', both
being synonymous with 'cuckold'.

111 **foot** walk

112 **cuckoo-birds** Cuckoos were known
for laying their eggs in other birds' nests,
and their song in late spring was taken as
a warning to married men. Cf. *LLL*
5.2.901–2: 'Cuckoo, cuckoo – O word of
fear / Unpleasing to a married ear.'

113–14 **Believe . . . sense** Johnson and
Collier (see t.n.) assign these words to
Nim. But here Pistol invites Page to
listen to what Nim has to tell him
before going.

116–23 In this, his last speech in the play,
Nim gives free rein to his fanciful uses

105–8 With . . . name] *this edn (RP); F lines* preuent: / with / name. /; *Capell lines* thou / heels. /
name! /; *Ard² lines* Prevent, / he, / heels. / name! /; *prose Pope*   113–14] *as Theobald; F lines* Nim:
/ sence. /; *Page* belieue him what he ses. Away sir Corporal Nym. Q; Away, Sir corporal. / Nym.
Believe . . . sense. *(Johnson);* Away, . . . Nym. / *Nym.* Believe . . . sense. *Collier*   114 SD] *Q (Exit
Pistoll:); not in F*   115 SD] *Capell*   116 SD] *Hanmer*   116–17 And . . . humours] Syr the humor
of it is, he loues your wife *Q*

have borne the humoured letter to her, but I have a
sword, and it shall bite upon my necessity. He loves
your wife, there's the short and the long. My name is   120
Corporal Nim. I speak, and I avouch 'tis true: my name
is Nim and Falstaff loves your wife. Adieu. I love not
the humour of bread and cheese. Adieu.   *Exit.*

PAGE   The humour of it, quoth 'a! Here's a fellow frights
     English out of his wits.   125

FORD [*aside*]   I will seek out Falstaff.

PAGE [*aside*]   I never heard such a drawling-affecting
     rogue.

FORD [*aside*]   If I do find it – well.

PAGE [*aside*]   I will not believe such a Cathayan, though   130

of 'humour' as an all-purpose word:
humour (116) meaning 'habit'; *humours*
(117) 'respects'; *humoured letter* (118)
'mendacious letter'; cf. *humour-letter* at
1.3.74–5; for *humour of bread and cheese*
see 122–3n.

119 **bite . . . necessity** strike when
needed. GWW suggests that *my* is a
compositorial misreading of 'any'.

120 **the short . . . long** the whole point;
proverbial (Dent, L419)

122–3 **I . . . cheese** My nature (*humour*) is
not that of a man content with the bare
necessities of life (*bread and cheese*);
possibly an allusion to the miserly
treatment received by Falstaff's followers. Dover Wilson (Cam¹), noting
that 'bread and cheese' was also 'a
name for the cuckoo-bread flower',
believes that Nim refers to Falstaff as
'the cuckoo in Page's nest', but the
explanation seems far-fetched.

124 **The . . . it** Instead of *Adieu* at 123, Q
has 'And theres the humor of it',
adopted by some editors in view of
Page's comment after Nim's exit. But
Nim's typical tag in *H5*, 'the humour
of it', is never used by him in F *MW*

(see note on Nim to the List of Roles);
Page refers to Nim's fourth and last
variation on it in his speech (122–3n.).
quoth 'a he said; *'a*, he (colloquial)

125 **his** its; referring to the English language, a variant of the common expression 'to be frightened out of one's wits'
(Dent, W583, with reference also to
2.2.264–5); cf. *MA* 5.2.55–6, 'Thou
hast frighted the word out of his right
sense'. The Q reading, 'humor' for
English, is attractive (a criticism of
Nim's constant misuse of the word
'humour'), but lacks textual support.

127 **drawling-affecting** whose affectation consists in repeating (the same
word all the time). The hyphenation in
F is significant: Nim's affected 'drawl'
is not a lengthening of the sound of
words, but a variation of the same
sounds to the detriment of sense.

130 **Cathayan** literally, a native of
Cathay (China), a jocular term of disparagement, reflecting distrust for
people from faraway countries; also
used by the drunken Toby Belch of
Olivia at *TN* 2.3.75

130–1 **though . . . man** The local parson

118–20 but . . . long] *not in Q*   119 my] any *(GWW)*   121 avouch 'tis true] *Q;* auouch; 'tis true *F*
123 cheese. Adieu.] *F (subst.);* cheese: / And theres the humor of it. *Q*   123 SD] *Q (Exit Nym.);*
not in F   124 quoth 'a!] *(quoth'a?);* quoth you: *Q*   125 English] humor *Q*   126, 129, 132 SD]
Capell   127, 130 SD] *Dyce*   130 Cathayan] *(Cataian)*

the priest o'the town commend him for a true man.

FORD [*aside*]   'Twas a good sensible fellow – well.

[MISTRESS PAGE *and* MISTRESS FORD *come forward.*]

PAGE   How now, Meg?

MISTRESS PAGE   Whither go you, George? Hark you.

MISTRESS FORD   How now, sweet Frank, why art thou   135
melancholy?

FORD   I melancholy? I am not melancholy. Get you home,
go.

MISTRESS FORD   Faith, thou hast some crotchets in thy
head now. – Will you go, Mistress Page?   140

MISTRESS PAGE   Have with you. You'll come to dinner,
George? [*aside to Mistress Ford*] Look who comes
yonder: she shall be our messenger to this paltry
knight.

MISTRESS FORD [*aside to Mistress Page*] Trust me, I   145
thought on her: she'll fit it.

Enter Mistress QUICKLY.

MISTRESS PAGE   You are come to see my daughter Anne?

QUICKLY   Ay, forsooth. And I pray, how does good
Mistress Anne?

was commonly consulted as a character referee (RP).
139–40 **crotchets . . . head** queer ideas;
proverbial (Dent, C843)
141 **Have with you** I'll go with you, let's
go (Dent, HH10).
You'll . . . dinner Shall you come back
home in time for the midday meal?
(*dinner*; see 1.1.181n.). The action of
Act 2 begins in the morning of the day
following that in which Act 1 takes
place, well before 10 a.m., the time

appointed for Falstaff's visit to
Mistress Page (2.2.77–80).
146 **fit it** be the right person for it
146.1 The timing of Quickly's entrance is a
matter for the actors to decide: the
exchange in asides between the two
wives at 142–6 suggests that she has been
sighted by them off stage, but comes into
the view of the audience only when
Mistress Page addresses her directly.
148 **forsooth** See 1.1.249n.

132.1] *Theobald*   134] How now sweet hart, how dost thou? *Q (cf. Mistress Ford at 135)*   135
sweet . . . thou] husband, how chaunce thou art so *Q*   137–8] *Pope; F lines* melancholy: / goe. /
140] head now. – Will] *Hanmer;* head, / Now: will *F*   141 come] come home *Oxf¹; come in (RP)*
142 SD] *Johnson*   142–3 Look . . . yonder] God saue me, see who yonder is *Q*   145 SD] *Capell*
146.1] *Q (after 144); not in F*

MISTRESS PAGE   Go in with us and see. We have an   150
 hour's talk with you.
 Exeunt Mistress Ford, Mistress Page and Mistress Quickly.
PAGE   How now, Master Ford?
FORD   You heard what this knave told me, did you not?
PAGE   Yes, and you heard what the other told me?
FORD   Do you think there is truth in them?   155
PAGE   Hang 'em, slaves! I do not think the knight would
 offer it, but these that accuse him in his intent towards
 our wives are a yoke of his discarded men – very rogues,
 now they be out of service.
FORD   Were they his men?   160
PAGE   Marry, were they.
FORD   I like it never better for that. – Does he lie at the
 Garter?
PAGE   Ay, marry, does he. If he should intend this voyage
 toward my wife, I would turn her loose to him, and   165
 what he gets more of her than sharp words, let it lie on
 my head.
FORD   I do not misdoubt my wife, but I would be loath to
 turn them together. A man may be too confident. I
 would have nothing lie on my head: I cannot be thus   170
 satisfied.

150–1 **We ... you.** We must talk together.
  A current idiom; cf. *JC* 2.2.121, 'I have
  an hour's talk in store for you.'
157 **offer it** attempt to do it
  in his intent of (evil) intentions
158 **yoke** pair, couple
  very true
161, 164 **Marry** See 1.1.192n.
162 **I ... better** I don't like it any better.
  lie lodge
164 **this voyage** these advances. The
  voyage of discovery is a common

metaphor in the language of seduction.
165 **turn . . . him** let her meet him.
  Farmyard language: 'turning loose of a
  cow and a bull in the same pasture'
  (Hibbard); see 'turn them together' at
  169.
166–7, 170 **lie on my head** be my
  responsibility; but Ford plays on the
  meaning 'be on my head', alluding to
  the cuckold's horns.
168 **misdoubt** doubt
170 **thus** so easily

150 We have] we would have *Hudson² (Walker)*; we'd have *Craig*   151 SD] *Q (Exit Mistresse Ford,*
Mis. Page, *and* Quickly.*); not in F*   162–3] *Pope; F lines* that, / Garter. /; [*aside*] I . . . that. [*to Page*]
Does . . . Garter? *(this edn)*

Enter HOST.

PAGE   Look where my ranting host of the Garter comes.
There is either liquor in his pate or money in his purse,
when he looks so merrily. – How now, mine host?

HOST   How now, bully rook? Thou'rt a gentleman. –   175
Cavaliero Justice, I say!

[*Enter* SHALLOW.]

SHALLOW   I follow, mine host, I follow. – Good even and
twenty, good Master Page. Master Page, will you go
with us? We have sport in hand.

HOST   Tell him, Cavaliero Justice, tell him, bully rook!   180

SHALLOW   Sir, there is a fray to be fought between Sir
Hugh the Welsh priest and Caius the French doctor.

FORD   Good mine host o' the Garter, a word with you.

HOST   What sayst thou, my bully rook?

---

172 **ranting** obstreperous; in Q 'ramping'
= 'extravagant' (*OED ppl. a.* 3)
173 **There . . . pate** either drink has gone
to his head; cf. Q 'Ther's either licker
in his hed'.
175 **How . . . gentleman** The Oxford editors reintroduce here Q's repeated
'God blesse you' (see t.n.), which may
have been omitted for censorial reasons,
but do not accept the plural 'rookes'; if
the Host is addressing both Page and
Ford, the F punctuation should be
adopted: the Host turns to Shallow
affirming that *he* is a gentleman. But
Dover Wilson's reading (Cam[1]) is
sounder: the Host greets Page and then
calls on the Justice who has been lagging behind. For *bully rook*, addressed

in turn to Page (175), Shallow (180) and
Ford (184), see 1.3.2n.
176, 180 **Cavaliero** Italian (*cavaliere*) for
'knight', confused with Spanish
caballero in the sense of 'gallant gentleman'
177–8 **Good . . . twenty** Good day twenty
times over. *Good even* seems inappropriate because the action takes place
before 'dinner', i.e. the midday meal.
But the greeting, especially in the form
'God den' used in Q, had lost its original application only to the afternoon
or evening.
179 **have . . . hand** anticipate entertainment, or we are getting ready a
trick
181 **fray** fight, contest

171.1] *Q (Enter Host and Shallow.); not in F; after* merrily. *at 174 Dyce; after* host? *Collier; Enter
Host, Shallow, and Slender. / Harness (after 174)*   172 ranting host] *(ranting-Host); ramping host
Q*   175–6 How . . . Justice,] *Cam[1] (subst.);* How now Bully-Rooke: thou'rt a Gentleman Caueliero
Iustice, *F;* God blesse you my bully rookes, God blesse you. Caueleria Iustice *Q;* God bless you,
bully-rook, God bless you! Thou'rt a gentleman. [*Enter Shallow.*] Cavaliero Justice, *Oxf*   176.1]
Collier[2]   177–8 Good . . . good] *(Good-euen, . . . (good);* M. Ford god den to you. God den an
twentie good *Q*   180 Cavaliero Justice] *(Caveleiro-Iustice);* cauelira Iustice *Q*

Ford and the Host talk apart.

SHALLOW   Will you go with us to behold it? My merry   185
host hath had the measuring of their weapons, and, I
think, hath appointed them contrary places; for, believe
me, I hear the parson is no jester. Hark, I will tell you
what our sport shall be. [*Shallow and Page talk apart,
Ford and Host come forward.*]

HOST   Hast thou no suit against my knight, my guest   190
cavaliero?

FORD   None, I protest. But I'll give you a pottle of burnt
sack to give me recourse to him – and tell him my name
is Brook, only for a jest.

HOST   My hand, bully: thou shalt have egress and regress   195
– said I well? – and thy name shall be Brook. It is a
merry knight. [*to all*] Will you go, myn-heers?

SHALLOW   Have with you, mine host.

PAGE   I have heard the Frenchman hath good skill in his
rapier.   200

SHALLOW   Tut, sir, I could have told you more. In these

---

186 **had . . . weapons** been appointed
umpire; see 1.4.110n.
187 **contrary** different; at a distance from
one another
188 **the . . . jester** Evans is not unskilled
in the use of weapons – a rumour that
may well have reached Caius's ears; see
2.3.1, 3n.
190–1 **guest cavaliero** Falstaff as a
lodger (*guest*) in the Host's inn. In F
'Caualeire', not 'Caualeiro' as at 176
and 180 (see n.). The Host is now using
the word in its correct Italian meaning,
'knight'.
192–3 **a . . . sack** a tankard holding half a
gallon of wine (see 8n.) – *burnt* is either

'mulled, heated with fire', or 'with
added burnt sugar'
193 **recourse** access
194 **Brook** For the implications of Ford's
assumed name see pp. 50–2.
195 **egress and regress** right of exit and
entrance; a common legal formula
(Dent, EE4). The Host displays his
fondness for legal terminology.
197 *****myn-heers** Dutch for 'gentlemen'.
Theobald's emendation of F's 'An-
heires' seems the best guess since the
Host takes pride in being polyglot.
198, 208 **Have with you** See 141n., with
the possible additional meaning
'enough said'.

---

184 SD] *Q (Ford and the Host talkes); not in F*   189 SD] *this edn (from Capell (subst.) and Oxf¹)*
190–1 my guest cavaliero] *(my guest-Caualeire);* My guest, my cauellira *Q*   192 SP] *Q (For.);*
Shal. F   194 Brook] *Q (Rooke);* Broome *F*   196 Brook] *Q (Brooke, throughout play);* Broome *F*
(throughout play)   197 SD] *this edn*   197 myn-heers] *Hanmer (Theobald);* An-heires *F;* on,
heirs *Warburton;* on, hearts *Steevens³ (Heath);* on, sirs *Halliwell;* Ameers *Cam¹ (Ard¹);* mijn'heers
Oxf

times you stand on distance – your passes, stoccadoes,
and I know not what. 'Tis the heart, Master Page, 'tis
here, 'tis here. I have seen the time, with my long
sword, I would have made you four tall fellows skip like   205
rats.

HOST   Here, boys, here, here! Shall we wag?

PAGE   Have with you; I had rather hear them scold than
fight.   [*Exeunt Host, Shallow and Page.*]

FORD   Though Page be a secure fool, and stands so firmly   210
on his wife's frailty, yet I cannot put off my opinion so
easily. She was in his company at Page's house, and
what they made there I know not. Well, I will look
further into't, and I have a disguise to sound Falstaff.
If I find her honest I lose not my labour. If she be   215
otherwise, 'tis labour well bestowed.   *Exit.*

---

202 **you . . . distance** The distance
between duellists is considered a matter of principle; *you* (and *your*) is used
generically, and *stand on* means 'attach
great importance'.
  passes, stoccadoes thrusts; a slur on
fashionable fencing terms
203 **'Tis the heart** 'What counts is the
spirit with which one fights.'
204 **I . . . time** a commonplace (Dent,
D81.1). Shallow's boast of his past
fighting (and sexual) exploits (see
2.3.38–44) is a feature of his character
inherited from *2H4* 3.2.17ff.
204–5 **long sword** heavy two-handed
sword – replaced in fashionable fencing by the rapier
205 **made . . . skip** made no fewer than
four lusty fellows (not Shallow's present auditors) run away; *you* is an ethic
dative for emphasis, cf. 202n. and
Abbott, 220. For *tall* see 1.4.23n.
207 **wag** go; see 1.3.6n.
209 SD In the Q version Page does

not exit with the Host and Shallow,
and instead of Ford's soliloquy at
210–16 there is an exchange of
civilities between Page and Ford,
who go together to dinner (cf. 141n.).
This entails that both the fight
between Caius and Evans and
Falstaff's assignation with Mistress
Ford are to take place not, as in the F
version, in the course of the same
morning as this scene, but early the
next day.
210 **secure** over-confident
210–11 **stands . . . frailty** There is
no need to suppose that *frailty* is a
misreading of 'fealty' or 'fidelity'.
Ford says that Page counts too much
on what is in fact his wife's weak
point.
213 **made** did, got up to (Hibbard)
214 **sound** sound out; sound the depth of.
Therefore *sound Falstaff* means
'inquire into Falstaff's plans'.

---

202 distance] your distance *(Oxf¹)*   208 hear] have *Hanmer*   than] *(then); than* see them *Collier²*
209 SD] *Rowe; Exit Host and Shallow. Q*   211 frailty] fealty *(Theobald);* fidelity *Collier²*   216 SD]
Rowe; Exeunt. F; Exit omnes. Q

2.2   *Enter* FALSTAFF *and* PISTOL.

FALSTAFF   I will not lend thee a penny.

PISTOL

Why then, the world's mine oyster,

Which I with sword will open.

FALSTAFF   Not a penny. I have been content, sir, you
should lay my countenance to pawn; I have grated upon   5
my good friends for three reprieves for you and your
coach-fellow Nim, or else you had looked through the
grate like a gemini of baboons. I am damned in hell
for swearing to gentlemen my friends you were good
soldiers and tall fellows. And when Mistress Bridget   10

2.2 The action of this scene, located in the Garter Inn, overlaps with the last part of 2.1: Pistol, having exited at 2.1.114, has gone straight to the Inn and is now talking with Falstaff, at the same time as the Host, Ford, Page and Shallow are still foretasting the sport they will have at the expense of Caius and Evans (2.1.172–216) and Mistress Page and Mistress Ford instruct Quickly about their replies to Falstaff's letters.

2–3 Faced with Falstaff's refusal to give him money, Pistol, reversing the meaning of the proverbial 'open an oyster with a dagger' (keep at a safe distance, Tilley, M777), affirms that the only alternative left him is to extract money from the world at large by using his sword. This speech is replaced in Q by 'I will retort the sum in equipage', which Theobald (followed by Hibbard) added to the text after 'open', as Pistol moves from bragging to pleading, assuring Falstaff that he will repay ('retort') the loan in some form. Hibbard remarks that 'Pistol seems to think it ["in equipage"] means "in equal payments" on the

instalment plan', but more probably what he has in mind is 'as your retinue' (*OED* Equipage *sb.* 11), i.e. going back without pay into Falstaff's service from which he had been dismissed at 1.3.78–81.

5   **lay . . . pawn** bank upon the credit (*OED* Countenance *sb.* 11) I enjoy in the world
      grated upon harassed, importuned (*OED* Grate *v.*[1] 4)

7   **coach-fellow** a horse yoked to the same carriage with another, i.e. companion, mate (*OED* Coach *sb* 6), cf. Page at 2.1.157–8 'these [Pistol and Nim] . . . are a yoke of his discarded men'. Theobald's emendation ('couch-fellow', i.e. bed-fellow) is unnecessary.
      had would have

8   **grate** prison-bars – punning on *grated* at 5 (see note)
      gemini of baboons pair (*gemini* meaning 'twins') of stupid apes; cf. 'Hang him, baboon', said by Falstaff of Poins in *2H4* 2.4.240.

10   **tall fellows** valiant men; see 1.4.23n.
      Mistress Bridget The name Bridget

2.2] *Scoena Secunda.* F   0.1] *Q (Enter Syr Iohn, and Pistoll); Enter* Falstaffe, Pistoll, Robin, Quickly, Bardolffe, Ford. *F*   1] *Pistol.* I will retort the sum in equipage. *Falstaff.* I will . . . penny. *Cam[1]* I will] Ile *Q*   2–3] *Steevens[3]; prose F;* I will retort the sum in equipage. *Q;* Why, then . . . open. – I will retort the sum in equipage. *Theobald;* I will retort the sum in equipage. / *Fal.* Not a penny. / *Pist.* Why then, . . . oyster, / Which . . . open. *Alexander*   7 coach-fellow] couch-fellow

lost the handle of her fan, I took't upon mine honour
thou hadst it not.

PISTOL   Didst not thou share? Hadst thou not fifteen
pence?

FALSTAFF   Reason, you rogue, reason. Thinkst thou I'll   15
endanger my soul gratis? At a word: hang no more
about me, I am no gibbet for you. Go – a short knife
and a throng – to your manor of Picked-hatch, go!
You'll not bear a letter for me, you rogue? You stand
upon your honour! Why, thou unconfinable baseness,   20
it is as much as I can do to keep the terms of my
honour precise. Ay, ay, I myself, sometimes, leaving
the fear of God on the left hand, and hiding mine

is mentioned in *CE* 3.1.31 as that of a
servant and in *MM* 3.2.79 with reference, presumably, to a whore. Pistol
steals from the menial and disreputable people among whom he moves.

11 **handle . . . fan** Fans had long handles
of ivory or precious metals, possibly
the only valuable object in the possession of such a person as Mistress
Bridget.
   took't . . . honour gave my word of
honour that

13–14 Falstaff is exposed as the master-
mind behind Pistol's thefts (and presumably those of Nim, who is hanged
for them in *H5*).

15 **Reason** not a verb but a noun (cf.
1.1.196n.): '[it is] right' (that Falstaff
should get some recompense for
endangering his soul by forswearing –
cf. 'I am damned in hell for swearing'
at 8–9)

15–16 **I'll . . . gratis** I should risk eternal
damnation without any reward

16 **At a word** in short (see 1.1.99n.); also
'I mean what I say' (see 1.3.14n.)

16–17 **hang . . . me** stop pestering me;
fasten no more crimes on me (Ard²)

17 **gibbet** gallows – quibbling on *hang
about*

17–18 **a . . . throng** the basic requirements for a pickpocket: a crowd
(*throng*) among which to move cutting
purse-strings

18 **manor of Picked-hatch** Pistol's
manor (country residence of the nobil-
ity) is but a disreputable house entered
through a half-door surmounted by a
row of pikes (*OED* Picked-hatch *sb.*);
with a possible pun on the 'manners' of
a place where what is 'picked' is not a
hatch, but people's pockets.

19–20 **stand upon** insist upon (your pretence to being honourable)

20 **unconfinable baseness** boundless
infamy

21 **as much . . . do** The emphasis is on *I*:
Falstaff contrasts himself with Pistol
(RP).

21–2 **terms . . . precise** my reputation of
honour unstained

22 **Ay, ay, I** in F 'I, I, I', but at the time
the affirmative 'ay' was spelt like the
pronoun, and the interjection 'ay, ay'
was used in the sense 'true it is that'.
Ultimately, though, it is up to the actor
whether to emphasize only one or all
three as personal pronouns.

22–3 **leaving . . . hand** disregarding the
fear of God

18 throng –] *(throng,)*; throng *Q;* thong *Pope*   Picked-hatch, go!] *Q (*pickt hatch, goe.*); Pickt-
hatch:* goe, *F*   22 Ay, ay, I] *Cam¹;* I, I, I *F;* I, I *Q;* I *Pope;* I, ay, I *White*   23 God] *Q;* heauen *F*

honour in my necessity, am fain to shuffle, to hedge,
and to lurch; and yet, you rogue, will ensconce your   25
rags, your cat-a-mountain looks, your red-lattice
phrases, and your bold beating oaths, under the shelter
of your honour! You will not do it! You!

PISTOL   I do relent. What would thou more of man?

[*Enter* ROBIN.]

ROBIN   Sir, here's a woman would speak with you.   30
FALSTAFF   Let her approach.

Enter Mistress QUICKLY.

24–5 **fain . . . lurch** likely to commit dishonest actions – such as cheating (*shuffle*), deceiving (*hedge* means 'use devious methods'), dissimulating (*lurch* means either 'lurk', 'hide' [*OED v.*[1] 1] or 'steal' [*OED v.*[1] 3])

25 **you rogue** both vocative and subject of the sentence. There is no need to emend either to 'you, rogue' or to 'you, you rogue'.

26 **cat-a-mountain looks** face (or figure) like a wildcat's – 'cat-a-mountain' described any wild feline animal, including the leopard and the panther, and was later used of any wild man from the mountains (*OED sb.* 2). Pistol had called Evans *mountain-foreigner* (see 1.1.148n.) and is now repaid by Falstaff in the same coin.

26–7 **red-lattice phrases** ale-house language. Instead of glass, tavern windows had wooden lattices painted red that served also as shop signs. Cf. *2H4* 2.2.79–81, where the page says of red-faced Bardolph ''A calls me . . . through a red lattice, and I could discern no part of his face from the window.'

27 **bold . . . oaths** oaths as violent (*bold*) as blows (*beating*). The hyphenation in F (see t.n.) suggested Hanmer's emendation 'bull-baiting', referring to the fights of trained dogs against bulls, a popular London entertainment.

29 **relent** not 'repent', a meaning of 'relent' for which *OED* gives a single example, but 'give way', i.e. 'renounce my arguments' (in Q 'recant')
would in Q 'wouldst'; the ending 'st' for the second person singular was frequently omitted in current speech.

29.1–31 Instead of the brief exchange with Robin, Q has a speech of Falstaff's in reply to Pistol: 'Well, gotoo, away, no more', which amounts to Pistol's final dismissal from his service and from the play. In the Q version Pistol is not present at Falstaff's interview with Quickly (32–126) and does not comment on it (127–9), neither does he appear disguised as Hobgoblin in the Herne's oak revels at 5.5.36.1–102. GWW sees in the silent presence of Pistol and Robin in this scene up to 130 'a sure sign of rewriting – or better yet – botching up'.

25–8 yet . . . You!] *F (subst.)*; yet you stand vpon your honor, you rogue. You, you. *Q*   25 yet, . . . will] yet you, rogue, will *Pope*; yet you, you rogue, will *Collier*[2]   27 bold beating] *(*bold-beating-*)*; bold-bearing *(Warburton)*; bull-baiting *Hanmer*; bowl-beating *(Cam*[1]*)*   29 relent] recant *Q* would] wouldst *Q*   29.1] *Rowe*   31.1] *Q; not in* F

179

QUICKLY   Give your worship good morrow.

FALSTAFF   Good morrow, goodwife.

QUICKLY   Not so, an't please your worship.

FALSTAFF   Good maid, then.   35

QUICKLY   That I am, I'll be sworn, as my mother was the
first hour I was born.

FALSTAFF   I do believe the swearer. What with me?

QUICKLY   Shall I vouchsafe your worship a word or two?

FALSTAFF   Two thousand, fair woman; and I'll vouch-   40
safe thee the hearing.

QUICKLY   There is one Mistress Ford, sir – I pray come
a little nearer this ways – I myself dwell with Master
Doctor Caius –

FALSTAFF   Well, on; Mistress Ford, you say –   45

QUICKLY   Your worship says very true. – I pray your
worship come a little nearer this ways.

32, 33 **good morrow** good morning, or
'good day'; Q has 'god den' and 'Good
den' respectively; see 2.1.177–8n.

33 **goodwife** like 'good woman', a current but rather condescending way of
addressing Mistress Quickly (see
1.4.124–6n.), who reacts by disclaim-
ing the use of the expression for her. Cf.
the distinction between *good man* and
goodman, meaning 'husband', 2.1.92n.

34 **an't** if it

35 **maid** unmarried woman, in contrast
with the literal meaning of 'wife'

36 ***That I am** I am in fact a maid, i.e.
'virgin'. These words, omitted in F,
are indispensable to justify what follows.

36–7 **as . . . born** Quickly's strong claim
(*I'll be sworn*) to virginity is contradicted by her confusing the proverbial
'as good a maid as her mother' (Dent,
M14) with 'as innocent as a new-born
babe' (Dent, B4) – a mother cannot be
a virgin.

38 **I . . . swearer** Ironical: Falstaff has
caught the contradiction in Quickly's
words by which she, or her mother,
had been swearing. He may have
understood her to say at 36 'as my
mother was *sworn* (i.e. swore) when I
was born'.
What with me? Why have you come
to me?

39 **vouchsafe** a Quicklyism: what she
means is 'beseech', 'be granted from',
and not 'grant', as Falstaff points out
by using the verb correctly at 40–1.

40 **fair woman** Falstaff has taken note of
Quickly's objection to *goodwife*, but his
use of *fair* is surely ironical; Q has 'faire
wife' at 33 and 'Faire maid' at 35.

41 **thee** Note Falstaff's instant assumption of superiority – or is it intimacy?
(RP).

43, 47 **this ways** mixing up 'this way' and
'go thy ways', a phrase of encouragement; see 130n.

45 **on** go on

32] Good you god den sir. *Q*   33] *(good-wife); Good den faire wife. Q*   34 an't please] ant like *Q*
35 Good] Faire *Q*   36 That . . . I'll] *Q (That I am Ile); Ile F*   36–7] *F lines* sworne, / borne. / ; *Q
lines* was / borne. /   45 on; Mistress] one Mistress *Halliwell (Douce)*

FALSTAFF   I warrant you, nobody hears. – Mine own
people, mine own people.

QUICKLY   Are they so? Now God bless them, and make   50
them his servants.

FALSTAFF   Well, Mistress Ford – What of her?

QUICKLY   Why, sir, she's a good creature – Lord, Lord,
your worship's a wanton! Well, God forgive you, and
all of us, I pray –   55

FALSTAFF   Mistress Ford, come, Mistress Ford.

QUICKLY   Marry, this is the short and the long of it: you
have brought her into such a canary as 'tis wonderful.
The best courtier of them all, when the court lay at
Windsor, could never have brought her to such a   60
canary – yet there has been knights, and lords, and
gentlemen, with their coaches, I warrant you – coach
after coach, letter after letter, gift after gift, smelling so
sweetly, all musk, and so rushling, I warrant you, in silk

48–9 **Mine . . . people** Falstaff reassures
Quickly that those present – Robin and
Pistol – are trustworthy because they
are his dependants. In Q, when
Quickly asks to speak 'in priuate',
Falstaff replies 'heeres none but my
owne houshold', meaning that all other
people in the inn would be loyal to him,
if they overheard the conversation.

50–1 *God . . . servants Cf. *Famous
Victories*, 579, 'God blesse thee, and
make thee his servant', suggesting that
in F 'heauen' replaced 'God' in conformity with the Profanity Act of 1606.

57 **the short . . . it** This is the full form
of the proverb; see 2.1.120n.

58, 60–1 **such a canary** such extremes
(i.e. unlike her usual behaviour).
Quickly probably means 'quandary'
and confuses it with 'canary', the name
of a lively Spanish dance (mentioned in
AW 2.1.74), as well as of the wine that

the Host proposes to drink with Falstaff
at 3.2.79. In *2H4* 2.4.26 Hostess
Quickly accuses Doll Tearsheet of having drunk 'too much canaries', a plural
form that accounts for the F spelling of
the word at 58 (see t.n.).

59–60 **when . . . Windsor** a possible allusion to previous Garter celebrations
like the one heralded by the preparations announced at 5.5.56–73; but
according to Caius (1.4.46–7, 53–5,
114) the court is already in residence at
Windsor during the action of the play.

61, 73 **has** a common form of singular
verb preceding a plural subject
(Abbott, 335)

64 **musk** perfume extracted from a gland
of the male deer
   rushling rustling (alluding to silk
court-dresses) in Quickly's version,
'perhaps by conflation with rushes
moving in the wind' (Ard²)

48–9] Say on I prethy, heeres none but my owne houshold. *Q*   50 Now God bless] *Q;* heauen-
blesse *F*   54 God] *Hibbard;* heauen *F; not in Q*   55 pray –] pray! *Cam*   56] Well, come Misteris
Ford, Misteris Ford. *Q;* Mistress Ford – come, Mistress Ford – *Cam*   58 canary] *(Oxf¹);* Canaries
F   64 rushling] rustling *Oxf*

and gold, and in such alligant terms, and in such wine 65
and sugar of the best and the fairest, that would have
won any woman's heart; and, I warrant you, they could
never get an eye-wink of her. I had myself twenty
angels given me this morning, but I defy all angels in
any such sort, as they say, but in the way of honesty; 70
and, I warrant you, they could never get her so much
as sip on a cup with the proudest of them all – and yet
there has been earls – nay, which is more, pensioners –
but, I warrant you, all is one with her.

FALSTAFF But what says she to me? Be brief, my good 75
she-Mercury.

QUICKLY Marry, she hath received your letter, for the
which she thanks you a thousand times; and she gives
you to notify that her husband will be absence from his

65 **alligant** Quickly's conflation of 'elegant' and 'eloquent', calling to mind 'alicant', the Spanish white wine from Alicante, which may well be the sweet *wine and sugar* mentioned at 65–6 as a tempting present from courtiers to Mistress Ford

68 **eye-wink** eye-flutter, as an acknowledgement; cf. *good eyes* and *oeillades*, 1.3.56–7n.

68–9 **twenty angels** ten pounds, with the usual quibble on the name of the coins; see 1.3.50n.

69 **defy** Quickly means 'deny', i.e. refuse, or 'despise', but the usual sense of 'challenge' is also present.

69–70 **in . . . but** (obtained) in any other way

70 **but . . . honesty** except honestly. Quickly's insistence on honesty is comparable to that of Falstaff and Pistol: three tricksters outdo each other in claiming honesty (RP).

72 **sip** to touch with her lips (without drinking)
proudest . . . all most eminent; a current phrase (Dent, P614.1)

73 **which is more** moreover; but

Quickly, like Dogberry in *MA* 4.2.80–2, uses it in the sense 'still more important', with reference to the social status of the *pensioners*

pensioners not, as generally glossed, 'gentlemen of the royal bodyguard', but Crown pensioners, known as the poor Knights of Windsor, who, in recognition of past services, were required to pray twice a day for the king in return for £18 per annum and clothes. In ranking them above earls, Quickly is not 'confused' (Ard²): she is flattering Falstaff, who must have been one of them (see pp. 20–1).

74 **all is one** They are all the same.

76 **she-Mercury** female messenger (Mercury was the messenger of the gods in classical mythology)

78–9 **gives . . . notify** bids you to take notice. Quickly conflates the common idiom 'gives you to understand' with 'notifies you' (cf. *Oth* 3.1.28–9, 'I shall seem to notify unto her').

79 **absence** absent; so Evans at 1.1.246. Is Quickly influenced by his confusion of the parts of speech? Or is this a compositor's misreading of final 'c' for final

69 this] *of a* Collier²   75 But . . . Be] Nay prethy be *Q*

house between ten and eleven.   80

FALSTAFF   Ten and eleven.

QUICKLY   Ay, forsooth; and then you may come and see
the picture, she says, that you wot of. Master Ford her
husband will be from home. Alas, the sweet woman
leads an ill life with him: he's a very jealousy man; she   85
leads a very frampold life with him, good heart.

FALSTAFF   Ten and eleven. Woman, commend me to
her; I will not fail her.

QUICKLY   Why, you say well. But I have another messenger to your worship. Mistress Page hath her hearty   90
commendations to you too; and let me tell you in your
ear she's as fartuous a civil modest wife, and one – I tell
you – that will not miss you morning nor evening
prayer, as any is in Windsor, whoe'er be the other; and
she bade me tell your worship that her husband is   95
seldom from home, but she hopes there will come a
time. I never knew a woman so dote upon a man –
surely I think you have charms, la; yes, in truth.

't' in the copy? It appears that Shakespeare in his handwriting sometimes
omitted the final 'e' in words ending
with 'ce' (RP).

80 **between . . . eleven** i.e. later the same
morning. In Q the assignation is
between eight and nine of the next day;
see 2.1.209 SDn.

82–3 **see the picture** The usual pretext
for visiting a stranger was to view some
remarkable object in the house.

83 **that . . . of** *wot*, supposedly the second
person present of the verb 'to wit', i.e.
know. There is a heavy hint of complicity in the phrase (RP).

84 **from** away from (also at 96)

85 **jealousy man** jealous man: an
Evansism rather than a Quicklyism
(see 79n.), but possibly Quickly is here
conflating 'jealous' with 'lousy'

86 **frampold** cross, disagreeable. *OED*
gives this as the earliest example of the
word; cf. *TNK* 3.5.58: 'Now to be
frampul, now to piss o'th' nettle' (RP).

89–90 **messenger** message (in Quicklyese)

90 **hath** gives, sends

92 **fartuous** Quickly's comic deforma-
tion of 'virtuous' ('virtue' was at times
spelt and pronounced 'vartue')

93 **miss you** *you* is merely for emphasis,
another case of 'ethic dative'; see
1.3.55n.

94 **whoe'er . . . other** whatever the competition (RP). By using *other* for the
plural, as was common at the time,
Quickly makes it sound as if there were
only one other virtuous wife in
Windsor.

98, 100 **charms** magic spells – at 98 Q has
'inchantments'

80 ten and eleven] eight and nine *Q*   81] So betweene eight and nine: *Q*   83–4 Master . . . home]
for then her husband goes a birding *Q*   85 jealousy man] *(*iealousie-man*)*   87–8] *F lines* eleuen. /
fail her. /

183

FALSTAFF   Not I, I assure thee. Setting the attraction of
    my good parts aside, I have no other charms.   100

QUICKLY   Blessing on your heart for't.

FALSTAFF   But I pray thee, tell me this: has Ford's wife
    and Page's wife acquainted each other how they love
    me?

QUICKLY   O God, no, sir: that were a jest indeed! They   105
    have not so little grace, I hope; that were a trick indeed!
    But Mistress Page would desire you to send her your
    little page, of all loves: her husband has a marvellous
    infection to the little page; and truly Master Page is an
    honest man – never a wife in Windsor leads a better life   110
    than she does: do what she will, say what she will, take
    all, pay all, go to bed when she list, rise when she list,
    all is as she will, and truly she deserves it, for if there
    be a kind woman in Windsor, she is one. You must send
    her your page, no remedy.   115

FALSTAFF   Why, I will.

QUICKLY   Nay, but do so then, and, look you, he may
    come and go between you both; and in any case have a
    nay-word, that you may know one another's mind, and
    the boy never need to understand anything; for 'tis not   120

---

100 **parts** physical and mental personal
    qualities
101 **Blessing** The proverbial form is
    'God's blessing' (Dent, G266), but see
    50–1n.
105 ***O . . . sir** It is more probable that
    these words, not found in F, were
    omitted from it for censorial reasons
    rather than added by the compiler of
    the Q version.
    that . . . indeed Are you joking? A
    common expression (Dent, J41.1); see
    Slender at 3.4.56–7.
106 **grace** sense of propriety (*OED sb.*
    12b)
108 **of all loves** for love's sake – an

emphatic expression found also in
MND 2.2.154, 'Speak, of all loves!'
109 **infection to** affection for; Quickly
    shares this blunder with Old Gobbo in
    MV 2.2.125–6 'He hath a great infec-
    tion . . . to serve –'.
111–12 **take all, pay all** a proverbial
    phrase (Dent, A203) meaning 'have
    full control in money matters'
112 **list** pleases
115 **no remedy** it can't be helped (Ard²),
    that's certain (Oxf¹, that compares
    1.3.30 in the sense 'no alternative'); cf.
    Dent, RR3.
119 **nay-word, that** private language or
    password (see 5.2.5), so that

100 I... charms] I vse no other inchantments Q   101 Blessing] God's blessing *(Oxf)*   105 O...
sir] *Q; not in F*   that] there *Q*

good that children should know any wickedness. Old
folks, you know, have discretion, as they say, and know
the world.

FALSTAFF   Fare thee well, commend me to them both.
There's my purse; I am yet thy debtor. – Boy, go along   125
with this woman. – This news distracts me.

                    [*Exeunt Mistress Quickly and Robin.*]

PISTOL   This punk is one of Cupid's carriers.
Clap on more sails, pursue, up with your fights,
Give fire! She is my prize, or ocean whelm them all! [*Exit.*]

FALSTAFF   Sayst thou so, old Jack? Go thy ways, I'll   130
make more of thy old body than I have done. Will they
yet look after thee? Wilt thou, after the expense of so
much money, be now a gainer? Good body, I thank

125 **yet** still (a common meaning of the
adverb at the time; see 132). Falstaff
apologizes for the small sum in his
purse.
126 **distracts me** 'diverts me', meaning
both 'perplexes' and 'amuses me', but
also suggesting the basic meaning of
'distract' in Shakespeare, i.e. 'drive
mad'
127–9 In the Q version Pistol is not on
stage (see 29.1–31n.). This speech
seems an authorial afterthought serving a dual purpose: to keep Pistol in the
play in view of his appearance as
Hobgoblin at 5.5.36.3; and to hint at
the reasons for his marriage to Hostess
Quickly that, given as a *fait accompli* in
H5, might well have disconcerted the
audience of that play. The conquest of
Quickly is described in terms of a sea
battle: the metaphor of a sailing vessel
for a female go-between is implicit in
the greeting to the Nurse approaching
Romeo and Mercutio in *RJ* 2.4.102, 'A
sail, a sail!'
127 **punk** prostitute, bawd. In view of
developments in *H5* (see 127–9n.),
Warburton emended to 'pink' (small
coasting vessel), in keeping with the

nautical imagery; but surely Pistol is
beyond such niceties.
Cupid's carriers messengers from
the god of love, i.e. panders
128 **Clap on** hoist (more sails for pursuit); cf. Troilus's nautical metaphor
in *TC* 1.1.103–4: 'Ourself the merchant, and this sailing Pandar / Our
doubtful hope, our convoy, and our
bark.'
fights canvas screens for the protection of the crew during sea-fights
129 Discharge the artillery: either I conquer her (*prize* meaning 'captured
prey'), or let the sea submerge (*whelm*
meaning 'overwhelm') all such ships.
130–5 Falstaff's self-addressed soliloquy
shares the same reassuring tone with
Pistol's comment on Quickly.
130 **Sayst thou so** Is it so? Falstaff had
started talking to himself, oblivious of
Pistol's presence, at 126.
Go thy ways an expression of self-
encouragement; see 43, 47n.
131 **make more** think more highly
132 **yet . . . thee** still consider you worthy
of their 'good eyes'; see 1.3.56–7n.
132–3 **expense . . . money** i.e. in food
and drink (Oxf[1])

126 SD] *Rowe; Exit Mistresse Quickly. Q*   127 SP] *(Pist.); Pist.[aside] Kittredge*   129 SD] *Rowe*

thee. Let them say 'tis grossly done – so it be fairly
done, no matter.   135

Enter BARDOLPH.

BARDOLPH   Sir John, there's one Master Brook below
would fain speak with you and be acquainted with you
– and hath sent your worship a morning's draught of
sack.

FALSTAFF   Brook is his name?   140

BARDOLPH   Ay, sir.

FALSTAFF   Call him in.   [*Exit Bardolph.*]
Such brooks are welcome to me, that o'erflows such
liquor. Ah ha, Mistress Ford and Mistress Page, have
I encompassed you? Go to, *via*!   145

Enter FORD *as* BROOK [*introduced by* BARDOLPH].

FORD   God bless you, sir.

FALSTAFF   And you, sir. Would you speak with me?

134 **grossly** clumsily, indelicately, but
  also with reference to the large size
  ('gross' meaning 'fat') of his body, and
  to the action undertaken (*'tis grossly
  done*), either in seducing the Windsor
  wives or in obtaining cash
134–5 **so ... done** provided that it is done
  successfully (*fairly*), as well as 'made
  handsomely' (of his body)
136 ***Brook** Ford's assumed name in the
  Q version is appropriate, since a brook
  is a small stream easily 'forded'. The
  reasons for the change from 'Brook' to
  'Broome' in F are discussed on pp.
  50–2.
137 **fain** like to, desire to
138–9 **draught of sack** cup of wine (for
  sack see   2.1.8n.).   Presumably
  Bardolph as drawer (151) enters carry-

ing the cup.
143 **brooks** The obvious pun on Ford's
  assumed name is conclusive evidence
  that the change to 'Broome' was forced
  upon the author at a late stage; see pp.
  51–2.
  o'erflows overflow with – the third
  person plural in *s* is extremely common
  in Shakespeare (Abbott, 333).
145 **encompassed**   compassed,   i.e.
  caught (*OED* Compass *v.*[1] 9), as in
  TGV 2.4.214, 'to compass her I'll use
  my skill', as well as 'outwitted', a usage
  for which *OED* (Encompass *v.* 5) gives
  this as the sole example
  via Italian: 'go!' said at the start of a
  competition, equivalent to 'go to' in
  the sense of 'hurry up' (Ard[2])
146 ***God** omitted in F; see 50–1n.

135.1] *Q; not in F*   138–9 a ... sack] a cup of sacke *Q*   143 brooks] *Q (Brookes)*; Broomes *F*
o'erflows] o'erflow with *Pope*   145 encompassed you] caught you a the hip *Q*   145.1] *Theobald
(subst.); Enter* Foord *disguised like* Brooke. *Q; not in F*   146 God bless] *Oxf*; 'Blesse *F*; God saue *Q*

FORD   I make bold, to press with so little preparation upon you.

FALSTAFF   You're welcome. What's your will? – Give us   150
leave, drawer.   [*Exit Bardolph.*]

FORD   Sir, I am a gentleman that have spent much; my name is Brook.

FALSTAFF   Good Master Brook, I desire more acquaintance of you.   155

FORD   Good Sir John, I sue for yours; not to charge you, for I must let you understand I think myself in a better plight for a lender than you are, the which hath something emboldened me to this unseasoned intrusion; for they say if money go before, all ways do lie open.   160

FALSTAFF   Money is a good soldier, sir, and will on.

FORD   Truth, and I have a bag of money here troubles me. If you will help to bear it, Sir John, take all, or half, for easing me of the carriage.

FALSTAFF   Sir, I know not how I may deserve to be your   165
porter.

FORD   I will tell you, sir, if you will give me the hearing.

FALSTAFF   Speak, good Master Brook; I shall be glad to be your servant.

148 **make bold** presume
  preparation forewarning
150 **What's . . . will?** a courteous form: 'What can I do for you?' (Oxf[1])
150–1 **Give us leave** Please, leave us; Falstaff uses a formal expression, as if he were not familiar with Bardolph, now the inn's drawer.
154–5 **I . . . you** another polite formula, used also by Bottom to the Fairies in *MND* 3.1.182, 188–9, 195
156 **charge** load (you with expense)
158–9 **something** somewhat, in some measure
159 **unseasoned** unseasonable, ill-timed

160 **if . . . open** a proverb (Dent, M1050)
161 Falstaff gives a proverbial turn to his reply; *will on* means 'will go forward'.
163 **take . . . half** Collier's transposition of *all* and *half* ignores the pretence at courtesy in Ford's speech: considering the bag of money a burden, he asks Falstaff to take it from him, or at least, if it is too heavy, to relieve him of half the load.
164 **carriage** burden of carrying it
167 **give . . . hearing** Ford treats Falstaff as a judge, who grants hearings to the parties in court.

151 SD] *Theobald*   163 all, or half] half, or all *Collier[2]*   165 Sir . . . may] O Lord, would I could tell how to *Q*

FORD Sir, I hear you are a scholar – I will be brief with 170
you – and you have been a man long known to me,
though I had never so good means as desire to make
myself acquainted with you. I shall discover a thing to
you, wherein I must very much lay open mine own
imperfection. But, good Sir John, as you have one eye 175
upon my follies, as you hear them unfolded, turn
another into the register of your own, that I may pass
with a reproof the easier, sith you yourself know how
easy it is to be such an offender.

FALSTAFF Very well, sir, proceed. 180

FORD There is a gentlewoman in this town, her husband's name is Ford.

FALSTAFF Well, sir.

FORD I have long loved her, and, I protest to you,
bestowed much on her, followed her with a doting 185
observance, engrossed opportunities to meet her, fee'd
every slight occasion that could but niggardly give me
sight of her: not only bought many presents to give her,
but have given largely to many, to know what she would
have given. Briefly, I have pursued her as love hath 190
pursued me, which hath been on the wing of all

---

170 **scholar** learned person; also the Host
at 1.3.2 had asked Falstaff to *speak
scholarly*, but this does not warrant the
Cam[1] editors' assumption that *MW* is
the remake of a lost earlier comedy in
which the equivalent of Falstaff was a
scholar or pedant
172 **had . . . desire** have always had a
greater wish than I have had means
173 **discover** reveal; cf. *lay open* at 174
and *unfolded* at 176.
177 **register** record – an allusion to the
book into which the 'recording angel'
enters the good actions and the sins of
men
177–8 **pass . . . easier** get off with a
milder reproof. Dent (I27) sees here a
reference to the proverb 'He that
speaks ill of another let him first think

of himself', but RP finds that the principle invoked is 'Judge not that ye be
not judged', referring to the pleas to
save the life of Claudio, condemned to
death for lechery, in *MM* 2.1.4–16 and
2.2.136–41.
178 **sith** an obsolete form of 'since'
185–6 **doting observance** deference
typical of an infatuated (*doting*) person
186 **engrossed** collected
186–7 **fee'd . . . occasion** procured (*fee'd*
means 'paid a fee for') even the slight-
est opportunity
187 **but niggardly** even grudgingly
189–90 **would have given** would have
liked to receive
191–2 **on . . . occasions** taking all possible opportunities

occasions. But whatsoever I have merited, either in my
mind or in my means, meed, I am sure, I have received
none – unless experience be a jewel, that I have
purchased at an infinite rate, and that hath taught me   195
to say this:
 Love like a shadow flies, when substance love
    pursues,
 Pursuing that that flies, and flying what pursues.

FALSTAFF   Have you received no promise of satisfaction
at her hands?   200

FORD   Never.

FALSTAFF   Have you importuned her to such a purpose?

FORD   Never.

FALSTAFF   Of what quality was your love, then?

FORD   Like a fair house built on another man's ground, so   205
that I have lost my edifice by mistaking the place where
I erected it.

FALSTAFF   To what purpose have you unfolded this to
me?

193 **meed** reward, recompense (an
emphatic transposition of object and
verb)
194–5 **that . . . that** Theobald and Cam[1]
place a semicolon or full stop after
jewel, beginning a new sentence with
the first *that* ('I have purchased *that*
. . ., and *that* [i.e.'it'] hath taught me
. . .'). But the F reading is correct:
'unless experience be a jewel that [i.e.
which] I have purchased . . ., and *that*
[experience] hath taught me . . .'.
197–8 The couplet versifies the proverb
'Love, like a shadow, flies one following and pursues one fleeing' (Dent,
L518), introducing a pun on *substance*:
1) the opposite of *shadow*; 2) wealth
(alluding to the sums he pretends to
have spent to secure the woman's
love).
199 **satisfaction** perhaps mildly euphemistic, like Juliet to Romeo in *RJ*

2.2.126: 'What satisfaction canst thou
have tonight?' (RP)
202 **importuned** impòrtuned; another
euphemistic expression; see 199n.
204 **quality** sort
205–7 Ford again in this case adapts a
proverbial saying: 'Who builds upon
another's ground loses both mortar
and stones' (Dent, G470). Little credit
has been given to the notion that this
alludes to Burbage's Theatre being
built on land the lease for which
expired in April 1597; it was then
demolished and its timbers were used
to build the Globe in 1599 (see note 1
on p. 20). The use of *erected* instead of
'built' at 207 may be a perhaps unconscious sexual innuendo; RP refers to
Tim 4.3.163–4: 'your activity may
defeat and quell / The source of all
erection', and cf. 3.5.38n.
208 **unfolded** revealed, told

194 jewel, that] Jewel that *F4;* Jewel *Rowe;* jewel; that *Theobald;* jewel. That *Cam[1]*

FORD   When I have told you that I have told you all. Some   210
      say that, though she appear honest to me, yet in other
      places she enlargeth her mirth so far that there is
      shrewd construction made of her. Now, Sir John, here
      is the heart of my purpose: you are a gentleman of
      excellent breeding, admirable discourse, of great   215
      admittance, authentic in your place and person,
      generally allowed for your many warlike, courtlike and
      learned preparations –

FALSTAFF   O, sir!

FORD   Believe it, for you know it. [*Points to the bag.*]   220
      There is money: spend it, spend it, spend more, spend
      all I have; only give me so much of your time in
      exchange of it, as to lay an amiable siege to the honesty
      of this Ford's wife. Use your art of wooing, win her to
      consent to you: if any man may, you may as soon   225
      as any.

FALSTAFF   Would it apply well to the vehemency of
      your affection that I should win what you would
      enjoy? Methinks you prescribe to yourself very
      preposterously.   230

FORD   O, understand my drift. She dwells so securely on

---

211 **appear . . . me** behaves as a chaste
   woman in my presence
212 **enlargeth her mirth** gives free rein
   to her wantonness
212–13 **there . . . her** (her behaviour)
   offers grounds for malicious interpre-
   tations (*shrewd construction*)
215–16 **of great admittance** having free
   access to the best society
216 **authentic** respectable (*OED a.* 1)
217 **allowed** recognized, approved
218 **learned preparations** scholarly
   accomplishments (*OED* Preparation
   sb. 4); see 170n.
223 **amiable** amorous; cf. *MA* 3.3.151–2
   'this amiable encounter'.

honesty chastity
224 **art of wooing** a possible allusion to
   Ovid's poem *Ars Amatoria*, considered
   a handbook of courtship, like the 'book
   of *Songs and Sonnets*' mentioned by
   Slender at 1.1.183–4
227 **apply well to** be appropriate to, fit in
   with
229 **Methinks** it seems to me that
229–30 **you . . . preposterously** a medical
   metaphor: you order precisely the worst
   medicine for your ailment; *preposterously*
   carries also the sense of 'perversely' (RP)
231 **drift** intention, purpose
231–2 **dwells . . . honour** relies so much
   on her reputation for honesty

218 preparations –] *this edn;* preparations. F   220 SD] *Oxf¹ (subst.)*   223 exchange] *Q3;* enchange
F   224 art] *(Art)*

the excellency of her honour, that the folly of my soul
dares not present itself; she is too bright to be looked
against. Now, could I come to her with any detection
in my hand, my desires had instance and argument to   235
commend themselves. I could drive her then from the
ward of her purity, her reputation, her marriage vow
and a thousand other her defences, which now are too
too strongly embattled against me. What say you to't,
Sir John?   240

FALSTAFF   Master Brook, I will first make bold with your
money. Next, give me your hand. And last, as I am a
gentleman, you shall, if you will, enjoy Ford's wife.

FORD   O good sir!

FALSTAFF   I say you shall.   245

FORD   Want no money, Sir John, you shall want none.

FALSTAFF   Want no Mistress Ford, Master Brook, you
shall want none. I shall be with her, I may tell you, by
her own appointment; even as you came to me, her
assistant, or go–between, parted from me. I say I shall   250
be with her between ten and eleven, for at that time the
jealous rascally knave her husband will be forth. Come

232 **folly . . . soul** wantonness of my feelings
233–4 **looked against** looked at (with an
  implicit comparison with the sun, that
  blinds those who look directly at it)
234 **detection** exposure (of her misbehaviour)
235–6 **had . . . themselves** would have
  evidence (*instance*) and good reasons
  (*argument*) to be well received
237 **ward** guard, defensive posture (in
  fencing); but 'also often used of a
  fortress or stronghold' (Ard²). RP
  compares the use of *ward* to indicate
  the defence of reputation in *TC*
  1.2.259, 267.
238–9 **too too** an emphatic repetition; cf.
  for example *LLL* 5.2.529 or *Ham*

1.2.129.
239 **embattled** in battle array (against an
  assault)
246, 247 **Want no** do not go short of, or
  without (*want* meaning 'lack')
250 **assistant** Q has instead 'spokes
  mate', i.e. mouthpiece.
251 **ten and eleven** See 80n. Here too Q
  has '8. and 9.', i.e. early the next morning.
252 **rascally** roguish; Q has 'Cuckally',
  i.e. 'cuckoldly', picked up from
  Falstaff's following speeches (256,
  260, 266), but see 258n. for the implications of *rascally*.
  forth out, away from home. Q has
  'from home', as at 84 and 96.

232 soul] suit *Collier²*   238–9 too too] *(too-too)*   250 assistant] spokes mate *Q;* spokesmate *Oxf*
251 ten and eleven] 8. and 9. *Q*   252 jealous rascally knave] *(iealious-rascally knave)*   rascally]
Cuckally *Q*   forth] *F;* from home *Q*

you to me at night: you shall know how I speed.

FORD   I am blessed in your acquaintance. Do you know
Ford, sir?   255

FALSTAFF   Hang him, poor cuckoldly knave, I know
him not. Yet I wrong him to call him poor: they say
the jealous wittolly knave hath masses of money, for the
which his wife seems to me well-favoured. I will use her
as the key of the cuckoldly rogue's coffer, and there's   260
my harvest-home.

FORD   I would you knew Ford, sir, that you might avoid
him if you saw him.

FALSTAFF   Hang him, mechanical salt-butter rogue! I

253 **at night** In fact the next visit of Ford
as Brook to Falstaff does not take place
the same evening but the next morning
(see 3.5). The confusion is due to the
survival in F of the time sequence
reflected in the Q version, where Falstaff's assignation with Mistress Ford
is fixed for the next morning (see 80n.),
so that *soone at night* here as well as at
271 in Q (see 253 t.n.) means 'tomorrow evening', i.e. shortly after Falstaff's ducking in the Thames. For this
reason in Q the action equivalent to 3.5
(Quickly's and Ford's second visits to
Falstaff) takes place *before* instead of
after that reflected in 3.4 (the
Fenton/Anne/Slender scene).
     speed fare
256 **cuckoldly** the adverbial form of
'cuckold' (see 266), i.e. husband of an
unfaithful wife
258 **wittolly** a pejorative equivalent of
cuckoldly, in so much as 'wittol' (283)
is a cuckold who knows and abets his
wife's infidelity; as such he can be
called a rogue (260, 264) or rascal – cf.
jealous rascally knave at 252.

258–9 **for the which** for which reason,
i.e. 'and this is why'
259 **well-favoured** good-looking, i.e.
attractive
260–1 **there's my harvest-home** This
will be the gathering in of my harvest
– the money in Ford's coffer, to which
Falstaff gains access through Ford's
wife ('harvest-home' in the sense of
'final collection of the harvest' is found
also in *1H4* 1.3.34, but in Q is replaced
by 'randeuowes', i.e. *rendez-vous*,
French for 'appointment', 'assignation'). Falstaff implies that the plundering of Ford's coffer is his only
reason for seeking an appointment
with Mistress Ford. Although Ford is
thus made aware of Falstaff's true
motives, his wife and Mistress Page are
never undeceived (RP).
264 **mechanical** base, vulgar (originally
'manual labourer'); cf. *2H4* 5.5.36
'most mechanical and dirty hand'
     salt-butter mean, cheap, avaricious.
Salted butter imported from Flanders
was considered of inferior quality,
used by people too poor or too mean to

253 at] soone at *Q*   256 cuckoldly] cuckally *Q*; cuckoldy *Q3*   260 cuckoldly rogue's] *(*Cuckoldly-
rogues); cuckally knaues *Q*; Cuckold-rogues *F2*   261 harvest-home] randeuowes *Q*

will stare him out of his wits, I will awe him with my   265
cudgel: it shall hang like a meteor o'er the cuckold's
horns. Master Brook, thou shalt know I will predominate over the peasant, and thou shalt lie with his wife.
Come to me soon at night: Ford's a knave, and I will
aggravate his style. Thou, Master Brook, shalt know   270
him for knave and cuckold. Come to me soon at night.

Exit.

FORD   What a damned epicurean rascal is this? My heart
is ready to crack with impatience. Who says this is
improvident jealousy? My wife hath sent to him, the
hour is fixed, the match is made: would any man have   275
thought this? See the hell of having a false woman: my
bed shall be abused, my coffers ransacked, my
reputation gnawn at; and I shall not only receive this
villainous wrong, but stand under the adoption of
abominable terms, and by him that does me this wrong.   280

go the expense of buying English butter (Ard[1], quoting Thomas Nashe,
Pierce Penniless, about a man pretending high social standards but living
with only 'salt butter and Holland
cheese in his chamber').

265 stare . . . wits frighten him with my
looks; see 2.1.125n. Oxf[1] compares *KL*
4.6.108, 'When I do stare, see how the
subject quakes'.

266 like a meteor both as an ominous
sign and as ready to fall on the head

267 thou shalt Falstaff's change of the
form of address to Master Brook from
you to *thou* 'displays his familiarity and
self-confidence' (Oxf[1]).

267–8 predominate over prevail on,
defeat; hinting as well, in connection
with *meteor*, at the astrological meaning: 'be in the ascendancy over' the

zodiac

268 peasant like *mechanical* (264), a term
of contempt

269, 271 soon at night early tonight
(Dent, S639.1), but see *at night*,
253n.

270 aggravate his style add to (*aggravate* meaning 'augment') his title; as
stated in the next sentence. Thanks to
Falstaff, Ford will add to the title of
knave, which he already has, that of
cuckold.

272 epicurean pleasure-loving (like the
followers of the doctrines of the Greek
philosopher Epicurus)

274 improvident rash, thoughtless

278 gnawn at destroyed, eaten away as if
by rats

279–80 stand . . . terms suffer being
called detestable names (Hibbard)

265–6 I . . . cudgel] Ile keepe him in awe / With this my cudgell *Q*   266–7 o'er . . . horns] Ore the
wittolly knaues head *Q*   271 SD] *Q (Exit Falstaffe.); not in F*

Terms, names! Amaimon sounds well; Lucifer, well;
Barbason, well; yet they are devils' additions, the
names of fiends. But cuckold? Wittol? Cuckold! The
devil himself hath not such a name! Page is an ass, a
secure ass; he will trust his wife, he will not be jealous.   285
I will rather trust a Fleming with my butter, Parson
Hugh the Welshman with my cheese, an Irishman with
my aqua-vitae bottle, or a thief to walk my ambling
gelding, than my wife with herself. Then she plots,
then she ruminates, then she devises; and what they   290
think in their hearts they may effect – they will break
their hearts but they will effect. God be praised for
my jealousy! Eleven o'clock the hour – I will prevent
this, detect my wife, be revenged on Falstaff and laugh
at Page. I will about it: better three hours too soon than   295
a minute too late. Fie, fie, fie! Cuckold, cuckold,
cuckold!   *Exit.*

281–2 **Amaimon . . . Barbason**
Amaimon (or Amamon), a name found
in Reginald Scot's *Discovery of
Witchcraft* (1584), and Lucifer, evoked
by Pistol at 1.3.73, are mentioned
together by Falstaff in *1H4* 2.4.336–7
where he ironizes on the Prince of
Wales 'that gave Amamon the basti-
nado and made Lucifer cuckold'. Of
Barbason, a name possibly derived
from that of a French knight, Nim says
in *H5* 2.1.54 'I am not Barbason, you
cannot conjure me.'

282 **additions** titles; cf. *style*, 270n.

283 **cuckold? Wittol?** See 258n.

285 **secure** over-confident; cf. *securely* at
231.

286–8 **trust . . . bottle** Flemings were
notorious for their over-fondness
for butter (cf. 3.5.110n.), Welshmen
for cheese (see 1.2.11–12n.), Irishmen
for strong liquor (*aqua-vitae* is Latin
for 'water of life', also the meaning

of *usquebaugh*, Gaelic for Irish
whisky).

288–9 **a . . . gelding** a curious anticipation
of the horse-stealing episode in 4.5.
It would be unwise to trust a thief with
the task of exercising (*walk*) a good riding horse (*ambling* means 'going at a
comfortable pace'; a *gelding* is a cas-
trated, and therefore gentle, horse).

292 ***God** the Q reading, replaced as
usual in F by 'Heauen'

293 **Eleven . . . hour** See 80n. In this
case Q avoids mentioning the hour of
the assignation, but confuses its own
time-scheme (see *at night*, 253n.) by
introducing before *better* at 295 the
words 'the time drawes on', suggesting
imminent or immediate action.

295 **about** go about, get a move on

295–6 **better . . . late** proverbial (Dent,
H745)

296 **Fie** a current expression of strong disapproval or disgust

---

283 cuckold? Wittol? Cuckold!] *Ard²;* Cuckold, Wittoll, Cuckold? *F;* Cuckold, Wittol-Cuckold! *Rowe*
292 God] *Q;* Heauen *F*   296–7 Fie . . . cuckold!] Gods my life cuckold, cuckold. *Q*

2.3　　　　　*Enter* Doctor CAIUS *and* RUGBY.

CAIUS　Jack Rugby!

RUGBY　Sir?

CAIUS　Vat is the clock, Jack?

RUGBY　'Tis past the hour, sir, that Sir Hugh promised to
　　meet.　　　　　　　　　　　　　　　　　　　　　　5

CAIUS　By gar, he has save his soul, dat he is no-come. He
　　has pray his Pible well, dat he is no-come. By gar, Jack
　　Rugby, he is dead already, if he be come.

RUGBY　He is wise, sir; he knew your worship would kill
　　him if he came.　　　　　　　　　　　　　　　　　10

CAIUS　By gar, de herring is no dead, so as I vill kill him.
　　Take your rapier, Jack; I vill tell you how I vill kill him.

RUGBY　Alas, sir, I cannot fence.

CAIUS　Villainy, take your rapier.

RUGBY　Forbear; here's company.　　　　　　　　　　15

Enter SHALLOW, PAGE, HOST *and* SLENDER.

2.3 The location is a field near Windsor, at
the opposite side of the town from the
place appointed to Evans for the duel,
but the time is deliberately left vague
(4–5: 'past the hour. . . that Sir Hugh
promised to meet'); duels were fought
at dawn, to avoid notice since they
were illegal; Caius says (33) he has
been staying 'two, tree hours', and the
fact that it must now be nearer nine
than eight in the morning is confirmed
by the arrival of the Host and the rest
straight from 2.1 (they have picked up
Slender on the way). In Q there is no
reference to Caius's having waited for
hours: the action is imagined as taking
place very early on the day after 2.2
(see 2.1.209 SDn.).

1, 3 Jack The use of *Jack* instead of

'John', not necessarily a term of abuse
as at 1.4.53, may denote Caius's ner-
vousness, perhaps in view of Evans's
reputation as a fighter, suggested by
Shallow at 2.1.188 ('the parson is no
jester').

6–8 Caius, in his Frenchified English
(though *Pible* for 'Bible' sounds like an
Evansism), is saying that the parson
must thank his devotions for not turning up (*he is no-come*), otherwise he
would already have been dead.

9–10 Cf. the proverb 'he is wise that is
ware' (Dent, T291).

11 de . . . him No herring is as dead as he
will be when killed by me – with reference to the saying 'as dead as a herring'
(Dent, H446)

14 Villainy See 1.4.63n.

2.3] *Scena Tertia. F* 0.1] *Q (Enter the Doctor and his man.); Enter Caius, Rugby, Page, Shallow,*
Slender, Host. F 11–12] Bully moy, mon rapier *Iohn Rugabie*, begar de / Hearing be not so dead as I
shall make him. *Q* 14 Villainy] *(Villanie);* Villan-a *Johnson;* Villain *Dyce²* 15.1] *Q (my Host);*
not in F

195

HOST   God bless thee, bully Doctor.

SHALLOW   God save you, Master Doctor Caius.

PAGE   Now, good Master Doctor.

SLENDER   'Give you good morrow, sir.

CAIUS   Vat be all you one, two, tree, four, come for?   20

HOST   To see thee fight, to see thee foin, to see thee traverse; to see thee here, to see thee there; to see thee pass
thy punto, thy stock, thy reverse, thy distance, thy
montant. Is he dead, my Ethiopian? Is he dead, my
François? Ha, bully? What says my Esculapius, my   25
Galen, my heart of elder, ha? Is he dead, bully stale, is
he dead?

16, 17 ***God** omitted in F, see 2.2.50–1n.
19 **'Give** God give; possibly Slender does
not use the full current form to show
his politeness.
morrow morning; see 2.2.32, 33n.
21–4 **foin . . . montant** The Host exhibits
his knowledge of fencing terminology:
the verbs *foin* and *traverse* mean to make
direct or sideways thrusts respectively;
pass as verb is 'use', 'show' with reference to different fencing moves; *punto*
(Italian) and *stock* direct thrusts; *reverse*
(cf. *punto reverso* in *RJ* 2.4.26) backward
thrust; *distance*, i.e. distance kept from
the opponent (see 2.1.202n.); *montant*
(French) upward thrust. Oxf[1] emends
thee pass to 'thy pass', since *pass* in fencing designated a type of thrust, referred
to by Shallow apropos of Caius's fencing skill (*your passes*, 2.1.202).
24 **Ethiopian** The Host shares Pistol's
partiality for exotic names (see
1.3.85n.). In other Shakespearean contexts (*TGV* 2.6.25, *MND* 3.2.257, *RJ*
1.5.46, *MA* 5.4.38) the word suggests a
dark complexion; is that the case of the
Frenchman Caius?
25 ***François** The Q reading (see t.n.) is
an attempt at reproducing a French

spelling, while 'Francisco' in F looks
like a misinterpretation of Crane's presumably correct transcript by a compositor unfamiliar with French.
Esculapius Aesculapius, the Latin
name of Asclepios, god of medicine
26 **Galen** famous Greek physician of the
second century, mentioned also by
Evans at 3.1.62 and by Falstaff in *2H4*
1.2.117
heart of elder The Host is playing on
the expression 'heart of oak' (*OED*
Heart *sb.* 3; cf. Dent, H309), the hard
core of the oak-tree, said of a strong
person; the elder was instead proverbial for its soft core ('the elder though
fullest of pith is farthest from strength',
Dent, E105.1), so that it could be hol-
lowed to make popguns ('elder-gun' at
H5 4.1.198). 'Heart of elder' means
therefore 'hollow heart' but Caius,
ignorant of the difference from 'heart
of oak', may take it as a compliment.
stale urine (*OED sb.*[5] 1), a jocular way
of calling a doctor since diagnoses were
based on the inspection of the patient's
'water' (see *2H4* 1.2.1–5). The Host
also plays on the other meanings of
stale, as decoy or dupe (*OED sb*[3].1, 5).

16 God bless] *Q;* 'Blesse *F*   17 God save] *Q;* 'Saue *F*   19 'Give] God give *(Oxf)*   22–3 thee pass
. . . stock,] *(*thee passe thy puncto, thy stock,*);* thee passe the punto. The stock, *Q;* thy pass, thy
punto, thy stock, *Oxf*[1]   25 François] *Q (*francoyes*);* Francisco *F* Esculapius] escuolapis *Q*   26
Galen] *(Galien);* gallon *Q* bully stale] *(*bully-Stale*);* bullies taile *Q*

CAIUS   By gar, he is de coward Jack-priest of the vorld: he
is not show his face.

HOST   Thou art a castalian king urinal – Hector of   30
Greece, my boy!

CAIUS   I pray you bear witness that me have stay – six or
seven – two, tree hours for him, and he is no-come.

SHALLOW   He is the wiser man, Master Doctor: he is a
curer of souls and you a curer of bodies. If you should   35
fight, you go against the hair of your professions. Is it
not true, Master Page?

28 **coward Jack-priest** most cowardly
knavish priest; cf. 1.4.109n. and *jackanape priest* at 1.4.102.

30–1 *****castalian . . . Greece** No satisfactory explanation has been found
for this expression, which must have
puzzled even the scribe Ralph Crane
when he hyphenated the first three
words, treating them as a single
attribute of the appellation *Hector of
Greece*, nonsensical in itself (since
Hector was not a Greek but a Trojan
hero) but equivalent to *bully Hector*
addressed by the Host to Falstaff at
1.3.11. Having just called Caius *bully
stale* – alluding to the doctor's diag-
nostic skill in 'casting' (cf. *OED* Cast
v. 40) his patients' urine (see 26n.) –
the Host, in his most emphatic vein,
may now be conflating *bully Hector*
and *bully stale* in gratifying Caius with
the title of the first of the nine
Worthies (see 1.3.11n.), attributed to
him as the supreme ruler of urinals
(*king urinal*). In turn the adjective
'castallian' (Q) or 'Castalion' (F) may
be the Host's transmogrification of
the 'casting' of urine into the water of
the Castalian spring on Mount
Parnassus, sacred to Apollo and the
nine Muses (Ard¹). The least unlikely
other readings suggested are:
'Castilion', with reference to Baldesar
Castiglione, famous for his book of
courtesy, *Il Cortegiano*, 1528, translated into English in 1561 (Oxf¹);
'Castilian', with reference to Philip II
of Castile, the Spanish king hated by
the English (Ard² after Farmer);
'Cardalion', with reference to Richard
Coeur de Lion, the most celebrated
English king (Hanmer).

32–3 **six or seven** Caius is calling on the
people present – actually no more than
six, even including among them,
besides the four newcomers, himself
and Rugby – to bear witness to the fact
that he has been waiting two or three
hours for Evans to turn up. RP offers
two alternative explanations of this
puzzling passage: '(1) *six or seven* could
be Caius's angry exaggeration of the
number of hours he has waited –
rapidly toned down to "two, three"
in response to general incredulity; (2)
six or seven may be a phrase intended
for deletion but inadequately marked,
and so included by Crane in his transcript.'

36 **against the hair** against the grain,
contrary to the principles; proverbial
(Dent, H18)

28 By . . . vorld] Begar de preest be a coward Iack knaue *Q*   30–1] *(*Thou art a Castalion-king-
Vrinall: *Hector* of *Greece* (my Boy)*)*; *Q lines* vrinall. / boy.*;* . . . *Hanmer;* . . . *Castillian*, king urinal; . . . *Capell;* . . . Castilian king, Urinal! . . . *Steevens²
(Farmer);* . . . Castalion [Castiglione] King Urinal Hector of Greece, . . . *Oxf¹*   32–3 stay – . . . –
two,] *(*stay, . . . , two*)*

PAGE   Master Shallow, you have yourself been a great
fighter, though now a man of peace.

SHALLOW   Bodykins, Master Page, though I now be old,   40
and of the peace, if I see a sword out, my finger itches
to make one. Though we are justices and doctors and
churchmen, Master Page, we have some salt of our
youth in us – we are the sons of women, Master Page.

PAGE   'Tis true, Master Shallow.   45

SHALLOW   It will be found so, Master Page. – Master
Doctor Caius, I am come to fetch you home. I am sworn
of the peace: you have showed yourself a wise physician, and Sir Hugh hath shown himself a wise and
patient churchman. You must go with me, Master   50
Doctor.

HOST   Pardon, guest justice. – A word, Monsieur
Mockwater.

CAIUS   Mockvater? Vat is dat?

HOST   Mockwater, in our English tongue, is valour, bully.   55

40 **Bodykins** euphemistic for 'by God's
body'
41, 48 **of the peace** a peace-lover, as *of
peace* at 39, with reference to his title of
Justice of the Peace; see 1.1.6n.
41–2 **my . . . one** I feel an impulse to
join in the fray. The expression 'my
fingers itch' is proverbial (Dent,
F237), and 'to make one' was current
for 'to take part' (Dent, MM2).
Shallow is again in a reminiscent mood
(see 2.1.204n.).
43 **salt** liveliness, spirit, or savour, i.e.
taste – possibly with a suggestion of
salaciousness, sexual drive
44 **we . . . women** proverbial (Dent, W637)
47–8 **sworn . . . peace** under oath to keep
the peace (as Justice; see 41, 48n.)
52 **guest justice** implying that Shallow,
Justice of the Peace 'in the County
of Gloucester' (1.1.4), not being a

Windsor resident, is a lodger at the
Garter Inn, like Falstaff, referred to by
the Host at 2.1.190–1 as *my guest
cavaliero*. Though Shallow is again
called by the Host *Master guest* at 66,
his stay under the same roof as Falstaff
seems unlikely; significantly Q has
'bully Iustice' for *guest justice* and simply 'M. *Shallow*' for *Master guest*.
53 **Mockwater** a jocular new coinage by
the Host modelled on current com-
pounded botanical names such as
'mock-chervil' or 'mock-saffron'
(*OED* Mock *a.* 2b), playing on the
medical practice of casting water; see
26n. and 30–1n. The agreement of Q
and F on the spelling 'Mock-water' (or
'Mocke-water') renders improbable
the suggested emendations 'Muck-
water' (urine used as manure) or
'make-water' (urinate because of fear).

52 guest] bully *Q* A word, Monsieur] *Q* (A word monsire); a Mounseur *F*; ah! Monsieur *Hanmer*
53 Mockwater] *Q* (mockwater); *F* (Mocke-/water); Muck-water *Steevens³ (Farmer)*; Make-water
Sisson (Cartwright)

CAIUS   By gar, then I have as much mockvater as de
Englishman. Scurvy Jack-dog priest! By gar, me vill
cut his ears.

HOST   He will clapper-claw thee titely, bully.

CAIUS   Clapper-de-claw? Vat is dat?   60

HOST   That is, he will make thee amends.

CAIUS   By gar, me do look he shall clapper-de-claw me,
for, by gar, me vill have it.

HOST   And I will provoke him to't, or let him wag.

CAIUS   Me thank you for dat.   65

HOST   And moreover, bully – but first, Master guest and
Master Page, and eke Cavaliero Slender, go you
through the town to Frogmore.

PAGE [*aside to Host*]   Sir Hugh is there, is he?

HOST [*aside to Page*]   He is there. See what humour he is   70
in; and I will bring the Doctor about by the fields. Will
it do well?

SHALLOW [*aside to Host*]   We will do it.

PAGE, SHALLOW, SLENDER   Adieu, good Master Doctor.

Exeunt all but Host, Caius [and Rugby].

56–7 **de Englishman** any Englishman
57 **Jack-dog priest** 'Jack-dog' means
male dog or mongrel, but here it seems
to be simply an 'improvement' on
Caius's previous exclamation *Jack-
priest*; see 28n.
59 **clapper-claw** scratch, beat, thrash
(*OED v.* 1); cf. *TC* 5.4.1
titely in no time; see 1.3.76n.
64 **wag** go (to the devil); see 1.3.6n.
66–8 **but . . . Frogmore** not an aside: the
Host pretends to Caius that he wants
to speak to him in private and must
therefore get rid of the other three by
sending them on some errand to a vil-

lage at the other side of the town
(Frogmore is south-east of Windsor).
Page and Shallow understand the
Host's game and the next three
speeches are in fact asides, spoken out
of Caius's hearing.
67 **eke Cavaliero** The Host adds formal
emphasis to his speech by using
Pistol's language (*eke*, archaic for
'also'; see 1.3.90n.) and, for Slender,
the same high-sounding title with
which he had addressed Shallow
(2.1.176,   180n.)   and   Falstaff
(2.1.190–1n.).

---

59 titely] *Q;* tightly *F*   66 bully – but] *Q (*bully, but*);* (Bully) but *F;* bully – [*To the others, aside*]
But *Capell (subst.)*   67 Cavaliero] *(*Caualeiro*);* cauellira *Q*   68 through . . . Frogmore.] all ouer the
fields to Frogmore? *Q*   69 SD] *Oxf¹*   70 SD] *Oxf¹*   73 SD] *Oxf¹*   74 SP] *Malone; All F; Shal.
Q; Page.Slen. / Capell*   74 SD] *Q (*Exit all but the Host and Doctor*); not in F; Exeunt Page, Shallow
and Slender / Rowe*

CAIUS　By gar, me vill kill de priest, for he speak for a　75
　　　　jackanape to Anne Page.
HOST　Let him die. Sheathe thy impatience. Throw cold
　　　　water on thy choler. Go about the fields with me
　　　　through Frogmore. I will bring thee where Mistress
　　　　Anne Page is, at a farmhouse a-feasting, and thou shalt　80
　　　　woo her. Cried game; said I well?
CAIUS　By gar, me dank you vor dat; by gar, I love you;
　　　　and I shall procure-a you de good guest: de earl, de
　　　　knight, de lords, de gentlemen, my patients.
HOST　For the which I will be thy adversary toward Anne　85
　　　　Page. Said I well?
CAIUS　By gar, 'tis good; vell said.
HOST　Let us wag then.
CAIUS　Come at my heels, Jack Rugby.　　　　　　　*Exeunt.*

76 **jackanape** i.e. Slender. At 1.4.102 Caius had called Evans *jackanape priest*, and see 1.4.100n.
78–9 **Go . . . Frogmore** If you go with me round by the fields beyond Frogmore. The Host, knowing that Caius has heard his instructions to the others about an unspecified errand in Frogmore (see 66–8n.), mentions the village to him as a place to be bypassed by a different route on the way to a farmhouse beyond it. Cf. 'about by the fields' at 71.
80 **at . . . a-feasting** Improvised entertainments at farms in the countryside were not infrequent.
81 **Cried game** No satisfactory explanation has been found for this, which sounds like a hunting or sporting expression. None of the emendations suggested (see t.n.) is convincing. The most likely guess is a hunting cry meaning 'the quarry (*game*) has been sighted' (*Cried* referring to the cry of

the dogs at the sight of it). Caius would take this to refer to *his* quarry, Anne Page, without realizing that for the Host he himself is the quarry.
84 **my patients** The Oxf emendation 'patiences', based on Q, is a 'Welsh plural' inappropriate to Caius. This is not an exclamation of impatience: Caius is telling the Host that he will recommend to his high-class patients (*earl, knight, lords, gentlemen*) that they lodge at the Garter Inn when visiting him in Windsor.
85 **adversary** the Host's joke: he is sure that Caius, with his poor knowledge of English, will understand *adversary* to mean 'advocate', a Latinate term played upon in *WT*, especially at 4.4.742: 'Advocate's the court word for a pheasant'. Cf. the 'explanations' of *Mockwater* and *clapper-claw* at 54–5 and 59–61.
89 Cf. 1.4.54 and 116.

75–6 for he . . . Page] He is make a foole of moy *Q*　77 die. Sheathe thy] die, but first sheth your *Q*
78–9 Go . . . Frogmore] com go with me / Through the fields to *Frogmore Q*　81 woo . . . game;] *(*wooe her: Cride-game,*); wear hir cried game: Q; woo her. Try'd Game; *Theobald;* woo her. Cry aim, *Warburton;* woo her. Cried I aim? *Halliwell (Douce);* woo her. Cried, Game? *Keightley;* woo her. Cried game? *Sisson*　84 my patients] mon patinces *Q;* my patiences *Oxf*　89] Alon, alon, alon. *Exit omnes. Q*

3.1   *Enter* EVANS *and* SIMPLE.

EVANS   I pray you now, good Master Slender's servingman, and friend Simple by your name, which way have
you looked for Master Caius, that calls himself Doctor
of Physic?

SIMPLE   Marry, sir, the Petty-ward, the Park-ward, every   5
way: Old Windsor way, and every way but the town
way.

EVANS   I most fehemently desire you, you will also look
that way.

SIMPLE   I will, sir.   [*Stands aside on the lookout.*]   10

EVANS   Jeshu pless my soul, how full of cholers I am, and

3.1 The location has changed to the other side of Windsor ('through the town to Frogmore', 2.3.68, and 'about the fields . . . through Frogmore', 2.3.78–9), a distance covered by Page and the rest during the time Evans has been talking to Simple at the beginning of this scene (1–34). In Q the Host seems to be accompanied by his drawer, Bardolph, who does not figure in SDs but is asked to take the swords from the contenders at the equivalent of 99.

0.1 Modern editors indicate, taking a hint from Shallow's remarks at 37 and 41, that Evans has a Bible in one hand and a rapier in the other, while Simple carries Evans's gown (see 33).

1–2 **good . . . name** Evans stresses his full knowledge of Simple's identity and status, while he has only Caius's word for the latter's profession (*calls himself Doctor* at 3).

5 **the Petty-ward** In the direction of Windsor Little Park (*Petty* means 'little', from French *petit*); this implies a contrast with Windsor Great Park,

alluded to in the expression *Park-ward*. Capell's emendation (see t.n.) 'city-ward' suggests that Simple has been looking in the direction both of the town and of the park, but is palaeographically untenable.

6 **Old Windsor** a village south of Frogmore, a couple of miles from Windsor

8–9 The expression *most fehemently desire* for 'insist that' and the emphatic repetition of *you* underline the parson's state of agitation.

11 ***Jeshu . . . soul** The compromise adopted by *Riv* between the readings of F and Q (see t.n.) is permissible: in his agitation (*trembling of mind*, 12) Evans would forget the impropriety of using the name of Jesus.

cholers a Welsh plural, like *melancholies* at 13. Craik (Oxf[1]) suggests that Evans, like Quickly at 1.4.86, is mixing up his humours: by *cholers* he does not mean anger but 'melancholy', the cold and dry humour that produces mental discomfort (trembling of the mind).

3.1] *Actus Tertius. Scoena Prima. F*   0.1] *Q (Enter Syr Hugh and Simple)*; *Enter Euans, Simple, Page, Shallow, Slender, Host, Caius, Rugby. F*   5 Petty-ward] *Halliwell (Collier)*; pittie-ward *F*; pitty-wary *F2*; city-ward *Capell*; pitty-way *(Mason)*; pit-way *Collier²*; Pitty-ward *Dyce*   Park-ward] *(Parke-ward)*; park-way *Collier²*   10 SD] *this edn*; Retiring / *Collier*; Exit. *Cam*   11 Jeshu . . . soul] *Riv*; 'Plesse my soule *F*; Ieshu ples mee *Q*

trempling of mind. I shall be glad if he have deceived
me. How melancholies I am. I will knog his urinals
about his knave's costard when I have good opportunities for the 'ork. Pless my soul!   15
[*Sings.*]   To shallow rivers, to whose falls
               Melodious birds sings madrigals –
               There will we make our peds of roses
               And a thousand fragrant posies.
               To shallow –   20
Mercy on me, I have a great dispositions to cry.
[*Sings.*]   Melodious birds sing madrigals –
               Whenas I sat in Babylon –
               And a thousand vagram posies.
               To shallow, etc.   25

13–14 **How . . . costard** From the context
it appears that in this case by *melancholies* (Welsh plural of the adjective
'melancholic') Evans means 'choleric'.
He is ready to knock (*knog*) the doctor's urinal (a glass vessel with a long
neck in which the patient's urine was
collected for inspection – see 2.3.26n.
'stale' and 2.3.30–1n.) about his head
(*costard* is derogatory for 'head', from
the name of a large apple). Taking *urinals* as a euphemism for 'privy parts'
(see 79–80n.), here Evans implicitly
threatens to castrate Caius, as did
Caius him at 1.4.105.

16–20, 22, 24–5, 28 Evans's melancholy
(21 'I have a great dispositions to cry')
suggests to him variations on two consecutive stanzas of Marlowe's famous
song 'Come live with me and be my
love': 'And we will sit upon the rocks, /
Seeing the shepherds feed their
flocks / By shallow rivers to whose falls
/ Melodious birds sing madrigals. //
And I will make thee beds of roses, /
And a thousand fragrant posies'. At 24
fragrant is confused with *vagram*, a
variant of 'vagrant' which has nothing

to do with *posies*, but fits in with the
wanderings of the Jews exiled from
Israel evoked by Psalm 137 – see 23n.;
etc. at 25 indicates that Evans goes on
singing till interrupted by Simple. A
musical setting of Marlowe's song in
William Corkine's *The Second Book of
Aires* (1612) is reproduced in Oxf[1],
Appendix B, p. 225.

23 The shallow rivers mentioned in
Marlowe's song get mixed up in
Evans's mind with the rivers of
Babylon in the melancholic Psalm
137: 'By the rivers of Babylon, there
we sat down, yea, we wept, when we
remembered Zion', or rather the first
line of the metrical version by
Sternhold and Hopkins, 'When as we
sate in Babylon the riuers round about,
/ And in remembrance of Sion the
tears for grief burst out'. A further
mental confusion is suggested by the
version of this line in Q: 'There dwelt
a man in *Babylon*', which is not from
the psalm but the beginning of the
popular 'Ballad of Constant Susanna',
quoted by Sir Toby Belch in *TN*
2.3.78–9.

16, 22, 28 SD] *Pope*   16–20] *Pope; prose (in italic) F*   21] Now so kad vdge me, my hart / Swelles
more and more. Mee thinkes I can cry *Q*   22–5] *Pope; prose (in italic) F*   23] There dwelt a man in
Babylon, *Q*   25 etc.] etc. [*Enter Simple.*] Cam

SIMPLE   Yonder he is coming, this way, Sir Hugh.

EVANS   He's welcome.

[*Sings.*]   To shallow rivers, to whose falls –
God prosper the right. What weapons is he?

SIMPLE   No weapons, sir. There comes my master,   30
Master Shallow, and another gentleman; from
Frogmore, over the stile, this way.

EVANS   Pray you, give me my gown – or else keep it in
your arms.

Enter PAGE, SHALLOW *and* SLENDER.

SHALLOW   How now, Master Parson? Good morrow,   35
good Sir Hugh. Keep a gamester from the dice and a
good student from his book, and it is wonderful.

SLENDER   Ah, sweet Anne Page!

PAGE   God save you, good Sir Hugh.

EVANS   God pless you from his mercy's sake, all of you.   40

---

26 Simple has sighted Caius at a distance
(*Yonder*), coming through the fields
bypassing Frogmore, as the Host had
suggested at 2.3.78–9.

29 *God prosper a standard expression
found, for example, in Q *2H4*
3.2.289–90; as usual F replaces *God*
with 'Heauen'.
What . . . he? Evans asks whether
Caius is flourishing a weapon, ready
for combat. Simple's reply indicates
that he cannot see anything in his
hands.

30–2 There . . . way Slender (*my master*),
Shallow and Page (*another gentleman*)
appear quite close at hand from a different direction from that of Caius,
having taken, as suggested by the Host
(2.3.67–8), a short cut through the
town of Windsor.

33–4 Apparently Evans had taken off

his gown in readiness for the duel;
when he sees that the rest are fully
dressed he wants to put it on again, but
finds it awkward because he has a
naked weapon in his hand (Cam²).

36–7 Keep . . . wonderful This phrase,
modelled on proverbial expressions on
the impossibility of keeping gamblers
from gaming or scholars from books,
has been interpreted as an indication
that, at this point, Evans pretends to be
reading the Bible. Cam¹ advances the
unlikely guess that Evans has been
reading from a book containing
Marlowe's song.

38 Presumably Slender repeats this pro-
pitiatory phrase (see 65 and 103) for
the benefit of Master Page.

40 from . . . sake Ard² quotes Psalms,
6.4: 'Oh save me for thy mercies'
sake'.

27–9 He's . . . he?] *so arranged mod. eds; prose F*   29 God] *Q;* Heauen *F*   34 arms.] arms. [*Reads in
a book.*] *Dyce (Collier)*   34.1] *Q; not in F*   39 God save] *Q;* 'Saue *F*   40 God pless] *Q;* 'Plesse *F*
mercy's sake] *Q (*mercies sake*); F (*mercy-sake*)*

SHALLOW   What, the sword and the word? Do you study
them both, Master Parson?

PAGE   And youthful still – in your doublet and hose, this
raw-rheumatic day?

EVANS   There is reasons and causes for it.   45

PAGE   We are come to you to do a good office, Master
Parson.

EVANS   Fery well; what is it?

PAGE   Yonder is a most reverend gentleman who, belike,
having received wrong by some person, is at most odds   50
with his own gravity and patience that ever you saw.

SHALLOW   I have lived fourscore years and upward; I
never heard a man of his place, gravity and learning so
wide of his own respect.

EVANS   What is he?   55

PAGE   I think you know him: Master Doctor Caius, the
renowned French physician.

EVANS   Got's will and his passion of my heart, I had as lief

41 **the sword . . . word** By *the word* is
meant the Word of God, i.e. the
Scriptures. Cf. *2H4* 4.2.10, 'Turning
the word to sword and life to death'.
Evans appears to be equipped both
with a weapon and with a Bible (see
0.1n.), and in the Q version (see t.n.)
Page comments on it with disapproval.

43 **in . . . hose** without a top garment,
such as a gown (see 33–4n.). 'To be
stripped to one's doublet and hose' was
a current expression (Dent, D570.1),
cf. *MA* 5.1.199–200: 'What a pretty
thing man is when he goes in his doublet and hose and leaves off his wit!'

44 **raw-rheumatic**   cold,   causing
rheumatism

46 **good office** service

49–67 This situation anticipates the mock
duel in *TN* 3.2, where Sir Toby Belch
and Fabian terrify Sir Andrew Aguecheek and Viola/Cesario by turns (RP).

49 **reverend gentleman** respectable
person. Page is pointing at Caius,
whom he sees approaching at a distance (*Yonder*; cf. 26n.).

50–1 **is . . . with** behaves in a way incon-
sistent with

52 **fourscore . . . upward** more than
eighty years. At *2H4* 3.2.210 Justice
Silence says that Shallow had entered
Clement's Inn 'fifty-five years ago',
which suggests that his age in that play
must have been about seventy.

53–4 **so . . . respect** having so completely
lost control over himself

58 **his . . . heart** *his* signifies God's. Evans
conflates the oaths 'God's passion' and
'Passion of my heart!' (Oxf[1]).

58–9 **I . . . porridge** You might as well speak
of a worthless thing. Another biblical
reminiscence (Genesis, 25): Esau sold his
birthright for 'a mess of pottage'.

41–2] *Pope; F lines* Word?/ Parson? /; *Pa.* What the word and the sword, doth that agree well? *Q*
45 for it.] in all things, I warrant you now. *Q*   58 his passion] his – Passion *Staunton*

you would tell me of a mess of porridge.

PAGE   Why?   60

EVANS   He has no more knowledge in Hibocrates and
Galen, and he is a knave besides – a cowardly knave as
you would desires to be acquainted withal.

PAGE   I warrant you, he's the man should fight with him.

SLENDER   O sweet Anne Page!   65

SHALLOW   It appears so by his weapons.

Enter CAIUS *and* HOST [*followed by* RUGBY].

Keep them asunder: here comes Doctor Caius.
They offer to fight.

PAGE   Nay, good Master Parson, keep in your weapon.

SHALLOW   So do you, good Master Doctor.

HOST   Disarm them, and let them question. Let them   70
keep their limbs whole and hack our English.

CAIUS   I pray you let-a me speak a word with your ear.
Vherefore vill you not meet-a me?

EVANS   Pray you, use your patience. In good time!

CAIUS   By gar, you are de coward, de Jack-dog, John ape.   75

61 **Hibocrates** Hippocrates, a famous
Greek physician (fifth century BC) to
whom are attributed the rules govern-
ing the medical profession

62 **Galen** another famous physician; see
2.3.26n.
a cowardly ... as as cowardly a knave
as

63 **desires** desire. Evans's indiscriminate
use of the 'Welsh plural' extends to
verbal forms as well as nouns.

64 **he's ... him** *he* refers to Evans, *him* to
Caius. Page pretends to realize only at
this stage that Evans is the *person* (50)
Caius intends to fight with, a pretence
seconded by Shallow at 66.

66.1 *****RUGBY** Rugby is called upon at 81 in
both F and Q versions. But Q has the
Host at the equivalent of 99 call upon
Bardolph, now in his service (see 3.1n.).

70 **question** discuss the matter between
themselves

70–1 **Let ... English** This pointed allu-
sion to the misuse of English by the
Welshman Evans and the Frenchman
Caius is assigned by Q to Shallow.

75 **Jack-dog ... ape** Caius is playing on
variations of *jackanape* (used at 1.4.102
and 2.3.76) and on the insults with
which he has already gratified Evans;
see 1.4.109n. and 2.3.57n.

59 porridge] pottage *Oxf*   64] Why Ile laie my life tis the man / That he should fight withall. *Q*   66.1
Enter . . . HOST] *Q (Enter Doctor and the Host, they offer to fight.); not in F   followed by* RUGBY] *Rowe
(subst.), opp.* 65   67 SD] *Q (see 66.1); not in F*   70–1 Let . . . English] *Shal.* Let . . . English *Q;* Let . . .
English. [*Shallow and Page take Caius's and Evans's rapiers*] *Oxf*   72 ear.] ear. [*Aside to Evans*] *(GWW)*
74 Pray] [*aside to Caius*] Pray *Cam*   patience. In] *Johnson;* patience in *F;* patience. [*Aloud*] In *Bowers*

EVANS [*aside to Caius*]   Pray you, let us not be laughing
stocks to other men's humours. I desire you in friendship, and I will one way or other make amends. [*aloud*]
By Jeshu, I will knog your urinal about your knave's
cogscomb.   80

CAIUS   *Diable*! Jack Rugby, mine host de Jarteer, have I
not stay for him to kill him? Have I not, at de place I
did appoint.

EVANS   As I am a Christians soul, now look you: this is the
place appointed, I'll be judgement by mine host of the   85
Garter.

HOST   Peace, I say, Gallia and Gaul, French and Welsh,
soul-curer and body-curer.

CAIUS   Ay, dat is very good, *excellent*.

HOST   Peace, I say, hear mine host of the Garter. Am I   90
politic? Am I subtle? Am I a Machiavel? Shall I lose my

79–80 **I . . . cogscomb** Cf. 13–14.
'Cockscomb', like *costard* at 14, stands
for 'head' (actually the fool's cap and
bells). Since Q prints 'knock' for *knog*
here it is unlikely that Evans, as some
suggest, meant to say in both contexts
'knock', i.e. twist the Doctor's privy
parts about his head.

81 *Diable*! cf. 1.4.62n. In this case too Q
has instead 'O Ieshu'.

81–2 **have . . . kill him** Did not I wait for
him in order to kill him?

82–3 **place . . . appoint** Apparently
Caius's challenge to Evans, by which
he appointed the Host of the Garter to
measure our weapon (1.4.109–10), mentioned also the place for the duel. The
Host in turn appointed a different
place for Evans.

85 **I'll . . . by** I call as witness

87 **Gallia and Gaul** There is no doubt
that the Host means the ancient names

of France and Wales, but in fact both
Gallia and *Gaul* designate France
(Shakespeare uses *Gallia* for France at
least a dozen times in *1H6*, *3H6*, *H5*
and *Cym*, while there is no other mention of Gaul in the plays). In his pretence at universal knowledge, the Host
either confuses *Gallia* with 'Galles',
which is the French and Italian name
for Wales, and reserves the rarer name
Gaul to indicate France, or takes *Gaul*
to be a form of 'Gawlia', a pseudo-
Welsh name for Wales (Oxf[1]). Q's
spellings, 'gawle and gawlia', are perhaps significant.

89 *excellent F's spelling 'excellant' indicates that Caius uses, in his sarcastic
remark, the French rather than the
English word.

91 **politic . . . Machiavel** The name of
Niccolò Machiavelli, the author of the
treatise *Il Principe* (1532, published in

76 SD] *Staunton*   Pray] Harke *Q*   78 SD] *Staunton*   79 By Jeshu] *Q; not in F*   urinal] vrinalls *Q*
80 cogscomb] *(Cogs-combe); cockomes, for missing your meetings and appointments Q*   81
Diable] O Ieshu *Q*   84 As . . . you] So kad vdge me *Q*   87 Gallia and Gaul] gawle and gawlia *Q;*
Gallia and Wallia *Hanmer;* Gwallia and Gaul *Rann (Farmer);* Gallia and Guallia *Collier*   89
excellent] *Oxf; F (excellant); Q (excellent)*   90–1 Peace . . . Machiavel] *Q lines* garter, /
Matchauil? /; *F lines* Garter, / Machiuell? /   91 politic . . . subtle] wise? am I polliticke *Q*

doctor? No, he gives me the potions and the motions.
Shall I lose my parson? My priest? My Sir Hugh? No,
he gives me the proverbs and the no-verbs. [*to Caius*]
Give me thy hand, terrestrial; so. [*to Evans*] Give me   95
thy hand, celestial; so. – Boys of art, I have deceived
you both: I have directed you to wrong places. Your
hearts are mighty, your skins are whole, and let burnt
sack be the issue. – Come, lay their swords to pawn.
Follow me, lads of peace, follow, follow, follow.   *Exit.*

SHALLOW   Afore God, a mad host. Follow, gentlemen,   101
follow.

SLENDER   O sweet Anne Page!

[*Exeunt Shallow, Slender and Page.*]

CAIUS   Ha, do I perceive dat? Have you make-a de sot of
us, ha, ha?   105

Italian in London in 1594), had
become in Elizabethan England a
byword for a master of subtle political
intrigue.

92 **motions** of the bowels, the result of
taking laxative potions. See *OED*
Motion *sb.* 11, and cf. 1.1.199n.

94 **proverbs . . . no-verbs** words of wis-
dom and words of warning (Cam²).
This seems the best explanation for *no-
verbs*, the Host's new coinage for the
sake of symmetry with *potions* and
motions at 92: if pro-verbs advise on
what to do (pro meaning 'in favour
of'), no-verbs advise on what *not* to do.

95 ***Give . . . terrestrial; so** The omission of this phrase from F (see t.n.) is a
printing-house accident, an obvious
case of eye-skip by the compositor.
Caius cures the body, man's earthly
(*terrestrial*) part, Evans the soul, his
heavenly (*celestial* – 96) part.

96 **Boys of art** learned fellows

98 **your . . . whole** Cf. the proverb 'It is
good sleeping in a whole skin' (Dent,
S530).

98–9 **let . . . issue** Let us put an end to it
by drinking together; for *burnt sack* see
2.1.192–3n.

99 **lay . . . pawn** a way of saying that the
weapons, collected from them by Page
and Shallow at 68–9, are no longer
needed. In Q, omitting the invitation
to drown the quarrel in a drink, these
words are addressed to Bardolph, now
a tapster at the Host's inn.

101 ***Afore God** This mild oath (calling
God to witness), found in Q and
replaced in F by a non-committal
'Trust me', is more suited to Shallow
than to Falstaff, to whom Q attributes
it at the equivalent of 1.3.30; see
1.3.30–1 t.n.

104 **sot** fool (*OED sb.*[1] 1); appropriately, a
word of French origin

94 SD] *Oxf*   95 Give . . . terrestrial; so.] *Theobald (subst.); Giue me thy hand terestiall, / So Q; not
in F*   95 SD] *Oxf*   96 hand, . . . – Boys] *(hand (Celestiall) so: Boyes); hand celestiall: / So boyes
Q*   98-9 and . . . lay] *Bardolfe laie Q*   100 lads] *Q; Lad F*   peace . . . follow.] peace, follow me. Ha,
ra, la. Follow. *Q*   100 SD] *Q (Exit Host.); not in F*   101 Afore God] *Q; Trust me F*   101–2
Follow . . . follow] come let vs goe *Q*   103 SD] *Neilson; Ex.* Shal.Slen.Page *and* Host. *Rowe*

EVANS　This is well, he has made us his vlouting-stog. I
　　desire you that we may be friends, and let us knog our
　　prains together to be revenge on this same scall, scurvy,
　　cogging companion, the host of the Garter.
CAIUS　By gar, with all my heart. He promise to bring me　　110
　　where is Anne Page; by gar, he deceive me too.
EVANS　Well, I will smite his noddles. Pray you follow.

　　　　　　　　　　　　　　　　　　　　　　　　　　　Exeunt.

3.2　　　*[Enter]* MISTRESS PAGE *[following]* ROBIN.

MISTRESS PAGE　Nay, keep your way, little gallant; you
　　were wont to be a follower, but now you are a leader.
　　Whether had you rather, lead mine eyes or eye your
　　master's heels?
ROBIN　I had rather, forsooth, go before you like a man　　5
　　than follow him like a dwarf.
MISTRESS PAGE　O, you are a flattering boy: now I see
　　you'll be a courtier.

106 **vlouting–stog** flouting-stock, i.e.
　　laughing-stock, a person to be flouted,
　　disregarded or despised. At 4.5.76
　　Evans uses *vlouting-stocks* in the sense
　　of 'jokes, mockeries'.
107–8 **knog . . . together** knock, i.e. put,
　　our heads together (to devise our
　　revenge)
108 **scall** Evans means 'scald', i.e.
　　affected by the *scall*, a scabby disease of
　　the scalp; the adjective is the equiva-
　　lent of 'scurvy', used as an insult. The
　　Welshman Fluellen calls Pistol 'scald
　　knave' no fewer than four times in *H5*,
　　at 5.1.5, 30, 32 and 53.
109 **cogging companion** lying or
　　wheedling fellow; for 'cogging' see
　　OED Cog *v.*³ 5 and 3.3.42; 'compan-
　　ion' is frequently used by Shakespeare
　　in a negative sense; see 'a rabble of his
　　companions' at 3.5.71.
112 **noddles** noddle (Welsh plural),

another jocular name for 'head', like
costard at 14 and *cogscomb* at 80
3.2 A transitional scene, timed to follow
　　directly after the previous ones and
　　intended to gather together in the
　　heart of Windsor most of the cast of the
　　play in view of its centrepiece: the
　　'buck-basket' scene. Q dispenses with
　　the meeting of Mistress Page escorted
　　by Robin with Ford (1–26); the latter
　　enters alone, saying 'The time drawes
　　on he should come to my house / . . . I
　　now will seek my guesse that comes to
　　dinner, / And in good time see where
　　they all are come', which introduces
　　the entrance SD at 44.
1　**keep your way** keep going ahead
3　**Whether . . . rather** Which would you
　　prefer?
5　**go . . . man** a sexual innuendo, appre-
　　ciated by Mistress Page as a courtier's
　　compliment

112 SD] *Q (Exit omnes); not in F*　**3.2**] *Scena Secunda. F*　0.1] *Ard²; Mist.Page, Robin, Ford, Page,
Shallow, Slender, Host, Euans, Caius. F; Enter Mistress* Page *and* Robin. *Rowe*

[*Enter* FORD.]

FORD   Well met, Mistress Page. Whither go you?

MISTRESS PAGE   Truly, sir, to see your wife. Is she at   10
home?

FORD   Ay, and as idle as she may hang together, for want
of company. I think if your husbands were dead you
two would marry.

MISTRESS PAGE   Be sure of that – two other husbands.   15

FORD   Where had you this pretty weathercock?

MISTRESS PAGE   I cannot tell what the dickens his name
is my husband had him of. – What do you call your
knight's name, sirrah?

ROBIN   Sir John Falstaff.   20

FORD   Sir John Falstaff?

MISTRESS PAGE   He, he; I can never hit on's name. There
is such a league between my goodman and he! Is your
wife at home indeed?

FORD   Indeed she is.   25

MISTRESS PAGE   By your leave, sir, I am sick till I see her.

[*Exit with Robin.*]

FORD   Hath Page any brains? Hath he any eyes? Hath he

12–13 **as idle . . . company** as bored as
she can be without falling completely
to pieces for lack (*want*) of company
(Hibbard)

16 **weathercock** alluding to the diminutive size and presumably the gaudy
appearance of the page

17 **what the dickens** the first recorded
occurrence of this common expression, where *dickens* is presumably a
euphemism for 'devil'

17–18 **his . . . of** the name of the person
from whom my husband had him. As
Quickly told Falstaff at 2.2.107–9,
Mistress Page asked for him to send
Robin because 'her husband has a mar-

vellous infection for the little page'.
Now she pretends not to remember
Falstaff's name. Craik (Oxf[1]) detects
here an allusion to the fact that the
knight's name in *1H4* was originally
Oldcastle and had to be changed to
Falstaff for censorial reasons (cf. 'I can
never hit on's name' at 22, and see pp.
28–30). Significantly Fluellen at *H5*
4.7.45–50 also says he cannot remember Falstaff's name.

19 **sirrah** See 1.1.253n.; particularly
appropriate when addressing a boy.

23 **league** bond of friendship
goodman husband; see 2.1.92n.

8.1] *Rowe*   21 Sir John Falstaff?] *Sir Iohn Falstaffe. F; (aside)* Sir . . . Falstaff! *Oxf[1]*   23 goodman]
good man *F4*   26 SD] *Rowe (Exeunt Mistress Page and Robin)*

any thinking? Sure they sleep, he hath no use of them.
Why, this boy will carry a letter twenty mile, as easy as
a cannon will shoot point-blank twelve score. He pieces   30
out his wife's inclination, he gives her folly motion and
advantage. And now she's going to my wife, and
Falstaff's boy with her. A man may hear this shower
sing in the wind: and Falstaff's boy with her! Good
plots they are laid, and our revolted wives share damna-   35
tion together. Well, I will take him, then torture my
wife, pluck the borrowed veil of modesty from the so-
seeming Mistress Page, divulge Page himself for a
secure and wilful Actaeon, and to these violent pro-
ceedings all my neighbours shall cry aim. [*Clock*   40
strikes.] The clock gives me my cue, and my assurance
bids me search: there I shall find Falstaff. I shall be
rather praised for this than mocked, for it is as positive
as the earth is firm that Falstaff is there. I will go.

---

30 **shoot...score** hit with direct aim (i.e.
horizontal) a target 240 (*twelve score*)
yards or paces away. Cf. *2H4* 3.2.46,
where hitting the target 'at
twelvescore' is considered an exceptional feat in archery.

30–1 **pieces out** a sartorial metaphor:
adds to (*OED* Piece *v.* 6)

31–2 **motion and advantage** encouragement (*OED* Motion *sb.* 9) and
opportunity (*OED* Advantage *sb.* 4)

33–4 **hear . . . wind** anticipate trouble (as
a storm can be forecast from the way
the wind blows; cf. *Tem* 2.2.19–20:
'another storm brewing, I hear it sing
i'th' wind').

34–5 **Good . . . laid** Those are good plots
which are laid.

35 **revolted wives** rebels against their
vows of marriage chastity; cf. *TC*
5.2.186 and *WT* 1.2.199

36 **torture** torment

37–8 **so-seeming** i.e. seeming modest

38 **divulge** proclaim (*OED v.* 1b)

39 **secure** See 2.2.285n.
Actaeon See 2.1.106n.

40 **shall cry aim** must look on with
approval; *cry aim* is a current phrase
(Dent, AA1) originated by the cry
'Aim' as applause for successful com-
petitors in archery contests. Cf. *KJ*
2.1.196.

40–1 SD The hour struck by the town
clock could be ten in the morning, if we
consider Quickly's message ('between
ten and eleven') at 2.2.80, which
Falstaff reports to Ford/Brook at
2.2.251; but Ford seems determined to
catch the lovers in the act when he
exclaims at 2.2.293 'Eleven o' clock the
hour', so the clock may now be striking
eleven.

---

35 plots . . . laid,] (plots, they are laide,); plots! They are laid; *Ard²*   37 veil] (vaile)   40–1 SD]
Capell (subst.)   41 cue] (Qu)

Enter SHALLOW, PAGE, HOST, SLENDER, CAIUS,
EVANS [*and* RUGBY].

SHALLOW, PAGE, *etc.*   Well met, Master Ford.   45

FORD   Trust me, a good knot. I have good cheer at home,
and I pray you all go with me.

SHALLOW   I must excuse myself, Master Ford.

SLENDER   And so must I, sir. We have appointed to dine
with Mistress Anne, and I would not break with her for   50
more money than I'll speak of.

SHALLOW   We have lingered about a match between
Anne Page and my cousin Slender, and this day we
shall have our answer.

SLENDER   I hope I have your good will, father Page.   55

PAGE   You have, Master Slender, I stand wholly for you.
– But my wife, Master Doctor, is for you altogether.

CAIUS   Ay, be-gar, and de maid is love-a me: my nursh-a
Quickly tell me so mush.

HOST   What say you to young Master Fenton? He capers,   60
he dances, he has eyes of youth, he writes verses, he
speaks holiday, he smells April and May: he will

---

46 **a good knot** a fine company of people;
possibly with an ironical overtone,
since Shakespeare generally uses the
word in the sense of 'conspiracy': see
Ford at 4.2.112.

50 **break with her** Slender means 'break
my promise to dine with her', but later
developments will prove the break to
be much more drastic.

52 **lingered** remained in town longer
than expected. Shallow and Slender
are not Windsor residents; see note on
Shallow in the List of Roles.

53 **cousin** nephew; see 1.1.6n.

56 **Master** Many editors adopt Q's read-

ing 'son' in view of *father* (i.e. father-
in-law) at 55.
I . . . you You have my full support.

58 **nursh-a** nurse, i.e. housekeeper; see
1.2.3n.

60 **capers** literally, leaps, i.e. exhibits
high spirits; cf. *R3* 1.1.12, 'He capers
nimbly in a lady's chamber'

62 **speaks holiday** uses witty language
suited to the best time of life; cf. *holiday-time* at 2.1.2, and 'holiday and lady
terms' in *1H4* 1.3.46
smells . . . May has all the freshness
of spring (Ard²)

44.1–2 *Enter . . .* EVANS] *Q (Doctor, and sir Hugh); not in F   and* RUGBY] *Malone*   45 SP] *(Shal.,
Page, &c.)*   46 Trust . . . knot] By my faith a knot well met *Q; as aside Ard²*   49–51] *Pope; F lines
Sir, / Anne, / mony / of. /*   56 Master Slender] (Mʳ *Slender); sonne Slender Q*   60 What] But
what *Q*   62 smells April] smelles / All April *Q*

carry't, he will carry't – 'tis in his buttons he will carry't.

PAGE   Not by my consent, I promise you. The gentleman
is of no having, he kept company with the wild Prince   65
and Poins. He is of too high a region, he knows too
much – no, he shall not knit a knot in his fortunes with
the finger of my substance. If he take her, let him take
her simply: the wealth I have waits on my consent, and
my consent goes not that way.   70

FORD   I beseech you heartily, some of you go home with
me to dinner. Besides your cheer you shall have sport:
I will show you a monster. Master Doctor, you shall go;
so shall you, Master Page, and you, Sir Hugh.

SHALLOW   Well, fare you well. We shall have the freer   75
wooing at Master Page's.   *Exeunt Shallow and Slender.*

63 **carry't** succeed in his intent; cf. *carry-
her*, 1.1.220–1n.
  'tis . . . buttons Though the meaning
is clear – 'it can be safely foreseen', or
'it is written in his face' (that he will
succeed) – the expression is puzzling;
buttons has been taken to mean 'May-
blossoms' (cf. 62), i.e. youth and vitality (Ard[2]), or buttons of a garment in
the sense 'he has it in him, buttoned
up, as it were, inside' (Ard[1]).
65 **is . . . having** has no substance, is broke
65–6 **kept . . . Poins** For Fenton as a companion of Prince Hal before his accession to the throne, see note on Fenton
in the List of Roles, and pp. 45–8.
66 **region** sphere, social status
66–7 **knows too much** is too accom-
plished in courtly behaviour (for
middle-class society)
67–8 **shall . . . substance** shall not
restore his fortune by the help of my
wealth: the image is from the practice
of asking a person to put a finger on a

knot while it is made secure by tying it
a second time (Oxf[1])
69 **simply** with no dowry
  waits on depends on
73 **monster** Falstaff is seen by Ford as
one of those prodigies of nature, i.e.
deformed or exotic beings, which were
exhibited at fairs as a popular entertainment. In *Tem* 2.2.30 Trinculo
speculates on the possibility of exploit-
ing Caliban in this way: 'There [in
England] would this monster make a
man', i.e. 'make a fortune for a man'.
74 After this speech Q inserts the brief
exchange, found in F at 3.3.219–20,
between Evans and Caius, about the
Doctor making the 'turd' (meaning
'third') in the company of Page and the
Parson.
75–6 **We . . . Page's** a comment that must
not be overheard by Caius, who appears
now pacified, as shown by his addressing Rugby at 77 as *John* instead of 'Jack',
the name he uses when impatient

63 buttons he] *(buttons, he);* betmes he *Q;* talons – he *(Cam[1]);* fortunes, he *Sisson* 64–6
gentleman . . . knows] gentleman is / Wilde, he knowes *Q* 69–70 consent, . . . consent] liking, and
my liking *Q* 72 you . . . sport] Ile shew you wonders *Q* 75] *Q inserts here Evans's and Caius's
speeches at 3.3.219-20, adding: Sir Hu,* In your teeth for shame, 75–6] *F (lined* well: / *Pages.* /);
wel, wel, God be with you, we shall haue the fairer / Wooing at Maister *Pages: Q;* Well . . . well.
[*Aside to Slender*] We . . . Page's *Oxf* 76 SD] *Q (Exit shallow and slender,); not in* F

CAIUS   Go home, John Rugby; I come anon.   [*Exit Rugby.*]
HOST   Farewell, my hearts. I will to my honest knight
    Falstaff, and drink canary with him.   *Exit.*
FORD [*aside*]   I think I shall drink in pipe-wine first with   80
    him: I'll make him dance. – Will you go, gentles?
ALL   Have with you to see this monster.   *Exeunt.*

3.3   *Enter* MISTRESS FORD *and* MISTRESS PAGE.

MISTRESS FORD   What, John! What, Robert!
MISTRESS PAGE   Quickly, quickly! Is the buck-basket –
MISTRESS FORD   I warrant. – What, Robert, I say!

[*Enter* JOHN *and* ROBERT *with a great buck-basket.*]

MISTRESS PAGE   Come, come, come.
MISTRESS FORD   Here, set it down.   5

79 **canary** Spanish wine from the Canary Islands
80–1 **drink . . . him** drink with him another sort of wine, coming from a cask (*pipe*), first (before the Host has time to do so). There is a pun on *pipe-wine*: 1) wine in a pipe or cask; 2) wine that has the effect of pipe-music, making people dance (see 81n.).
81 **make him dance** Ford plays on the fact that *canary* is the name both of a wine and of a lively dance; see 2.2.58, 60–1n.
82 **Have with you** Let's go with you; see 2.1.141n.
3.3 Located in Ford's house, this is the central scene of the play. In the Q version Mistress Page is not present from the beginning, neither does Robin come in to announce the arrival of his master. Mistress Page enters only at the equivalent of 85 SD and from that moment the action in the two versions

proceeds along parallel lines except for the concluding speeches (219–26): after accepting Ford's invitation to dinner and that of Page's for the next day, in Q Caius and Evans do not indulge in their plan of revenge on the Host, but Evans ends the scene by remarking that 'M.F*ordes* is Not in his right wittes'.
2 **buck-basket** dirty-linen basket. 'Buck' meant to soak clothes or wash them in lye for bleaching (*OED* Buck *v.*[1] 1) and was later used as a noun to designate the clothes waiting for this treatment (*OED* Buck *sb.*[3] 3).
2–3 Mistress Page is asking whether the buck-basket is ready, and Mistress Ford reassures her (*I warrant*) before she has time to finish her sentence.
3 *****Robert** F's reading 'Robin' may be a mistaken expansion of an abbreviated form in the copy, by attraction of *Robin* in the massed entrance SD (see 0.1 t.n.).

77 SD] *Capell*   79 SD] *Q (Exit host.); not in F*   80 SD] *Johnson*   82 SP] PAGE, CAIUS *and* EVANS *Oxf*   3.3] *Scena Tertia. F*   0.1] *Capell; Enter Mistresse Ford, with two of her men, and a great buck basket. Q; Enter M.Ford, M.Page, Seruants, Robin, Falstaffe, Ford, Page, Caius, Euans. F; Enter Mistress* Ford, *Mistress* Page, *and Servants with a basket. Rowe*   3 Robert] *Bowers; Robin F*   3.1] *Ard*[2] *(subst.), after Q at 0.1*

MISTRESS PAGE   Give your men the charge; we must be
    brief.

MISTRESS FORD   Marry, as I told you before, John and
    Robert, be ready here hard by in the brew-house, and,
    when I suddenly call you, come forth and, without any   10
    pause or staggering, take this basket on your shoulders.
    That done, trudge with it in all haste, and carry it
    among the whitsters in Datchet Mead, and there empty
    it in the muddy ditch close by the Thames side.

MISTRESS PAGE   You will do it?   15

MISTRESS FORD   I ha' told them over and over, they lack
    no direction. – Be gone, and come when you are called.

                            [*Exeunt John and Robert.*]

                    [*Enter* ROBIN.]

MISTRESS PAGE   Here comes little Robin.

MISTRESS FORD   How now, my eyas-musket, what news
    with you?   20

ROBIN   My master, Sir John, is come in at your back door,
    Mistress Ford, and requests your company.

MISTRESS PAGE   You little Jack-a-Lent, have you been
    true to us?

ROBIN   Ay, I'll be sworn. My master knows not of your   25

6   **charge** instructions
9   **hard by** nearby
     brew-house outhouse used for brew-
     ing liquor
11   **staggering** hesitating (*OED* Stagger
     v. I.2); but she knows that Falstaff's
     added weight in the basket may well
     make them stagger
13   **whitsters** whiteners, i.e. professional
     bleachers of clothes
     Datchet Mead a meadow by the
     Thames next to Windsor Little Park
19   **eyas-musket** young sparrow-hawk;

'musket' is the male sparrow-hawk,
and 'eyas' was a young hawk taken
from the nest for training – in *Ham*
2.2.339 the children actors are called
'little eyases'.

23   **Jack-a-Lent** puppet – used affection-
     ately like *weathercock* at 3.2.16. A Jack-
     a-Lent (a current figurative expression
     since 1555, Dent, J9) was originally a
     dummy set up to be pelted during
     Lent, and Falstaff at 5.5.127 uses
     the word in the sense of 'laughing-
     stock'.

13 Datchet] *Rowe; Dotchet* F   17 SD] *Johnson (subst.); Ser.* I warrant you misteris. *Exit seruant.* Q
17.1] *Rowe*

being here, and hath threatened to put me into everlasting liberty if I tell you of it; for he swears he'll turn
me away.

MISTRESS PAGE   Thou'rt a good boy. This secrecy of
thine shall be a tailor to thee, and shall make thee a new   30
doublet and hose. – I'll go hide me.

MISTRESS FORD   Do so. – Go tell thy master I am alone.
                                                           [*Exit Robin.*]

Mistress Page, remember you your cue.

MISTRESS PAGE   I warrant thee: if I do not act it, hiss me.

MISTRESS FORD   Go to, then. We'll use this unwhole-   35
some humidity, this gross watery pumpion; we'll teach
him to know turtles from jays.   [*Exit Mistress Page.*]

Enter FALSTAFF.

FALSTAFF   Have I caught thee, my heavenly jewel? Why,
now let me die, for I have lived long enough: this is the
period of my ambition. O this blessed hour!   40

MISTRESS FORD   O sweet Sir John!

FALSTAFF   Mistress Ford, I cannot cog, I cannot prate,

26–7 **put . . . liberty** i.e. dismiss me; *everlasting* is not an ignorant blunder, like
Dogberry's 'everlasting redemption'
in *MA* 4.2.56–7, but adds to the irony
of the expression.

34 Mistress Page, getting ready for her
exit, is prompted to use theatrical language by Mistress Ford's mention of
cue at 33.

35 **use** treat (as he deserves); see *OED v.*
17*a*. RP suggests that the F reading
'vse' is a misreading of 'vese', i.e.
'pheeze', meaning 'fix' (see 1.3.9n.).

36 **pumpion** pumpkin – an alternative
form with a more comically solemn
sound

37 **turtles from jays** Turtle-doves were
emblematic of faithfulness (see
2.1.72n.), bright-coloured jays of
moral looseness; cf. *Cym* 3.4.49–50:
'some jay of Italy / Whose mother was
her painting'.

38 **Have . . . jewel** Falstaff adapts the first
line of the second song in Sir Philip
Sidney's *Astrophil and Stella*, by inserting in it the word *thee* (omitted in Q).

40 **period** full stop, i.e. end, achievement

41 Mistress Ford's ironical mimicry of
Slender's 'O sweet Anne Page'; cf.
3.1.38, 65, 103 (GWW).

42, 64 **cog** lie, fawn; see *cogging companion* 3.1.109n.

---

32 so. – Go] *(so: go)*; so. [*Exit Mistress Page*] / (*To Robin*) Go *Oxf¹*   32 SD] *Rowe, opp. 33*   33
cue] *(Qu)*   34 I warrant] [*within*] I warrant *Oxf¹*   35 use] *(vse)*; vese *(i.e. pheeze) (RP)*   36
pumpion] pumpkin *Oxf*   37 SD] *Rowe, opp. 34*   37.1] *Q (Enter Sir Iohn.); not in F*   38 caught
thee,] caught *Q*

Mistress Ford; now shall I sin in my wish: I would thy
husband were dead – I'll speak it before the best lord:
I would make thee my lady.   45

MISTRESS FORD   I your lady, Sir John? Alas, I should be
a pitiful lady.

FALSTAFF   Let the court of France show me such
another! I see how thine eye would emulate the
diamond: thou hast the right arched beauty of the brow   50
that becomes the ship-tire, the tire-valiant, or any tire
of Venetian admittance.

MISTRESS FORD   A plain kerchief, Sir John: my brows
become nothing else, nor that well neither.

FALSTAFF   By the Lord, thou art a tyrant to say so. Thou   55
wouldst make an absolute courtier, and the firm fixture
of thy foot would give an excellent motion to thy gait,
in a semi-circled farthingale. I see what thou wert if

---

44 **I'll . . . lord** I am ready to proclaim it
publicly; it sounds like a replacement
of the oath preserved in Q: 'By the
Lord' (see t.n., and cf. 55), in order to
avoid the blasphemous quibble Lord
(i.e. God)/lady (woman).

45 **I would . . . lady** Falstaff seems to
have been rather prone to making such
declarations to high and low, as the
Hostess Mistress Quickly reminds him
in *2H4* 3.1.91–2: 'thou didst swear to
me then . . . to marry me and make me
my lady thy wife'.

51 **becomes the ship-tire** suits a fashionable headdress (*OED* Tire *sb.*[1] 3,
from 'attire') in the form of a ship
tire-valiant A nonce compound, it
seems to refer to a particularly impos-
ing (valiant) sort of headdress (tire).
Oliver (Ard[2]), in view of *ship-tire*, sus-
pects a concealed pun on 'gallant' or
'top gallant', the flag borne on the main

mast of a ship.

52 **of Venetian admittance** accepted in
Venice, at the time the centre of fashion

53 **kerchief** head-kerchief or scarf

55 ***By the Lord** Falstaff's frequent oath
in *1* and *2H4*, suppressed in the F version; cf. 44n.
a tyrant cruel, with a possible pun on
tire at 51 (Cam[1]). The Q reading 'a traitor' (see t.n.) may have been prompted
by *1H4* 1.2.146, 'By the Lord, I'll be a
traitor then' (Oxf[1]).

56 **absolute** perfect

56–7 **the . . . foot** your way of putting
your foot firmly down on the
ground: throughout this speech
Falstaff is using a particularly affected
language.

58 **semi-circled farthingale** an ample
and long skirt or petticoat supported
by whalebones, flat at the front and
hooped at the back

44–5 I'll . . . lady] By the Lord, Ide make thee my Ladie *Q*   51 tire-valiant] *(*Tyre-valiant*)*; tire
vellet *Q*; tire-volant *(Steevens)*; tire-velvet *(Tollet)*; tire-gallant *(Oxf)*   51–2 tire of . . . admittance]
Venetian attire *Q*   53–4] *Pope; F lines* Iohn: / neither. /   55 By . . . tyrant] *Collier;* Thou art a
tyrant *F;* By the Lord thou art a traitor *Q*

Fortune thy foe were not, Nature thy friend. Come,
thou canst not hide it.   60

MISTRESS FORD   Believe me, there's no such thing in me.

FALSTAFF   What made me love thee? Let that persuade
thee there's something extraordinary in thee. Come, I
cannot cog and say thou art this and that, like a many
of these lisping hawthorn buds that come like women   65
in men's apparel, and smell like Bucklersbury in simple
time. I cannot – but I love thee, none but thee; and thou
deservest it.

MISTRESS FORD   Do not betray me, sir; I fear you love
Mistress Page.   70

FALSTAFF   Thou mightst as well say I love to walk by the
Counter gate, which is as hateful to me as the reek of a
lime-kiln.

MISTRESS FORD   Well, heaven knows how I love you, and
you shall one day find it.   75

FALSTAFF   Keep in that mind, I'll deserve it.

MISTRESS FORD   Nay, I must tell you, so you do; or else
I could not be in that mind.

59 **Fortune . . . friend** F2 corrects the
mispunctuation in F, which has caused
a number of misunderstandings and
attempts at emendation (see t.n.), due
also to Falstaff's affected transposition
of verb and object in an expression
based on the current phrase 'Fortune
is not my foe' (Dent, F607.1). What he
suggests is that while friendly nature
has endowed Mistress Ford with
beauty, adverse fortune has prevented
her from being a lady.

64 **a many** many. The use of the indefi-
nite article before words indicating
numbers or quantities is frequent in
Shakespeare; see Abbott, 87.

65 **lisping hawthorn buds** budding
would-be courtiers (*hawthorn buds*)
affecting a lisp

66–7 **Bucklersbury . . . time** perfumed
like Bucklersbury – the City street
where herbs were on sale – in summer,
i.e. newly supplied with aromatic
plants used as medicinal simples (see
1.4.58n.). Cf. the Host's description of
Fenton at 3.2.60–3.

72 **Counter** the debtor's prison in
Southwark, across the Thames from
the City, in very unsavoury surround-
ings
reek ill-smelling smoke

59 thy foe . . . friend] *F2;* thy foe, were not Nature thy friend *F;* thy foe were not, nature is thy
friend *Pope;* thy foe, were but nature thy friend *(Staunton);* thy foe were, not Nature, thy friend
Alexander; (thy foe) were – not Nature – thy friend *Ard²;* thy foe, were, with nature, thy friend *Oxf;*
thy foe were Nature thy friend *Oxf¹;* thy foe were not, and Nature thy friend *(RP)*   63 thee there's]
*Q (*thee / Ther's*);* thee. Ther's *F*   73 lime-kiln] *Rowe;* lime kill *Q;* Lime-kill *F*   74–5] *F lines*
you, / it. /   77–8] *F lines* doe; / minde. /

[*Enter* ROBIN.]

ROBIN   Mistress Ford, Mistress Ford, here's Mistress
        Page at the door, sweating, and blowing, and looking   80
        wildly, and would needs speak with you presently.

FALSTAFF   She shall not see me; I will ensconce me
        behind the arras.

MISTRESS FORD   Pray you do so; she's a very tattling
        woman. *Falstaff hides behind the arras.*   85

                Enter MISTRESS PAGE.

        What's the matter? How now?

MISTRESS PAGE   O Mistress Ford, what have you done?
        You're shamed, you're overthrown, you're undone for
        ever!

MISTRESS FORD   What's the matter, good Mistress Page?   90

MISTRESS PAGE   O well-a-day, Mistress Ford, having an
        honest man to your husband, to give him such cause of
        suspicion!

MISTRESS FORD   What cause of suspicion?

MISTRESS PAGE   What cause of suspicion? Out upon   95
        you: how am I mistook in you!

MISTRESS FORD   Why, alas, what's the matter?

MISTRESS PAGE   Your husband's coming hither, woman,
        with all the officers in Windsor, to search for a gentleman
        that he says is here now in the house, by your consent, to 100
        take an ill advantage of his absence. You are undone.

81 **presently** immediately
82 **ensconce** hide (as at 2.2.25)
83 **arras** woven tapestry hung in front of
   the wall – obviously at some distance
   because Falstaff manages to hide and
   fall asleep behind it in *1H4* 2.4.504–50,
   and Polonius, hiding behind the arras

in the Queen's bedchamber, is killed
like a rat (*Ham* 3.4.7–30)
95–6 **Out upon you** shame on you – a
   variant of the very common exclamation of impatience 'out upon it'; see
   1.4.153–4n.

78.1] *Capell; Within. / Rob. (as SP) F2*   85 SD] *Q (Falstaffe stands behind the aras.); not in F*
85.1] *F2; after 73 Q; not in F; Enter Mistress* Page *and* Robin. *Malone*   87–9] *F lines* done? / euer. /
95–6] *F lines* vpon you: / in you? /   100–1 house ... absence.] *(house; ... consent ... absence:);*
house: his wifes sweet hart. *Q*

MISTRESS FORD   'Tis not so, I hope.

MISTRESS PAGE   Pray heaven it be not so, that you have
such a man here. But 'tis most certain your husband's
coming, with half Windsor at his heels, to search for   105
such a one. I come before to tell you. If you know yourself clear, why, I am glad of it; but if you have a friend
here, convey, convey him out. Be not amazed, call all
your senses to you, defend your reputation, or bid
farewell to your good life for ever.   110

MISTRESS FORD   What shall I do? There is a gentleman,
my dear friend; and I fear not mine own shame so much
as his peril. I had rather than a thousand pound he were
out of the house.

MISTRESS PAGE   For shame, never stand 'you had rather   115
and you had rather'! Your husband's here at hand:
bethink you of some conveyance – in the house you
cannot hide him. – O, how have you deceived me! –
Look, here is a basket: if he be of any reasonable stature,
he may creep in here, and throw foul linen upon him,   120
as if it were going to bucking; or – it is whiting time –
send him by your two men to Datchet Mead.

---

102 In Q, before replying, Mistress Ford,
whispers to Mistress Page 'Speak
louder', so that they can be overheard
by Falstaff. See 4.2.14–15n.
107 **clear** innocent
friend euphemism for 'lover'. More
explicitly in Q, at the equivalent of
100–1, Mistress Page says that Ford is
going to search the house for 'his wifes
sweet hart' (see 100–1 t.n.).
108 **convey** Cf. the cant use of the verb
(i.e. steal) at 1.3.26.
amazed bewildered
110 **good life** comfort
112 **my dear friend** The placing of the
phrase is ambiguous: it can be either a
way of addressing Mistress Page or a

reference to the *gentleman*, i.e. Falstaff,
the friend of line 107, who is listening
behind the arras.
113 **a thousand pound** a frequent
hyperbole in Shakespeare (Dent,
T248.1), e.g. Falstaff in *1H4*
2.4.147–8, 'I would give a thousand
pound I could run as fast', and cf. *MA*
1.1.90 and 3.5.24–5, *2H6* 3.3.13, *Ham*
3.2.286–7
115 **stand** waste time (by saying), or 'rely
on' such expressions (cf. *stands* at
2.1.210)
121 **bucking** washing; see 2n.
whiting time time for bleaching
clothes; cf. *whitsters*, 13n.

102] Speak louder. But I hope tis not true Misteris *Page. Q*   115 For shame] Gode body woman *Q*
115–16 stand . . . rather!] stand what shal I do, and what shall I do. *Q*

219

MISTRESS FORD   He's too big to go in there. What shall
I do?

FALSTAFF [*Comes out of hiding.*]   Let me see't, let me   125
see't, O let me see't! I'll in, I'll in. – Follow your friend's
counsel. I'll in.

MISTRESS PAGE   What, Sir John Falstaff? (*aside to him*)
Are these your letters, knight?

FALSTAFF [*aside to her*]   I love thee, and none but thee.   130
Help me away. Let me creep in here. I'll never –
Goes into the basket, they put clothes over him.

MISTRESS PAGE   Help to cover your master, boy. – Call
your men, Mistress Ford. – You dissembling knight!
[*Exit Robin.*]

MISTRESS FORD   What, John! Robert, John!

[*Enter* JOHN *and* ROBERT.]

Go, take up these clothes here, quickly. Where's the   135
cowl-staff? – Look how you drumble! Carry them to
the laundress in Datchet Mead; quickly, come.

[*Enter* FORD, PAGE, CAIUS *and* EVANS.]

FORD   Pray you, come near. If I suspect without cause,

129 **Are . . . letters** 'Is this the way you
keep your protestations of love to me in
your letter?'
130 ***and . . . thee** a phrase in Q possibly
accidentally omitted by the printers of
F, substantially identical to Falstaff's
protestation to Mistress Ford at 67
133 SD Robin is not on stage in Q and no
exit for him is marked in F. It seems
appropriate that he should leave qui-
etly before the arrival of Ford and the

others and not wait till the basket is
carried out at 146 SD.
136 **cowl-staff** a wooden pole passed
through the handles of a tub (*cowl*) or
basket for two men to carry on their
shoulders
  drumble lag, move slowly (*OED*
v.[1] 1). The Oxford editors, by taking
Look to be a misreading of 'Lord' (see
t.n.), make of this sentence not a warning but a disparaging comment.

125 SD] *Capell (starting from his Concealment)*   128 SD] *Q (Aside); not in F*   129 Are . . . knight?]
Fie sir Iohn is this your loue? Go too. Q   130 SD] *(Malone, subst.)*   130–1 thee, . . . thee. Help] *Q;*
thee, helpe *F*   131 SD] *Q (Sir Iohn goes into the basket, they put cloathes ouer him, the two men carries*
it away: Foord meetes it, and all the rest, Page, Doctor, Priest, Slender, Shallow.); not in F   133 SD]
Capell (subst.); in 146 SD Ard²   134.1] *Capell (subst.); Exit* Robin. Re-enter *Servants. / Malone*
136 Look] Lord *(Oxf)*   137.1] *Rowe*   138–40] F *lines* cause, / iest, / this? /

why, then make sport at me, then let me be your jest, I
deserve it. – How now? Whither bear you this?   140
SERVANT   To the laundress, forsooth.
MISTRESS FORD   Why, what have you to do whither they
bear it? You were best meddle with buck-washing!
FORD   Buck? I would I could wash myself of the buck!
Buck, buck, buck! Ay, buck! I warrant you, buck – and   145
of the season too, it shall appear.
                        [*Exeunt John and Robert with the basket.*]
Gentlemen, I have dreamed tonight; I'll tell you my
dream. Here, here, here be my keys: ascend my
chambers, search, seek, find out. I'll warrant we'll
unkennel the fox. Let me stop this way first. [*Locks the*   150
door.] So, now escape!
PAGE   Good Master Ford, be contented; you wrong yourself too much.
FORD   True, Master Page. – Up, gentlemen, you shall see
sport anon. Follow me, gentlemen.   [*Exit.*]

142 **what . . . do** What business is it
of yours? A current phrase (Dent,
DD14, quoting *TS* 1.2.223–4 and
3.2.216).
143 **You . . . meddle** ironical: indeed, you
are the person to deal . . .
144–5 **Buck? . . . you, buck** Ford is playing on the meaning of *buck* as a noun,
which has nothing to do with washing,
but is the male deer or stag, an emblem
of cuckoldry because of its horns.
146 **of the season** in the rutting season,
i.e. when the buck's antlers have
reached maximum growth (Oxf[1])
147 **tonight** this last night
150 **unkennel** dislodge from cover
(used of a fox, *OED v.* 1); cf. *Ham*
3.2.81.
151 ***escape** The F reading is 'vncape',
which some commentators, adopting

slight variants (see t.n.), take as the
equivalent of *unkennel* at 150, i.e. a
further incitement to look for the
intruder. But Daly's emendation
adopted here, implying a possible
misreading of the copy, accounts for
the previous sentence, *Let me stop*
etc., and is dramatically more effective: Ford locks the front door and
defies the hidden intruder to escape.
RP finds palaeographically more convincing Sisson's emendation 'uncase'
(i.e. dislodge, cf. *unkennel the fox* at
150), and quotes Ben Jonson,
Volpone, 5.12.55: 'The fox shall here
uncase'.
152 **be contented** restrain yourself
152–3 **you . . . much** Cf. 1.1.294n.
154 **True** ironical: 'Indeed, I suffer too
much wrong.'

141 SP] *(Ser.); John Ard*[2]   144–6] *F lines* y[e] Buck: / you Bucke, / appeare. /   146 SD] *Rowe*
(subst.) 150–1 SD] *Capell (subst.)*   151 escape] *Daly;* vncape *F;* uncouple *Hanmer;* uncope
Cam[1]; uncase *Sisson;* uncoop *Oxf* 152–5] *F lines* contented: / much. / Gentlemen, / anon: /
Gentlemen. /   155 SD] *Capell*

221

EVANS   By Jeshu, this is fery fantastical humours and   156
jealousies.

CAIUS   By gar, 'tis no the fashion of France; it is not
jealous in France.

PAGE   Nay, follow him, gentlemen; see the issue of his   160
search.   [*Exeunt Page, Caius and Evans.*]

MISTRESS PAGE   Is there not a double excellency in this?

MISTRESS FORD   I know not which pleases me better,
that my husband is deceived, or Sir John.

MISTRESS PAGE   What a taking was he in, when your   165
husband asked who was in the basket!

MISTRESS FORD   I am half afraid he will have a need of
washing: so throwing him into the water will do him a
benefit.

MISTRESS PAGE   Hang him, dishonest rascal! I would all   170
of the same strain were in the same distress.

MISTRESS FORD   I think my husband hath some special
suspicion of Falstaff's being here, for I never saw him
so gross in his jealousy till now.

MISTRESS PAGE   I will lay a plot to try that, and we will   175
yet have more tricks with Falstaff. His dissolute disease
will scarce obey this medicine.

156, 195 ***By Jeshu** Evans's characteristic oath, omitted in F in conformity
with the Profanity Act; cf 2.2.50–1n.

165 **taking** state (of agitation or fear),
OED vbl. sb. 4b

166 **who . . . basket** Ford had asked no
such question, but only 'Whither bear
you this?' at 140, and in the equivalent
passage in Q 'who goes heare? whither
goes this?' But, reporting to Ford as
Brook at 3.5.93–5, Falstaff says 'the
jealous knave . . . asked them once or
twice what they had in their basket'.
Mistress Page, using *who* instead of
what, attributes to Ford what should

have been the question for him to
ask.

167–8 **need of washing** a common joke
on the befouling effects of a fright; cf.
Sir Thomas More, 2.1.45: 'they smell
for fear already'.

170–1 **all . . . strain** all those who share
the disposition (to lechery)

174 **gross** exaggerated; playing also on
the 'grossness' (bulk) of Falstaff

175 **try** test

176 **dissolute disease** lechery (see
170–1n.), considered a sort of illness

177 **obey** respond to

---

156 By Jeshu] *Q; not in F*   156–7 this . . . jealousies] these are iealosies & distemperes *Q*   158–9] *F
lines* France: / France. /   161 SD] *Capell; Exit omnes: Q opp. 157*   163–4] *F lines* better, / Iohn. /
166 who] what *Harness*

MISTRESS FORD   Shall we send that foolish carrion
 Mistress Quickly to him, and excuse his throwing into
 the water, and give him another hope, to betray him to   180
 another punishment?
MISTRESS PAGE   We will do it: let him be sent for tomorrow eight o'clock to have amends.

Enter FORD, PAGE, CAIUS *and* EVANS.

FORD   I cannot find him. Maybe the knave bragged of that
 he could not compass.   185
MISTRESS PAGE [*aside to Mistress Ford*]   Heard you that?
MISTRESS FORD   You use me well, Master Ford, do you?
FORD   Ay, I do so.
MISTRESS FORD   Heaven make you better than your
 thoughts.   190
FORD   Amen.
MISTRESS PAGE   You do yourself mighty wrong, Master
 Ford.
FORD   Ay, ay; I must bear it.
EVANS   By Jeshu, if there be anypody in the house, and in   195

178 ***foolish carrion** a humorous rather
 than insulting use of *carrion* for 'old
 body'; F's 'foolishion' is a mistake
 caused by the running together of the
 two words.
182–3 **tomorrow . . . clock** When
 Quickly carries the message to Falstaff
 (still suffering from the ducking in the
 Thames) early the next morning, she
 gives the time as 'between eight and
 nine' (3.5.44), and shortly after, in the
 same scene (122), Ford remarks to him
 ''Tis past eight already'. Q does not
 mention in 3.3 the time of the new
 assignation. Apparently Quickly's visit
 to Falstaff (the equivalent of 3.5.20–53)
 takes place the same evening of the
 ducking, so that she appoints the meeting for 'to morrow sir, betweene ten

and eleuen'. But the rest of the scene
 (equivalent to 3.5.54–141) must refer
 to the next morning, because when
 Falstaff speaks of 'Another appointment of meeting, / Between ten and
 eleuen is the houre' Ford reacts with
 'Why sir, tis almost ten alreadie.' For
 further time discrepancies between Q
 and F see 2.2.253n. and 293n.
184–5 **that . . . compass** that which he
 could not achieve
187–8 Both Mistress Ford's question and
 Ford's acquiescence are ironical (like
 the next exchange at 189–91): Ford is
 still unconvinced.
192 **You . . . wrong** Cf. Master Page at
 152–3.
194 **bear** endure (the reproach)

178 foolish] *F2;* foolishion *F*   183 eight] by eight *F2*   183.1] *Q (Enter all); not in F*   186 SD]
Capell   187 do you?] do you not? *Oxf¹*   189 you] me *(Capell)*   195 By Jeshu] *Q; not in F*

the chambers, and in the coffers, and in the presses,
heaven forgive my sins at the day of judgement!

CAIUS   Be gar, nor I too; there is nobodies.

PAGE   Fie, fie, Master Ford, are you not ashamed? What
spirit, what devil, suggests this imagination? I would   200
not ha' your distemper in this kind, for the wealth of
Windsor Castle.

FORD   'Tis my fault, Master Page, I suffer for it.

EVANS   You suffer for a pad conscience. Your wife is as
honest a 'omans as I will desires among five thousand,   205
and five hundred too.

CAIUS   By gar, I see 'tis an honest woman.

FORD   Well, I promised you a dinner. Come, come, walk
in the park, I pray you pardon me; I will hereafter make
known to you why I have done this. Come, wife, come,   210
Mistress Page, I pray you pardon me, pray heartily
pardon me.

PAGE [*to Caius and Evans*]   Let's go in, gentlemen; but
trust me, we'll mock him. [*to all*]   I do invite you
tomorrow morning to my house to breakfast; after,   215

---

196 **presses** cupboards

197 **heaven . . . judgement** As Shaheen
notes (143), Evans quotes the Lord's
Prayer (from Luke, 11.4: 'And forgiue
vs our sinnes'), with a further biblical
reference (2 Peter, 2.9: 'To reserve the
vniust vnto the daye of iudgement to
be punished'), but in fact he means
the contrary: 'if there is somebody in
the house, may heaven *not* forgive my
sins. . .'.

200 **spirit** i.e. evil spirit, fiend

201 **distemper** Jealousy is considered an
illness, like lechery in the case of
Falstaff at 176; in fact *dis-temper* is
most appropriate, since its basic meaning is 'lack of temper', i.e. lack of

moderation, control.

203 **fault** weakness or misfortune, like
distemper at 201

205 **will desires** would wish to find

208–9 **walk . . . park** go for a walk in
Windsor Park till dinner-time

212 Probably Cam[1] is right in marking
at this point the exit for Mistress
Page and Mistress Ford, since they
are obviously not included in Page's
invitation for the next morning at
214–17.

213 **Let's go in** Let's go in for dinner
(after walking in the park). In stage
directions 'go in' means 'to leave the
stage'.

197] I am an arrant Iew: Now God plesse me *Q*   211 heartily] *(*hartly*)*   212 me.] me. *Mistress
Ford and Mistress Page go to prepare dinner. Cam[1]*   213 SD] *Oxf*   214 SD] *Oxf (To Ford, Caius, and
Evans)*

we'll a-birding together, I have a fine hawk for the
bush. Shall it be so?

FORD　Anything.

EVANS　If there is one, I shall make two in the company.

CAIUS　If there be one or two, I shall make-a the turd.　　220

FORD　Pray you go, Master Page.

　　　　　　　　　　　　　　　[Exeunt all but Evans and Caius.]

EVANS　I pray you now remembrance tomorrow on the
lousy knave, mine host.

CAIUS　Dat is good, by gar, with all my heart.

EVANS　A lousy knave, to have his gibes and his　225
mockeries!　　　　　　　　　　　　　　　　　　*Exeunt.*

3.4　　　　　　*Enter* FENTON *and* ANNE PAGE.

FENTON

I see I cannot get thy father's love,
Therefore no more turn me to him, sweet Nan.

216　**a-birding** go shooting small birds
216–17　**hawk . . . bush** a hawk trained to
drive birds into bushes, where they
could be shot with small guns
('birding-pieces'; see 4.2.53)
219　**make two** Evans misuses the idiom
'to make one in a company', i.e. to be
member of a group, misleading Caius
into further equivocations.
220　**turd** The comic effect of Caius's mispronunciation of 'third' is confirmed in
Q, where the two speeches at 219–20 are
inserted after the equivalent of 3.2.74,
and Caius says 'I sall make de tird'; 'tird'
and 'turd' are identical in pronunciation.
222–6　These speeches, not in Q, echo
3.1.104–12 and anticipate 4.5.69–84,
where Evans and Caius take their
revenge on the Host by telling how he
has been swindled by his German

lodgers.
225–6　**his gibes . . . mockeries!** Cf.
4.5.76, *gibes and vlouting-stocks.*
3.4　The Quarto version of this scene does
not follow 3.3 but is placed after the
equivalent of 3.5; Mistress Quickly is
present from the beginning and
Master and Mistress Page enter
together with Shallow and Slender, so
that Fenton is soon dismissed after
being briefly given the opportunity of
speaking to Mistress Page. When the
Pages leave, Slender courts Anne, but
is called off with Shallow and Anne by
Mistress Quickly, who concludes the
scene with a brief soliloquy. The transposition of 3.4 and 3.5 is due to the different time-scale in the two texts; see
2.2.253n. and pp. 66–77.
2　**turn** refer

219–20] *S.Hu* If there be one in the company, I shal make two: / *Doc.* And dere be ven to, I sall make
de tird: *Q, at 3.2.75*　221 SD] *Hibbard; Exit with Page. Ard² (Cam¹)*　225–6] By so kad vdgme, M.
Fordes is / Not in his right wittes: / *Exit omnes: Q*　3.4] *Scoena Quarta. F*　0.1] *Rowe; Enter
Fenton, Anne, Page, Shallow, Slender, Quickly, Page, Mist. Page. F; Enter* M. *fenton, page, and
mistresse Quickly. Q, after the equivalent of 3.5*

ANNE   Alas, how then?

FENTON   Why, thou must be thyself.
He doth object I am too great of birth,
And that, my state being galled with my expense,   5
I seek to heal it only by his wealth.
Besides these, other bars he lays before me:
My riots past, my wild societies –
And tells me 'tis a thing impossible
I should love thee, but as a property.   10

ANNE   Maybe he tells you true.

FENTON
No, God so speed me in my time to come!
Albeit I will confess thy father's wealth
Was the first motive that I wooed thee, Anne,
Yet, wooing thee, I found thee of more value   15
Than stamps in gold or sums in sealed bags.
And 'tis the very riches of thyself
That now I aim at.

ANNE   Gentle Master Fenton,
Yet seek my father's love, still seek it, sir.
If opportunity and humblest suit   20
Cannot attain it, why then – hark you hither –
[*They talk apart.*]

3   **be thyself** act independently
4   **too . . . birth** a gentleman – boon companion of Prince Hal; see 8 and note on Fenton in the List of Roles
5   **state being galled** estate being reduced (literally 'made sore by chafing')
7   **bars** impediments, objections
10   **property** capital owned; means to an end (*OED sb.* 4)
12   ***God . . . come** May God favour (*speed*) me in future only if I speak true (*so*); as usual *God* is replaced in F by 'heauen'.

16   **stamps in gold** gold coins, stamped with the image of the sovereign
     sealed sealèd
17   **riches** wealth (singular, from French *richesse*)
20   **opportunity** catching the most favourable occasion
21 SD   Anne interrupts her speech and takes Fenton aside (*hither*) upon seeing Shallow and the rest approach. Cam[1] considers the line complete and uninterrupted, meaning '(if all else fail,) come back to me (*hither*)'.

7 Besides these,] Besides, these *Oxf¹ (Walker)*   12 SP] *Q3; not in F, but line indented*   God] *(Oxf);* heauen *F*   20 opportunity] importunity *Hanmer*   21 then – hark] *Theobald (subst.);* then harke *F* 21 SD] *Rowe*

[*Enter* SHALLOW, SLENDER *and* Mistress QUICKLY.]

SHALLOW   Break their talk, Mistress Quickly. My kins-
man shall speak for himself.

SLENDER   I'll make a shaft or a bolt on't. 'Slid, 'tis but
venturing.   25

SHALLOW   Be not dismayed.

SLENDER   No, she shall not dismay me: I care not for that,
but that I am afeard.

QUICKLY [*to Anne*]   Hark ye, Master Slender would speak
a word with you.   30

ANNE   I come to him. – [*aside*] This is my father's choice.
O, what a world of vile ill-favoured faults
Looks handsome in three hundred pounds a year!

QUICKLY   And how does good Master Fenton? Pray you,
a word with you.   [*She draws Fenton aside.*]   35

SHALLOW [*to Slender*]   She's coming; to her, coz. O boy,
thou hadst a father!

SLENDER   I had a father, Mistress Anne, my uncle can tell
you good jests of him. – Pray you, uncle, tell Mistress
Anne the jest how my father stole two geese out of a   40
pen, good uncle.

SHALLOW   Mistress Anne, my cousin loves you.

SLENDER   Ay, that I do, as well as I love any woman in
Gloucestershire.

---

24 **I'll . . . on't.** 'I'll do it [propose mar-
riage] by any means.' Proverbial
(Dent, S264), from archery: using
either a shaft (long slim arrow) or a bolt
(thicker arrow shot by a crossbow)
'Slid a mild oath: by God's eyelid
24–5 **'tis but venturing** There is no
harm in trying.
33 **three . . . year** Though there are allusions to Slender's family wealth (see
for example 1.1.256n.), his yearly
income is nowhere stated so definitely.

36 **to her, coz** a phrase of encouragement
(see 1.3.52n.), and for *coz* (cousin, as at
42) see 1.1.6n. and 1.1.21n.
37 **thou . . . father** 'an exhortation [to
marriage] which Slender mistakes for a
prompt' (Oxf[1]); cf. *Son* 13.14, 'You
had a father, let your son say so'. From
Slender's words at 1.1.256–8 it appears
that his father is dead.
38, 41 **uncle** This is as vague a definition
of relationship as 'cousin'; see 1.1.6n.

21.1] *Rowe; Enter M.Page his wife, M.Shallow, and Slender. Q*   22–3] *F lines Quickly, / himselfe. /*
27–8] *F lines* me: / affeard. /   29 SD] *Ard[2]*   31 SD] *Capell*   34–7] *F lines Fenton? / you. / Coz:*
/ father. /   35 SD] *Capell (subst.)*   36 SD] *Ard[2]*

227

SHALLOW   He will maintain you like a gentlewoman.   45

SLENDER   Ay, that I will, come cut and long-tail, under the degree of a squire.

SHALLOW   He will make you a hundred and fifty pounds jointure.

ANNE   Good Master Shallow, let him woo for himself.   50

SHALLOW   Marry, I thank you for it, I thank you for that good comfort. – She calls you, coz; I'll leave you.

ANNE   Now, Master Slender.

SLENDER   Now, good Mistress Anne.

ANNE   What is your will?   55

SLENDER   My will? 'Od's heartlings, that's a pretty jest indeed! I ne'er made my will yet, I thank God: I am not such a sickly creature, I give God praise.

ANNE   I mean, Master Slender, what would you with me?

SLENDER   Truly, for mine own part, I would little or   60
nothing with you. Your father and my uncle hath made motions: if it be my luck, so; if not, happy man be his dole. They can tell you how things go better than I can. – You may ask your father: here he comes.

---

46 **come . . . long-tail** proverbial (Dent, C938), meaning any kind of dog or horse, whether their tails are cut or grown long

46–7 **come . . . squire** 'as well as anyone else of a squire's rank can do, whoever he may be . . . *Under* (*OED prep.* 16) is "in accordance with"' (Oxf¹)

49 **jointure** the part of the husband's estate settled by marriage contract on the wife should she be widowed. Oxf¹ remarks that it would normally be one third of the husband's estate, so if, as Anne suggests at 33, Slender's yearly worth is £300, her jointure should be £100 and not £150.

52 **good comfort** Shallow takes it as a good omen that Anne wishes to be wooed by Slender directly rather than

by proxy, so he tells him *She calls you*.

53, 54 **Now** a form of greeting

55 **will** wish – foolishly Slender takes it in the sense 'last will and testament'

56 **'Ods heartlings** The diminutive 'heartling' is a euphemism for the oath 'God's heart'.

56–7 **that's . . . indeed** See 2.2.105n.

57, 58 ***God** as at 12, replaced by 'Heauen' in F

60–1 **little or nothing** have nothing to do

62 **motions** proposals; see 1.1.199n.

62–3 **happy . . . dole** a common proverb (Dent, M158) meaning 'may fate (*dole* means 'destiny', *OED* Dole *sb.*¹ 4) reward the lucky (*happy*) man', used by Shakespeare also in *TS* 1.1.139–40, *1H4* 2.2.76, *WT* 1.2.163

46 Ay . . . will] I be God that I vill *Q*   57, 58 God] *Oxf, after Q;* Heauen *F*

[*Enter* PAGE *and* MISTRESS PAGE.]

PAGE

    Now, Master Slender, – love him, daughter Anne –   65

    Why, how now? What does Master Fenton here?

    You wrong me, sir, thus still to haunt my house.

    I told you, sir, my daughter is disposed of.

FENTON   Nay, Master Page, be not impatient.

MISTRESS PAGE

    Good Master Fenton, come not to my child.   70

PAGE

    She is no match for you.

FENTON

    Sir, will you hear me?

PAGE   No, good Master Fenton. –

    Come, Master Shallow; come, son Slender, in. –

    Knowing my mind, you wrong me, Master Fenton.

                        [*Exit with Shallow and Slender.*]

QUICKLY [*to Fenton*]   Speak to Mistress Page.   75

FENTON

    Good Mistress Page, for that I love your daughter

    In such a righteous fashion as I do,

    Perforce, against all checks, rebukes and manners,

    I must advance the colours of my love

    And not retire. Let me have your good will.   80

ANNE   Good mother, do not marry me to yond fool.

71–2 These are in fact three half-lines. It is up to the actors to decide where to place the major pause. The present line division has been adopted on the assumption that Fenton is stunned by Page's statement, and then his plea is cut short by Page, who disregards him, turning immediately to Shallow. But this could be acted otherwise: Fenton completes with his plea Page's verse line, and an ominous pause comes after Page's firm rejection of it.

78 **against . . . manners** in spite of (*against*) all obstacles (*checks*) and rebukes, as well as contrary to (*against*) common courtesy (*manners*)

79–80 **advance . . . retire** Military metaphors are frequent in the language of love and courtship; *advance the colours* means raise the flag (before a battle).

64.1] *Rowe*   66 Fenton] *Q3; Fenter F*   74 SD] *Rowe (subst.)*   75 SD] *Oxf*

MISTRESS PAGE   I mean it not, I seek you a better husband.

QUICKLY [*aside*]   That's my master, Master Doctor.

ANNE

     Alas, I had rather be set quick i'th' earth,   85
     And bowled to death with turnips.

MISTRESS PAGE

     Come, trouble not yourself, good Master Fenton,
     I will not be your friend, nor enemy.
     My daughter will I question how she loves you,
     And as I find her, so am I affected.   90
     Till then, farewell, sir; she must needs go in,
     Her father will be angry.

FENTON   Farewell, gentle mistress; farewell, Nan.

                 [*Exeunt Mistress Page and Anne.*]

QUICKLY   This is my doing, now. 'Nay,' said I, 'will you
cast away your child on a fool, and a physician? Look   95
on Master Fenton!' This is my doing.

FENTON

     I thank thee, and I pray thee once tonight
     Give my sweet Nan this ring. – There's for thy pains.

QUICKLY   Now heaven send thee good fortune! [*Exit Fenton.*]

85 **set . . . earth** buried alive (*quick*). The image is from the barbarous torture which consisted of burying a person alive, with only the head above ground, and either letting him die of starvation (the sentence passed on Aaron the Moor in *Tit* 5.3.78–82) or pelting the head with stones or the like; see *bowled*, 86.

87 Warburton (followed by Cam²) suggested that Mistress Page addresses the first four words to Anne in reply to her plea, then turns to Fenton.

90 **affected** inclined

93 SD Rowe anticipates the exit of the two women at the end of the previous line, to account for the fact that they do not answer Fenton's farewell.

95 **fool . . . physician** Johnson suggested to emend *and* to 'or', in view of the current saying (Dent, M125) 'Every man is either a fool or a physician to himself'. But Quickly wants to stress the double danger of a fool (Slender) and a physician (Caius) who is also a fool.

97 **once tonight** at some time this evening, as in *1H4* 5.2.72, 'once ere night'

98 **There's . . . pains.** Fenton's tip to Quickly must have been generous, judging from the Q version where, exiting before the rest of the characters on stage, he tells her 'Here nurse, theres a brace of angels to drink', i.e. two gold coins worth ten shillings each (see 1.3.50n.).

84 SD] *Bowers*   87–8] *prose F*   87 yourself, good] yourself. Good *Warburton*   93 SD] *Rowe, opp.*
92   95 and] or *Hanmer (Johnson)*   95–6] *F lines* Physitian: / doing. /   99 SD] *F2, opp. 98*

A kind heart he hath: a woman would run through fire   100
and water for such a kind heart. But yet I would my
master had Mistress Anne, or I would Master Slender
had her; or, in sooth, I would Master Fenton had her.
I will do what I can for them all three, for so I have
promised and I'll be as good as my word – but   105
speciously for Master Fenton. Well, I must of another
errand to Sir John Falstaff from my two mistresses –
what a beast am I to slack it!   *Exit.*

3.5   *Enter* FALSTAFF.

FALSTAFF   Bardolph, I say!

                    [*Enter* BARDOLPH.]

BARDOLPH   Here, sir.
FALSTAFF   Go fetch me a quart of sack; put a toast in't.
                                        [*Exit Bardolph.*]
Have I lived to be carried in a basket like a barrow of
butcher's offal, and to be thrown in the Thames? Well,   5

100–1 **run . . . water** a common expres-
    sion (Dent, F285), derived ultimately
    from Psalms 66.12
105 **be . . . word** keep my promise;
    another current expression (Dent,
    W773.1) frequent in Shakespeare
106 **speciously** specially (a Quicklyism
    repeated at 4.5.104)
    of go on
107–8 **errand . . . slack it** In fact, accord-
    ing to F, Quickly postpones her errand
    to Falstaff till the next morning, as it
    appears from 3.5.24–5; not so in Q,
    where this scene is placed after the
    next (see 3.4n.), so that she has already
    delivered her two mistresses' messages

to him.
108 **slack** postpone
3.5 The location is the Garter Inn, and the
    time early next morning (see Quickly's
    good morrow at 25), though Falstaff
    seems not yet fully recovered from
    the ducking. In the Q version the
    first part of this scene (placed before
    3.4; see 3.4n.) takes place in the
    evening of the same day as 3.3; see
    3.3.182–3n.
3 **quart** two pints
    toast piece of hot toasted bread used
    as a sop in wine
4 **barrow** barrow-load (of butcher's
    waste)

---

108 SD] *(Exeunt)*   3.5] *Scena Quinta. F   0.1] Q (Enter sir Iohn Falstaffe.); Enter Falstaffe,*
Bardolfe, Quickly, Ford. F; Enter Sir Iohn Falstaffe and Bardolfe. Q2   1–2] Fal: Bardolfe brew me a
pottle sack presently: / Bar: With Egges sir? / Fal: Simply of itselfe, Ile none of these pullets sperme
/ In my drinke: goe make haste. Q (at 26–30 in F)   1.1] Cam¹   3 SD] *Theobald*

231

if I be served such another trick, I'll have my brains
ta'en out and buttered, and give them to a dog for a
New Year's gift. 'Sblood, the rogues slighted me into
the river with as little remorse as they would have
drowned a blind bitch's puppies, fifteen i'the litter; and   10
you may know by my size that I have a kind of alacrity
in sinking: if the bottom were as deep as hell, I should
down. I had been drowned, but that the shore was
shelvy and shallow – a death that I abhor, for the water
swells a man – and what a thing should I have been,   15
when I had been swelled? I should have been a moun-
tain of mummy!

[*Enter* BARDOLPH *with sack.*]

BARDOLPH   Here's Mistress Quickly, sir, to speak with
you.

FALSTAFF   Come, let me pour in some sack to the   20
Thames water, for my belly's as cold as if I had swallowed snowballs for pills to cool the reins. – Call her in.

BARDOLPH   Come in, woman.

6–7 **I'll . . . buttered** i.e. I'll consider my
brains as titbits to feed animals (cf.
butcher's offal at 5). This is the first
occurrence of the expression (Dent,
B602.1), and only later did 'buttered
brains' became synonymous with foolishness (Ard[1]).

8   **New Year's gift** New Year's Day was
the time for giving presents.
***'Sblood** This strong oath (by God's
or Christ's blood), omitted by F, is
used repeatedly by Falstaff in the
unexpurgated version of *1H4*, e.g. at
1.2.72, 2.2.35, 2.4.244.
slighted in Q 'slided'; a pun, or
rather, as Hibbard remarks, a port-
manteau word combining the mean-

ings 'treated contemptuously' (*OED*
Slight *v.* 3c) and 'slid', i.e. let down
(into the water)

9   **remorse** compunction

10   **a . . . puppies** the blind puppies of a
bitch

11   **you** 'An indication that the soliloquy is
directly addressed to the audience'
(Oxf[1])

12   **as . . . hell** a current phrase (Dent,
H397.1); cf. *MM* 3.1.93, 'A pond as
deep as hell'

14   **shelvy** sloping gently

17   **mummy** dead flesh or pulpy mass
(*OED sb.*[1] 1b and 1c)

22   **reins** loins, kidneys (considered the
seat of lust)

6–7 I'll . . . buttered] Ile giue them leaue to take out my braines and butter them *Q*   8 'Sblood] *Q;*
not in F   slighted] slided *Q;* sleighted *(Cam[1])*   10 blind bitch's] *Q,* F *(*blind bitches*);* bitch's blind
Theobald   16–17 I should . . . mummy] By the Lord a mountaine of money. Now is the Sacke
brewed? *Q*   17.1] *Capell*23.1] *Q; not in* F

Enter Mistress QUICKLY.

QUICKLY   By your leave, I cry you mercy! Give your
worship good morrow.   25

FALSTAFF   Take away these chalices. Go, brew me a
pottle of sack finely.

BARDOLPH   With eggs, sir?

FALSTAFF   Simple of itself. I'll no pullet sperm in my
brewage.   [*Exit Bardolph.*]
How now?   31

QUICKLY   Marry, sir, I come to your worship from
Mistress Ford.

FALSTAFF   Mistress Ford? I have had ford enough. I was
thrown into the ford, I have my belly full of ford.   35

QUICKLY   Alas the day, good heart, that was not her fault.
She does so take on with her men: they mistook their
erection.

FALSTAFF   So did I mine, to build upon a foolish
woman's promise.   40

QUICKLY   Well, she laments, sir, for it, that it would
yearn your heart to see it. Her husband goes this morn–

---

24 **cry you mercy** a current phrase of
apology for intruding on privacy
25 **morrow** morning; see 3.5n.
26 **chalices** goblets or tankards. Since
Falstaff had asked for a *quart* (see 3n.),
Bardolph must have brought in at 17
SD two tankards containing a pint each.
27 **pottle** Falstaff is doubling his dose of
drink: a pottle was the equivalent of
four pints.
finely probably heated with the addition of ginger; *brewage* (30) is the name
for a concocted beverage
29 **Simple of itself** with no addition (of
eggs)
pullet sperm i.e. egg
34, 35 **ford** shallow water; Falstaff is punning on the name Ford in the same way
as he did with Brook at 2.2.143–4.

35 **have . . . ford** Falstaff says that his
belly is full of shallow water, implying
also the current expression 'to have a
bellyful' (Dent, B306) in the sense of
'to have had enough, to be sick and
tired' of something.
36 **Alas the day** a common expression
(Dent, AA3) of biblical origin (e.g.
Jeremiah, 30.7, 'Alas, for this day'),
found at least ten times in Shakespeare's
plays, also in the form 'Alack the day'
good heart poor thing (referring to
Mistress Ford)
37 **take on with** scold; cf. 4.2.20
38 **erection** Quickly means 'direction',
but Falstaff plays on the sexual implications of the mistake.
42 **yearn** move to compassion (*OED v.*[1] 7)
42–3 **Her . . . a-birding** cf. 3.3.215–18

23.1] *Q; not in F*   24–7] *F lines* mercy? / morrow. / Challices: / finely. /   30 SD] *Capell*

233

ing a-birding. She desires you once more to come to
her, between eight and nine. I must carry her word
quickly; she'll make you amends, I warrant you.   45

FALSTAFF   Well, I will visit her; tell her so, and bid her
think what a man is. Let her consider his frailty, and
then judge of my merit.

QUICKLY   I will tell her.

FALSTAFF   Do so. Between nine and ten, sayst thou?   50

QUICKLY   Eight and nine, sir.

FALSTAFF   Well, be gone. I will not miss her.

QUICKLY   Peace be with you, sir.   *Exit.*

FALSTAFF   I marvel I hear not of Master Brook; he sent
me word to stay within. I like his money well. – By the   55
mass, here he comes.

Enter FORD *as* BROOK.

FORD   God save you, sir.

FALSTAFF   Now, Master Brook, you come to know what
hath passed between me and Ford's wife.

FORD   That indeed, Sir John, is my business.   60

FALSTAFF   Master Brook, I will not lie to you. I was at
her house the hour she appointed me.

FORD   And how sped you, sir?

FALSTAFF   Very ill-favouredly, Master Brook.

---

47 **consider his frailty** Cf. 2.1.210–11n.
Falstaff's application to himself of the
common saying (Dent, F363) from
Matthew 26.41, 'Flesh is frail', is
found also in *1H4* 3.3.166–8: 'Thou
seest I have more flesh than another
man, and therefore more frailty.' But
here he takes as a *merit* (48) his ability
to resist such weakness by his determination to commit sinful actions.

52 **miss** fail

55–6 ***By the mass** an oath suppressed
in F

57 ***God save** The F reading 'Blesse'
replaces what was considered a blasphemous expression.

63 ***how sped you** How did you get on?
The omission of *how* in F looks like a
printing-house accident rather than a
way of asking 'did you succeed?'

64 **ill-favouredly** badly; cf. *ill-favoured*,
meaning 'ugly', 1.1.279–80n.

53 SD] *Q (Exit mistresse Quickly.); not in F* 55–6 By . . . comes] *Oxf;* By the masse here he is *Q;*
Oh, heere he comes *F* 56.1] *Q (Enter Brooke.); not in F* 57] *Q;* Blesse you sir *F;* God bless you,
sir *Oxf* 58–9] *F lines* know / wife. / 61–2] *F lines* you, / me. / 63 how sped] *Q;* sped *F*

FORD   How so, sir? Did she change her determination?   65

FALSTAFF   No, Master Brook, but the peaking cornuto
her husband, Master Brook, dwelling in a continual
'larum of jealousy, comes me in the instant of our
encounter, after we had embraced, kissed, protested,
and, as it were, spoke the prologue of our comedy; and   70
at his heels a rabble of his companions, thither pro-
voked and instigated by his distemper, and, forsooth,
to search his house for his wife's love.

FORD   What, while you were there?

FALSTAFF   While I was there.   75

FORD   And did he search for you, and could not find you?

FALSTAFF   You shall hear. As good luck would have it,
comes in one Mistress Page, gives intelligence of Ford's
approach; and in her invention, and Ford's wife's
distraction, they conveyed me into a buck-basket.   80

FORD   A buck-basket?

FALSTAFF   By the Lord, a buck-basket! Rammed me in

---

65 **determination** opinion, decision
66 **peaking** skulking, mean-spirited
(*OED a.* 1), with a possible allusion to
'peak', meaning 'horn'
cornuto cuckold (from Italian, meaning 'horned creature')
68 **'larum** alarum, i.e. alarm, warning of
danger
comes me in comes in; *me* is an ethic
dative: see 1.3.55n.
69 **encounter** meeting (possibly with a
sexual innuendo)
protested made declarations (of love)
71 **companions** cf. 3.1.109n.
72 **distemper** once again, jealousy as a
disease, i.e. madness; see 3.3.201n.
77 **good luck** Q has 'God' instead of *good
luck*, but the current expression, used
by Falstaff in *1H4* 2.4.221, was 'as the
devil would have it' (Dent, D221.1).

79–80 **in . . . distraction** The preposition
in ('by' in Q) is made to do double
service: it applies to the state of agitation (*distraction*) Mistress Ford is *in*,
and, by attraction, to the resourceful-
ness (*invention*) of Mistress Page
thanks to which Falstaff was conveyed
in the buck-basket. Hanmer's emendation (see t.n.), 'direction' for *distraction*, justifies the use of 'by' both for
Mistress Page's invention of the buck-
basket trick and for Mistress Ford's
giving orders for its disposal, but is
unsupported by the original readings.
82 *****By the Lord** another oath suppressed in F and replaced by 'Yes'
Rammed thrust, possibly punning on
'ram' (male horned animal); see *bell-
wether* at 101

---

66 cornuto] *(Curnuto)*   72–3 and, forsooth . . . love] And what to do thinke you? to search for his
wiues loue. Euen so, plainly so *Q*   77 good luck] God *Q*   79 in] by *Q*   80 distraction] *Q, F;*
direction *Hanmer (Warburton)*   82 By the Lord] *Q;* Yes: *F*

with foul shirts and smocks, socks, foul stockings, greasy napkins, that, Master Brook, there was the rankest compound of villainous smell that ever offended   85 nostril.

FORD   And how long lay you there?

FALSTAFF   Nay, you shall hear, Master Brook, what I have suffered to bring this woman to evil for your good. Being thus crammed in the basket, a couple of Ford's   90 knaves, his hinds, were called forth by their mistress, to carry me in the name of foul clothes to Datchet Lane. They took me on their shoulders, met the jealous knave their master in the door, who asked them once or twice what they had in their basket. I quaked for fear lest the   95 lunatic knave would have searched it; but Fate, ordaining he should be a cuckold, held his hand. Well, on went he for a search, and away went I for foul clothes. But mark the sequel, Master Brook. I suffered the pangs of three several deaths: first, an intolerable fright   100 to be detected with a jealous rotten bell-wether; next, to be compassed like a good bilbo in the circumference

---

84 **that** so that
85 **compound . . . smell** not mixture of evil smells but mixture of ill-smelling ingredients; *of villainous smell* is an adjectival phrase defining *compound*
91 **knaves, his hinds** Both *knaves* and *hinds* meant 'servants', though frequently used contemptuously.
92 **in the name** under the disguise
    Datchet Lane leading to Datchet Mead; see 3.3.13n.
94–5 **asked . . . basket** See 3.3.166n.
96–7 **Fate . . . cuckold** alluding to the current saying 'Cuckolds come by destiny'. Dent (C889) quotes John Grange, *Golden Aphroditis* (1577), 'As Cuckoldes come by destinie, so

Cuckowes sing by kinde [i.e. by their nature]', echoed by the Clown in *AW* 1.3.62–3: 'Your marriage comes by destiny, / Your cuckoo sings by kind.'
101 **with** by
    rotten bell-wether diseased (mad) ram, with a bell tied round its neck, leading the flock; the allusion to Ford noisily leading the 'rabble of his companions' (71) is the more insulting since bell-wethers were generally castrated.
102 **compassed** bent in a circle (*OED* Compass *v.*[1] 14)
    good bilbo a sword (see 1.1.150n.) so good that it would bend into a circle, *hilt to point* (103), without snapping

---

84 greasy] *Q, F;* and greasy *Rowe*   85 smell] *Q, F;* smells *Hanmer*   89 to bring . . . good] by the Lord for your sake *Q*   100 several] egregious *Q*   101 with] by *Rowe*   jealous] *(*iealious*)*

of a peck, hilt to point, heel to head; and then, to be
stopped in like a strong distillation with stinking
clothes that fretted in their own grease. Think of that,   105
a man of my kidney, think of that – that am as subject
to heat as butter – a man of continual dissolution and
thaw: it was a miracle to scape suffocation. And in the
height of this bath – when I was more than half stewed
in grease, like a Dutch dish – to be thrown into the   110
Thames and cooled, glowing hot, in that surge like a
horseshoe – think of that – hissing hot – think of that,
Master Brook.

FORD   In good sadness, sir, I am sorry that for my sake
you have suffered all this. My suit, then, is desperate: 115
you'll undertake her no more?

FALSTAFF   Master Brook, I will be thrown into Etna, as
I have been into Thames, ere I will leave her thus. Her
husband is this morning gone a-birding; I have

103 **peck** a circular container capable of
holding a peck, i.e. a quarter of a
bushel, of dry goods
104–5 **stopped . . . clothes** corked
(*stopped*) in like liquid exuding a potent
smell distilled from (*with*) stinking
clothes
105 **fretted . . . grease** fermented (*OED*
Fret *v*.[1] 7, 10) in their own grease,
another variant of the saying 'He fries
in his own grease' (Dent, G433); see
2.1.59–60n.
106 **kidney** nature, constitution (*OED sb.*
2). The expression 'of the same (of my
own) kidney' was current from *c.* 1531
(Dent, K31).
106–7 **as subject . . . butter** cf. the
proverb 'To melt like butter before the
sun' (Dent, B780)
107 **dissolution** liquefaction (through
perspiration)

110 **Dutch dish** The Dutch had the reputation of being overfond of butter.
111 **surge** water (agitated by Falstaff's
body being thrown into it). The F
reading 'serge' (see t.n.) was emended
by Capell to 'forge', in connection with
the image of the forging of a horseshoe
(112).
114 **sadness** seriousness (the normal
meaning of the word at the time). The
expression 'in sadness' (Dent SS1),
current since 1544, is played upon in
RJ 1.1.199–204.
116 **undertake** approach (with specific
intent)
117–18 **I will . . . Thames** Etna is the
famous volcano in Sicily. The phrase
gives a solemn classical ring to the
expression of biblical origin 'to go
through fire and water'; see
3.4.100–1n.

108 it . . . scape] by the Lord it was maruell I / Escaped *Q*   111 surge] *(serge); forge (Capell)*   112
think . . . hot] thinke of that hissing heate *Q*

received from her another embassy of meeting: 'twixt　120
eight and nine is the hour, Master Brook.

FORD　'Tis past eight already, sir.

FALSTAFF　Is it? I will then address me to my appointment. Come to me at your convenient leisure, and you
shall know how I speed; and the conclusion shall be　125
crowned with your enjoying her. Adieu. You shall have
her, Master Brook. Master Brook, you shall cuckold
Ford.　　　　　　　　　　　　　　　　　　　*Exit.*

FORD　Hum – ha! Is this a vision? Is this a dream? Do I
sleep? Master Ford, awake; awake, Master Ford!　130
There's a hole made in your best coat, Master Ford.
This 'tis to be married, this 'tis to have linen and buck-
baskets! Well, I will proclaim myself what I am. I will
now take the lecher. He is at my house, he cannot scape
me – 'tis impossible he should. He cannot creep into a　135
half-penny purse, nor into a pepperbox. But, lest the
devil that guides him should aid him, I will search
impossible places. Though what I am I cannot avoid,
yet to be what I would not shall not make me tame. If I
have horns to make one mad, let the proverb go with　140
me: I'll be horn-mad.　　　　　　　　　　　　*Exit.*

---

120 **embassy** embassage, i.e. message

122 Ford's remark is relevant to establish the time of the action; see 3.3.182–3n.

125 **speed** get on; cf. 63n.

125–6 **the . . . crowned** from the well-known Latin tag *Finis coronat opus*, current in English as 'the end crowns all' (Dent, E116); *La fin couronne les oeuvres*, the French equivalent, are the dying words of Clifford in *2H6* 5.2.28. Cf. *TC* 4.5.224 and *AW* 4.4.35–6.

131 **There's . . . coat** Proverbially, 'To pick a hole in a man's coat' (Dent, H522) meant to discover a hidden fault in a person, and in this sense is used by Fluellen of Pistol in *H5* 3.6.84.

136 **half-penny purse** small purse for small coins

136–7 **lest . . . aid him** Cf. 95–7: Ford echoes Falstaff, replacing Fate with the devil as Falstaff's assistant.

138 **what I am** i.e. a cuckold, as he had implicitly proclaimed himself at 133; Ford's elaborate syntax at this point seems intended to avoid the mention of the word cuckold

140 **one** Editors have taken this to be a printer's misreading of 'me' in the copy (see t.n.), but Ford is referring to the current expression in general terms (*proverb*), 'to be horn-mad', for which see 1.4.45n.

---

128 SD] *Q; not in F*　140 one] me *Halliwell (Dyce)*

4.1   *Enter* MISTRESS PAGE, Mistress QUICKLY
                and WILLIAM.

MISTRESS PAGE   Is he at Master Ford's already, thinkst
thou?
QUICKLY   Sure he is by this, or will be presently. But
truly he is very courageous mad about his throwing into
the water. Mistress Ford desires you to come suddenly.   5
MISTRESS PAGE   I'll be with her by and by: I'll but bring
my young man here to school. Look where his master
comes; 'tis playing day, I see.

[*Enter* EVANS.]

How now, Sir Hugh, no school today?
EVANS   No, Master Slender is let the boys leave to play.   10
QUICKLY   God's blessing of his heart!

4.1 Q omits this whole scene, which in fact
is unnecessary to the development of
the plot. See pp. 6–7 on the significance
of this as a kind of interlude meant to
stress the main stylistic feature of the
play, its quality of verbal pyrotechnics.
This is evidenced in the linguistic peculiarities of the different characters, from
Mistress Quickly to Parson Evans, from
Pistol to Doctor Caius, and in the verbal inventiveness of Falstaff himself,
which reaches its highest point in the
description of his ducking in the
Thames in 3.5. The time is about eight
in the morning, when children were
taken to school, and the location a
Windsor street leading from Page's
house to Evans's school.
1   **Master Ford's** The F reading 'M.
Fords' is ambiguous; Master Ford
seems more likely since he is the house
owner, but the Oxford editors prefer
'Mistress' because Mistress Page
intends to visit her and not her husband.

3   **presently** immediately; see 3.3.81.
4   **courageous mad** furious; *courageous*
is used similarly by ignorant speakers
in *MND* 4.2.27, 'O most courageous
day', and *MV* 2.2.10, 'the most courageous fiend'
5   **suddenly** at once
6–7   **I'll but . . . man** I'll come as soon as
I have taken my boy.
8   **playing day** holiday
10   **is . . . play** 'asked that the boys be
given a holiday' (Hibbard). Pre-
sumably Slender wanted Evans to be
free from his duties as a schoolteacher
in order to devote himself to arranging
his match with Anne Page.
11   ***God's . . . heart!** a current formula
(Dent, G266), and a favourite of
Mistress Quickly, who uses it at
2.2.101, as well as in *2H4* 2.4.303. The
apostrophe before 'Blessing' in F (see
t.n.) suggests that 'God's', present in
the copy, was suppressed by the
printer for the reason given in
2.2.50–1n.

4.1] *Actus Quartus. Scoena Prima. F*   0.1–2] *Rowe; Enter Mistris Page, Quickly, William, Euans. F*
1 Master] *(M.); Mistress Oxf*   8.1] *Rowe, after 9*   11 God's blessing] *(Oxf);* 'Blessing F

239

MISTRESS PAGE   Sir Hugh, my husband says my son
    profits nothing in the world at his book. I pray you, ask
    him some questions in his accidence.

EVANS   Come hither, William. Hold up your head, come.   15

MISTRESS PAGE   Come on, sirrah, hold up your head.
    Answer your master, be not afraid.

EVANS   William, how many numbers is in nouns?

WILLIAM   Two.

QUICKLY   Truly, I thought there had been one number   20
    more, because they say ''Od's nouns'.

EVANS   Peace your tattlings. What is 'fair', William?

WILLIAM   *Pulcher.*

QUICKLY   Polecats? There are fairer things than polecats,
    sure.   25

EVANS   You are a very simplicity 'oman; I pray you,
    peace. – What is *lapis*, William?

WILLIAM   A stone.

EVANS   And what is 'a stone', William?

WILLIAM   A pebble.   30

EVANS   No, it is *lapis*; I pray you remember in your prain.

WILLIAM   *Lapis.*

---

13 **book** presumably *A Short Introduction
of Grammar . . . to attain the knowledge
of the Latin tongue* by William Lilly and
John Colet (1549, frequently
reprinted), which Edward VI commanded to be used in all schools (Ard²)

14 **accidence** the first part of the grammar, dealing with inflexions

15 **William** Was the name chosen
because Shakespeare (obviously familiar with Lilly and Colet's *Grammar*)
had a similar experience as a schoolboy?

16 **sirrah** See 3.2.19n.

19 **Two** The answer is correct; Ard²
quotes Lilly and Colet: 'In Nounes be
two Numbers, the Singular and the
Plurall'.

21 **'Od's nouns** ''Od's 'ouns' is the
euphemistic form of the strong oath 'By

God's (i.e. Christ's) wounds'; cf.
''Sblood', 3.5.8n. Quickly equivocates on
both *numbers* ('three', not *two*, is an odd
number) and *nouns* (''ouns' in the oath).

22 **tattlings** prattling (Evans's Welsh
plural); cf. 'tittle-tattling' (prattling) in
WT 4.4.246

23 *Pulcher* The word is given as an example
of noun–adjective in Lilly and Colet.

24 **Polecats** Polecats were considered as
vermin, and the word was used abu-
sively in the sense of prostitutes; see
Ford at 4.2.175. The word was presumably pronounced 'pullcats', allowing for the confusion with *pulcher.*

26 **simplicity 'oman** simple (i.e. stupid)
woman. As usual, Evans takes the
noun for the adjective.

27, 31, 32 *lapis* another word quoted as
an example in Lilly and Colet

EVANS　That is a good William. What is he, William, that
does lend articles?

WILLIAM　Articles are borrowed of the pronoun, and be　　35
thus declined: *Singulariter nominativo hic, haec, hoc.*

EVANS　*Nominativo hig, haeg, hog,* pray you mark.
Genitivo huius. Well, what is your accusative case?

WILLIAM　*Accusativo hinc –*

EVANS　I pray you have your remembrance, child:　　40
accusativo hing, hang, hog.

QUICKLY　'Hang-hog' is Latin for bacon, I warrant you.

EVANS　Leave your prabbles, 'oman. – What is the focative case, William?

WILLIAM　O – *vocativo –* O –　　45

EVANS　Remember, William; focative is *caret.*

QUICKLY　And that's a good root.

EVANS　'Oman, forbear.

MISTRESS PAGE　Peace.

EVANS　What is your genitive case plural, William?　　50

WILLIAM　Genitive case?

EVANS　Ay.

WILLIAM　*Genitivo horum, harum, horum.*

35–6 William's speech is a nearly verbatim quotation from Lilly and Colet,
which he has learnt by heart. Latin:
'The singular nominative case [of the
pronoun meaning "this"] is *hic, haec,
hoc.'* Evans repeats it in his Welsh
accent.

39 *hinc –* Either William cannot remember the rest of the paradigm, which is
actually '*hunc,* hanc, hoc', and Evans
prompts him but repeats in his Welsh
accent William's mistake (at 41 *hing* is
hinc, for 'hunc'), or Evans interrupts
him to correct that mistake, and *hing* at
41, as Pope suggests, is a printer's misreading of 'hung' in the copy.

42 '**Hang-hog**' . . . **bacon** Quickly's
equivocation caused by Evans's Welsh

accent may contain an allusion to the
story of a man named Hog who, sentenced to death, tried to save his life by
claiming kinship with Sir Nicholas
Bacon; the latter's reply became
proverbial: 'Hog is not Bacon till it be
well hanged' (Ard[2]).

43 **prabbles** cf. *pribbles and prabbles,*
1.1.50n.

46 *caret* Latin: is lacking. Latin pronouns
have no vocative case, but Evans
should have omitted *is,* which is
already implicit in the verbal form.
Quickly understands 'focative is *caret*'
as 'the word for *fucking* is *carrot*' (vulgar for 'penis'), which prompts her
comment at 47, *a good root* being
another euphemism for 'penis'.

37 *haeg] Oxf[1]; hag F* 39 *hinc –] this edn; hinc. F;* hunc *Halliwell* 41 *hing]* hung / *Pope* 42 Latin]
F3 *(Latine);* latten F 53 *Genitivo] Singer; Genitiue F*

QUICKLY   'Vengeance of Jenny's case, fie on her! Never
name her, child, if she be a whore.   55

EVANS   For shame, 'oman.

QUICKLY   You do ill to teach the child such words. – He
teaches him to hick and to hack, which they'll do fast
enough of themselves, and to call 'whore 'm'! – Fie
upon you!   60

EVANS   'Oman, art thou lunatics? Hast thou no under-
standings for thy cases, and the numbers of the gen-
ders? Thou art as foolish Christian creatures as I would
desires.

MISTRESS PAGE [*to Quickly*]   Prithee hold thy peace.   65

EVANS   Show me now, William, some declensions of your
pronouns.

WILLIAM   Forsooth, I have forgot.

EVANS   It is *qui, quae, quod*. If you forget your *qui*s, your
*quae*s, and your *quod*s, you must be preeches. Go your   70
ways and play, go.

MISTRESS PAGE   He is a better scholar than I thought he
was.

EVANS   He is a good sprag memory. Farewell, Mistress
Page.   75

54 '**Vengeance of** a plague on; a common
locution (Dent, VV2), frequent in
Shakespeare, euphemistic for 'God's
vengeance on'
    Jenny's case Quickly interprets the
words *genitive case* as a gross allusion to
the vagina (*case*) of a whore, since prostitutes were mostly known by diminutive nicknames.
58 **to hick . . . hack** Quickly takes
the nominative case of the pronoun to
mean to hiccup (for drunkenness) and
to go whoring; see *hack* at 2.1.45n.
59 **whore 'm** fuck them; Quickly's interpretation of the plural genitive *horum*
61 **lunatics** mad; cf. Evans at 4.2.118,

where he means 'madness'. In this
passage Evans revels in 'Welsh
final *s*', extended to verbal forms
(*desires*, 64).
69–70 **your *qui*s . . . *quod*s** Oliver (Ard²)
suggests that, if pronounced by
Evans as 'keys', 'case' and 'cods',
the pronominal forms would imply
indecent allusions to 'penis', 'vagina'
(see 54n.) and 'testicles' respectively.
70 **preeches** i.e. 'breeched', short for
'whipped with his breeches down'
74 **is** has
    sprag smart; recorded by *OED* (Sprag
a.) as a mispronunciation of 'sprack' in
this sense

54 Jenny's] *Capell;* Ginyes *F;* Guney's / *Theobald;* Jinny's *Ridley;* Ginny's *Ard²*   59 whore 'm] *this
edn;* horum *F;* whorum *Oxf*   61 lunatics] *Capell;* Lunaties *F;* lunacies *Rowe*   62 of the] and the
Collier²; of thy *(White)*   65 SD] *Munro*   69 quae] *Pope;* que *F*   quis] *(Quies)*   70 quaes] *Pope;*
Ques *F*   preeches] preeched *(White)*

MISTRESS PAGE   Adieu, good Sir Hugh.   [*Exit Evans.*]
Get you home, boy.   [*Exit William.*]
Come, we stay too long.   *Exeunt.*

4.2   *Enter* FALSTAFF *and* MISTRESS FORD.

FALSTAFF   Mistress Ford, your sorrow hath eaten up
my sufferance. I see you are obsequious in your love
and I profess requital to a hair's breadth, not only,
Mistress Ford, in the simple office of love, but in all the
accoutrement, compliment and ceremony of it. But are   5
you sure of your husband now?
MISTRESS FORD   He's a-birding, sweet Sir John.
MISTRESS PAGE [*within*]   What ho, gossip Ford, what ho!
MISTRESS FORD   Step into the chamber, Sir John.
[*Exit Falstaff.*]

4.2 Falstaff's second trial, once again in
Ford's house. In the Q version the
scene opens with Mistress Page giving
instructions to her servants about the
handling of the buck-basket. The lines
do not figure in F and, from what
Mistress Ford says at 89–91 and 94–5,
there is no need for the basket to be visible on the stage from the beginning of
the scene, as Oxf[1] postulates (see 0.1
t.n.) – it can be fetched in at 108; see
108.2n.
1–2 **eaten . . . sufferance** atoned for,
made me forget what I suffered
2 **obsequious** compliant to my wishes
(*OED a.* 1)
3 **profess requital** undertake to re-
quite you (RP)
to . . . breadth exactly, in full; a cur-

rent phrase (Dent, H29)
5 **accoutrement** literally 'apparel', i.e.
the social forms in which the 'simple
office of love' (4) is apparelled
compliment F's spelling 'complement', a term meaning 'consummation' (*OED sb.* 3), was indifferently
used also for *compliment*, i.e. courteous
language, which accords with *accoutrement* and *ceremony*, while consummation is implicit in 'the simple office
of love' at 4.
8 **gossip** friend – a term of endearment
among women (*OED sb.* 2)
9 **chamber** inner room, possibly a closet
like that of Doctor Caius in 1.4; see
1.4.35n. Q has instead 'behind the
arras', as at 3.3.83.

76 SD] *Steevens*[3]   77 SD] *Oxf*   **4.2**] *Scena Secunda. F*   0.1] *Rowe; Enter Falstoffe, Mist. Ford,*
Mist. Page, Seruants, Ford, Page, Caius, Euans, Shallow. F; Enter misteris Ford and her two men. Q;
The buck-basket brought out. Enter Falstaff and Mistress Ford. Oxf[1]   1–6] *Mis. For.* Do you heare?
when your M. comes take vp this basket as you did before, and if your M. bid you set it downe, obey
him. / *Ser.* I will forsooth. / *Enter Syr Iohn.* / *Mis. For.* Syr *Iohn* welcome. / *Fal.* What are you sure
of your husband now? *Q*   5 accoutrement] *Capell;* accustrement *F*   compliment] *(*complement*)*
8 SD] *Rowe*   9] Gods body here is misteris *Page,* / Step behind the arras good sir *Iohn. Q*   9 SD]
Rowe; He steps behind the arras. Q

Enter MISTRESS PAGE.

MISTRESS PAGE   How now, sweetheart, who's at home   10
besides yourself?

MISTRESS FORD   Why, none but mine own people.

MISTRESS PAGE   Indeed?

MISTRESS FORD   No, certainly. – [*Whispers.*] Speak
louder.   15

MISTRESS PAGE   Truly, I am so glad you have nobody
here.

MISTRESS FORD   Why?

MISTRESS PAGE   Why, woman, your husband is in his old
lines again: he so takes on yonder with my husband, so   20
rails against all married mankind, so curses all Eve's
daughters, of what complexion soever, and so buffets
himself on the forehead, crying 'peer out, peer out!',
that any madness I ever yet beheld seemed but tame-
ness, civility and patience to this his distemper he is in   25
now. I am glad the fat knight is not here.

MISTRESS FORD   Why, does he talk of him?

MISTRESS PAGE   Of none but him, and swears he was
carried out, the last time he searched for him, in a
basket; protests to my husband he is now here, and hath   30
drawn him and the rest of their company from their
sport, to make another experiment of his suspicion. But

---

12 **people** household dependants; cf.
Falstaff reassuring Quickly, 2.2.48–9n.

14–15 **Speak louder** so as to be heard by
Falstaff. Q gives these words to
Mistress Ford during the buck-basket
scene; see 3.3.102n.

20 **lines** fits of temper (*OED* Line *sb.*[2] 29).
There is no need to adopt Theobald's
emendation to 'lunes' (implying a
minim misreading by the compositor);
used also by Shakespeare in *WT*
2.2.28, i.e. fits of madness.

so . . . with harangues angrily, scolds;
cf. 3.5.37.

23 **peer out** peep out (*OED* Peer *v.*[2] 2),
addressed by Ford to his budding
horns

25 **to . . . distemper** 'compared with the
frenetic condition'; *his* is supereroga-
tory, either introduced for emphasis
or interpolated by the printer's in-
advertency. As for *distemper*, see
3.5.72n.

32 **experiment** trial

9.1] *F2; after 7, Q; not in F*   14 SD] *Theobald (subst.)*   14–15 Speak louder] *at 3.3.102, Q*   20
lines] vaine *Q;* lunes *Theobald*   25 this his] this *(Collier)*

I am glad the knight is not here: now he shall see his own foolery.

MISTRESS FORD   How near is he, Mistress Page?   35

MISTRESS PAGE   Hard by, at street end. He will be here anon.

MISTRESS FORD   I am undone: the knight is here.

MISTRESS PAGE   Why, then you are utterly shamed and he's but a dead man. What a woman are you! Away with   40
him, away with him: better shame than murder.

MISTRESS FORD   Which way should he go? How should I bestow him? Shall I put him into the basket again?

Enter FALSTAFF.

FALSTAFF   No, I'll come no more i'the basket. May I not go out ere he come?   45

MISTRESS PAGE   Alas, three of Master Ford's brothers watch the door with pistols, that none shall issue out, otherwise you might slip away ere he came. – But what make you here?

FALSTAFF   What shall I do? I'll creep up into the   50
chimney.

MISTRESS FORD   There they always use to discharge their birding-pieces.

MISTRESS PAGE   Creep into the kiln-hole.

FALSTAFF   Where is it?   55

36 **street end** the end of the street; a kind of compound replacing the genitive construction (Abbott, 430)
37 **anon** directly, at once
38 **undone** ruined
43 **bestow** dispose of
49 **make you** are you doing; cf. 2.1.213n. Mistress Page pretends indignation; see 3.3.129n.
52–3 **use . . . birding-pieces** Firing the guns used in bird-hunting up chim-

neys served a double purpose: to make sure the weapons were unloaded and to remove the soot from the chimneys. Q has 'Fowling peeces', heavier guns for hunting larger fowl.
54 SP *Though F assigns the speech to Mistress Ford, the suggestion to hide Falstaff in the oven through its door (*kiln-hole*) must come from Mistress Page; see 56.

43.1] *Rowe*   44–5] *F lines* Basket: / come? /   53 birding-pieces] Fowling peeces *Q*   54 SP] *Dyce*
(Malone); speech continued to Mistress Ford F   54 kiln-hole] *(*Kill-hole*)*

MISTRESS FORD   He will seek there, on my word.
Neither press, coffer, chest, trunk, well, vault, but he
hath an abstract for the remembrance of such places
and goes to them by his note. There is no hiding you in
the house.   60

FALSTAFF   I'll go out, then.

MISTRESS PAGE   If you go out in your own semblance
you die, Sir John – unless you go out disguised.

MISTRESS FORD   How might we disguise him?

MISTRESS PAGE   Alas the day, I know not: there is no   65
woman's gown big enough for him. Otherwise he
might put on a hat, a muffler and kerchief, and so
escape.

FALSTAFF   Good hearts, devise something; any extrem-
ity rather than a mischief.   70

MISTRESS FORD   My maid's aunt, the fat woman of
Brentford, has a gown above.

MISTRESS PAGE   On my word, it will serve him. She's as
big as he is – and there's her thrummed hat and her
muffler too. – Run up, Sir John.   75

MISTRESS FORD   Go, go, sweet Sir John. Mistress Page

---

57 **press** large cupboard
58 **abstract** inventory list (like *note* at 59)
62 SP *F assigns this speech to Mistress
Ford. Greg accepts the F speech prefix, but assigns the last five words
('unless you go out disguised') to
Mistress Page.
65 **Alas the day** See 3.5.36n.
67 **muffler** scarf covering the lower part
of the face (*OED sb.* 1a)
kerchief linen head-cover (*OED sb.*
1); see 77, 'linen for your head'
69 **Good hearts** a pleading term; Q has
'For Gods sake'
69–70 **any . . . mischief** proverbial:
'Better an inconvenience than a mis-

chief' (Dent, I62); cf. 'better shame
than murder' at 41
71–2 **the . . . Brentford** a village formerly
named Brainford twelve miles east of
Windsor, now a large suburb of
London on the Thames. Q's reading,
'Gillian of Brainford', was suggested
by the name of the main character in
the ribald poem by Robert Copland,
Jyl of Breyntfords Testament (c. 1560).
But 'Brainford' may conceal a pun on
Ford's name: the fat woman is a creation of his brain.
74 **thrummed** fringed with loose ends of
yarn

62 SP] *Malone, after Q (Mi.Pa.); Mist. Ford. F*   63 John – unless] *(Iohn,* vnlesse*);* John. */ Mistress
Page.* Unless *(Greg)*   69–70 Good . . . extremity] For Gods sake deuise any extremitie, *Q*   71 the
fat woman] Gillian *Q*   72 Brentford] *Capell;* Brainford *Q, F, throughout play*   76–9] *Mis.Pa.* Come
goe with me sir *Iohn,* Ile helpe to dresse you. */ Fal.* Come for God sake, any thing. *Q*

and I will look some linen for your head.

MISTRESS PAGE   Quick, quick! We'll come dress you
     straight; put on the gown the while.   *[Exit Falstaff.]*

MISTRESS FORD   I would my husband would meet him   80
     in this shape! He cannot abide the old woman of
     Brentford; he swears she's a witch, forbade her my
     house and has threatened to beat her.

MISTRESS PAGE   Heaven guide him to thy husband's
     cudgel and the devil guide his cudgel afterwards.   85

MISTRESS FORD   But is my husband coming?

MISTRESS PAGE   Ay, in good sadness is he, and talks of
     the basket too, howsoever he hath had intelligence.

MISTRESS FORD   We'll try that; for I'll appoint my men
     to carry the basket again to meet him at the door with   90
     it, as they did last time.

MISTRESS PAGE   Nay, but he'll be here presently. Let's
     go dress him like the witch of Brentford.

MISTRESS FORD   I'll first direct my men what they shall
     do with the basket. Go up, I'll bring linen for him   95
     straight.

MISTRESS PAGE   Hang him, dishonest varlet! We cannot
     misuse him enough.   *[Exit Mistress Ford.]*

---

77 **look** look for, search out

79, 96 **straight** directly

79 **the while** in the meantime
     SD In the Q version Mistress Page
     exits with Falstaff to help him with his
     disguise, and Mistress Ford remains on
     stage to face Ford and his companions,
     while the servants she had instructed at
     the beginning of the scene (see 4.2n.)
     come in carrying the basket.

81 **shape** attire (i.e. disguise)

87 **in good sadness** seriously, in earnest;
     see 3.5.114n.

88 **howsoever** by whatever means
     intelligence information; as at 140,
     and cf. *gives intelligence* at 3.5.78

89 **try** test; also 'try to find out who gave
     the information'

92 **presently** in a moment; see 4.1.3

97 **dishonest** unchaste, lecherous; a
     deliberate use of the word in contrast
     with *honest* (i.e. chaste) at 100
     varlet Significantly, Mistress Page
     gratifies Falstaff with the same term of
     abuse used by Pistol at 1.3.91, imply-
     ing utter social degradation.

98 ***misuse him** ill-treat him (the ab-
     sence of *him* in F seems an accidental
     omission)
     SD Mistress Ford's exit may be
     placed here or at 96 (where Capell and
     other editors place it). What matters is

79 SD] *F2 (Exit); Exit Mis.Page, & Sir Iohn. Q*   94 direct] *Q3; direct direct F*   97–8] *F lines*
Varlet, / enough: /   98 misuse him] *F2;* misuse *F*   98 SD] *Capell, opp. 96*

247

We'll leave a proof, by that which we will do,
Wives may be merry and yet honest too.　　　　　100
We do not act that often jest and laugh;
'Tis old but true: 'Still swine eats all the draff'.　　[*Exit.*]

[*Enter* MISTRESS FORD *with* JOHN *and* ROBERT.]

MISTRESS FORD　　Go, sirs, take the basket again on your
　　shoulders. Your master is hard at door; if he bid you
　　set it down, obey him. Quickly, dispatch.　　[*Exit.*]
JOHN　Come, come, take it up.　　　　　　　　106
ROBERT　Pray heaven it be not full of knight again.
JOHN　I hope not, I had as lief bear so much lead.

[*Enter* FORD, PAGE, SHALLOW, CAIUS *and* EVANS *at
one door, and* JOHN *and* ROBERT *go and fetch in the
basket at another.*]

FORD　　Ay, but if it prove true, Master Page, have you
　　any way then to unfool me again? – Set down the　　110

that Mistress Page must be left alone
on the stage to deliver directly to the
audience the only rhymed quatrain in
the scene (99–102). This provides a
formal statement of the moral of the
play and of the reason for its title:
quickness of wit in women is not to be
confused with immoral behaviour – a
principle that Queen Elizabeth would
have been the first to subscribe to.
101　**act** commit improper actions
102　**old but true** The current expression
was 'Not so old as true' (Dent, O34.1,
quoting Henry Porter, *Two Angry
Women of Abingdon* (1599?): ''Tis an
olde Proverbe, & not so old as true').
Still . . . draff It is the quiet pig that
eats up the hog's-wash, i.e. those who
efface themselves are the real malefac-

tors. Proverbial from 1546 (Dent, S681)
104　**hard at door** right at the door (*OED*
Hard *adv.* 6). Cf. *Hard by* at 36.
108　**had as lief** would as willingly
108.1　CAIUS not included in the Q SD
(see t.n.) and mute throughout the
scene, but his presence in Ford's company is required by what is said at the
end of 3.3, and his name is listed in the
F massed entry direction at the beginning of this scene.
108.2–3　**and . . . basket** Since the servants
don't know how heavy the basket is
(107–8), either they fetch it in at this
point or it was brought in at the beginning of the scene, as Oxf[1] suggests; see
4.2n. and 0.1 t.n.
110　**unfool me** a Shakespearean coinage:
make me less of a fool. Obviously Page

102 SD] *Capell*　102.1] *Q (subst.), at 0.1; here as in Capell (Re-enter Mistress* Ford *with her two
Men); Enter Ser.* F2, *after 105*　104–5 if . . . him] *cf. Q at 1–6*　105 SD] *Capell; Exeunt Mrs. Page
and Mrs. Ford. / Theobald*　106, 108 SP] *Ard²; 1 Ser.* F　107 SP] *Ard²; 2 Ser.* F　108 as lief] *F2;
liefe as* F　108.1 *Enter . . .* EVANS] *Rowe; Enter M.Ford, Page, Priest, Shallow, the two men carries the
basket, and Ford meets it. Q*　108.1–3 *at one . . . another*] *this edn after Q (see 108.1)*

248

basket, villains. Somebody call my wife. Youth in a
basket! O you panderly rascals, there's a knot, a gin, a
pack, a conspiracy against me. Now shall the devil be
shamed. – What, wife, I say! Come, come forth: behold
what honest clothes you send forth to bleaching!   115
PAGE   Why, this passes, Master Ford! You are not to go
loose any longer, you must be pinioned.
EVANS   Why, this is lunatics, this is mad as a mad dog.
SHALLOW   Indeed, Master Ford, this is not well indeed.
FORD   So say I too, sir.   120

[*Enter* MISTRESS FORD.]

Come hither, Mistress Ford – Mistress Ford, the
honest woman, the modest wife, the virtuous creature
that hath the jealous fool to her husband! I suspect
without cause, mistress, do I?

has been warning Ford that if this
time, too, no intruder is found in the
house, he will look like a fool. Ford
retorts that likewise if his suspicions
prove true he will be considered a fool
for being a cuckold.
111 *villains F has 'villaine:': a common
misreading of final 's' as a comma or
semicolon, substituted by the printer
with a colon.
111–12 Youth . . . basket! first example
of a proverbial phrase alluding ironically to an adventurous lover (Dent,
Y51), possibly from such popular
sixteenth-century interludes as *Lusty
Juventus*, whose central figure (the
type of the prodigal son) was called
'Youth'
112 panderly pimping, bawdy
  knot band; see 3.2.46n.
  gin snare, trap; many editors prefer
  F2's reading 'ging', meaning 'gang'
  (*OED* Ging *sb.* 3)

113–14 shall . . . shamed proverbial:
  'Speak truth and shame the devil'
  (Dent, T566); cf. Hotspur in *1H4*
  3.1.58, 61
114 What . . . say Nobody had heeded
  Ford's request to call his wife at 111.
  Mistress Ford might enter at this
  point, but most editors delay her
  entrance till 120, when Ford addresses
  her directly. There is no direction in F,
  while in the Q version she is already on
  stage (see 79 SDn.). The timing of
  entrances and exits could be left to the
  discretion of the actors.
116 this passes It surpasses belief, is
  incredible; see 1.1.278n.
117 pinioned tied up; the usual 'cure' for
  madmen at the time
118 lunatics lunacy; see 4.1.61n.
  mad as . . . dog a common phrase;
  Dent (M2.1) records it from 1529
123 to as

111 villains] *Collier²*; villaine *F*   112 gin] ging *F2*; gang *Oxf*   120.1] *Hanmer; after 118 Theobald;
after I say! at 114 (this edn)*   121–2 Mistress Ford, . . . creature] Misteris *Ford* the modest woman, /
Misteris *Ford* the vertuous woman, *Q*   123 jealous] *(iealious)*

MISTRESS FORD   God be my witness you do, if you   125
  suspect me in any dishonesty.

FORD   Well said, brazen-face, hold it out! – Come forth,
  sirrah! [*Pulls clothes from the basket.*]

PAGE   This passes.

MISTRESS FORD   Are you not ashamed? Let the clothes   130
  alone.

FORD   I shall find you anon.

EVANS   'Tis unreasonable! Will you take up your wife's
  clothes? Come, away!

FORD   Empty the basket, I say.   135

PAGE   Why, man, why?

FORD   Master Page, as I am a man, there was one conveyed out of my house yesterday in this basket. Why
  may not he be there again? In my house I am sure he is:
  my intelligence is true, my jealousy is reasonable. –   140
  Pluck me out all the linen.

MISTRESS FORD   If you find a man there, he shall die a
  flea's death. [*They empty the basket.*]

125 ***God** Oxf's emendation of F's
'Heauen' to 'God' is supported by the
Q reading 'Gods my record' (see t.n.),
and by Mistress Ford's indignant tone,
though Shaheen (143) refers to
Romans, 1.9: 'Heaven be my witness'.
127 **brazen-face . . . out** ironical: 'Keep
up your pretence, you impudent
woman'. The expression 'He has a
brazen face' was current from 1563
(Dent, F8), and cf. *LLL* 5.2.395: 'Can
any face of brass hold longer out?'
129 See 116n.
133–4 **take . . . clothes** Evans 'means
"pick up your wife's dirty clothes", but
what he says is "lift up your wife's
dress", the preliminary to sexual inter-

course' (Hibbard). Cf. the same equivocation at *TS* 4.3.162: 'Take up my
mistress' gown to his master's use!'
136 SP ***F** assigns the speech to '*M.Ford*'
(Mistress Ford?), presumably an oversight for '*M.Page*' (Master Page), to
whom its pleading tone is much more
appropriate.
140 **intelligence** information; see 88n.
141 **me** for me; not necessarily an ethic
dative; see 1.3.55n.
142–3 **he . . . death** Recalling the expression 'die a dog's death' (Dent, D509),
i.e. wretchedly, Mistress Ford under-
takes to kill the intruder with her own
fingers, since he cannot be larger than
a flea.

125 God . . . do] *Oxf (after Q):* Heauen be my witnesse you doe *F;* I Gods my record do you *Q*
127–8 Come forth, sirrah] You youth in a basket, come out here, / Pull out the cloathes, search *Q*
128 SD] *Rowe (subst.)*   133 'Tis unreasonable] Ieshu plesse me *Q*   take] pull *Q*   135–6] *Pa.* Fie
M.*Ford* you are not to go abroad if you be in these fits. / *Sir Hu.* By so kad vdge me, tis verie
necessarie / He were put in pethlem. *Q*   136 SP] *Oxf (Lambrechts);* M.*Ford.* F   137 a man] an
honest man *Q*   143 SD] *this edn*

PAGE   Here's no man.

SHALLOW   By my fidelity, this is not well, Master Ford,   145
this wrongs you.

EVANS   Master Ford, you must pray, and not follow the
imaginations of your own heart: this is jealousies.

FORD   Well, he's not here I seek for.

PAGE   No, nor nowhere else but in your brain.   150

FORD   Help to search my house this one time. If I find not
what I seek, show no colour for my extremity, let me for
ever be your table-sport. Let them say of me 'As jealous
as Ford, that searched a hollow walnut for his wife's
leman'. Satisfy me once more, once more search with   155
me.   [*Exeunt John and Robert with basket.*]

MISTRESS FORD   What ho, Mistress Page, come you and
the old woman down; my husband will come into the
chamber.

FORD   Old woman? What old woman's that?   160

MISTRESS FORD   Why, it is my maid's aunt of Brentford.

FORD   A witch, a quean, an old cozening quean! Have I
not forbid her my house? She comes of errands, does

---

145 **By my fidelity** Shallow's improvement on the oath 'By my faith' or 'In
faith'

146 **wrongs** disgraces (Hibbard); cf.
1.1.294n. and 3.3.152–3, 192

147 **pray** to exorcise the devil that pos-
sesses him

147–8 **follow . . . heart** alluding to
Jeremiah, 13.10: 'They folowe the
wicked imaginations of their owne
heart'.

149 **here** in the basket (but must be else-
where in the house)

152 **show . . . extremity** (If I) find no reasonable ground for my extravagance
(*OED* Colour *sb.* 12b, and Extremity
sb. 5)

153 **table-sport** laughing stock for your
jokes at table

153–4 **Let . . . Ford** Cam² compares *TC*
3.2.195–6: 'let them say . . . "As false
as Cressid"'.

154 **hollow walnut** proverbially the
most unlikely hiding place; cf. *Ham*
2.2.254: 'I could be bounded in a nut-
shell'.

155 **leman** lover (archaic, used of unlaw-
ful relations)

162 **quean** disreputable woman, bawd or
prostitute
cozening cheating; *cozenage* and *cozened* occur repeatedly in the reports
of the horse-stealing episode at
4.5.61–88

163 **errands** Their nature is always
looked upon with suspicion; see
Simple's errand at 1.4.70 and
Quickly's at 3.4.107.

---

156 SD] *Ard²*   161 it . . . of] my maidens Ant, *Gillia* of *Q*

she? We are simple men, we do not know what's
brought to pass under the profession of fortune-telling.　165
She works by charms, by spells, by the figure, and such
daubery as this is, beyond our element: we know nothing. – Come down, you witch, you hag, you! Come
down, I say!

MISTRESS FORD　Nay, good sweet husband – good　170
gentlemen, let him not strike the old woman.

Enter FALSTAFF, *disguised like an old woman,*
and MISTRESS PAGE.

MISTRESS PAGE　Come, mother Prat, come, give me your
hand.

FORD　I'll prat her! [*Beats him.*] Out of my door, you
witch, you rag, you baggage, you polecat, you runnion,　175
out, out! I'll conjure you, I'll fortune-tell you!

[*Exit Falstaff.*]

165 **under the profession** in the name
166 **figure** astrological sign (*OED sb.* 14)
　from which horoscopes are cast
167 **daubery** false outward show (*OED*
　Daub *v.* 7)
　beyond our element outside our
　sphere, incomprehensible; a common
　phrase (Dent, E107); cf. *TN* 3.1.57–9,
　'[You] are out of my welkin – I might say
　"element", but the word is overworn.'
171 ***not strike** The omission of *not* in F
　looks like a printing-house accident.
171.1–2 Mistress Page's speech at 172–3
　suggests that she is helping Falstaff in
　his disguise to descend from *above*,
　implying the presence on the stage of
　stairs visible to the audience. See note
　3 on p. 21.
172 **mother Prat** In Q the old woman of
　Brainford is always called Gillian (see
　71–2n.). The change to Prat in F seems

intended to avoid identification with a
character known to the public through
other sources. The choice of the new
name was probably prompted by its
jocular implications, 'prat[s]' meaning
'buttocks' (*OED* Prat *sb²*).
174 **I'll prat her** a repetition, most likely
　in threatening tone, of a name or noun
　previously used, as Pistol does at *H5*
　4.4.28–9: 'Master Fer! I'll fer him,
　and firk him, and ferret him.'; cf. *I'll*
　fortune-tell you at 176.
175 **rag** worthless person; no need to
　accept F3's 'hag', used at 168
　polecat whore; see 4.1.24n.
　runnion an abusive term for a woman,
　possibly from French *rongneux*, i.e.
　scurvy, found as 'ronyon' at *Mac* 1.3.6
　and as 'roynish' (of a man) at *AYL* 2.2.8
176 **conjure** use charms upon (an activity
　attributed to mother Prat)

171 not] *Q3; not in F*　171.1–2] *Q (Enter Falstaffe disguised like an old woman, and misteris Page with*
him, Ford beates him, and hee runnes away.); not in F　174 SD] *Q, see 171.1–2*　175 rag] *(Ragge);*
Hagge *Q3;* Hag *F3*　runnion] ronyon *Capell*　176 SD] *F2; Q at 171.1–2*

MISTRESS PAGE   Are you not ashamed? I think you have
    killed the poor woman.

MISTRESS FORD   Nay, he will do it. 'Tis a goodly credit
    for you!   180

FORD   Hang her, witch!

EVANS   By yea and no, I think the 'oman is a witch indeed.
    I like not when a 'oman has a great peard – I spy a great
    peard under her muffler.

FORD   Will you follow, gentlemen? I beseech you, follow,   185
    see but the issue of my jealousy. If I cry out thus upon
    no trail, never trust me when I open again.

PAGE   Let's obey his humour a little further. Come,
    gentlemen.   *Exeunt all but Mistress Ford and Mistress Page.*

MISTRESS PAGE   By my troth, he beat him most pitifully.   190

MISTRESS FORD   Nay, by th'mass, that he did not: he
    beat him most unpitifully, methought.

MISTRESS PAGE   I'll have the cudgel hallowed and hung
    o'er the altar: it hath done meritorious service.

179–80 **'Tis ... you!** 'ironical: it does you
    great credit' (Hibbard)
182 **By ... no** The expression is used by
    Shallow (see 1.1.80n.) and adapted by
    Mistress Quickly, 1.4.87–8n.
183 **spy** Oxf¹ emends to 'spied' (an easy
    misreading of 'spie' in the copy)
    'because Falstaff is no longer in
    sight'.
184 ***her** F reads 'his', which may be
    Evans's confusion, but more likely
    Shakespeare's slip or a printer's mis-
    reading of 'hir', an alternative spelling
    of *her*, in the copy.
185 **follow** follow me
186 **issue** final outcome
186–7 **cry . . . again** hunting imagery:

cry out is the barking of the hounds,
trail the scent of the quarry, *open* the
first barking of the hounds when they
think they have found the scent. The
locution 'never trust me when' is very
common in Shakespeare (Dent,
T558.1).
188 **obey his humour** humour him, i.e.
    comply with his whims
190 ***By my troth** replaced in F, for the
    usual reasons, by 'Trust me'
193–4 **cudgel ... altar** This canonization
    of the cudgel as a holy relic is con-
    trasted by Cam² with Falstaff's threat,
    at 2.2.265–7, saying that his cudgel
    'shall hang like a meteor o'er the cuck-
    old's horns'.

177–8] *F lines* asham'd? / woman. /   182 By ... no] By Ieshu *Q*   183 spy] *(spie)*; espied *Q;*
spied *Oxf¹*   184 her] *Q;* his *F*   188–9] *F lines* further: / Gentlemen. /   189 SD] *Q (Exit omnes.);*
not in F; Exeunt. F2   190 By my troth] *Q;* Trust me *F*   pitifully] extreamly *Q*

MISTRESS FORD   What think you? May we, with the   195
warrant of womanhood and the witness of a good
conscience, pursue him with any further revenge?

MISTRESS PAGE   The spirit of wantonness is sure scared
out of him. If the devil have him not in fee-simple, with
fine and recovery, he will never, I think, in the way of   200
waste, attempt us again.

MISTRESS FORD   Shall we tell our husbands how we have
served him?

MISTRESS PAGE   Yes, by all means, if it be but to scrape
the figures out of your husband's brains. If they can   205
find in their hearts the poor unvirtuous fat knight
shall be any further afflicted, we two will still be the
ministers.

MISTRESS FORD   I'll warrant they'll have him publicly
shamed, and methinks there would be no period to the   210
jest should he not be publicly shamed.

MISTRESS PAGE   Come, to the forge with it, then shape
it: I would not have things cool.   *Exeunt.*

196–7 **witness . . . conscience** a phrase
of scriptural origin, suggesting such
proverbs as 'Conscience is witness
enough' (Tilley, C603)

198 **spirit of wantonness** demon of lust;
cf. *spirit* at 3.3.200.

199–200 **fee-simple . . . recovery** legal
terminology: absolute possession, with
no possibility of termination or transfer (of the property concerned)

200–1 **in . . . waste** The legal metaphor is
continued: *waste* (*OED sb.* 7) is an act
of damage by a tenant to the owner's
property. Mistress Page compares
Falstaff's attempt at their virtue to
wilful damage to property.

204–5 **scrape the figures** erase the

fancies or imaginings; cf. *JC* 2.1.231:
'Thou hast no figures nor no fan-
tasies'.

206 **find . . . hearts** decide; a common
expression (Dent, HH14) frequent in
Shakespeare

208 **ministers** agents, executants

210 **period** appropriate end; see 3.3.40n.

212–13 a brilliant adaptation of the current saying 'Strike while the iron is
hot' (Dent, I94), from the forging of
metals: the new *jest* must be first
devised (put into the forge), then ham-
mered into shape as soon as possible.
Cf. *3H6* 5.1.49: 'strike now, or else the
iron cools'.

---

212 it, then shape] it then, shape *Hanmer*   213 SD] *Exit both. Q*

4.3   *Enter* HOST *and* BARDOLPH.

BARDOLPH   Sir, the German desires to have three of your
horses. The Duke himself will be tomorrow at court,
and they are going to meet him.

HOST   What duke should that be comes so secretly? I hear   5
not of him in the court. Let me speak with the gentlemen – they speak English?

BARDOLPH   Ay, sir. I'll call him to you.

HOST   They shall have my horses, but I'll make them pay,
I'll sauce them. They have had my house a week at   10
command. I have turned away my other guests: they
must come off, I'll sauce them. Come.   *Exeunt.*

4.3 This brief scene in the Garter Inn,
preserved in both the Quarto and the
Folio versions, opens up yet another
subplot, curiously marginal in respect
of the main action, or actions, of the
play. If, as most commentators agree,
it was introduced for the sake of a specific topical reference (see pp. 26–7),
one wonders why it should not have
been cut when the topical allusions it
contained were no longer of interest to
new audiences. In fact the trick played
on the Host of the Garter by the
German cozeners gives the crowning
touch to the central theme of the play,
that of the deceiver deceived, represented in the first place by Falstaff, and
also in varying measure by most of the
other main characters, from Master
Ford to Parson Evans, from Mistress
Page to Doctor Caius, and even
Bardolph and Nim. It is appropriate
that the Host, presented as the wise
arbiter of Windsor quarrels, should in
his turn also be cheated.

1   **German desires** Most editors since

Capell have emended to 'Germans
desire', in view of the fact that, as
stated in Q, the request comes from
'three Gentlemen' (see t.n.). But
Bardolph uses the singular presumably
referring to the one acting as their
spokesman.

4   **comes** that comes. For the omission of
the relative pronoun see Abbott, 244.

7   **him** Q has 'them'. Once again
Bardolph refers to the one he has been
talking to, rather than to all three of
them.

9, 11   **sauce them** charge them extortion-
ate prices (*OED* Sauce *v.* 4a, giving
only this example)

9–10   **at command** at their disposal. But
obviously Falstaff, and presumably
Shallow and Slender, are still lodging at
the Garter, and the guests turned away
must be later newcomers; either the
Host is exaggerating, or by *houses* (the F
reading for Q 'house' at 9) he means
'rooms', as he jocularly describes
Falstaff's chamber (*his house*) at 4.5.5.

11   **come off** pay up

4.3] *Scena Tertia. F*   1–2 the . . . horses] heere be three Gentlemen come from the Duke the
Stanger sir, would haue your horse *Q*   1 German desires] *(Germane desires);* Germans desire
Capell   6 they] do they *Q*   7 him] them *Q*   8 They . . . pay] No *Bardolfe,* let them alone *Q*   9
house] *Q;* houses *F*   10–11 they must . . . Come] They shall haue my horses *Bardolfe,* / They must
come off, Ile sawce them *Q*   11 come off] *Q, F;* count off *Hanmer (Warburton);* not come off *Capell*

4.4   *Enter* PAGE, FORD, MISTRESS PAGE,
                          MISTRESS FORD *and* EVANS.

EVANS   'Tis one of the best discretions of a 'oman as ever
    I did look upon.
PAGE   And did he send you both these letters at an
    instant?   5
MISTRESS PAGE   Within a quarter of an hour.
FORD
    Pardon me, wife. Henceforth do what thou wilt:
    I rather will suspect the sun with cold
    Than thee with wantonness. Now doth thy honour
        stand,
    In him that was of late an heretic,
    As firm as faith.   10
PAGE   'Tis well, 'tis well, no more.
    Be not as extreme in submission as in offence.
    But let our plot go forward. Let our wives
    Yet once again, to make us public sport,
    Appoint a meeting with this old fat fellow,   15
    Where we may take him and disgrace him for it.

4.4 Apparently located in Page's house, this is one of the rare verse-scenes in the play – except for all of Evans's speeches (1–2, 19–22, 65–7, 78–9) and a few by other characters (3–5, 16–18, 80). The Q version, omitting 1–5 and shortening the rest of the scene, follows the same pattern and introduces at the end three rhyming couplets not present in F. It is just possible to imagine that this scene adapts and extends a similar one in a different early version of a play or entertainment where Evans had no part (see pp. 71–80).

1   'Tis . . . 'oman She is one of the best instances of feminine discretion (i.e. good sense).

3–4   **at an instant** at the same time
7   ***with cold** of being cold; F's 'gold' is an obvious error
9   **heretic** misbeliever
11–12 The first line is hypermetrical, so that Capell suggested treating *submission* as a quadrisyllable, and considering *as in offence* as a separate short line. But line 11 sounds like a *sententia*, i.e. a precept quoted by Page in prose form. A better metrical regularization is the one proposed by RP, who divides the lines after 'submission' and after 'forward', so that *Let our wives* becomes an independent short line, such as is found when a speech takes a new turn.

4.4] *Scena Quarta. F*   0.1] *Enter Ford, Page, their wiues, Shallow, and Slender. Syr Hu. Q*   7 cold]
Rowe; gold *F*   11–12] *Capell lines* submission, / offence. / wives /; submission / forward. / wives /
(RP)

FORD   There is no better way than that they spoke of.

PAGE   How? To send him word they'll meet him in the
park at midnight? Fie, fie, he'll never come.

EVANS   You say he has been thrown in the rivers, and has   20
been grievously peaten, as an old 'oman. Methinks
there should be terrors in him, that he should not come.
Methinks his flesh is punished, he shall have no desires.

PAGE   So think I too.

MISTRESS FORD

Devise but how you'll use him when he comes   25
And let us two devise to bring him thither.

MISTRESS PAGE

There is an old tale goes that Herne the hunter,
Sometime a keeper here in Windsor Forest,
Doth, all the winter time, at still midnight,
Walk round about an oak, with great ragg'd horns,   30
And there he blasts the trees, and takes the cattle,
And makes milch-kine yield blood and shakes a chain
In a most hideous and dreadful manner.
You have heard of such a spirit, and well you know,
The superstitious idle-headed eld   35
Received and did deliver to our age
This tale of Herne the hunter for a truth.

---

24 **use** treat
26 **Herne the hunter** The *tale* or legend
seems to be of Shakespeare's own
invention. Q spells 'Horne', somewhat
too obviously allusive, while *Herne*
suggests the heron, a water bird that
could be found on the Thames banks.
27 **Sometime** formerly
28 **still** quiet, silent
29 **ragg'd** jagged
30 **blasts** withers, or strikes as with light-

ning
takes bewitches (Ard², comparing
with 'taking', i.e. being bewitched, at
KL 3.4.60)
31 **milch-kine** dairy cattle
shakes a chain typical of ghosts or
evil spirits; cf. 'roaring, shrieking,
howling, jingling chains' at *Tem*
5.1.233
34 **idle-headed eld** ignorant people of
earlier ages (*OED* Eld *sb.*² 5b)

26–7] *Q3; prose F*   26 Herne] *Horne Q, throughout play*   29 ragg'd horns] *(*rag'd-hornes*);* jag'd
horns *Capell*   30 trees] *Hanmer;* tree *F*   31 makes] *F2;* make *F*

PAGE
    Why, yet there want not many that do fear
    In deep of night to walk by this Herne's oak.
    But what of this?
MISTRESS FORD   Marry, this is our device: 40
    That Falstaff at that oak shall meet with us,
    Disguised like Herne, with huge horns on his head.
PAGE
    Well, let it not be doubted but he'll come,
    And in this shape; when you have brought him thither,
    What shall be done with him? What is your plot?
MISTRESS PAGE   45
    That likewise have we thought upon, and thus:
    Nan Page my daughter, and my little son,
    And three or four more of their growth, we'll dress
    Like urchins, oafs and fairies, green and white,
    With rounds of waxen tapers on their heads   50
    And rattles in their hands. Upon a sudden,
    As Falstaff, she and I are newly met,
    Let them from forth a sawpit rush at once
    With some diffused song; upon their sight
    We two in great amazedness will fly;   55
    Then let them all encircle him about,
    And fairy-like to pinch the unclean knight,
    And ask him why, that hour of fairy revel,
    In their so sacred paths he dares to tread

---

37 **want not** are (literally: are not lacking)
41 *This line, missing in F presumably because of a compositorial oversight, is supplied from Q, as it provides the indication of Falstaff's *shape* (43) at Herne's oak, essential to the play.
47 **growth** age (and size)
48 **urchins** goblins, elves, i.e. male fairies (*OED* Urchin *sb*. 1c)
    oafs children of elves; hence oafs were considered changelings.

49 **rounds** circlets
52 **sawpit** pit across which timber was laid to be sawn (Oxf[1])
53 **diffused** diffusèd; either 'divided into musical parts', or 'confused', 'mixed'
56 **to pinch** The *to* is redundant, and seems to have been inserted for the sake of the metre, unless it be taken, as some editors did (see t.n.), to be an intensive prefix: 'to-pinch' meaning pinch repeatedly.
    unclean corrupt; see 5.5.90n.

41] *Q (Horne); not in F*   43 shape; when] *Capell;* shape, when *F;* shape when *F2*   48 oafs]
(Ouphes)   56 to pinch] too, pinch *Warburton;* to-pinch *Steevens[2] (Tyrwhitt)*

In shape profane.

MISTRESS FORD   And till he tell the truth   60
Let the supposed fairies pinch him sound
And burn him with their tapers.

MISTRESS PAGE   The truth being known,
We'll all present ourselves, dishorn the spirit,
And mock him home to Windsor.

FORD   The children must
Be practised well to this, or they'll ne'er do't.   65

EVANS   I will teach the children their behaviours, and I
will be like a jackanapes also, to burn the knight with
my taber.

FORD

That will be excellent, I'll go buy them vizards.

MISTRESS PAGE

My Nan shall be the queen of all the fairies,   70
Finely attired in a robe of white.

PAGE

That silk will I go buy – [*aside*] and in that time

---

59 SP *F assigns this speech to Ford, but
it is clear from the context that the
speaker must be his wife.
60 **supposed** supposèd
   sound soundly
62 **dishorn** remove the horns; a symbolic
action, the stag's horns being the signs
of his sexual potency
   spirit i.e Falstaff, identified with the
   spirit of wantonness; see 4.2.198n.
66 **jackanapes** literal: tame monkey
entertaining people at fairs with its
tricks. At 1.4.102 Caius had called
Evans *jackanape priest* and at 2.3.76 he
had used the same term for Slender.
Now Evans is ready to accept that role
in its original sense.
67 **taber** Evans's pronunciation of 'taper'

evokes the 'tabor', a musical instru-
ment (small drum) mentioned repeatedly in the Bible.
68 **vizards** masks
69–70 This speech suggests that the
author's original intention had been to
make Anne impersonate the Fairy
Queen in the Garter masque (5.5.37–73)
and that he only later transferred the
role to Mistress Quickly (see pp. 52–5).
Significantly in Q Page says at this point:
'my daughter *Anne*, / Shall like a litle
Fayrie be disguised', and again 'in a robe
of white / Ile cloathe my daughter', with
no mention of the Queen of Fairies.
70 **attired** attirèd
71 **time** Theobald's emendation, 'tire', i.e.
attire, robe, is ingenious but unnecessary.

---

59 SP] *Rowe; Ford. F*   65 I . . . behaviours] So kad vdge me the deuises is excellent *Q*   68] *Pope; F
lines* excellent, / vizards. /   69–70] *Rowe³; prose F*   71–2] *Mis. For.* But who will buy the silkes to tyre
the boyes? / *Pa.* That will I do, and in a robe of white / Ile cloath my daughter, and aduertise *Slender* /
To know her by that signe, and steale her thence, *Q*   71 SD] *Pope, opp. 72*   time] tire *Theobald*

Shall Master Slender steal my Nan away,
And marry her at Eton. – Go, send to Falstaff straight.
FORD
    Nay, I'll to him again in name of Brook: 75
    He'll tell me all his purpose. Sure, he'll come.
MISTRESS PAGE
    Fear not you that. Go get us properties
    And tricking for our fairies.
EVANS   Let us about it. – It is admirable pleasures and
    ferry honest knaveries.   *[Exeunt Page, Ford and Evans.]*
MISTRESS PAGE   Go, Mistress Ford,
    Send quickly to Sir John to know his mind.
                          [Exit Mistress Ford.]
    I'll to the Doctor: he hath my good will,
    And none but he, to marry with Nan Page.
    That Slender, though well landed, is an idiot –   85
    And he my husband best of all affects.
    The Doctor is well moneyed, and his friends
    Potent at court: he, none but he, shall have her,
    Though twenty thousand worthier come to crave her.
                                  [Exit.]

---

73 **Eton** across the Thames from Windsor

74 **Nay** or rather. The stress is on *I'll*: Ford will *again* personally visit Falstaff rather than *send* to him, as suggested by Page at 73.

75 **purpose** intentions

76 **properties** a theatrical term still in use (props): the equipment required for a performance

77 **tricking** costumes and ornaments

79 **ferry honest knaveries** Evans's brilliant involuntary oxymoron (the adjective contradicting the noun – knavery cannot be honest)

81 **quickly** Some editors capitalize the word since in fact Mistress Quickly is sent to give Falstaff the assignation at Herne's oak.

84 **well landed** rich in landed properties; balancing *well moneyed*, wealthy, said of Doctor Caius (86)

85 **affects** likes; see 2.1.100n.

88 **worthier** more deserving, rather than better endowed with money or land (Oxf[1])

78–9] *Pope; F lines* it, / knaueries.   79 SD] *Rowe*   81 quickly] Quickly *Theobald*   81 SD] *Rowe*
82–3, 86–7] *Mis. Pa.* And in that Maske Ile make the Doctor steale my daughter *An*, & ere my husband knowes it, to carrie her to Church, and marrie her. *Q, before 71*   88 SD] *F2*

4.5   *Enter* HOST *and* SIMPLE.

HOST   What wouldst thou have, boor? What, thick-skin?
Speak, breathe, discuss – brief, short, quick, snap.

SIMPLE   Marry, sir, I come to speak with Sir John Falstaff
from Master Slender.   5

HOST   There's his chamber, his house, his castle, his
standing-bed, and truckle-bed: 'tis painted about with
the story of the Prodigal, fresh and new. Go, knock and
call: he'll speak like an anthropophaginian unto thee.
Knock, I say.   10

SIMPLE   There's an old woman, a fat woman, gone up into
his chamber. I'll be so bold as stay, sir, till she come
down. I come to speak with her indeed.

HOST   Ha? A fat woman? The knight may be robbed, I'll
call. – Bully knight, bully Sir John! Speak from thy   15
lungs military: art thou there? It is thine host, thine
Ephesian, calls.

4.5 This scene, once again in the Garter
Inn, links up with 4.3, as the conclusion of the horse-stealing subplot. The
main difference in Q is that Evans and
the Doctor enter in reverse order to
bring the bad news (their revenge for
the trick played on them by the Host).

1   **thick-skin** blockhead, synonymous
     with *boor*. Puck calls Bottom 'the shal-
     lowest thick-skin of that barren sort' in
     MND 3.2.13.

2   **Speak, breathe, discuss** three syn-
     onymous verbs. For *discuss* see 1.3.89n.
     brief . . . snap The Host's addiction to
     sequences of synonyms extends to
     adjectives and adverbs; *snap* is both, in
     the sense of 'quick' or 'quickly', con-
     nected with the verb 'to snip'; cf. *LLL*
     5.1.59–60: 'snip, snap, quick and home.'

5   **his castle** ironical reference to the
     proverb 'A man's house is his castle'
     (Dent, M473)

6   **truckle-bed** a small bed on castors
     that could be stored under the regular
     standing-bed

6–7 **'tis . . . Prodigal** It was common to
     have rooms decorated either with wall-
     paintings or with painted wall-hang-
     ings (frequently misnamed 'arras'; see
     the one behind which Falstaff hides at
     3.3.85 SD). See also those mentioned
     by Falstaff at *2H4* 2.1.143–5 to replace
     Hostess Quickly's 'tapestries of my
     dining-chambers' which she is going
     to pawn for his sake: 'and for thy walls,
     a pretty slight drollery, or the story of
     the Prodigal'. The parable of the
     Prodigal son, from Luke, 15 (see
     4.2.111–12n.), was a favourite subject
     for such decorations.

8   **anthropophaginian** literally, canni-
     bal, man-eater – used by the Host as
     the 'ogre' in children's stories

11   **stay** wait

14   **Bully** a favourite word with the Host;
     see 1.3.2n.

15   **lungs military** an emphatic inversion
     typical of the Host's style

16   **Ephesian** The page (Robin) calls
     Falstaff's boon companions in East-

4.5] *Scena Quinta. F*   0.1] *Q; Enter Host, Simple, Falstaffe, Bardolfe, Euans, Caius, Quickly. F*

FALSTAFF [*above*]   How now, mine host?

HOST   Here's a Bohemian-Tartar tarries the coming
down of thy fat woman. Let her descend, bully, let her   20
descend. My chambers are honourable. Fie! Privacy?
Fie!

Enter FALSTAFF.

FALSTAFF   There was, mine host, an old fat woman even
now with me, but she's gone.

SIMPLE   Pray you, sir, was't not the wise woman of   25
Brentford?

FALSTAFF   Ay, marry, was it, mussel-shell. What would
you with her?

SIMPLE   My master, sir, my master, Master Slender, sent
to her, seeing her go thorough the streets, to know, sir,   30
whether one Nim, sir, that beguiled him of a chain, had
the chain, or no.

FALSTAFF   I spake with the old woman about it.

cheap 'Ephesians . . . of the old church'
at *2H4* 2.2.150. The reputation of
Ephesians as corrupt comes from
Paul's warning to them against their
'former conversation' with 'the old
man which is corrupt' (Ephesians,
4.22). By calling himself Ephesian the
Host reminds Falstaff of their habit of
drinking together; see 3.2.78–9: 'I will
to my honest knight Falstaff, and drink
canary with him.'
17 SD Falstaff's reply from above confirms the impression that the play was
conceived for a playing space on two
levels, possibly joined by a staircase in
view of the audience; see 4.2.171.1–2n.
18 **Bohemian-Tartar**   Tartar   from
Bohemia – the usual nonsensical play
on exotic national names, practised also
by Pistol (see *Phrygian Turk* at 1.3.85)

tarries awaits
20 **Privacy** concealment (*OED sb.* 3) of
improper behaviour
24 **wise woman** fortune-teller, skilled in
magic arts
26 **mussel-shell** a variant of 'egg-shell',
for 'empty-headed person'
26–7 **What . . . her** Cf. Falstaff to Quickly
at 2.2.38: *What with me?*
28 *****master, Master Slender** Simple
must give the full title, 'Master
Slender', of his master – saying only,
as in F, 'my master Slender' would be
too familiar (RP).
29 **thorough** an archaic alternative form
of 'through'
30 **beguiled . . . chain** robbed him of a
chain; Slender does not mention a
chain when reporting how he was
robbed in a tavern at 1.1.116–70.

17 SD] *Q2 (he speakes aboue)*; *Enter* Falstaff *Rowe*; *within Oxf* 21.1] *Q (Enter Sir Iohn.), after
23; not in F* 28 My . . . Slender] *this edn (RP)*; Marry sir my maister *Slender Q*; My Master (Sir)
my master *Slender F*; My master, sir, master Slender *Steevens²*

SIMPLE   And what says she, I pray, sir?

FALSTAFF   Marry, she says that the very same man that   35
beguiled Master Slender of his chain – cozened him
of it.

SIMPLE   I would I could have spoken with the woman
herself. I had other things to have spoken with her too,
from him.   40

FALSTAFF   What are they? Let us know.

HOST   Ay, come. Quick!

SIMPLE   I may not conceal them, sir.

HOST   Conceal them, or thou diest.

SIMPLE   Why, sir, they were nothing but about Mistress   45
Anne Page, to know if it were my master's fortune to
have her, or no.

FALSTAFF   'Tis, 'tis his fortune.

SIMPLE   What, sir?

FALSTAFF   To have her, or no. Go, say the woman told   50
me so.

SIMPLE   May I be bold to say so, sir?

FALSTAFF   Ay, sir Tike; who more bold?

SIMPLE   I thank your worship; I shall make my master
glad with these tidings.   [*Exit*]

HOST   Thou art clerkly, thou art clerkly, Sir John. Was
there a wise woman with thee?

---

35 **cozened** cheated – synonymous with
beguiled
42 SP *In F *Fal.*, i.e. Falstaff, which is
obviously mistaken
42 **conceal** Simple means the opposite:
reveal; and the Host jocularly humours
him.
47 **fortune** Simple means 'good luck';
Falstaff means 'chance'.
51 **bold to say** cf. Simple's *bold as stay* at
11
52 *sir . . . **bold** The arguments in favour

of Reed's emendation, based substan-
tively on the Q reading 'tike' for F
'like' (see t.n.), are set out in *TxC*,
347–8. Falstaff humorously addresses
Simple as an ancient knight (cf. Pistol's
Sir Actaeon at 2.1.106), the boldest of
them all. Tike, the Elizabethan term
for 'mongrel', alludes to Simple's
appearance.
55 **clerkly** scholarly; cf. 1.3.2, *Speak
scholarly*, and 2.2.170n.

35 chain –] *(Chaine,)*   38 spoken] spoke *of (Oxf¹)*   41] *(I: come: quicke.)*   42 SP] *Rowe; Fal.* F
43 or] and *Hanmer*   52 Ay, sir Tike;] *Reed;* I sir: like F; I tike, *Q;* Ay, sir Tike; like *Steevens²*
(Farmer)   54 tidings.] tydings, God be with you sir. *Q*   54 SD] *Rowe*   55 ¹art] *Q;* are F

FALSTAFF   Ay, that there was, mine host; one that hath
taught me more wit than ever I learnt before in my life;
and I paid nothing for it neither, but was paid for my   60
learning.

Enter BARDOLPH.

BARDOLPH   Out alas, sir: cozenage, mere cozenage!
HOST   Where be my horses? Speak well of them, varletto.
BARDOLPH   Run away with the cozeners: for so soon as I
came beyond Eton, they threw me off from behind one   65
of them, in a slough of mire, and set spurs and away,
like three German devils, three Doctor Faustasses.
HOST   They are gone but to meet the Duke, villain, do not
say they be fled. Germans are honest men.

Enter EVANS.

EVANS   Where is mine host?   70
HOST   What is the matter, sir?
EVANS   Have a care of your entertainments. There is a

---

59 **was paid** i.e. in kind, by being beaten;
but the Host is unaware of the equivocation. Ard² refers to the proverb
'Bought wit is best' (Tilley, W545).

61 **Out alas** See 1.4.33n.; replacing 'O
Lord' in Q.
mere cozenage nothing but a cheat

62 **varletto** The Host Italianizes the
English term of abuse 'varlet' (see
1.3.91n.); the correct form is *valletto*,
i.e. personal male attendant or usher,
with no derogatory implications.

64–5 **from . . . them** 'Bardolph was evidently riding pillion . . . in order to
bring the horses back to Windsor once
the Germans had met the Duke'
(Oxf¹).

66 **Doctor Faustasses** alluding to
Marlowe's very popular play, *Doctor
Faustus* (see 1.1.122n.), where the

Doctor plays a number of tricks by
magic, among them having a man
attempting his life dragged in through
mud and dirt. Most editors emend to
'Doctor Faustuses', but possibly
Bardolph, in coining the plural form of
the name, as well as playing on 'asses',
is thinking also of Falstaff (a name
spelt 'Faulstof' or 'Faulstafe' in
Stationers' Register entries), who has
dismissed him.

68.1 In Q Caius enters and delivers his
message before Evans. If it is true that
Evans's *Cozen-Garmombles* is a covert
allusion to the Duke of Württemberg
(see 72–3), it would have more point if
it came not before but after Caius's
mention of 'a Duke de Jarmany' (82–3).

71 **your entertainments** the people you
entertain as guests in the Inn

60.1] *Q; not in F; Enter Bardolph muddy. Oxf* 61 Out alas] O Lord *Q* 66 Faustasses] Faustuses
mod. eds 68.1] *Q (Enter Sir Hugh.), after 86; not in F*

friend of mine come to town tells me there is three sorts
of Cozen-Garmombles, that has cozened all the hosts
of Readings, of Maidenhead, of Colebrook, of horses   75
and money. I tell you for good will, look you: you are
wise, and full of gibes and vlouting-stocks, and 'tis not
convenient you should be cozened. Fare you well.   *Exit.*

Enter CAIUS.

CAIUS   Vere is mine host de Jarteer?
HOST   Here, master Doctor, in perplexity and doubtful   80
dilemma.
CAIUS   I cannot tell vat is dat, but, by gar, it is tell-a me

72–3 *three . . . Cozen-Garmombles
The F reading (see t.n.) offers only a
pointless pun on 'German cozeners'
(Cozen-Iermans) and 'cousins-german', i.e. first cousins, close relatives,
referring to the proverb 'Call me cousin
but cozen me not' (Dent, C739), played
upon in *R3* 4.4.223 and *1H4* 1.3.254–5.
The Oxford editors (*TxC*, 348) suspect
that this replaced the Q reading either
by censorial intervention or when the
allusion contained in it had lost its top-
icality; *sorts of* has a contemptuous ring,
and the joke on 'cousins-german'/
'Cozen-Germans' is more effective
when 'Germans' is turned by Evans
into *Garmombles*, transforming 'German nobles' into 'geremumble', a term
of abuse used by Thomas Nashe of
Gabriel Harvey in his *Strange News*
(Nashe, *Works*, I.321). At the same
time there is a suggestive reference
to 'Mömpelgard', the German count
(later Duke of Württemberg) who
aspired to be elected Knight of the
Garter (see pp. 26–7).
74 **Readings** Reading (Welsh plural),
then a village sixteen miles west of

Windsor, now a sizeable town
Maidenhead six miles north-west of
Windsor
Colebrook now Colnbrook, some
four miles east of Windsor
76 **wise . . . vlouting-stocks** a wise man
(of the same kind as Simple's *wise
woman* at 24) fond of mockeries (*gibes*;
see 3.3.225) and of making laughing-
stocks of people (3.1.106n.). The
heavy irony of the passage, reflected
also in *for good will* (out of friendship)
at 75, and *convenient* (proper, fitting) at
77, is Evans's revenge for the trick
played on him and Caius, a revenge
promised at 3.1.104–12 and confirmed
at 3.3.222–6.
79–80 **perplexity . . . dilemma** more
synonyms from the Host: *dilemma*, i.e.
perplexity of choice (cf. *AW* 2.6.74–5,
'I will presently pen down my dilem-
mas'), is necessarily *doubtful*, i.e.
uncertain; but some gloss 'apprehen-
sive' (*OED* Doubtful *a.* 5)
81, 84 *by gar** Caius's usual oath, though
present only in Q (see t.n.), seems
appropriate in these cases
81 **it . . . me** I am told

72–3 three . . . Garmombles] *Q (*cosen garmombles*);* three Cozen-Iermans *F*   73–5 hosts . . .
money] *(*Readins*);* Host of Maidenhead & Readings *Q*   74 Colebrook] *(*Cole-brooke*);* Colnbrook
Oxf   77 SD] *Q; not in F*   77.1] *Q (Enter Doctor), after 68; not in F*   78 Jarteer] *(*Iarteere*);* gartyr
Q   81 by gar] *Q (*begar*); not in F*

dat you make grand preparation for a Duke de Jarmany.
By my trot, der is no Duke that the court is
know to come. By gar, I tell you for good will. Adieu.   *Exit.*
HOST   Hue and cry, villain, go! – Assist me, knight, I am   85
undone! – Fly, run, hue and cry, villain, I am undone!

Exit [with Bardolph].

FALSTAFF   I would all the world might be cozened, for I
have been cozened and beaten too. If it should come to
the ear of the court how I have been transformed, and
how my transformation hath been washed and cud-   90
gelled, they would melt me out of my fat drop by drop,
and liquor fishermen's boots with me. I warrant they
would whip me with their fine wits till I were as crest-
fallen as a dried pear. I never prospered since I forswore
myself at primero. Well, if my wind were but long   95
enough, I would repent.

Enter Mistress QUICKLY.

Now, whence come you?

82 **grand** great (Caius is thinking in
French)
   Jarmany Germany. The F spelling
'Iamany' tries to suggest the French
pronunciation.
83–4 **is know to come** knows to be coming (rather than 'to have come'; cf.
4.3.4).
85 **Hue and cry** the usual expression for
'Raise the alarm'
   villain addressed to Bardolph
89 **transformed** first into dirty washing
and then into the wise woman of
Brentford
91 **melt . . . fat** deflate my pretence at a
high social status
92 **liquor** grease
93–4 **as crest-fallen . . . pear** a mixed
metaphor: *crest-fallen* applies to a

defeated cock, and for the image of the
shrivelled pear see Prince Hal's joke
reported in *2H4* 2.2.1–9, comparing
Falstaff to a withered apple-john. RP
also compares 'French withered pears'
at *AW* 1.1.161, and suggests a sub-
merged pun 'pear'/'peer', as in the
extended passage depending on this
pun in *Tom a' Lincoln* (*MSR*,
ll.961–93) in a scene heavily indebted
to the Falstaff scenes in *1* and *2H4*.
94–5 **forswore . . . primero** swore
(falsely) that I had not cheated playing
primero (a table-game), and was found
out
95–6 **my . . . enough** I had breath enough
left in me; Q completes the sentence
with 'to say my prayers', which is what
Falstaff means.

82 Duke de Jarmany] *(Duke de Iamanie)*; Garmaine Duke *Q*   84 By gar] *Q (begar)*; *not in F*   84
SD] *Q*; *not in F*   86 SD] *Q (Exit)*; *not in F*; *Exeunt Host and Bardolph. / Capell*   96 enough]
inough to say my prayers *Q*   96.1] *Q, after 97; not in F*

QUICKLY   From the two parties, forsooth.

FALSTAFF   The devil take one party and his dam the
other, and so they shall be both bestowed. I have suf-   100
fered more for their sakes, more than the villainous
inconstancy of man's disposition is able to bear.

QUICKLY   And have not they suffered? Yes, I warrant,
speciously one of them. Mistress Ford, good heart, is
beaten black and blue, that you cannot see a white spot   105
about her.

FALSTAFF   What tellst thou me of black and blue? I was
beaten myself into all the colours of the rainbow, and I
was like to be apprehended for the witch of Brentford.
But that my admirable dexterity of wit, my counter-   110
feiting the action of an old woman, delivered me, the
knave constable had set me i'the stocks, i'the common
stocks, for a witch.

QUICKLY   Sir, let me speak with you in your chamber,
you shall hear how things go, and, I warrant, to your   115
content. Here is a letter will say somewhat – good
hearts, what ado is here to bring you together! Sure, one

98 **parties** interested persons; Oxf[1] remarks that Shakespeare generally uses
'party' for 'person' for comic effect

99 **The . . . dam** 'The devil take . . .' is an
expression frequently used by
Shakespeare (Dent, DD11), and for
'The devil and his dam' see 1.1.138n.

100 **bestowed** lodged (in the place they
deserve)

101–2 **villainous . . . disposition**
wretched inconstant state of man's
mind

104 **speciously** See 3.4.106n.
good heart poor thing, as at 3.5.36

105 **beaten . . . blue** a current idiom for
'beaten soundly' (Dent, B160)
that so that

108 **all . . . rainbow** another idiomatic

expression (Dent, C519)

109 **apprehended for** taken to be;
arrested for being

110 **But that** were it not that

110–11 **counterfeiting . . . woman**
mimicking the way of moving of old
women (witches, though old in
appearance, were believed to move
with great agility)

114 **let** if you will let

116 **content** satisfaction

116–17 **good hearts** See 104; Quickly
leaves it uncertain whether she means
both women and Falstaff, or only Mistress Ford and Falstaff.

117 ***is here** F's 'here is' is either an accidental transposition or a mistake for
'there is'.

103 And] O Lord sir, *Q;* O Lord, sir, and *Oxf*   103–4 have . . . Ford] they are the sorowfulst
creatures / That euer liued: specially mistresse *Ford Q*   109–13 Brentford. But . . . stocks,]
Theobald (subst.); Braineford, but . . . stocks, *F;* Brainford, and set in the stockes. *Q*   117 is here]
(Oxf[1]); here is *F*

of you does not serve heaven well, that you are so
crossed.   119

FALSTAFF   Come up into my chamber.   *Exeunt.*

4.6   *Enter* HOST *and* FENTON.

HOST   Master Fenton, talk not to me: my mind is heavy
   – I will give over all.

FENTON
   Yet hear me speak. Assist me in my purpose,
   And, as I am a gentleman, I'll give thee
   A hundred pound in gold more than your loss.   5

HOST   I will hear you, Master Fenton, and I will, at the
   least, keep your counsel.

FENTON
   From time to time I have acquainted you
   With the dear love I bear to fair Anne Page,
   Who mutually hath answered my affection –   10
   So far forth as herself might be her chooser –
   Even to my wish. I have a letter from her
   Of such contents as you will wonder at,

119 **crossed** thwarted; possibly an ironical allusion to the already famous 'star-crossed lovers' of Verona, *RJ* Prologue 6. See also Hermia's comment 'O cross!' on Lysander's mention of the proverbial 'The course of love never did run smooth' in *MND* 1.1.134–6 (RP).

4.6 Another scene in verse, except for two speeches in prose by the Host (four in the Q version, which echoes it closely). It is difficult to decide whether the use of verse is merely meant to emphasize Fenton's higher social status, or whether this is a survival from an earlier entertainment all in verse (see pp. 73–8). As in the previous scene, the location is apparently the Garter Inn, by now the headquarters of the Herne's oak plot, and the action takes place while Falstaff, unconscious of the trap prepared for him, is talking upstairs with Mistress Quickly.

2 **give over all** have nothing more to do with it: at 3.2.60–3 the Host maintained that Fenton was the best candidate for Anne Page's hand, and that he would *carry't.*

5 **more . . . loss** over and above your expenses (or perhaps 'after refunding you for the loss of your horses'). Fenton is counting on Anne Page's dowry if the Host is successful in assisting him to marry her.

7 **keep your counsel** not divulge what you tell me

10 **answered** returned

11 **So far forth** as far

13 **contents** stressed on the second syllable, though meaning 'subject'

4.6] *Scena Sexta. F*   0.1] *Q; Enter Fenton, Host. F*

The mirth whereof so larded with my matter
That neither singly can be manifested   15
Without the show of both, wherein fat Falstaff
Hath a great scene; the image of the jest
I'll show you here at large. Hark, good mine host:
Tonight at Herne's oak, just 'twixt twelve and one,
Must my sweet Nan present the Fairy Queen –   20
The purpose why is here – in which disguise,
While other jests are something rank on foot,
Her father hath commanded her to slip
Away with Slender, and with him at Eton
Immediately to marry – she hath consented. Now, sir,   25
Her mother – ever strong against that match
And firm for Doctor Caius – hath appointed

14 the amusing contents of which (the plot against Falstaff) are so intermingled with my own concerns (the plan he is going to confide to the Host)

16 **the show of** showing, telling
  ***wherein** borrowed from Q in a different context, corresponding to 24–5 (see facsimile of Q, sig. G1v 6–8). The Cambridge editors (Cam[1], 128) maintained that the passage at 16–17, from 'fat Falstaffe' to 'scene' (as well as its equivalent in Q, at G1v 6, 'Wherein fat *Falstaffe* had a mightie scare'), 'is obviously a hasty addition in both texts', and that 'if the F. passage be omitted, verse and sense are improved'. But the mention of Falstaff is indispensable at this point to introduce the circumstances of the Herne's oak *jest*, and it is typical of Shakespeare to see it in theatrical terms, as a *great scene* on the stage.

17 **image . . . jest** form the jest will take
18 **at large** in detail

20 **present . . . Queen** act the part of the Fairy Queen. Since the part is in fact entrusted not to Nan but to Mistress Quickly (in this case there is also no mention of the Fairy Queen in the Q version), the impression that the substance of this verse-scene, as of 4.4, may be a survival from a different entertainment is reinforced; see 4.4.69–70n. and pp. 52–5.

21 **here** 'Perhaps Fenton points to the letter from Anne' (Ard[2]).

22 **something . . . foot** taking place (*on foot*) in a number of ways (*something* means 'somewhat'; *rank*, as an adverb, means 'profusely')

25 **Now, sir** Hypermetrical, it could be considered a short line beginning a new paragraph, or, as in F, two extra syllables in the previous line; see t.n. and cf. 4.4.11–12n.

26 ***ever** always ('still' in Q); in F 'euen', but final *r* and final *n* are easily confused in Elizabethan handwriting

16 wherein fat Falstaff] *Q; fat Falstaffe F; Fat Sir Iohn Falstaffe F2; Fat Falstaff in't Irving*   17 great scene] mightie scare *Q; great scene in it Capell; great share Dyce[2]; great scare Craig*   21 in which disguise] And in a robe of white this night disguised *Q*   25–6] *Malone lines* consented. / sir, / match /; consented. / match / *Ard[2]*   26 ever strong] *Pope;* euen strong *F;* still *Q*   27–33 hath . . . Doctor] in a robe of red / By her deuice, the Doctor must steale her thence, / And she hath giuen consent to goe with him *Q*

That he shall likewise shuffle her away
While other sports are tasking of their minds,
And at the dean'ry, where a priest attends,   30
Straight marry her: to this her mother's plot
She, seemingly obedient, likewise hath
Made promise to the Doctor. Now thus it rests:
Her father means she shall be all in white
And, in that habit, when Slender sees his time   35
To take her by the hand and bid her go,
She shall go with him. Her mother hath intended –
The better to denote her to the Doctor,
For they must all be masked and vizarded –
That quaint in green she shall be loose enrobed,   40
With ribbons pendant flaring 'bout her head;
And when the Doctor spies his vantage ripe,
To pinch her by the hand, and on that token
The maid hath given consent to go with him.

HOST

Which means she to deceive, father or mother?   45

FENTON

Both, my good host, to go along with me.

---

28 **shuffle** smuggle, remove secretly (*OED v.* 5b)
29 **tasking of** occupying
30 **dean'ry** deanery; Ard[1] sees in the three mentions of the word in the play a specific reference to the deanery attached to St George's Chapel at Windsor Castle, presumably accessible to Caius as a courtier
     attends is waiting (including the ecclesiastical meaning: 'officiates')
33 **thus it rests** The situation is this.
35 **habit** costume
38 ***denote** indicate; F's 'deuote' is a case of a letter turned upside down or misread.
39 **masked and vizarded** wearing fancy dresses and face-masks (*vizards*; see

4.4.68n.)
40 **quaint** i.e quaintly, elegantly (the usual meaning in Shakespeare)
     in green Q has instead 'in a robe of red'. The divergences between the two texts in the colours of Anne's disguise continue in the next act. At 4.4.69–70 Mistress Page had decided that Nan should wear 'a robe of white', and only later did she suspect her husband of planning to have her *stolen* by Slender; see pp. 53–4.
41 **pendant** hanging (from her head)
     flaring blowing in the air
43 **To pinch** As at 36, *To* stands for 'He is to', but for *To pinch* see 4.4.56n.
     token sign

---

38 denote] *Capell;* deuote *F*   41 ribbons pendant] *(*Ribonds-pendant*); Q (*ribones pendant*)

And here it rests: that you'll procure the vicar
To stay for me at church, 'twixt twelve and one,
And, in the lawful name of marrying,
To give our hearts united ceremony.   50

HOST

Well, husband your device; I'll to the vicar.

Bring you the maid, you shall not lack a priest.

FENTON

So shall I evermore be bound to thee;

Besides, I'll make a present recompense.   *Exeunt.*

5.1   *Enter* FALSTAFF *and* Mistress QUICKLY.

FALSTAFF   Prithee, no more prattling. Go, I'll hold: this
is the third time – I hope good luck lies in odd numbers.
Away, go! They say there is divinity in odd numbers,
either in nativity, chance or death. Away!

QUICKLY   I'll provide you a chain, and I'll do what I can   5
to get you a pair of horns.

FALSTAFF   Away, I say; time wears. Hold up your head,
and mince.   [*Exit Mistress Quickly.*]

---

47 **here it rests** This is the point (of my request); cf. 33n.
48 **stay** wait (see 1.1.191)
49 **lawful . . . marrying** proper form of celebration
50 **united ceremony** the rite of union, i.e. marriage
51 **husband your device** carry on the plan you have devised
52 **Bring you** if you bring
54 **present** immediate
5.1 Missing in Q, like the next three scenes, this is a continuation of the previous two: Mistress Quickly, having delivered her message to Falstaff in his upstairs chamber in the Garter Inn, has just come down and is taking her leave.
1 **hold** keep (the appointment)
2 **third time** proverbial: 'The third

time pays for all' (Dent, T319), cf. *TN* 5.1.37
good . . . numbers another proverb: 'There is luck in odd numbers' (Dent, L582)
3 **divinity** divine power (*OED sb.* 3)
4 **either . . . death** i.e. it is a good thing to be born, to undertake something, or to die on an odd-numbered day
5 **provide . . . chain** See 4.4.31n.; but F has no direction for Falstaff, when impersonating Herne the hunter, to shake any chains.
7 **wears** runs out (*OED* Wear *v.*[1] 19)
7–8 **Hold . . . mince** Walk away like a proper lady, erect and taking quick short steps. In *MV* 3.4.67–8 Portia speaks of turning 'two mincing steps / Into a manly stride'.

49 marrying] marriage *Oxf*[1] *(Walker)*   **5.1]** *Actus Quintus. Scoena Prima. F*   0.1] *Rowe; Enter Falstoffe, Quickly, and Ford. F*   8 SD] *Rowe, opp. 6*

[*Enter* FORD *as* BROOK.]

How now, Master Brook? Master Brook, the matter
will be known tonight or never. Be you in the park   10
about midnight, at Herne's oak, and you shall see wonders.

FORD   Went you not to her yesterday, sir, as you told me
you had appointed?

FALSTAFF   I went to her, Master Brook, as you see, like a   15
poor old man, but I came from her, Master Brook, like
a poor old woman. That same knave, Ford her husband, hath the finest mad devil of jealousy in him,
Master Brook, that ever governed frenzy. I will tell you
he beat me grievously, in the shape of a woman; for in   20
the shape of man, Master Brook, I fear not Goliath with
a weaver's beam, because I know also life is a shuttle. I
am in haste: go along with me, I'll tell you all, Master
Brook. Since I plucked geese, played truant and
whipped top, I knew not what 'twas to be beaten till   25
lately. Follow me, I'll tell you strange things of this
knave Ford, on whom tonight I will be revenged, and I

13 **yesterday** More confusion in the
play's timing. Falstaff's second assignation with Mistress Ford was fixed
'between eight and nine' in the morning, while Ford was supposed to go *a-
birding* (3.5.41–51, 117–22); Falstaff
tells Ford disguised as Brook 'Come to
me at your convenient leisure, and you
shall know how I speed' (3.5.124–5).
At 4.5.1–21 he has just returned to the
Garter Inn from his misadventure, still
disguised as the wise woman of
Brentford, so that it must be some time
later in the same day. Shortly after, in
the same scene (4.5.96 SD), Mistress
Quickly joins him and he takes her up
to his room, which she leaves only at
the beginning of the present scene
(1–8). Ford's mention of *yesterday* only

five lines later is an example of 'stage
time' replacing 'real' time.
21–2 **Goliath . . . beam** a reminiscence of
1 Samuel, 17.7: 'And the shaft of his
[Goliath's] speare was like a weauers
beame' (i.e. the wooden roller in a
loom)
22 **I . . . shuttle** Falstaff is consciously (as
indicated by *also*) making a further
Biblical reference, this time to Job, 7.6:
'My daies are swifter then a weauers
shuttle'. For the possible significance
of these allusions see note 3 on p. 29.
24–6 **Since . . . lately** 'From the time I
was a schoolboy' (caning was a normal
educational method). Plucking feath-
ers from a live goose was a boy's dare,
and the string with which tops were set
spinning was called the whip.

8.1] *Rowe (subst.)*   21 Goliath] *(Goliah)*

will deliver his wife into your hand. Follow – strange
things in hand, Master Brook! – Follow.   *Exeunt.*

5.2   *Enter* PAGE, SHALLOW *and* SLENDER.

PAGE   Come, come: we'll couch i'the castle ditch till we
see the lights of our fairies. Remember, son Slender,
my daughter –

SLENDER   Ay, forsooth. I have spoke with her and we
have a nay-word how to know one another. I come to   5
her in white, and cry 'mum'; she cries 'budget'; and by
that we know one another.

SHALLOW   That's good too. But what needs either your
'mum' or her 'budget'? The white will decipher her
well enough. – It hath struck ten o'clock.   10

PAGE   The night is dark: lights and spirits will become it
well. God prosper our sport. No man means evil but
the devil, and we shall know him by his horns. Let's
away; follow me.   *Exeunt.*

5.3   *Enter* MISTRESS PAGE, MISTRESS FORD *and* CAIUS.

MISTRESS PAGE   Master Doctor, my daughter is in

28–9 **strange . . . hand** Extraordinary
doings are afoot.
5.2 The action takes place later in the day
(ten in the evening; see 10), presumably on the way to Windsor Park.
1   **couch** lie hidden
castle ditch presumably the ditch at
the park side of Windsor Castle
2, 11 ***lights** The plural seems necessary,
in view of *obscured lights* at 5.3.14.
3   ***my daughter** – The absence of
punctuation in F indicates that Page is
interrupted by Slender, but the omission of 'daughter' (restored in F2) is
probably accidental.
5   **nay-word** password; see 2.2.119n.
6, 9 '**mum**' . . . '**budget**' 'Mumbudget'

was 'the name of a children's game in
which silence was required' (*OED sb.*).
The expression 'To play mumbudget'
is recorded from 1559 (*OW*, 551a; cf.
Dent, M1311). See 5.5.194–5.
9   **The . . . her** Her white robe will mark
her out.
11 **become** suit
12 ***God prosper** 'Heauen' in F; see
3.1.29n.
13 **know . . . horns** a way of calling
Falstaff 'devil', by adapting the
proverb 'The devil is known by his
horns' (Tilley, D252; not in Dent)
5.3 This scene is practically simultaneous
with 5.2, somewhere in Windsor.

5.2] *Scena Secunda. F* 0.1] *(Enter Page, Shallow, Slender.)*   2 lights] *Oxf¹;* light *F*   3 my
daughter –] *Oxf¹;* my *F;* my daughter. *F2*   11 lights] *Oxf;* Light *F*   12 God] *Oxf;* Heauen *F*   5.3]
Scena Tertia. F 0.1] *(Enter Mist. Page, Mist. Ford, Caius.)*

273

green: when you see your time, take her by the hand,
away with her to the deanery and dispatch it quickly.
Go before into the park. – We two must go together.

CAIUS   I know vat I have to do. Adieu.   5

MISTRESS PAGE   Fare you well, sir.   [*Exit Caius.*]
My husband will not rejoice so much at the abuse of
Falstaff as he will chafe at the Doctor's marrying my
daughter. But 'tis no matter: better a little chiding than
a great deal of heartbreak.   10

MISTRESS FORD   Where is Nan now, and her troop of
fairies? And the Welsh devil Hugh?

MISTRESS PAGE   They are all couched in a pit hard by
Herne's oak, with obscured lights, which, at the very
instant of Falstaff's and our meeting, they will at once   15
display to the night.

MISTRESS FORD   That cannot choose but amaze him.

MISTRESS PAGE   If he be not amazed, he will be mocked;
if he be amazed, he will every way be mocked.

MISTRESS FORD   We'll betray him finely.   20

MISTRESS PAGE

Against such lewdsters and their lechery
Those that betray them do no treachery.

---

3   **deanery** See 4.6.30n.
7   **abuse** ill-treatment
8   **chafe** be angry
9–10 **better . . . heartbreak** Ard[2] sus-
pects a proverb, such as 'Better once a
mischief than always an inconvenience' (Tilley, M995; not in
Dent).
12   **Welsh devil** Cam[2] remarks that 'The
word "devil" must here be used in a
weakened sense as meaning a mischie-
vous spirit (*OED sb* 4b)'. For Evans's
disguise as a Satyr (5.5.36.1) see 5.4.0.1n.
*Hugh 'Herne' in F must be a wrong
expansion of an abbreviated form of
'Hugh' in the copy ('H.' or 'Hu.', as in
SPs).

13   **couched** hidden; see 5.2.1n.
14   **obscured lights** covered lanterns
17   **cannot choose but** is bound to; a
locution very frequent in Shakespeare
(Dent, CC11)
amaze frighten
18, 19 **mocked** meaning 'deceived' at 18
and 'ridiculed as well as deceived'
(*every way*) at 19
20   **betray** deceive
21   **lewdsters** lascivious (lewd) persons;
this is the first recorded use of the word
in *OED*.
21–2 a rhyming couplet pointing out, like
the quatrain at 4.2.99–102, the moral
of the story. Both speeches characterize Mistress Page as the really wise

---

6 SD] *F2, opp. 5*   12 Welsh devil Hugh] *Capell;* Welch-deuill Herne *F; Welch* devil *Evans /
Theobald;* Welsh devil *Ard[1]*

MISTRESS FORD   The hour draws on. To the oak, to the
oak!   *Exeunt.*

5.4   *Enter* EVANS *[disguised] and* [Children *as*] Fairies.

EVANS   Trib, trib, fairies. Come, and remember your
parts: be pold, I pray you, follow me into the pit, and
when I give the watch-'ords do as I pid you.
Come, come, trib, trib.   *Exeunt.*

5.5   *Enter* FALSTAFF *with buck's horns on his head.*

FALSTAFF   The Windsor bell hath struck twelve, the
minute draws on. Now the hot-blooded gods assist me!

wife, in contrast to the more adventurous Mistress Ford, motivated by her
determination to mock a husband out
of his jealousy.
5.4 The time is about two hours later than
that indicated at 5.2.10, and the location is near the sawpit mentioned at
4.4.52.
0.1 *disguised* The modern addition to
the SD is warranted by Q's '*as a Satyr*'
at 5.5.36.1, but it is hard to guess what
his disguise would have been like. In
classical mythology Satyrs were goat-
footed demi-gods with small horns,
addicted to chasing nymphs, an inappropriate impersonation by a parson
and schoolteacher instructing children
of both sexes. Probably Evans was simply wearing a horned mask, which
would account for *Welsh devil* at 5.3.12
and for *Welsh goat* at 5.5.136.
1 **Trib** trip, i.e. walk mincingly; see
5.1.7–8n, and cf. *MND* 5.1.421, 'Trip
away', addressed to the fairies
2 **into the pit** Craik (Oxf[1]) detects a hidden joke, 'pit' being used by Shake-

speare in other contexts (e.g. *Ham*
4.5.133, *KL* 4.6.128) to signify 'hell',
and Evans being the *devil*; see 0.1n.
3 **watch-'ords** watchword, signal
(Evans's plural)
5.5 The location is Herne's oak in
Windsor Park, the time midnight, as
indicated in l.1.
0.1 *buck's . . . head* Q has '*a Bucks head
vpon him*', but it does not seem likely
that Falstaff's face is covered by a mask
in that shape, and the word 'head' by
itself could mean 'antlers of a deer'
(*OED* Head *sb*. 6). Oxf adds '*and bearing a chain*', in view of 'shakes a chain'
at 4.4.31 and of Quickly's undertaking
at 5.1.5, but there is no mention of
chains in Q nor in the rest of the play,
so they are better forgotten.
1 **Windsor bell** presumably the clock
heard striking by Ford at 3.2.40–1 SD
2 **minute** appointed moment (*OED* sb[1]
1c)
  hot-blooded gods lustful gods of
ancient mythology. Falstaff produces
for his own benefit a sample of his

5.4] *Scena Quarta. F* 0.1] *Ard*[2] *(subst.)*; *Enter Euans and Fairies. F*; *Enter Sir Hugh Evans disguised as
a satyr, and William Page and other children disguised as fairies Oxf ('as a satyr' from Dyce, see Q at
5.5.36.1)* 5.5] *Scena Quinta. F* 0.1] *this edn after Q (Enter sir Iohn with a Bucks head vpon him);
Enter Falstaffe, Mistris Page, Mistris Ford, Euans, Anne Page, Fairies, Page, Ford, Quickly, Slender,
Fenton, Caius, Pistoll. F*; *Enter Sir John Falstaff, disguised as Herne, with horns on his head, and bearing a
chain. Oxf* 2 hot-blooded gods] *(hot-bloodied-Gods)*; hot-bloodied-god *F4*; hot-blooded God *Rowe*

Remember, Jove, thou wast a bull for thy Europa: love
set on thy horns. O powerful love, that in some respects
makes a beast a man, in some other a man a beast! You   5
were also, Jupiter, a swan for the love of Leda: O
omnipotent love, how near the god drew to the complexion of a goose! A fault done first in the form of a
beast – O Jove, a beastly fault! – and then another fault
in the semblance of a fowl: think on't, Jove, a foul fault!   10
When gods have hot backs, what shall poor men do?
For me, I am here a Windsor stag, and the fattest, I
think, i'the forest. Send me a cool rut-time, Jove, or
who can blame me to piss my tallow? – Who comes
here? My doe?   15

Enter MISTRESS FORD *and* MISTRESS PAGE.

scholarship (see Ford's remark, 'I hear you are a scholar', at 2.2.170), identifying himself with Jove, the father of the pagan gods.

3–10 Falstaff recalls the two best-known rapes of earthly women committed by Jove: in the shape of a white bull ('in the form of a beast', 8–9) the god induced Europa, the daughter of Agenor, king of Phoenicia, to ride on his back and carried her away to Crete; and in the shape of a swan ('in the semblance of a fowl', 10) Jove (*Jupiter*, 6) raped Leda, wife of Tyndarus king of Sparta.

3–4 love . . . horns It was love that induced you to wear horns (symbolizing not cuckoldry but sexual potency, like the stag's, or buck's horns).

5 makes a beast a man 'transforms a dull man into a witty one' (Oxf[1]); playing on *bull* (3) meaning 'beast'
a man a beast 'transforms a wise man into a fool' (Oxf[1]), or into a lustful animal; cf. *TNK* 1.1.232–3, 'being sensually subdued / We lose our human title' (RP).

7–8 complexion . . . goose appearance and nature of a goose (i.e. stupid). Dent (G369) refers to the phrase 'All his geese are swans', noting that Ard[1] cites John Lyly, *Midas* (1592), 4.1.47f, 'Love made *Iupiter* a goose, and *Neptune* a swine, and both for love of an earthlie mistresse'; and compares 'To make a swan a crow' (S1028.1); see *RJ* 1.2.87.

9 beastly fault filthy sin; punning on 'beast' meaning 'bull'

10 foul fault like *beastly fault* (9, i.e. 'filthy sin'), punning on *fowl* meaning 'swan' (6): F spells 'fowle-fault'.

11 When . . . backs if even gods are lustful (see *hot-blooded gods*, 2n.)

13 rut-time mating season

14 piss my tallow melt my fat away. Stags at mating time urinate frequently and grow lean. Dent (T66) notes that the phrase in its literal sense is recorded as from *c.* 1450 in *OED* Piss *v.* 2b.

15 doe female deer

10 foul fault] *(fowle-/fault)*   15.1] *Q (Enter mistris* P*age, and mistris* F*ord); not in* F

MISTRESS FORD   Sir John, art thou there, my deer, my
male deer?

FALSTAFF   My doe with the black scut! Let the sky rain
potatoes, let it thunder to the tune of 'Greensleeves',
hail kissing-comfits and snow eringoes. Let there come   20
a tempest of provocation, I will shelter me here.

MISTRESS FORD   Mistress Page is come with me, sweetheart.

FALSTAFF   Divide me like a bribed buck, each a haunch.
I will keep my sides to myself, my shoulders for the   25
fellow of this walk, – and my horns I bequeath your
husbands. Am I a woodman, ha? Speak I like Herne the
hunter? Why, now is Cupid a child of conscience: he
makes restitution. As I am a true spirit, welcome!

A noise of horns within.

16, 17 **deer** hart, punning on 'dear'
18 **scut** the tail of a deer; referring to
Mistress Ford's black hair, but with a
hidden allusion to 'tail' meaning 'cunt'
(*OED* Tail *sb*[1] 5c)
19 **potatoes** Sweet (or Spanish) potatoes
were thought to have aphrodisiac qualities, alluded to also in *TC* 5.2.56.
tune of 'Greensleeves' a love ballad;
see 2.1.54–6n.
20 **kissing-comfits** sweetmeats used to
sweeten the breath
eringoes candied roots of the sea-
holly (*eryngium maritimum*), frequently mentioned in later plays as a
powerful aphrodisiac
21 **provocation** sexual temptation
here i.e. in Mistress Ford's arms. In
the darkness, Falstaff has not realized that
she is accompanied by Mistress Page.
22–3 **sweetheart** punning on 'hart', i.e.
'deer'; see 16, 17n.
24 **bribed buck** stolen (*OED* Bribe *v.* 1)
deer (which had to be divided up
quickly to avoid apprehension), recalling the deer-stealing episode at
1.1.104–5 (see 1.1.14n.)

haunch buttock
25 **my . . . myself** perhaps meaning 'to
keep on my own side' for protection
and defence (Cam[2])
26 **fellow . . . walk** keeper of this part of the
forest. The shoulders of prey were traditionally part of the keeper's fee in authorized hunting; Falstaff hints that the
keeper may connive at the theft (24n.).
26–7 **horns . . . husbands** by making
them cuckolds
27 **woodman** hunter (*OED sb.* 1), but
also womanizer (*OED sb.* 1b); used in
this sense by Lucio of the Duke in
MM 4.3.162
28 **Cupid . . . conscience** The infant god
of love keeps his word (literally, is a
conscientious child).
29 **makes restitution** compensates for
what was withheld (on the two previous occasions, 3.3, 4.2)
true spirit loyal man; but also the
'spirit', i.e. reincarnation of Herne the
hunter
29 SD ***horns*** The sound of hunting horns
is only in the Q direction, while *rattles*
were mentioned at 4.4.50 as the fairies'

16–17] *F lines* Deere?) / male-Deere?/   21 here.] here. (*embracing her*) / *Capell*   24 bribed buck]
*(*brib'd-Bucke); bribe-buck *Theobald*   29 SD] *Q (There is a noise of hornes, the two women run
away); not in F; A noise of rattles within. Oxf*[1]

277

MISTRESS PAGE   Alas, what noise?   30
MISTRESS FORD   Heaven forgive our sins!
FALSTAFF   What should this be?
MISTRESS FORD, MISTRESS PAGE   Away, away!

They run away.

FALSTAFF   I think the devil will not have me damned, lest
the oil that's in me should set hell on fire; he would   35
never else cross me thus.

Enter EVANS *as a Satyr,* ANNE *and* Children *as*
Fairies, Mistress QUICKLY *as the Queen of Fairies,*
PISTOL *as Hobgoblin.*

QUICKLY
Fairies black, grey, green and white,
You moonshine revellers and shades of night,

instruments. But horns were regularly used to produce noises offstage in Elizabethan playhouses, and they are certainly responsible for the '*noise of hunting*' that disperses the fairies at 102.4, another SD peculiar to Q.
31 Cf. 3.3.197n.
36 **cross** thwart; cf. 4.5.119n.
36.1 **Satyr* For Evans's disguise see 5.4.0.1n.
36.3 **PISTOL as Hobgoblin* Pistol does not figure either in the SD or in the text of Q, where in one case (42) the equivalent of his speech is given to '*Sir Hu.*', i.e. Evans. In the F version instead he is given three speeches (42–6, 83 and 88), all correctly prefixed '*Pist.*', and his role in the fairy show is indicated by Quickly at 41, but there is no trace of his characteristic bombastic language. Possibly his reintroduction here was an authorial second thought, intended to fill out a role present in a previous version of a

Garter entertainment (see pp. 21–4).
37 SP Like Evans, who has lost his Welsh accent, Quickly in this scene has none of the Quicklyisms that characterize her throughout the play, and does not take part in the final comedy of mockery and deception (103–239). Her speech prefixes at 37 and 90 – '*Qui.*' in F and '*Quic.*' in Q – are unequivocal, but the two speeches which have no equivalent in Q – at 55–76 and 84–7 – bear in F the prefix '*Qu.*' This could mean 'Queen (of the Fairies)', and be a survival from a text in which the speeches were not attributed to her, in the same way as the other two speeches were probably not meant to be spoken by Quickly.
37 In this opening line there is no mention of red which, according to Q (at the equivalent of 4.6.27 and 5.5.102.2; see 4.6.27–33 t.n. and 5.5.102.1–5 t.n.), was the colour of the robe by which Caius should have recognized Anne.

30] *Mis.Pa.* God forgiue me, what noise is this? *Q*   31 Heaven] God *Oxf*   33 SD] *Q, (see 29 SD)*; not in F   34–6] *Pope; F lines* damn'd, / fire; / thus. /   36.1–3] *this edn after Q (Enter sir Hugh like a Satyre, and boyes drest like Fayries, mistresse Quickly, like the Queene of Fayries: they sing a song about him, and afterward speake.); Enter Fairies. F*   37, 90 SP] *(Qui.); Q (Quic.); Queen / Collier (Harness); Anne / Halliwell (Harness);* MISTRESS QUICKLY *as Queen of Fairies Oxf¹*   37 green and] green, red and *(RP)*

You orphan heirs of fixed destiny,
Attend your office and your quality.   40
Crier Hobgoblin, make the fairy oyez.

PISTOL

Elves, list your names; silence, you airy toys.
Cricket, to Windsor chimneys shalt thou leap:
Where fires thou find'st unraked and hearths unswept,
There pinch the maids as blue as bilberry –   45
Our radiant queen hates sluts and sluttery.

FALSTAFF

They are fairies, he that speaks to them shall die.
I'll wink and couch: no man their work must eye.

RP suggests that 'red' was accidentally omitted after *green*: its restoration would make this line into a tetrameter, the metre of the rest of this and of the following speeches.

38 **shades** spirits

39 **orphan . . . destiny** parentless (fairies were not born of men) inheritors (i.e. executants by immemorial tradition) of specific tasks
fixed fixèd

40 **Attend** attend to
your office . . . quality your function and your particular task (cf. 39n.)

41 **Crier Hobgoblin** Hobgoblin, known also as Puck or Robin Goodfellow (as in *MND*), was a spirit addicted to playing pranks, who acted as messenger or herald (*Crier* is town-crier) in the fairy world. In Q Hobgoblin is taken to be the same as 'Satyr', Evans's disguise (see 5.4.0.1n.): at the equivalent of this line (see facsimile, sig. G2r 25) Evans is addressed as '*Puck*'.
oyez An Old French word, meaning 'hark ye', shouted by the crier to alert the townspeople; here pronounced as monosyllable, to rhyme with *toys*.

42 **list your names** Listen for your names being called (to assign a task to each).

airy toys insubstantial creatures; cf. *MND* 3.1.161, 'aery spirit', and 5.1.3, 'fairy toys'

43 **Cricket** appropriately the spirit of chimneys; but in Q (facsimile, sig. G2r 25) the task is assigned to '*Peane*'; see 49n.
leap pronounced 'lep' to near-rhyme with 'unswept' (44)

44 **unraked** with the embers not covered with ashes to keep them alive (*OED* Rake v^1 5)

45 **pinch . . . blue** the punishment inflicted by fairies; see 4.5.105n.
bilberry a plant producing dark blue edible berries, known in Scotland as 'blaeberry' and in North America as 'blueberry'

46 **queen** Queen of Fairies; but the homage to Queen Elizabeth is implicit, as at 59–60
sluttery squalor, disorder (in Q 'sluttish huswiferie')

47–8 Falstaff's rhymed couplet (absent in Q), referring to the popular belief that being received in the spirit world was an omen of death, may be another survival from an earlier version of this masque-like scene.

48 **wink and couch** close my eyes and lie down

39 orphan heirs] Ouphen-heirs *Theobald (Warburton)*; ouphs, and heirs *Keightley* 42, 83, 88 SP] *(Pist.); Eva. / Theobald; Puck (Harness);* HOBGOBLIN *Oxf*; PISTOL *as Hobgoblin Oxf^1; Sir Hu. Q (in corresponding speech at 42 only)*

EVANS

Where's Pead? Go you, and where you find a maid
That ere she sleep has thrice her prayers said,   50
Raise up the organs of her fantasy:
Sleep she as sound as careless infancy.
But those as sleep and think not on their sins,
Pinch them, arms, legs, backs, shoulders, sides and
    shins.

QUICKLY   About, about!   55
Search Windsor Castle, elves, within and out.
Strew good luck, oafs, on every sacred room,
That it may stand till the perpetual doom
In state as wholesome as in state 'tis fit,
Worthy the owner and the owner it.   60
The several chairs of Order look you scour
With juice of balm and every precious flower;
Each fair instalment, coat and several crest,
With loyal blazon, evermore be blest.

49 **Pead** Bead, a name alluding to the diminutive size of the fairy. The Q spelling (for 'Bede' in F) suggests that the actor's accent was the means by which Falstaff was able to recognize him as a *Welsh fairy* (81) since, as in the case of Pistol and Quickly, in Evans's speeches at 49–54, 77–80 and 88 there is no trace of the linguistic peculiarities that characterize him in the rest of the play.

51 Grant her sweet dreams
52 **Sleep she** may she sleep
    careless carefree
53 **as** who (*OED adv.* 24), and cf. Abbott, 112
55 Go about your business.
56–73 Cf. Oberon's blessing of Theseus's palace in *MND* 5.1.401–20.
57 **oafs** See 4.4.48n.
58 **perpetual doom** Day of Judgement

59 in a well-preserved condition (*state*) as is suited (*fit*) to its dignity (*state*)
60 an explicit homage to Queen Elizabeth, the owner of Windsor Castle. Cf. *MND* 5.1.419–20: 'And the owner of it ["this Palace", 418] blest / Ever shall in safety rest'.
61 **several ... Order** each of the twenty-four stalls in the choir of St George's Chapel in Windsor Castle, one for each knight of the Order of the Garter
    look you make sure that you (also at 65)
62 **balm** aromatic herb
63 **instalment** place, represented by a stall (see 61n.)
    coat ... crest coat of arms fixed to the back of each stall, and a separate heraldic device decorating the helmet placed on top of the stall
64 **With loyal blazon** together with each

49 Pead] *Q (but 'Come hither P*eane* in an earlier speech corresponding to 42); Bede F*   51 Raise] Rein *Hanmer (Warburton);* Rouse *Collier²* fantasy:] *Theobald (*fantasie;*);* fantasie F   55, 84 SP] *(Qu.);* Queen / *Collier;* Anne / *Halliwell;* MISTRESS QUICKLY *as Queen of Fairies Oxf¹*   57 oafs] *(Ouphes)*   59 In state] In site *Hanmer*

And nightly, meadow-fairies, look you sing,   65
Like to the Garter compass, in a ring.
Th'expressure that it bears, green let it be,
More fertile-fresh than all the field to see;
And *Honi soit qui mal y pense* write
In em'rald tufts, flowers purple, green and white,   70
Like sapphire, pearl and rich embroidery,
Buckled below fair knighthood's bending knee:
Fairies use flowers for their charactery.
Away, disperse. But till 'tis one o'clock,
Our dance of custom round about the oak   75
Of Herne the hunter let us not forget.

EVANS
Pray you, lock hand in hand, yourselves in order set;
And twenty glow-worms shall our lanterns be
To guide our measure round about the tree. –
But stay, I smell a man of middle earth.   80

banner bearing the coat of arms, hanging from the wall above the stall, an emblem of loyalty to the monarch

65 *nightly*, at night (rather than 'every night'). The F reading (see t.n.) may mean 'fairies that haunt the meadows at night'.

66 **compass** circle: the emblem of the Order of the Garter is a blue ribbon bearing a motto worn as a garter just below the knee (see 72)

67 **expressure** expression, appearance; referring to the 'fairy rings', circular patches where the grass appears greener and brighter than in the rest of the meadow

69 *Honi . . . pense* 'Shame to him who thinks evil of it', the motto in archaic French (which became proverbial in English; see Dent, S277) chosen, according to tradition, by Edward III, the founder of the Order of the Garter in or about 1344, when some courtiers

made ironical comments seeing him pick up a lady's garter which had fallen to the floor during a dance; *pense* is pronounced as disyllabic.

70 **em'rald tufts** bright green bunches of grass
flowers monosyllabic

72 See 66n.

73 **charactery** writing, stressed on the second syllable

75 **dance of custom** customary dance

77 **Pray you** hypermetrical: since Evans uses the expression about a dozen times in the rest of the play, it may have been added here to a pre-existing text meant for a different character, to justify its attribution to Evans

79 **measure** dance

80 **man . . . earth** mortal man, i.e. not a fairy; the earth was conceived as being mid-way between heaven and hell.

65 nightly, meadow-fairies] *Capell;* Nightly-meadow-Fairies *F*   68 More] *F2;* Mote *F*   70 em'rald tufts] *(*Emrold-tuffes*)*

FALSTAFF   Heavens defend me from that Welsh fairy,
lest he transform me to a piece of cheese!
PISTOL
Vile worm, thou wast o'erlooked even in thy birth.
QUICKLY
With trial fire touch me his finger end:
If he be chaste, the flame will back descend   85
And turn him to no pain; but if he start,
It is the flesh of a corrupted heart.
PISTOL
A trial, come.
EVANS   Come, will this wood take fire?
They put the tapers to his fingers, and he starts.
FALSTAFF   O, o, o!
QUICKLY
Corrupt, corrupt, and tainted in desire!   90
About him, fairies, sing a scornful rhyme,
And, as you trip, still pinch him to your time.

The fairies' song
Fie on sinful fantasy,
Fie on lust and luxury!

81–2 This prose speech of Falstaff, like
his *O, o, o!* at 89, sounds like a later
insertion, breaking up the sequence of
rhymed couplets (*earth* at 80 rhymes
with *birth* at 83) in which all of this part
of the scene, from 37 to 102, is written.
81 **Welsh fairy** See 49n.
82 **transform . . . cheese** the usual joke
on the Welsh fondness for cheese; cf.
1.2.11–12n.
83 **o'erlooked** bewitched, subjected to
the evil eye (*OED* Overlook *v*.7)
84 **trial fire** The ordeal by fire was a test of
the prowess or the innocence of a man.
me an ethic dative; see 1.3.55n.
86 **turn him to** put him to (*OED* Turn *v*.
43b)

88 **wood** i.e. Falstaff's finger
88 SD *Some modern editors consider this
direction, found only in Q, incorrect,
and maintain that only Evans puts his
taper to Falstaff's finger. Once again, the
decision must be left to the actors.
90 **tainted in desire** made unclean by
lust; cf. *unclean knight* at 4.4.56.
91 **About him** circle him round about;
get to work on him (see 55n.)
92 **trip** See 5.4.1n.
still continually (the usual meaning of
the adverb at the time)
93 **fantasy** desire (*OED sb.* 7)
94 **luxury** lechery; from Latin *Luxuria*,
one of the seven deadly sins

81–2] *Pope; F lines* Fairy, / Cheese. /   81 Heavens defend] God blesse *Q*   88 SD] *Q; not in F*
92 SD] *(The Song)*   93–102] *F lines* Luxurie: / desire, / aspire, / higher. / villanie. / about, / out. /

Lust is but a bloody fire,   95
Kindled with unchaste desire,
Fed in heart, whose flames aspire,
As thoughts do blow them, higher and higher.
Pinch him, fairies, mutually,
Pinch him for his villainy.   100
Pinch him and burn him and turn him about,
Till candles and starlight and moonshine be out.

[*During the song*] *they pinch him, and* [CAIUS] *comes one way
and steals away a boy in green, and* SLENDER *another way
takes a boy in white;* FENTON [*comes in and*] *steals
Mistress Anne. A noise of hunting is heard within, and all
the Fairies run away. Falstaff pulls off his buck's head, and
rises up.*

95 **bloody fire** fire in the blood
97 **aspire** ascend (*higher and higher*, 98)
98 **blow** like bellows, swell
99 **mutually** all together, in unison (*OED adv.* 2)
102.1–6 *This long stage direction, found only in Q, requires several adjustments, especially in the colour of the costumes. Mistress Page had told Caius that Anne would be dressed in green, while Q had 'in a robe of red' (4.6.40n., and cf. 5.3.1–2, not in Q); from the beginning Page had chosen white for his daughter, while the compiler of this SD has Slender take away '*a boy in greene*', and adds that Fenton '*steales misteris Anne, being in white*'. In fact the colour by which Fenton should recognize Anne is never mentioned in F; in contrast, in Q, in the scene equiv-

alent to 4.6, Fenton informs the Host that Page wants her in white for Slender, but shortly after adds that he has agreed with Nan that 'by a robe of white . . . I shalbe sure to know her' (facsimile, sig. G1v 21–3). The confusion is obvious, so that it seems wiser to accept the F colour scheme, leaving Anne free, whatever her costume, to run to Fenton, who enters undisguised, as soon as she sees him.
102.5 *Falstaff . . . head* The form and timing of the 'dis-horning' of Falstaff is an option left to the actor or producer. Oxf[1], for example, places it at 111, when Ford says 'Here are his horns, Master Brook', while Oxf suggests that Falstaff should remove his headgear only when he acknowledges that he is made an ass, at 119.

102.1–5 *During . . . away.*] *this edn after Q (Here they pinch him, and sing about him, & the Doctor comes one way & steales away a boy in red. And Slender another way he takes a boy in greene: And Fenton steales misteris Anne, being in white. And a noyse of hunting is made within: and all the Fairies runne away.); not in F*   102.5–6 *Falstaff . . . up*] *Q; not in F; Sir John rises and starts to run away. Oxf, at 102.5; He takes off the horns. Oxf, opp. 119; Falstaff rises and begins to run away. Oxf[1], at 102.5; He [Ford] removes the horns from Falstaff's head. Oxf[1], after* horns, Master Brook. *at 111*

Enter PAGE, FORD, MISTRESS PAGE *and*
MISTRESS FORD.

PAGE

Nay, do not fly – I think we have watched you now.
Will none but Herne the hunter serve your turn?

MISTRESS PAGE

I pray you, come, hold up the jest no higher. –   105
Now, good Sir John, how like you Windsor wives?
See you these, husband? [*Points to the horns.*]
                              Do not these fair yokes
Become the forest better than the town?

FORD   Now, sir, who's a cuckold now? Master Brook,
Falstaff is a knave, a cuckoldly knave. Here are his   110
horns, Master Brook. And, Master Brook, he hath
enjoyed nothing of Ford's but his buck-basket, his
cudgel and twenty pounds of money, which must be
paid to Master Brook. His horses are arrested for it,
Master Brook.   115

MISTRESS FORD   Sir John, we have had ill luck, we could
never meet. I will never take you for my love again, but
I will always count you my deer.

103 **watched you** spied upon you (*OED*
    Watch *v.* 11a) to catch you in the act
104 **serve your turn** do for you, a current
    phrase (Dent, TT25) frequent in
    Shakespeare
105 **hold . . . higher** prolong the jest no
    further
107 **yokes** antlers, shaped like the handles
    of a plough (*OED* Yoke *sb.* 4)
108 **Become** suit; adorn
109–15 **Master . . . Brook** Ford is mim-
    icking Falstaff's tone and language in
    the previous interviews with him when
    he was disguised as Brook, 2.2.146–
    271, 3.5.57–128, 5.1.9–29.
110 **cuckoldly knave** See 2.2.256. There

the expression was used by Falstaff of
Ford, who now applies it to the would-
be deceiver deceived.
114 **arrested for it** impounded (*OED*
    Arrest *v.* 11) till the money be returned.
    At 2.1.83–6 Mistress Page had sug-
    gested that Falstaff should be made to
    run into such expenses in his courtship
    'till he hath pawned his horses to mine
    host of the Garter'; see 2.1.86n. In Q
    (facsimile, sig. G3v 28–9) Mistress
    Ford asks her husband to 'Forgiue
    [Falstaff] that sum', and he agrees.
117 **meet** i.e. to make love (*OED v.* 11e)
118 **deer** the usual quibble on 'dear'; see
    16, 17n.

102.7–8] *Capell; And enters* M. *Page,* M. *Ford, and their wiues,* M. *Shallow, Sir Hugh. Q; not in F*
103–4] *Rowe; prose F*   107 SD] *Hanmer (subst.)*   109–11 Now . . . horns, Master Brook.] *Pope; F*
lines now? / knaue, / *Broome*: /   117 meet] *(meete); mate Cam[1]*

FALSTAFF   I do begin to perceive that I am made an ass.

FORD   Ay, and an ox too: both the proofs are extant.   120

FALSTAFF   And these are not fairies. I was three or four
times in the thought they were not fairies, and yet the
guiltiness of my mind, the sudden surprise of my
powers, drove the grossness of the foppery into a
received belief, in despite of the teeth of all rhyme and   125
reason, that they were fairies. See now how wit may be
made a Jack-a-Lent when 'tis upon ill employment!

EVANS   Sir John Falstaff, serve Got, and leave your
desires, and fairies will not pinse you.

FORD   Well said, fairy Hugh.   130

EVANS   And leave you your jealousies too, I pray you.

FORD   I will never mistrust my wife again, till thou art
able to woo her in good English.

FALSTAFF   Have I laid my brain in the sun and dried it,

119–20 **I am . . . too** Both expressions, 'To make an ass of' and 'To make an ox of', were current. The first (Dent, A379.1) is frequent in Shakespeare, notably as used by Bottom in *MND* 3.1.120–1 or by Hostess Quickly accusing Falstaff in *2H4* 2.1.37. The second (Dent, O108.1; cf. *OED* Ox *sb.* 4a), in the sense of both 'making a fool of' and 'being cuckolded', is frequently associated with the first (Dent, O105.1, citing John Lyly, *Midas*, 4.1.148f: 'It might bee hard to iudge whether he were more Ox or Asse'). Cf. Thersites on the cuckold Menelaus, in *TC* 5.1.56–60: 'to what form . . . should wit larded with malice . . . turn him to? To an ass, were nothing, he is both ass and ox; to an ox, were nothing, he is both ox and ass.'

120 **both . . . extant** i.e. the horns prove that he is both a fool in wearing them and deceived like a cuckold – with a pun on *extant*, both 'in existence' and 'prominent' (of the horns; see *OED* Extant *adj.* 1)

121 **these are** implying that only some of the 'fairies' have left the stage at 102.5 – some are still present, though one can be sure only of Evans (*fairy Hugh*, 130), who reveals himself at 128–9

124 **powers** understanding
grossness . . . foppery crudeness of the hoax (Cam[2])

125 **received belief** article of faith (*OED* Received *ppl. adj.*, meaning 'accepted as true')

125–6 **in . . . reason** contrary to all common sense; combining the two expressions 'In spite of one's teeth' (Dent, S764) and 'To have neither rhyme nor reason' (Dent, R98)

127 **Jack-a-Lent** 'butt for every one to throw at' (Onions); see 3.3.23n.

128–9, 131 Evans, finally undisguised, returns to his linguistic eccentricities, such as the Welsh plurals (*desires*, 129, *jealousies*, 131) and is teased for them by Ford (132–3).

134 **laid . . . it** Cf. 'I'll have my brains ta'en out and buttered', 3.5.6–7n.

121 And . . . fairies] *separate line F;* Why then these were not F*airies? Q*   I was] By the Lord I was *Q*

that it wants matter to prevent so gross o'erreaching as   135
this? Am I ridden with a Welsh goat too? Shall I have a
coxcomb of frieze? 'Tis time I were choked with a piece
of toasted cheese.

EVANS   Seese is not good to give putter – your belly is all
putter.   140

FALSTAFF   'Seese' and 'putter'? Have I lived to stand at
the taunt of one that makes fritters of English? This is
enough to be the decay of lust and late-walking through
the realm.

MISTRESS PAGE   Why, Sir John, do you think, though we   145
would have thrust virtue out of our hearts by the
head and shoulders, and have given ourselves without
scruple to hell, that ever the devil could have made you
our delight?

FORD   What, a hodge-pudding? A bag of flax?   150

MISTRESS PAGE   A puffed man?

PAGE   Old, cold, withered and of intolerable entrails?

135 **wants matter** lacks means (as well as
 brains)
 so gross o'erreaching such a crude
 deception
136 **ridden with** harassed by
 Welsh goat Evans's satyr mask must
 have resembled a goat's head; see
 5.4.0.1n. The abundance of goats
 (instead of sheep) in Wales and the
 mountainous nature of the country
 were objects of scorn; see *mountain-
 foreigner*, 1.1.148n.
137 **coxcomb of frieze** a fool's cap made
 of coarse woollen cloth (a cheap product of Wales)
137–8 **choked . . . cheese** another jocular
 allusion to the Welsh fondness for
 cheese; see 82n.
139 **Seese . . . give putter** It is bad
 (unhealthy) to add cheese to butter.
142 **makes . . . English** chops the English

language into bits fried in batter
143 **decay** end
 late-walking going whoring at night
145–6 **though . . . have** if we *had* wished
 to (RP)
146–7 **thrust . . . shoulders** eradicated
 virtue from our hearts; from the current idiom 'To thrust out by the head
 and shoulders' (Dent, H274)
147–9 **given . . . delight** even if we had
 wanted a lover, that the devil himself
 could have made us choose you
150 **hodge-pudding** pudding (cf. 2.1.26)
 stuffed mith mixed ingredients
 bag of flax sack full of flax
151 **puffed** stuffed, inflated
152 **Old, cold, withered** Cf. the Lord
 Chief Justice's description of Falstaff
 in *2H4* 1.2.178–86.
 intolerable excessive (*OED adj.* 1c),
 said of Falstaff's paunch (*entrails*)

150 SP] MISTRESS FORD *(Oxf)*   150 hodge-pudding] hog's pudding *Pope;* hog-pudding *Collier*
flax] *F;* flux *(Cam¹)*

FORD   And one that is as slanderous as Satan?

PAGE   And as poor as Job?

FORD   And as wicked as his wife?   155

EVANS   And given to fornication, and to taverns, and sack,
and wine, and metheglins, and to drinkings, and swearings, and starings; pribbles and prabbles?

FALSTAFF   Well, I am your theme: you have the start of
me. I am dejected, I am not able to answer the Welsh   160
flannel, ignorance itself is a plummet o'er me. Use me
as you will.

FORD   Marry, sir, we'll bring you to Windsor to one
Master Brook that you have cozened of money, to
whom you should have been a pander. Over and above   165
that you have suffered, I think to repay that money will
be a biting affliction.

PAGE   Yet be cheerful, knight: thou shalt eat a posset
tonight at my house, where I will desire thee to laugh
at my wife that now laughs at thee. Tell her Master   170
Slender hath married her daughter.

---

153 **slanderous as Satan** Shaheen (146)
notes that Satan slandered God when
he told Eve (Genesis, 3.4–5) that God
knew that, by eating the fruit of the
tree of knowledge, she and Adam, far
from dying, should 'be as gods'. Also,
more generally, Satan is the father of
all lies.

154 **poor as Job** a biblical allusion turned
proverbial (Dent, J60). In *2H4* 1.2.126
Falstaff tells the Lord Chief Justice: 'I
am as poor as Job'.

155 **wicked . . . wife** Job's wife had
advised him to blaspheme God (Job,
2.9)

157 **metheglins** metheglin (Evans's
plural): strong spiced drink from
fermented honey produced in
Wales

157–8 **swearings and starings** insulting

behaviour by swearing and glaring at
people: Welsh plural of a standard
phrase (Dent, SS21)

158 **pribbles and prabbles** Evans's
coinage; see 1.1.50n.

159 **theme** subject of derision
start of advantage over; 'To have the
start of' is another stock phrase (Dent,
S828)

160 **dejected** humbled

160–1 **Welsh flannel** coarse Welsh cloth
(alluding to Evans); see 137n.

161 **ignorance . . . me** I am sunk so low
that ignorance itself cannot sink (like a
plummet) to my level

165 **should** were to

166 **¹that** that which

168 **eat a posset** drink a nightcap; see
1.4.7n.

161 is . . . o'er me] has a plume o' me *(Johnson)*; is a planet o'er me *(Farmer)*

MISTRESS PAGE [*aside*]   Doctors doubt that: if Anne Page
be my daughter, she is, by this, Doctor Caius's wife.

Enter SLENDER.

SLENDER   Whoa, ho, ho, father Page!

PAGE   Son, how now? How now, son, have you dis-   175
patched?

SLENDER   Dispatched? I'll make the best in
Gloucestershire know on't – would I were hanged, la,
else!

PAGE   Of what, son?   180

SLENDER   I came yonder at Eton to marry Mistress Anne
Page – and she's a great lubberly boy! If it had not
been i'the church, I would have swinged him – or he
should have swinged me. If I did not think it had
been Anne Page, would I might never stir. – And 'tis a   185
postmaster's boy.

PAGE   Upon my life, then, you took the wrong.

SLENDER   What need you tell me that? I think so, when I

172 **Doctors doubt that** ironical: 'things
may turn out differently', a variant of
the saying 'That is but one doctor's
opinion' (Dent, D426); Mistress Page
implies that Doctor Caius knows better.
173.1 In Q Caius enters first and Slender
second, after the equivalent of 207:
similar inverted entrances in Q have
been noted for Evans and Caius at 4.5;
see 4.5.n. and 4.5.68.1n.
174 **father Page** Slender's addressing
Page as father-in-law in order to tell
him that he is no such thing for him has
a pathetic ring.
175–6 **dispatched** settled the business
(*OED* Dispatch *v.* 10)
177–8 **the . . . Gloucestershire** the gentry of Gloucestershire, i.e. those
known to him and Shallow; a reminder
that Slender and Shallow are only vis-

itors on business to Windsor. Shallow
had been informed at 5.2 of Page's plan
for Slender, and it is strange that he
should not be present at this stage; in
Q his name figures in the direction at
102.7–8, but he does not speak.
178 **on't** of it – prompting Page's question
at 180: *Of what?*
182 **great lubberly** big loutish (*great*
meaning big for his young age)
183 **swinged** thrashed
185 **would . . . stir** another stock phrase
(Dent, S861), found also in *KJ*
1.1.145; cf. 'would I were hanged, la,
else' at 178–9.
186 **postmaster's boy** stable-boy of the
man in charge of post-horses
187 **took the wrong** Page means 'mistook
the instructions', but Slender understands 'got the wrong person'.

172 SD] *Theobald*   172 Doctors doubt that] *separate line in F*   173.1] *Q, after the equivalent of 201–
7; not in F*   175–6] *F lines* Sonne, / dispatch'd? /

took a boy for a girl! If I had been married to him, for
all he was in woman's apparel, I would not have had   190
him.

PAGE   Why, this is your own folly. Did I not tell you how
you should know my daughter by her garments?

SLENDER   I went to her in white, and cried 'mum', and
she cried 'budget', as Anne and I had appointed. – And   195
yet it was not Anne, but a postmaster's boy.

MISTRESS PAGE   Good George, be not angry: I knew of
your purpose, turned my daughter into green, and
indeed she is now with the Doctor at the deanery, and
there married.   200

Enter CAIUS.

CAIUS   Vere is Mistress Page? By gar, I am cozened, I ha'
married *un garçon*, a boy, *un paysan*, by gar! A boy it is
not Anne Page. By gar, I am cozened.

MISTRESS PAGE   Why, did you take her in green?

CAIUS   Ay, by gar, and 'tis a boy! By gar, I'll raise all   205
Windsor.

FORD   This is strange. Who hath got the right Anne?

189–90 **for all** even though
190–1 **would . . . him** would have refused
to treat him as a wife. Cf. 'to have and
to hold from this day foreward' in the
marriage service in the Book of
Common Prayer (RP).
194 ***in white** The emendation, here as at
198 and 204 (see t.n.), is indispensable,
since F's 'green' is the colour by which
Mistress Page had told Caius he would
recognize Anne. Q's 'red' is also incon-
sistent; see 37n.
194–5 **'mum'** . . . **'budget'** the agreed
nay-word; see 5.2.5–10 and notes.
196 Craik (Oxf¹) marks Slender's exit

here. But this seems unnecessary: he as
well as Caius may well remain, though
silent and crestfallen, till the end, if for
no other reason, in order to fill the
stage in the absence of Quickly,
Shallow and the Host of the Garter.
202 **married** Caius is doubly fooled,
because apparently he has actually
gone through the marriage ceremony.
un paysan French: a peasant, used
contemptuously
202–3 **A . . . Page** Caius means, in his
peculiar English, 'Anne Page is not a
boy'; for other possible readings see t.n.
205 **raise** call to arms

192–3] *F lines* folly, / daughter, / garments? /   194 white] *Rowe³;* greene *F;* red *Q*   196 boy.] boy.
[*Exit*] *Oxf¹*   198 green] *Rowe³;* white *F*   200.1] *Q, after the equivalent of 173; not in F*   202 *un
garçon*] *(*oon Garsoon*) Capell   un paysan*] *F (*oon pesant*), Capell   by gar! A boy it*] *this edn;* by gar. A
boy, it *F;* by Gar. A boy! It *Oxf;* by gar, a boy. It *Oxf¹*   204 SP] (*M. Page*); PAGE *Oxf*   take] not take
Pope   green] *Pope;* white *F*   206 Windsor.] Windsor. [*Exit*] *Capell*

Enter FENTON *and* ANNE PAGE.

PAGE   My heart misgives me. – Here comes Master
Fenton. – How now, Master Fenton?

ANNE

Pardon, good father – good my mother, pardon.   210

PAGE   Now, mistress, how chance you went not with
Master Slender?

MISTRESS PAGE

Why went you not with Master Doctor, maid?

FENTON

You do amaze her. Hear the truth of it:
You would have married her most shamefully   215
Where there was no proportion held in love.
The truth is, she and I, long since contracted,
Are now so sure that nothing can dissolve us.
Th'offence is holy that she hath committed,
And this deceit loses the name of craft,   220
Of disobedience, and unduteous title,
Since therein she doth evitate and shun
A thousand irreligious cursed hours
Which forced marriage would have brought upon her.

FORD

Stand not amazed, here is no remedy.   225
In love the heavens themselves do guide the state:

208–39 The final part of the play is in blank verse interspersed with odd rhymed couplets, but at 208–9 and 211–12 Page, in his indignation, breaks up the rhythmical pattern.
214 **amaze** bewilder; cf. *amazed* at 225
216 **proportion held** reciprocation
217 **contracted** betrothed
218 **sure** firmly bound together
220 **deceit** deception
craft scheming, cunning
221 **unduteous title** breach of duty (*title*

is synonymous with *name* at 220)
222 **evitate** avoid (synonymous with *shun*)
223 **cursed** cursèd
225 **here is** in this case there is (the current phrase is 'There's no remedy', Dent, RR3; cf. 1.3.30n.)
226–7 a sententious rhymed couplet: Ford takes over from Mistress Page the task of stating the moral of the play; see 5.3.21–2n.
226 **guide the state** rule

207.1] *Q (Anne.); not in F*   211–12] *F lines* Mistris: / Slender?   221 title] guile *Collier²*   225 amazed, here] amazed. There *(Oxf¹)*

Money buys lands, and wives are sold by fate.

FALSTAFF   I am glad, though you have ta'en a special
stand to strike at me, that your arrow hath glanced.

PAGE

Well, what remedy? Fenton, God give thee joy!   230
What cannot be eschewed must be embraced.

FALSTAFF

When night-dogs run, all sorts of deer are chased.

MISTRESS PAGE

Well, I will muse no further. – Master Fenton,
God give you many, many merry days!
Good husband, let us every one go home,   235
And laugh this sport o'er by a country fire,
Sir John and all.

FORD   Let it be so, Sir John.
To Master Brook you yet shall hold your word,
For he tonight shall lie with Mistress Ford.   *Exeunt.*

---

227 based on proverbial lore: 'He that has
gold may buy land' (Dent, G286), and
'Marriage and hanging go by destiny'
(Dent, M682)

229 **stand** position from which to shoot
(Falstaff as a deer being the quarry)
glanced struck obliquely, without
piercing the mark

230 ***God . . . joy!** This is the conven-
tional expression recorded since 1440
(Dent, JJ2): F's 'heauen' replaced
'God' because of the 1606 Profanity
Act. The use of *thee* marks Page's
acceptance of Fenton (RP).

231 What cannot be avoided must be

accepted; proverbial as 'What cannot
be cured must be endured' (Dent,
C922)

232 Falstaff's last speech in the play is a
personal principle turned into proverbial form: when hunting dogs are
released at night ('squires of the
night's body' was the definition
Falstaff had given of himself and his
companions in *1H4* 1.2.24) they will
fall on any prey – with the usual pun
on 'deer'/'dear', 16, 17n.

233 **muse** grumble, or wonder

234 ***God** 'Heauen' in F; see 230n.

230–1] *Rowe³; prose F*   230, 234 God] *this edn (RP, suggested by Q);* heauen *(Heauen 234) F*   237
so, Sir John.] *(so* (Sir *Iohn:));* so. – Sir John, *Theobald*

APPENDIX
THE FIRST QUARTO (1602)

The First Quarto (1602) of *The Merry Wives of Windsor* is repro-
duced in reduced photographic facsimile from the copy in the
Henry E. Huntington Library, San Marino, California (press-
mark 69331). The Huntington copy is reproduced full-size in
Shakespeare's Plays in Quarto, ed. Michael J.B. Allen and
Kenneth Muir (Berkeley, Los Angeles and London, 1981). A
full-size photo-lithographic facsimile of the H. Huth copy of the
Quarto (British Library, London, press-mark Huth 48) was first
published by William Griggs in 1888, with an introduction by
P.A. Daniel, and a photographic facsimile of the same copy by
W.W. Greg (Oxford, 1957, 1963).

The Quarto consists of title-page (sig. A2) and 52 pages of
text (sigs. A3–G4v).

Top-of-page references indicate: 1) Quarto scene numbers –
followed by dash (–) if scene continues on next page; preceded
by dash if scene follows from previous page; enclosed between
dashes if scene follows from previous page and continues on
next. 2) Roughly equivalent passages in the Folio text showing
act/scene/line numbers as in the present edition.

Scene numbers are placed in the margin at the beginning of
each new Quarto scene.

A more detailed list of parallel passages in the two texts is
illustrated in the table on pp. 324–5. The left-hand column indicates in sequence the characters present in the different sections
of each individual Quarto scene; sometimes changes due to the
entrance of new characters are indicated by a solidus (/), and

more marked divisions within single scenes by a double solidus (//). Passages in Folio roughly equivalent to Quarto readings (frequently in a different order) are listed on the right. **Bold** designates passages transferred to Quarto scenes from different Folio contexts, *italics* passages in Folio completely reworded in Quarto. In the Quarto column, characters that, though present, do not speak are in *italics*, and enclosed in square brackets if not mentioned in Quarto stage directions.

A
Moſt pleaſaunt and
excellent conceited Co-
medie, of Syr *Iohn Falſtaffe*, and the
merrie Wiues of *Windſor*.

Entermixed with ſundrie
variable and pleaſing humors, of Syr *Hugh*
the Welch Knight, Iuſtice *Shallow* , and his
wiſe Couſin M. *Slender*.

With the ſwaggering vaine of Auncient
Piſtoll, and Corporall *Nym*.

By *William Shakeſpeare*.

As it hath bene diuers times Acted by the right Honorable
my Lord Chamberlaines ſeruants. Both before her
Maieſtie, and elſe-where.

LONDON
Printed by **T. C.** for Arthur Iohnſon, and are to be ſold at
his ſhop in Powles Church-yard, at the ſigne of the
Flower de Leuſe and the Crowne.
1 6 0 2.

sc. 1

A pleasant conceited Co-
medie, of Syr *Iohn Falstaffe*, and the
merry Wiues of *VVindsor*.

Enter Iustice Shallow, *Syr* Hugh, *Maister* Page,
and Slender.

Shal. NEre talke to me, Ile make a star-cham-
ber matter of it.
The Councell shall know it.   (mee.
Pag. Nay good maister *Shallow* be perswaded by
slen. Nay surely my vncle shall not put it vp so.
Sir Hu. Wil you not heare reasons M. *Slenders* ?
You should heare reasons.
Shal. Tho he be a knight, he shall not thinke to
carrie it so away.
M. *Page* I will not be wronged. For you
Syr, I loue you, and for my cousen
He comes to looke vpon your daughter.
Pa. And heres my hand, and if my daughter
Like him so well as I, weel quickly haue it a match:
In the meane time let me intreat you to soiourne
Here a while. And on my life Ile vndertake
To make you friends.
Sir Hu. I pray you M. *Shallowes* let it be so,
A 3   The

A pleasant Comedie, of

The matter is pud to arbitarments.

The firft man is M. *Page*, videlicet M. *Page*.   (tyr.

The fecond is my felfe, videlicet my felfe.

And the third and laft man, is mine hoft of the gar-

Enter Syr Iohn *Falftaffe,* Piftoll, Bardolfe, *and* Nim.

Here is fir *Iohn* himfelfe now, looke you.

Fal. Now M. *Shallow*, youle complaine of me to the Councell, I heare?

Shal. Sir *Iohn*, fir *Iohn*, you haue hurt my keeper, Kild my dogs, ftolne my deere.

Fal. But not kiffed your keepers daughter.

Shal. Well this fhall be anfwered.

Fal. Ile anfwere it ftrait. I haue done all this. This is now anfwred.

Shal. Well, the Councell fhall know it.   (counfell,

Fal. T'were better for you were knowne in

Youle be laught at.

Sir Hu. Good vrdes fir *Iohn*, good vrdes.

Fal. Good vrdes, good Cabidge.

Slender I brake your head,

What matter haue you againft mee?

Slen. I haue matter in my head againft you and your cogging companions, *Piftoll* and *Nym*. They carried mee to the Tauerne and made mee drunke, and afterward picked my pocket.

Fal. What fay you to this *Piftoll*, did you picke Mafter *Slenders* purfe *Piftoll*?

Slen. I by this handkercher did he. Two faire fhouell boord fhillings, befides feuen groats in mill fixpences.   *Fal.*

the merry Wiues of windfor.

Fal. What fay you to this *Piftoll*?

Pift. Sir *Iohn*, and Maifter mine, I combat craue Of this fame laten bilbo. I do retort the lie Euen in thy gorge, thy gorge, thy gorge.

Slen. By this light it was he then.

Nym. Syr my honor is not for many words, But if your run bace humors of me, I will fay mary trap. And there's the humor of it.

Fal. You heare thefe matters denide gentlemē, You heare it.

Enter Miftreffe Foord, *Miftreffe* Page, *and her daughter* Anne.

Pa. No more now, I thinke it be almoft dinner time, For my wife is come to meet vs.

Fal. Miftreffe *Foord*, I thinke your name is, If I miftake not.

                                    Syr Iohn *kiffes her.*

Mif. Ford. Your miftake fir is nothing but in the Miftreffe. But my husbands name is *Foord* fir.

Fal. I fhall defire your more acquaintance. The like of you good mifteris *Page*.

Mif. Pa. With all my hart fir *Iohn*. Come husband will you goe? Dinner ftaies for vs.

Pa. With all my hart, come along Gentlemen.

                        Exit all, but Slender and
                                    miftreffe Anne.
                                                      Anth.

A pleasant Comedie, of

Anne. Now forsooth why do you stay me?
What would you with me?
Slen. Nay for my owne part, I would litle or no-
thing with you. I loue you well, and my vncle can
tell you how my liuing stands. And if you can loue
me why so. If not, why then happie man be his
dole.
An. You say well M. slender.
But first you must giue me leaue to
Be acquainted with your humor,
And afterward to loue you if I can.
Slen. Why by God, there's neuer a man in chri-
stendome can desire more. What haue you Beares
in your Towne mistresse Anne, your dogs barke so?
An. I cannot tell M. Slender, I thinke there be.
Slen. Ha how say you? I warrant your afeard of
a Beare let loose, are you not?
An. Yes trust me.
Slen. Now that's meate and drinke to me,
Ile run yon to a Beare, and take her by the muscell,
You neuer saw the like.
But indeed I cannot blame you,
For they are maruellous rough things.
An. Will you goe into dinner M. slender?
The meate staies for you.
Slen. No faith not I. I thanke you,
I cannot abide the smell of hot meate
Ne're since I broke my shin. Ile tel you how it came
By my troth. A Fencer and I plaid three venies
For a dish of stewd prunes, and I with my ward
Defending my head, he hot my shin. Yes faith.

Enter

---

the merry wiues of Windsor.

Enter Maister Page.

Pa. Come, come Maister Slender, dinner staies for
you.
Slen. I can eate no meate, I thanke you.
Pa. You shall not choose I say.
Slen. Ile follow you sir, pray leade the way.
Nay be God misteris Anne, you shall goe first,
I haue more manners then so, I hope.
An. Well sir, I will not be troublesome.

Exit omnes.

sc. 2

Enter for Hugh and Simple, from dinner.

Sir Hu. Harke you Simple, pray you beare this letter
to Doctor Cayus house, the French Doctor. He is
well vp along the street, and enquire of his house
for one mistris Quickly, his woman, or his try nurse,
and deliuer this Letter to her, it is about Maister
Slender. Looke you, will you do it now?
Sim. I warrant you Sir.
Sir Hu. Pray you do, I must not be absent at the
grace.
I will goe make an end of my dinner,
There is pepions and cheese behinde.

Exit omnes.

sc. 3

Enter for Iohn Falstaffes Host of the Garter,
Nym, Bardolfe, Pistoll, and the boy.

Fal. Mine Host of the Garter.

B   Host.

298

A pleasant Comedie, of

Host. What is my bully Rooke?
Speake scholerly and wisely.
Fal. Mine Host, I must turne away some of my
followers.
Host. Discard bully, *Hercules* cashire,
Let them wag, trot, trot.
Fal. I sit at ten pound a weeke.
Host. Thou art an Emperour *Cæsar*, *Pheser* and
Kesar bully.
Ile entertaine *Bardolfe*. He shall tap, he shall draw.
Said I well, bully *Hector*?
Fal. Do good mine Host.
Host. I haue spoke. Let him follow. *Bardolfe*
Let me see thee froth, and lyme. I am at
A word. Follow, follow.
             Exit Host.

Fal. Do *Bardolfe*, a Tapster is a good trade,
An old cloake will make a new Ierkin,
A withered seruingman, a fresh Tapster:
Follow him *Bardolfe*.
Bar. I will sir, Ile warrant you Ile make a good
shift to liue.
             Exit Bardolfe.

Pist. O base gongarian wight, wilt thou the spic-
ket wild?
Nym. His minde is not heroick. And theres the
humor of it.
Fal. Well my Ladde, I am almost out at the
heeles.
Pist. Why then let cybes insue.
Nym. I thanke thee for that humor.

             Fal.

---

the merry wiues of windsor.

Fal. Well I am glad I am so rid of this tinder
Boy.
His stealth was too open, his filching was like
An vnskilfull singer, he kept not time.
Nym. The good humor is to steale at a minuts
rest.
Pist. Tis so indeed *Nym*, thou hast hit it right.
Fal. Well, afore God, I must cheat, I must cony-
catch.
Which of you knowes *Foord* of this Towne?
Pist. I ken the wight, he is of substance good.
Fal. Well my honest Lads, Ile tell you what
I am about.
Pist. Two yards and more.
Fal. No gibes now *Pistoll*: indeed I am two yards
In the wast, but now I am about no wast:
Briefly, I am about thrift your rogues you,
I do intend to make loue to *Foords* wife,
I espie entertainment in her. She carues, she
Discourses. She giues the lyre of inuitation,
And euery part to be construed rightly is, I am
Syr *Iohn Falstaffes.*
Pist. He hath studied her well, out of honestie
Into English.
Fal. Now the report goes, she hath all the rule
Of her husbands purse. She hath legians of angels.
Pist. As many diuels attend her.
And to her boy say I.
Fal. Heere's a Letter to her. Heere's another to
misteris *Page.*

             B 2

             Who

A pleasant Comedie, of

Who euen now gaue me good eies too, examined
my exteriors with such a greedy intentiō, with the
beames of her beautie, that it seemed as she would
a scorged me vp like a burning glasse. Here is another Letter to her, shee beares the purse too. They
shall be Exchechers to me, and Ile be cheaters to
them both. They shall be my East and West Indies,
and Ile trade to them both. Heere beare thou this
Letter to mistresse Foord. And thou this to mistresse
Page. Weele thriue Lads, we will thriue.

Pist. Shall I sir Panderowes of Troy become?
And by my sword were steele.
Then Lucifer take all.

Nym. Here take your humor Letter againe,
For my part, I will keepe the hauior
Of reputation. And theres the humor of it.

Fal. Here sirrha beare me these Letters titely,
Saile like my pinnice to the golden shores:
Hence slaues, auant. Vanish like hailstones, goe.
Falstaffe will learne the humor of this age,
French thrift you rogue, my selfe and skirted Page.
                  Exit Falstaffe,
                  and the Boy.

Pist. And art thou gone? T'easter Ile haue in pouch
When thou shalt want, bace Phrygian Turke.

Nym. I haue operations in my head, which are
    humors of reuenge.

Pist. Wilt thou reuenge?

Nym. By Welkin and her Fairies.

Pist. By wit, or sword?

Nym. With both the humors I will disclose this
loue to Page. Ile poses him with Iallowes,
                      And

---

the merry wiues of windsor.

And theres the humor of it.

Pist. And I to Foord will likewise tell
How Falstaffe varlot vilde,
Would haue her loue, his doue would proue,
And eke his bed desile.

Nym. Lets vs about it then.   (on.
Pist. Ile second thee : sir Corporall Nym troope
                  Exit omnes.

sc. 4

Enter Mistresse Quickly, and Simple.

Quic. M. Slender is your Masters name say you?
Sim. I indeed that is his name.
Quic. How say you? I take it thee is somewhat a
    weakly man?

And he has as it were a whay coloured beard.
Sim. Indeed my maisters beard is kane colored.
Quic. Kane colour, you say well.
And is this Letter from sir Iom, about Misteris An,
Is it not?
Sim. I indeed is it.
Quic. So: and your Maister would haue me as
it were to speak to misteris Anne concerning him :
I promisse you my M. hath a great affectioned mind
to mistresse Anne himselfe. And if he should know
that I should as they say, giue my verdit for any one
but himselfe, I should heare of it throughly : For
I tell you friend, he puts all his priuities in me.
Sim. I by my faith you are a good faie to him.
Quic. Am I? and you knew all yow'd say so :
Washing, brewing, baking, all goes through my
Or else it would be but a woe house.   (hands,
Sim. I bethrow me, one woman to do all this,
                      Is

B 3

Is very painfull.

Qui. Are you auised of that? I, I warrant you,
Take all, and paie all, all goe through my hands,
And he is such a honest man, and he should chance
To come home and finde a man here, we should
Haue no who with him. He is a parlowes man.

Sim. Is he indeed?

Qui. Is he quoth you? God keepe him abroad:
Lord blesse me, who knocks there?
For Gods fake step into the Counting-houfe,
While I goe fee whofe at doore.

He steps into the Counting-houfe.

What *Iohn Rugby, Iohn,*
Are you come home fir alreadie?

And she opens the doore.

Doct. I begar I be forget my oyntment,
VVhere be *Iohn Rugby*?

Enter Iohn.

Rug. Here fir, do you call?

Doc. I you be *Iohn Rugbie*, and you be *Iack Rugby*
Goe run vp met your heeles, and bring away
De oyntment in de vindoe present:
Make haft *Iohn Rugbie*. O I am almost forget
My fimples in a boxe in de Counting-houfe:
O *Iefhu* vat be here, a deuella, a deuella?
My Rapier *Iohn Rugby*, Vat be you, vat make
You in my Counting-houfe?

Qui. Iefhu blesse me, we are all vndone.

Sim. O Lord fir no? I am no theefe,
I am a Seruingman:

My

My name is *Iohn Simple*, I brought a Letter fir
From my M.*Slender*, about misteris *Anne Page*
Sir: indeed that is my comming.

Doc. I begar is dat all? *Iohn Rugby* giue a ma pen
An Inck:tarche vn petit tarche a little.

The Doctor writes.

Sim. O God what a furious man is this?

Qui. Nay it is wellhe is no worse:
I am glad he is fo quiet.

Doc. Here giue dat same to fir *Hu*, it be ver chalenge
Begar tell him I willcut his nafe, will you?

Sim. I fir, Ile tell him fo. (may,

Doc. Dat be vell, my Rapier *Iohn Rugby*, follow

Exit Doctor.

Qui. VVell my friend, I cannot tarry, tell your
Maifter Ile doo what I can for him,
And fo farewell.

Sim. Mary will I, I am glad I am got hence.

Exit omnes.

sc. 5

Enter Mistresse Page, reading of
a Letter.

(reafon,

Mis. Pa. Miftresse *Page*, I loue you. Aske me no
Becaufe they impoffible to alledge. Your faire,
And I am fat. Yon loue fack, fo do I:
As I am sure I haue no mind but to loue,
So I know you haue no hart but to grant (knowes
A fouldier doth not vfe many words, where a
A letter may ferue for a fentence. I loue you,
And fo I leaue you.

Yours Syr Iohn Falstaffe.

Now

A pleasant Comedie, of

Now Iefhu bleffe me, am I metliomorphifed?
I thinke I knowe not my felfe. Why what a Gods
name doth this man fee in me, that thus he fhootes
at my honeftie? Well but that I knowe my owne
heart, I fhould fcarcely perfwade my felfe I were
hand. Why what an vnreafonable woolfack is this.
He was neuer twice in my companie, and if then I
thought I gaue fuch affuraunce with my eies, Ide pul
them out, they fhould neuer fee more holie daies.
Well, I fhall truft fat men the worfe while I liue for
his fake. O God that I knew how to be reuenged of
him. But in good time, heeres miftreffe *Foord*.

Enter Miftreffe Foord.

Mif.For. How now Miftris *Page*, are you reading
Loue Letters? How do you woman?
Mif.Pa. O woman I am I know not what:
In loue vp to the hard eares. I was neuer in fuch a
cafe in my life.
Mif.Ford. In loue, now in the name of God with
whom?
Mif.Pa. With one that fweares he loues me,
And I muft not choofe but do the like againe:
I prethie looke on that Letter.
Mif.For. Ile match your letter iuft with the like,
Line for line, word for word. Only the name
Of mifteris *Page*, and mifteris *Foord* difagrees:
Do me the kindnes to looke vpon this.
Mif.Pa. Why this is right my letter.
O moft notorious villaine!
Why what a bladder of iniquitie is this?
Lets be reuenged, if we liue weel be reuenged.
O Lord

the merry Wiues of Windsor.

O Lord if my husband fhould fee this Letter,
Ifaith this would euen giue edge to his Iealoufie.

Enter Ford, Page, Piftall and Nym.

Mif.Pa. See where our husbands are,
Mine's as far from Iealoufie,
As I am from wronging him.
Piff. Ford the words I fpeake are fort:
Beware, take heed, for *Falftaff* loues thy wife:
When *Piftall* lies do this.
Ford. Why fir my wife is not young,
Piff. He wooes both yong and old, both rich and
None comes amis. I fay he loues thy wife: (poore
Faire warning did I giue, take heed,
For fommer comes, and Cuckoo birds appeare:
Page belieue him what he fes. Away fir Corporall
(*Nym.*
Exit Piftall.

Nym. Syr the humor of it is, he loues your wife,
I fhould ha borne the humor Letter to her:
I fpeake and I auouch tis true: My name is *Nym*,
Farwell, I loue not the humor of bread and cheefe:
And theres the humor of it.   *Exit Nym.*
Pa. The humor of it, quoth you:
Heres a fellow frites humor out of his wits.
Mif.Pa. How now fweet hart, how dooft thou?

Enter Miftreffe Quickly.

Pa. How now man? How do you miftris *Ford*?
Mif.For. Well I thanke you good M.*Page*,
How now husband, how chaunce thou art fo me-
lancholy?
Ford. Melancholy, I am not melancholy.
Goe get you in, goe.
Mif.For. God faue me, fee who yonder is:
C   Weele

A pleasant Comedie, of

Weele set her a worke in this businesse.

Mis. Pa. O the else serue excellent.

Now you come to see my daughter *An* I am sure.

Quic. I forsooth that is my comming.

Mis. Pa. Come go in with me. Come Mis. *Ford.*

Mis. For. I follow you Mistresse *Page.*

　　Exit Mistresse Ford, Mis. Page, and Quickly.

For. M. *Page* did you heare what these fellowes

Pa. Yes M. *Ford,* what of that sir?　　(said?

For. Do you thinke it is true that they told vs?

Pa. No by my troth do I not,

I rather take them to be paltry lying knaues,

Such as rather speakes of enuie,

Then of any certaine they haue

Of any thing. And for the knight, perhaps

He hath spoke merrily, as the fashion of fat men

Are : But should he loue my wife,

Ifaith I de turne her loose to him :

And what he got more of her,

Then ill lookes, and shrowd words,

Why let me beare the penaltie of it.

For. Nay I do not mistrust my wife,

Yet I de be loth to turne them together,

A man may be too confident.

　　Enter Host and Shallow.

Pa. Here comes my ramping host of the garter,

Ther's either licker in his hed, or mony in his purse,

That he lookes so merrily. Now mine Host?

Host. God blesse you my bully rookes, God blesse

Cauelero Iustice I say.　　(you.

Shal. At hand mine host, at hand. M. *Ford* god den

God den an twentie good M. *Page.*　　(to you.

　　　　　　　　　　　　　　　　　I tell

the merry wiues of Windsor.

I tell you sir we haue sport in hand.

Host. Tell him caueliro Iustice : tell him bully

Ford. Mine Host a the garter :　　(rooke.

Host. What ses my bully rooke?

Ford. A word with you sir.

　　　　Ford and the Host talkes.

Shal. Harke you sir, Ile tell you what the sport

Doctor *Caywu* and sir *Hu* are to fight,　　(shall be,

My merrie Host hath had the measuring

Of their weapons, and hath

Appointed them contrary places. Harke in your

　Host. Hast thou no shute against my knight,　(eare:

My guess, my caueliro :

For. None I protest : But tell him my name

Is *Brooke,* onlie for a Iest.

　Host. My hand bully : Thou shalt

Haue egres and regres, and thy

Name shall be *Brooke* : Sed I well bully Hector?

Shal. I tell you what M. *Page,* I beleeue

The Doctor is no Iester, heele laie it on :

For tho we be Iustices and Doctors,

And Church men, yet we are

The sonnes of women M. *Page.*

　Pa. True maister *Shallow:*

Shal. It will be found so maister *Page:*

Pa. Maister *Shallow* you your selfe

Haue bene a great fighter,

Tho now a man of peace:

Shal. M. *Page* I haue seene the day that yong

Tall fellowes with their stroke & their passado,

I haue made them trudge Maister *Page,*

A tis the hart, the hart doth all : I

　　　　　　　　C 2　　　　　　　　　Haue

A pleasant Comedie, of

Haue seene the day, with my two hand sword
I would a made you foure tall Fencers
Skippe like Rattes.

Hoſt. Here boyes, ſhall we wag, ſhall we wag, ſhall we wag?

Shal. Ha with you mine hoſt.

       Exit Hoſt and Shallow.

Pa. Come M. *Ford,* ſhall we to dinner?
I know theſe fellowes ſticks in your minde.

For. No in good ſadneſſe ti not in mine:
Yet for all this Ile try it further,
I will not leaue it fo:
Come M. *Page,* ſhall we to dinner?

Pa. With all my hart ſir, Ile follow you.

         Exit omnes.

sc. 6

Enter Syr Iohn, and Piſtoll.

Fal. Ile not lend thee a peny.

Piſt. I will retort the ſum in equipage.

Fal. Not a pennie : *I* haue beene content you
ſhuld lay my countenance to pawne : I haue grated
vpon my good friends for 3. repriues, for you and
your Coach-fellow *Nym,* elſe you might a looked
thorow a grate like a geminy of babones. I am damned in hell for ſwearing to Gentlemen your good
ſouldiers and tall fellowes : And when miſtriſſe *Bri-
get* loſt the handle of her Fan, *I* tooke on my ho-
thou hadſt it not.

Piſt. Didſt thou not ſhare ? hadſt thou not fif-
teene pence?

Fal. Reaſon you rogue, reaſon.
Doeſt thou thinke Ile indanger my ſoule gratis?
In briefe, hang no more about mee, I am no gybit
for you. A ſhort knife and a throng to your manner of

the merry wiues of windſor.

of pickt hatch, goe. Youle not beare a Letter for me
you rogue you : you ſtand vpon your honor. Why
thou vnconfinable baſeneſſe thou, tis as much as I
can do to keep the termes of my honor precife. I, I
my felfe fometimes, leauing the feare of God on
the left hand, am faine to fhuffle, to filch & to lurch.
And yet you ſtand vpon your honor, you rogue.
You, you.

Piſt. I do recant : what woulſt thou more of man?

Fal. Well, goe too, away, no more.

      Enter Miſtreſſe Quickly.

Quic. Good you god den ſir.

Fal. Good den faire wife.

Quic. Not ſo ant like your worſhip.

Fal. Faire mayd then.

Quic. That I am Ile be ſworne, as my mother
The firſt houre I was borne.   (was

Sir I would ſpeake with you in priuate.

Fal. Say on I prethy, heeres none but my owne
houſhold.

Quic. Are they fo? Now God bleſſe them, and
make them his ſeruants.

Syr I come from Miſtreſſe *Ford.*

Fal. So from Miſtreſſe *Ford.* Goe on.

Quic. I ſir, ſhe hath ſent me to you to let you
Vnderſtand ſhe hath receiued your Letter, (dit.
And let me tell you, ſhe is one ſtands vpon her cre-

Fal. Well, come Miſteris *Ford.* Miſteris *Ford.*
Hath bene led in a fooles paradice.

Fal. Nay prethy be briefe my good fine *Mercury.*

Quic. Mary ſir, ſhee d haue you meet her between
eight and nine.   C 3   *Fal.*

A pleasant Comedie, of

Fal. So betweene me eight and nine: (birding,
Ouic. I forsooth, for then her husband goes a
Fal. Well commend me to thy mistris, tel her
I will not faile her: Boy giue her my purse.
Ouic. Nay sir it haue another arant to do to you
From mistris Page:
Fal. From mistris Page? I prethy what of her?
Ouic. By my troth I think you work by inchant-
Els they could neuer loue you as they doo: (ments,
Fal. Not I, assure thee: letting the attraction of my
Good parts aside, rise no other inchantments:
Ouic. Well sir, she loues you extremely:
And let me tell you, shees one that feares God,
And her husband giues her leaue to do all:
For he is not halse so ielousie as M. Ford is: (Ford,
Fal. But harke thee, hath misteris Page & mistris
Acquainted each other how dearly they loue me?
Ouic. O God no sir: there were a iest indeed:
Fal. Well fat wel, commend me to misteris Ford,
I will not faile her say,
Ouic. Godbe with your worship.
      Exit Mistresse Quickly.

Enter Bardolfe.

Bar. Sir heer's a Gentleman,
One M. Brooke, would speak with you,
He hath sent you a cup of sacke.
Fal. M. Brooke, hees welcome: Bid him come vp,
Such Brookes are alwaies welcome to me:
A luck, will thy old bodie yet hold out?
Wilt thou after the expence of so much mony
B: now a gainer? Goodbodie I thanke thee,
And Ile make more of thee then I ha done:
           Ha

the merry wiues of window.

Ha, ha, misteris Ford, and misteris Page, haue
I caught you at the tip? go too.
   Enter Foord disguisfed like Brooke.
For. Godsaue you sir.
Fal. And you too, would you speak with me?
Fal. Mary would I sir, I am somewhat bolde to
My name is Brooke.   (trouble you,
Fal. Good M. Brooke your verie welcome.
For. Ifaith sir I am a gentleman and a traueller,
That haue seen somewhat. And I haue often heard
That if mony goes before, all waies lie open:
Fal. Mony is a good souldier sir, and will on.
For. Ifaith sir, and I haue a bag here,
Would you wood helpe me to beare it.
Fal. O Lord, would I could tell how to deserue
To be your porter.
For. That may you easily sir Iohn: I haue an ear-
Sure to you. But good sir Iohn when I haue (nest
Told you my griefe, cast one eie of your owne
Estate, since your selfe knew what tis to be
Such an offender,
Fal. Verie well sir, proceed.
For. Sir I am deeply in loue with one Fords wife
Of this Towne. Now sir Iohn you are a gentleman
Of good discoursing, well beloued among Ladies,
A man of such parts that might win 2 o. such as she.
Fal. O good sir.   (loue
For. Nay beleeue it sir Iohn, for tis time. Now my
Is so grounded vpon her, that without her loue
I shall hardly liue.
Fal. Hate you importuned her by any means?
    Ford. No neuer Sir.
            Fal. Of

A pleasant Comedie, of

Fal. Of what qualities is your loue then?

Ford. I faith fir, like a faire house set vpon
Another mans foundation.   (me?

Fal. And to what end haue you vnfolded this to

For. O fir, when I haue told you that, I told you
For she fir stands so pure in the firme state (all:
Of her honestie, that she is too bright to be looked
Againft: Now could I come against her
With some detectió, I should sooner perswade her
From her marriage vow, and a hundred such nice
T carmes that she else stand vpon.

Fal. Why would it apply well to the vertuesie
of your affection,   (ioy?
That another should posesse what you would en-
Meethinks you prescribe verie proposterously
To your selfe.

For. No fir, for by that meanes should I be certaine of that which I now mildoubt.

Fal. Well M.*Brooke*, Ile first make bold with your
Next giue me your hand. Lastly, you shall (mony,
And you shall enioy *Fords* wife.

For. O good fir.

Fal. M. *Brooke*, I say you shall.

Ford. Want no mony Syr *Iohn*, you shall want

Fal. Want no Misteris *Ford* M.*Brooke*, (none.
You shall want none. Euen as you came to me,
Her sookes mate, her go between parted from me:
I may tell you M.*Brooke*, I am to meet her
Between 8. and 9. for at that time the Iealous
Cuckally knaue her husband wilbe from home,
Come to me soone at night, you shall know how
I speed M. *Brooke*.

                    Ford.

the merry wiues of windsor.

Ford. Sir do you know *Ford*?   (him not,

Fal. Hang him poore cuckally knaue, I know
And yet I wrong him to call him poore. For they
Say the cuckally knaue hath legions of angels,
For the which his wife seemes to me well fauored,
And Ile vse her as the key of the cuckally knaues
Coffer, and ther's my randeuowes.

Ford. Meethinkes fir it were very good that you
that you might shun him.   (knew

Fal. Hang him cuckally knaue, Ile stare him
Out of his wits, Ile keepe him in awe
With this my cudgell: It shall hang like a meator
Ore the wittolly knaues head, M. *Brooke* thou shalt
See I will predominate ore the peasant,
And thou shalt lie with his wife. M.*Brooke*
Thou shalt know him for knaue and cuckold,
Come to me soone at night.

                  Exit Falstaffe.

Ford. What a damned epicurians is this?
My wife hath sent for him, the plot is laid:
Page is an Asse, a foole. A secure Asse,
Ile sooner truft an Irishman with my
Aquauita bottle, Sir *Hu* our parson with my cheese,
A theefe to walk my ambling gelding, then my wife
With her selfe: then she plots, then she ruminates,
And what she thinkes in her hart she may effect,
Shee le breake her hart but she will effect it.
God be praised, God be praised for my iealoufie:
Well Ile goe preuent him, the time drawes on,
Better an houre too soone, then a minit too late,
Gods my life cuckold, cuckold.

                Exit Ford.

    D   *Enter*

A pleaſant Comedie, of

sc.7

Enter the Doctor and his man.

Doc. Iohn Rugbie goe looke met your eies ore de
And ſpie and you can ſee de parſon. (ſtall,

Rug. Sir I cannot tell whether he be there or no,
But I ſee a great many comming.

Doc. Bully moy, mon rapier *Iohn Rugabie*, begar
Hearing be not ſo dead as I ſhall make him. de

Enter Shallow, Page, my Hoſt, and Slender.

Pa. God ſaue you M. Doctor *Cayus*.

Shal. How do you M. Doctor? (thee,

Hoſt. God bleſſe thee my bully doctor, God bleſſe

Doc. Vat be all you, Van to tree com for, a?

Hoſt. Bully to ſee thee fight, to ſee thee foine, to
ſee thee trauerſe, to ſee thee here, to ſee thee there,
to ſee thee paſſe the punto. The ſtock, the reuerſe,
the diſtance: the montnce is a dead my francoyes?
Is a dead my Ethiopian? Ha what ſes my gallon?
my eſcuolapis? Is a dead bullies taile, is a dead?

Doc. Begar de preeſt be a coward Iack knaue,
He dare not ſhew his face.

Hoſt. Thou art a caſtallian king vrinall.
Hector of *Greece* my boy.

Shal. He hath ſhowne himſelfe the wiſer man
M. Doctor:
Sir *Hugh* is a Parſon, and you a Phiſition. You muſt
Goe with me M. Doctor.

Hoſt. Pardon bully Iuſtice. A word monſire

Doc. Mockwater, vat me dat? (mockwater.

Hoſt. That is in our Engliſh tongue, Vallor bully,
vallor.

Doc.

the merry wiues of windſor.

Doc. Begar den I haue as mockuater as de Engliſh
Iack dog, knaue.

Hoſt. He will claperclaw thee titely bully.

Doc. Claperclawe, vat be dat?

Hoſt. That is, he will make thee amends.

Doc. Begar I do looke he ſhal claperclaw me dē,
And Ile prouoke him to do it, or let him wag:
And moreouer bully, but M. *Page* and M. *Shallow*,
And eke cauellira *Slender*, go you all ouer the fields
to Frogmore?

Pa. Sir *Hugh* is there, is hee?

Hoſt. He is there: goe ſee what humor hee is in,
Ile bring the Doctor about by the fields:
Will it do well?

Shal. We wil do it my hoſt. Farwel M. Doctor.

Exit all but the Hoſt and Doctor.

Doc. Begar I will kill de cowardly Iack preeſt,
He is make a foole of moy.

Hoſt. Let him die, but firſt ſheth your impatience,
Throw cold water on your collor, com go with me
Through the fields to *Frogmore*, and Ile bring thee
Where miſtris *An Page* is a feaſting at a farm houſe,
And thou ſhalt wear hir cried game: ſed *I* wel bully

Doc. Begar excellent vel: and if you ſpeak pour
moy, I ſhall procure you de geſſe of all de gentelmē
mon patinces. I begar *I* ſall.

Hoſt. For the which Ile be thy aduerſary
To miſteris *An Page*: Sed *I* well?

Doc. I begar excellent.

Hoſt. Let vs wag then.

Doc. Alon, alon, alon.

Exit omnes.

D 2 *Enter*

A pleafant Comedie, of

sc. 8

Enter Syr Hugh and Simple.

Sir Hu. I pray you do fo much as fee if you can (efpie
Doctor Cayus comming, and giue me intelligence,
Or bring mee vrde: i, you pleafe now.
Sim. I will Sir.
Sir Hu. Iethu ples mee, how my hart trobes, and
And then fhe made him bedes of Rofes, (trobes,
And a thou, and fragrant pofes,
To fhallow riueres. Now fo kad vdge me, my hart
Swelles more and more. Mee thinkes I can cry
Verie well. There dwelt a man in *Babylon*,
To fhallow riuers and to falles,
Melodious birds fing Madrigalles,
Comming hither as faft as they can. (fword,
Sir Hu. Then it is verie neceffary I put vp my
Pray giue me my cownetoo, marke you.

Enter Page, fhallow, and Slender.

Pa. Godfaue you Sir *Hugh.*
Shal. Godfaue you M. parfon. (now.
Sir Hu. God pleffe you all from his mercies fake
Pa. What the word and the fword, doth that a-
gree well?
Sir Hu. There is reafons and caufes in all things,
I warrant you now.
Pa. Well Sir *Hugh*, we are come to craue
Your helpe and furtherance in a matter.
Sir Hu. What is I pray you?
Pa. Ifaith tis this fir *Hugh*. There is an auncient
friend of ours, a man of verie good fort, fo at oddes
with

---

with one patience, that I am fure you would hartily
grieue to fee him. Now Sir *Hugh*, you are a fcholler
well red, and verie periwafiue, we would intreate
you to fee if you could intreat him to patience.
Sir Hu. I pray you who is it? Let vs know that.
Pa. I am fhure you know him, tis Doctor *Cayus.*
Sir Hu. I had as leeue you fhould tel me of a meffe
He is an arrant lowfie beggerly knaue: (of poredge,
And he is a coward befide.
Pa. Why lle laie my life tis the man
That he fhould fight withall.

Enter Doctor and the Hoft, they
offer to fight.

Shal. Keepe them afunder, take away their wea-
Hoft. Difarme, let them queftion. (pons.
Shal. Let them keep their limbs hole, and hack
our Englifh.
Doc. Hark van vrd in your eare. You be vn daga
And de tack, coward preft.
Sir Hu. Hark you, let vs not be laughing ftockes
to other mens humors. By Iefhu I will knock your
vrinals about your knaues cockcomes, for miffing
your meetings and appointments.
Doc. O let h ..m mi hoft of de garter, *Iohn Rogoby*,
Haue I not met hum at de place he make apoint,
Haue I not?
Sir Hu. So kad vdge me, this is the pointment
Witnes by my Heft of the garter. (place,
Hoft. Peace I fay gawle and gawle, French and
Soule cure r. and b. die curer. (Wealch,
Doc. This is verie braue, excellent.
Hoft. Peace I fay, hear mine hoft of the garter,
         Am

D 3

A pleasant Comedie, of

Am I wife? am I polliticke? am I Matchauil?
Shall I lose my doctor? No, he giues me the motions
And the potions. Shall I lose my parson, my sir Hu?
No, he giues me the prouerbes, and the nouerbes:
Giue me thy hand terestiall,
So giue me thy hand celestiall:
So boyes of art I haue deceiued you both,
I haue directed you to wrong places,
Your hearts are mightie, your skins are whole,
Bardolfe laie their swords to pawne. Follow me lads
Of peace, follow me. Ha, ra, la. Follow.   *Exit Host.*
  Shal. Afore God a mad host, come let vs goe.
  Doc. I begar haue you mocka may thus?
I will be cuen met you my lack Host.
  Sir Hu. Giue me your hand Doctor *Caius,*
We be all friends:
But for mine hosts foolish knauery, let me alone.
  Doc. I dat be vell begar I be friends, (*Exit omnis*

sc. 9

                  Enter M. Foord.
  For. The time drawes on he shuld come to my
Well wife, you had best worke closely,   (house,
Or I am like to goe beyond your cunning:
I now wil seek my guesse that comes to dinner,
And in good time see where they all are come.
  Enter Shallow, Page, host, Slender, Doctor,
               and sir Hugh.
By my faith a knot, well met: your welcome all.
  Pa. I thanke you good M. *Ford.*
  For. Welcome good M. *Page.*
  Pa. I thanke you sir, she is very well at home.
  Slen. Father *Page* I hope I haue your consent
For Misteris *Anne?*
                      P a.

the merry wiues of windsor.

  Pa. You haue sonne *Slender,* but my wife here,
Is altogether for maister Doctor.
  Doc. Begar I tanck her hartily:
  Host. But what say you to yong Maister *Fenton?*
He capers, he daunces, he writes verses, he smelles
All April and May: he wil cary it, he wil cary it,
Tis in his beemes he wil carie.
  Pa. My host not with my cosent: the gentleman is
Wilde, he knowes too much: If he take her,
Let him take her simply: for my goods goes
With my liking, and my liking goes not that way.
  For. Well I pray go home with me to dinner:
Besides your cheare Ile shew you wonders: Ile
Shew you a monster. You shall go with me
  M. Page, and so shall you sir *Hugh,* and you Maister
Doctor.   (two:
  S. Hu If there be one in the company, I shal make
  Doc. And dere be ven to, I sall make de tird:
  Sir Hu, In your teeth for shame,   (fairer
  Shal. wel, wel, God be with you, we shall haue the
Wooing at Maister *Pages:*
          Exit Shallow and Slender,
  Host Ile to my honest knight sir *Iohn Falstaffe,*
And drinke Canary with him.   *Exit host.*
  Ford. I may chance to make him drinke in pipe
Wine come gentlemen.   *Exit omnes.*   (wine,
  Enter Mistresse Ford, with two of her men, and
            a great buck basket.
  Mis. For. Sirha, if your M. aske you whither
You cary this basket, say to the Launderers,
I hope you know how to bestow it?
  Ser. I warrant you misteris.   *Exit servant:*
                      Mis. Ford

sc. 10

Mis.For. Go get you in, Well sir Iohn,
I beleeue I shall serue you such a trick,
You shall haue little mind to come againe.
        Enter Sir Iohn.
Fal. Haue I caught my heauenlie Iewel?
Why now let me die. I haue liued long inough,
This is the happie houre: I haue desired to see,
Now shall I sin in my wish,
I would thy husband were dead.
Mis. For. Why how then sir Iohn?
Fal. By the Lord, I de make thee my Ladie.
Mis. For. Alas sir Iohn, I should be a verie simple
    Ladie.
Fal. Go too, I see how thy eie doth emulate
    the Diamond.
And how the arched bent of thy brow
Would become the ship tire, the tire veller,
Or anie Venetian attire, I see it.   (better.
Mis. For. A plaine kercher sir Iohn, would fit me
Fal. By the Lord thou art a traitor to saie so:
What made me loue thee? Let that perswade thee
Ther's somewhat extraordinaire in thee: Go too
I loue thee:
Mistris Ford, I cannot cog, I cannot prate, like one
Of these fellowes that smels like Bucklers-berie,
In simple time, but I loue thee,
And none but thee.
Mis. For. Sir Iohn, I am afraid you loue misteris
    Fal. I thou mightest as well faie   (Page.
I loue to walke by the Counter gate,
Which is as hatefull to me
As the reake of a lime kill.
                                    Enter

Enter Mistresse Page.

Mis.Pa. Mistresse Ford, Mis.Ford, where are you?
Mis.For. O Lord step aside good sir Iohn.
    Falstaffe stands behind the aras.
How now Misteris Page whats the matter?
Mis.Pa. Why your husband woman is comming,
With halfe Windsor at his heeles,
To looke for a gentleman that he sees
Is hid in his house: his wifes sweet hart.
Mis.For. Speak louder. But I hope tis not true
    Misteris Page.
Mis.Pa. Tis too true woman. Therefore if you
Haue any here, away with him, or your vndone for
    euer.
Mis.Pa. Alas mistresse Page, what shall I do?
Here is a gentleman my friend, how shall I do?
Mis.Pa. Gode body woman, do not stand what
shall I do, and what shall I do: Better any shift, rather
then you shamed. Looke heere, here's a buck-bas-
ket, if thee be a man of any reasonable sise, heele in
here.
    Mis.For. Alas I feare he is too big.
    Fal. Let me see, let me see, Ile in, Ile in,
Follow your friends counsell.   (Aside.
Mis.Pa. Fie sir Iohn is this your loue? Go too.
    Fal. I loue thee, and none but thee:
Helpe me to conuey me hence,
Ile neuer come here more.

E   Sir

A pleafant Comedie, of

Sir Iohn goes into the basket, the two men carries it away: Foord meetes it, and all thereſt, Page, Doctor, Prieſt, Slender, Shallow.

Ford. Come pray along, you ſhall ſee all.
How now who goes heare? whither goes this?
Miſ. For. Now let it go, you had beſt meddle with buck-waſhing.

Ford. Buck, good buck, pray come along,
Maiſter Page take my keyes: helpe to ſearch. Good
Sir Hugh pray come along, helpe a little, a little,
Ile ſhew you all.

Sir Hu. By Ieſhu theſe are iealoſies & diſtempers.
                  Exit omnes.

Miſ. Pa. He is in a pittifull taking.
Miſ. I wonder what he thought
Whé my husband bad them ſet downe the basket.
Miſ. Pa. Hang him diſhoneſt ſlaue, we cannot vſe
Him bad inough. This is excellent for your
Husbands iealouſie.

Mi. For. Alas poore foule: it grieues me at the hart,
But this will be a meanes to make him ceaſe
His iealous fits, if Falſtaffes loue increaſe.
Miſ. Pa. Nay we will ſend to Falſtaffe once again,
Tis great pittie we ſhould leaue him:
What wiues may be merry, and yet honeſt too.
Mi. For. Shall we be códemnd becauſe we laugh?
Tis old, but true: ſtill ſowes eate all the draffe.
                  Enter all.

Miſ. Pa. Here comes your husband, ſtand aſide.
For. I can find no body within, it may be he lied.
Miſ. Pa. Did you heare that?   Miſ. For.

the merry wiues of Windſor.

Miſ. For. I, I, peace.
For. Well Ile not let it go, fo, yet Ile trie further,
S. Hu. By Ieſhu if there be any body in the kitchin
Or the cuberts, or the preſſe, or the buttery,
I am an arrant Iew: Now God pleſſe me:

You ſcrue me well, do you not?
Pa. Fie M. Ford you are too blame:
Miſ. Pa. I faith tis not well M. Ford to fuſpect
Her thus without cauſe.
Doc. No by my troti be no vell:
For. Well I pray beare with me, M. Page pardó me.
I ſuffer for it, I ſuffer for it: (now:
Sir Hu. You ſuffer for a bad conſcience looke you
Ford. Well I pray no more, another time Ile tell
          you all:
The meane time go dine with me, pardó me wife,
I am ſorie. M. Page pray goe in to dinner,
Another time Ile tell you all.
Pa. Well et it be fo, and to morrow I inuite you all
To my houſe to dinner: and in the morning weele
A birding, I haue an excellent Hauke for the buſh.
Ford. Let it be fo: Come M. Page, come wife:
I pray you come in all, your welcome, pray come
Sir Hu. By fo kad vegne, M. Ford is   (in.
Not in his right wittes:
                  Exit omnes:

        Enter Sir Iohn Falſtaffe.   sc.11
Fal. Bardolfe brew me a poule ſack preſently:
Bar. With Egges ſir?
Fal. Simply of it felfe, Ile none of theſe pullets
In my drinke: goe make haſte.   (ſperme
Haue I liued to be carried in a basket
        E 2   And

A pleasant Comedie, of

and throwne into the Thames like a barow of But-
chers offoll. Well, and I be serued such another
tricke, Ile giue them leaue to take out my braines
and butter them, and giue them to a dog for a new-
yeares gift. Sblood, the rogues slided me in with as
little remorse as if they had gone to drowne a blind
bitches puppies in the litter: and they might know
by my size I haue a kind of alacritie in sinking: and
the bottom had bin as deep as hell I should downe.
I had bene drowned, but that the shore was shelue
and somewhat shallowe : a death that I abhorre.
For you know the water swelles a man : and what a
thing should I haue bene whe I had bene swelled?
By the Lord a mountaine of money. Now is the
Sacke brewed?

Bar. I sir, there's a woman below would speake
with you.

Fal. Bid her come vp. Let me put some Sacke
among this cold water, for my belly is as cold as if I
had swallowed snow-balles for pilles.

Enter Mistresse Quickly.

Now whats the newes with you?

Qui. I come from misteris *Ford* forsooth.

Fal. Misteris *Ford,* I haue had *Ford* enough,
I haue bene throwne into the *Ford,* my belly is full
Of *Ford:* she hath tickled mee.

Qui. O Lord sir, she is the sorrowfullest woman
that her seruants misfooke, that euer liued. And sir,
she would desire you of all loues you will meet her
once againe, to morrow sir, betweene ten and eleuen, and she hopes to make amends for all.

Fal. Ten, and eleuen, saiest thou?

Qui. I

---

the merry wiues of Windsor.

Qui. I forsooth.
Fal. Well, tell her Ile meet her. Let her but think
Of mans frailtie : Let her iudge what man is,
And then thinke of me. And so farwell.
Qui. Youle not faile sir?
                Exit mistresse Quickly.
Fal. I will not faile. Commend me to her.
I wonder I heare not of M. *Brooke,* I like his
Mony well. By the maske here he is.
                Enter Brooke.
For. God saue you sir.
Fal. Welcome good M. *Brooke.* You come to
    know how matters goes.
Ford. Thats my comming indeed sir *Iohn.*
Fal. M. *Brooke* I will not lie to you sir,
I was there at my appointed time.
For. And how sped you sir?
Fal. Verie ilfauouredly sir.
For. Why sir, did she change her determination?
Fal. No M. *Brooke,* but you shall heare. After we
had kissed and imbraced, and as it were euen amid
the prologue of our incounter, who should come,
but the iealous knaue her husband, and a rabble of
his companions at his heeles, thither prouoked and
instigated by his distemper. And what to do thinke
you? to search for his wiues loue. Euen so, plainly
so.
For. While eye were there?
Fal. Whilst I was there.
For. And did he search and could not find you?
Fal. You shall heare sir, as God would haue it,
A litle before comes me one *Pages* wife,
                      Giues

E 3

the merry Wiues of Windsor.

For. Is this a dreame? Is it a vision?
Maister _Ford_, maister _Ford_, awake maister _Ford_,
There is a hole made in your best coat M._Ford_,
And a man shall not only endure this wrong,
But shall stand vnder the taunt of iames,
Lucifer is a good name, _Barbifon_ good: good
Diuels names: But cuckold, wittold, godefo
The diuel himfelfe hath not fuch a name:
And they may hang hats here, and napkins here
Vpon my hornes: Well Ick home, I feit him,
And vnleffe the diuel him felfe fhould aide him,
Ile fearch vnpoffible places: Ile about it,
Leaft I repent too late:

                          Exit omnes.   sc. 12

Enter M.Fenton, Page, and mistresse
                 quickly,   (resolue,
Fen: Tell me sweet _Nan_, how doest thou yet
Shall foolish _Slender_ haue thee to his wife?
Or one as wise as he, the learned Doctor?
Shall such as they enioy thy maiden hart?
Thou knowst that I haue alwaies loued thee deare,
And thou hast of times fwore the like to me.
_An:_ Good M. _Fenton_, you may assure your selfe
My hart is setled vpon none but you,
Tis as my father and mother pleafe:
Get their confent, you quickly shall haue mine.
Fen: Thy father thinks I loue thee for his wealth,
Tho I must needs confesse at first that drew me,
But since thy vertue wiped that trash away,
I loue thee _Nan_, and so deere is it fet,
That whilft I liue, I nere shall thee forget.

                                Quic: Godes

A pleafant Comedie, of

Giues her intelligence of her husbands
Approach: and by her inuention, and _Fords_ wiues
Diftraction, conueyd me into a buck basket.
Ford. A buck basket!
Fal. By the Lord a buck basket, rammed me in
With foule shirts, ftokins, greafie napkins,
That M. _Brooke_, there was a compound of the most
Villanous fmel, that euer offended nostrill.
Itcell you M. _Brooke_, by the Lord for your fake
I fuffered three egregious deaths: Firft to be
Crammed like a good bilbo, in the circomference
Of a pack, Hilt to point, heele to head: and then to
Beftewed in my owne greafe like a Dutch difh:
A man of my kidncy; by the Lord it was maruell I
Efcaped fuffocation; and in the heat of all this,
To be throwne into Thames like a horfhoo hot:
Maifter _Brooke_, thinke of that hissing heate, Maifter
Brooke.
Ford. Well fir then my flute is void?
Youle vndertake it no more?
Fal. M. _Brooke_, Ile be throwne into Etna
As I haue bene in the Thames,
Ere I thus leaue her: I haue receiued
Another appointment of meeting,
Betweene ten and eleuen is the houre.
Ford. Why fir, tis almoft ten alreadie:
Fal. Is it? why then will I addreffe my felfe
For my appointment: M._Brooke_ come to me foone
At night, and you fhall know how I fpeed,
And the end fhall be, you fhall enioy her loue:
You fhall cuckold _Ford_: Come to mee fooner at
at night.   _Exit Falftaffe._   Ford

313

A pleasant Comedie, of

Gods pitie here comes her father.

Enter M. Page his wife, M. Shallow, and Slender.

Pa. M. *Fenton* I pray what make you here?
You know my answere fir, shees not for you:
Knowing my vow, to blame to vse me thus.

Fen. But heare me speake fir.

Pa. Pray fir get you gon: Come hither daughter,
Sonne *Slender* let me speak with you.   *(they whisper.*

Qui. Speake to Misteris *Page.*

Fen. Pray misteris *Page* let me haue your cōsent.

Mif. Pa. I faith M. *Fentō* tis as my husband pleafe.
For my part Ile neither hinder you, nor further

Qui. How say you this was my doings?   *(you.*
I bid you speake to misteris *Page.*

Fen. Here nurfe, theres a brace of angels to drink,
Woorke what thou canst for me, farwell. *(Exit Fen.*

Pa. By my troth fo I will, good hart.   *(Slider*
Pa. Come wife, you an I will in, weele leaue M.
And my daughter to talke together. M. *Shallow,*
You may ftay fir if you pleafe.

Exit Page and his wife.

Shal. Mary I thanke you for that:
To her coufin, to her.

Slen. I faith I know not what to fay.

An. Now M. *Slender,* whats your will?   *(An.*

Slen. Godefo theres a Ieft indeed: why mifteris
I neuer made wil yet: I thik God I am wife inough
Shal. Fie cuffe fie, thou art not right,   *(for that.*
O thou hadft a father.

Slen. I had a father mifteris *Anne,* good vncle
Tell the Ieft how my father ftole the goofe out of
The henloft. All this is nought, harke you miftreffe
Anne.   *Shal.*

the merry wiues of windsor.

Shal. He will make you ioynter of three hundred pound a yeare, he fhall make you a Gentlewoman.

Slend. I be God that I vill, come cut and long
taile, as good as any is in *Gloifterfhire,* vnder the degree of a Squire.

An. O God how many groffe faults are hid,
And couered in three hundred pound a yeare?

Well M. *Slender,* within a day or two Ile tell you
more.

Slend. I thanke you good mifteris *Anne,* vncle I
fhall haue her.

Qui. M. *Shallow,* M. *Page* would pray you to
come you, and you M. *Slender,* and you miftris *An.*

Slend. Well Nurfe, if youle fpeake for me,
Ile giue you more then Ile talke of.

Exit omnes but Quickly.

Qui. Indeed I will, Ile fpeake what I can for you,
But fpecially for M. *Fenton* :
But fpecially of all for my Maifter.
And indeed I will do what I can for them all three.
Exit.

sc.13

Enter mifteris Ford and her two men.

Mif. For. Do you heare? when your M. comes
take vp this basket as you did before, and if your M.
bid you fet it downe, obey him.

Ser. I will forfooth.
Enter Syr Iohn.

Mif. For. Syr *Iohn* welcome.

Fal. What are you fure of your husband now?

Mif. For. He is gone a birding fir *Iohn,* and I hope
will not come home yet.

F   *Enter*

Enter mistresse Page.

Gods body here is misteris *Page*,
Step behind the arras he is good sir *Iohn*.
  He steps behind the arras.

Mis.Pa. Misteris *Ford*, why woman your husband
is in his old vaine againe, hees comming to search
for your sweet heart, but I am glad he is not here.

Mis.Ior. O God misteris *Page* the knight is here,
What shall I do?

Mis.Pa. Why then you'r vndone woman, vnles
you make some meanes to shift him away,

Mis.For. Alas I know no meanes, vnlesse
we put him in the basket againe.

Fal. No Ile come no more in the basket.

Ile creep vp into the chimney. (*sing peeces.*

Mis.For. There they vse to discharge their Fow-
Fal. Why then Ile goe out of doores.

Mis.Pa. Then your vndone, your but a dead man.

Fal. For Gods sake deuise any extremitie,
Rather then a mischiefe.

Mis.Pa. Alas I know not what meanes to make,
If there were any womans apparell would fit him,
He might put on a gowne and a muffler,
And so escape.

Mis.For. Thats wel remembred, my maids Aunt
Gillian of Brainford, hath a gowne about.

Mis.Pa. And he is altogether as fat as she.

Mis.For. I that will serue him of my word.

Mis.Pa. Come goe with me sir *Iohn*, Ile helpe to
dresse you.

Fal. Come for God sake, any thing.

 Exit Mis. Page, & Sir Iohn. *Enter*

Enter M. Ford, Page, Priest, Shallow, the two men
carries the basket, and Ford meets it.

For. Come along I pray you, shal know the cause,
How now whither goe you? Ha whither go you?
Set downe the basket you slaue,

You panderly rogue set it downe. (thus:

Mis.For. What is the reason that you vse me
For. Come hither set downe the basket,

Misteris *Ford* the modest woman,

Misteris *Ford* the vertuous woman,

She that hath the iealous foole to her husband,
I mistrust you without cause do I not?

Mis.For. I Gods my record do you. And if
you mistrust me in any ill sort.

Ford. Well said brazen face, hold it out,

You youth in a basket, come out here, (cloathes?
Pull out the cloathes, search.

Hu. Ieshu plesse me, will you pull vp your wiues
Pa. Fie M. *Ford* you are not to go abroad if you
be in these fits.

Sir Hu. By so kad vdge me, tis verie necessarie
He were put in pethlem.

For. M. *Page*, as I am an honest man M. *Page*,
There was one conuyed out of my house heere yesterday out of this basket, why may he not be here
now?

Mi. For. Come mistris *Page*, bring the old woma~
For. Old woman, what old woman? (downe.

Mi. For. Why my maidens Aunt, *Gillia of Brainford.*

A witch, haue I not forewarned her my house,
Alas we are simple we, we know not what

          Is

F 2

Ford. Well wife, heere take my hand, vpon my
foule I loue thee dearer then I do my life, and ioy I
hnue so true and constant wife, my iealousie shall
neuer more offend thee.

Mi.For. Sir I am glad, & that which I haue done,
Was nothing else but mirth and modestie.

Pa. I mister is *Ford*, *Falstaffe* hath all the griefe,
And in this knauerie my wife was the chiefe.

Mi.Pa. No knauery husband, it was honest mirth.

Hu. Indeed it was good passimes & merriments.

Mis.For. But sweete heart shall wee leaue olde
Falstaffe so?

Mis.Pa. O by no meanes, send to him againe.

Pa. I do not thinke heele come being so much
deceiued.

For. Let me alone, Ile to him once againe like
Brooke, and know his mind whether heele come
or not.   (come.

Pa. There must be some plot laide, or heele not

Mis.Pa. Lets alone for that. Heare my deuice,
Of haue you heard since *Horne* the hunter dyed,
That women to affright their litle children,
Ses that she walkes in shape of a great stagge.
Now for that *Falstaffe* hath bene so deceiued,
As that he dares not venture to the house,
Weele send him word to meet vs in the field,
Disguisd like *Horne*, with huge horns on his head,
The houre that be iust betweene twelue and one,
And at that time we will meet him both:
Then would I haue you present there at hand,
With litle boyes disguisd and dressed like Fayries,
For to affright fat *Falstaffe* in the woods.

                                               And

F 3

Is brought: to passe vnder the colour of fortune.
Telling. Come downe you witch, come downe.

Enter Falstaffe disguisd like an old woman, and mi-
steris Page with him, Ford beates him, and hee
runnes away.

Away you witch get you gone.   (indeed,
Sir *Hu.* By Ieshu I verily thinke she is a witch
I espied vnder her muffler a great beard.

Ford. Pray come helpe me to search, pray now.

Pa. Come weele go for his minds sake.

                                   Exit omnes.

Mi.For. By my troth he beat him most extreamly.

Mi.Pa. I am glad of it, what shall we proceed any
further?

Mi.For. No faith, now if you will let vs tell our
husbands of it. For mine I am sure hath almost fretted himselfe to death.

sc.14

Mi.Pa. Content, come weele goe tell them all,
And as they agree, so will we proceed.   *Exit both.*

            Enter Host and Bardolfe.

Bar. Syr heere be three Gentlemen come from
the Duke the Stranger sir, would haue your horse.

Host. The Duke, what Duke? let me speake with
the Gentlemen, do they speake English?

Bar.   Ile call them to you sir.

Host. No *Bardolfe*, let them alone, Ile sauce them:
They haue had my house a weeke at command,
I haue turned away my other guests,
They shall haue my horses *Bardolfe*,
They must come off, Ile sauce them.   *Exit omnes.*

sc.15

Enter Ford, Page, their wines, Shallow, and Slen-
der, Syr Hu.

                                            Ford.

316

A pleasant Comedie, of

And then to make a period to the iest.
Tell *Falstaffe* all, I thinke this will do best.
Pa. Tis excellent, and my daughter *Anne*,
Shall like a litle Fayrie be disguised.
Mif. Pa. And in that Maske Ile make the Doctor
steale my daughter *An*, & ere my husband knowes
it, to carrie her to Church, and marrie her. (boyes?
Mif. For. But who will buy the silkes to tyre the
Pa. That will I do, and in a robe of white
Ile cloath my daughter, and aduertise *Slender*
To know her by that signe, and steale her thence,
And vnknowne to my wife, shall marrie her.
Hu. So kad vdge me the deuifes is excellent.
I will also be there, and be like a Iackanapes,
And pinch him most cruelly for his lecheries.
Mif. Pa. Why then we are reueng'd sufficiently.
First he was carried and throwne in the Thames,
Next beaten well, I am sure youle witnes that.
Mi. For. Ile lay my life this makes him nothing fat.
Pa. Well lets about this stratagem, I long
To see deceit deceiued, and wrong haue wrong.
For. Well send to *Falstaffe*, and if he come thither,
Twill make vs smile and laugh one moneth togi-
ther.   *Exit omnes.*

sc.16   *Enter Host and Simple.*

Host. What would thou haue boore, what think-(skin?
Speake, breath, discus, short, quick, briefe, snap.
Sim. Sir, I am sent frō my M. to sir *Iohn Falstaffe.*
Host. Sir *Iohn*, theres his Castle, his standing bed,
his trundle bed, his chamber is painted about with
the storie of the prodigall, fresh and new, go knock,
heele speake like an Antropophiginian to thee:
                                          Knocke

the merry Wiues of Windsor.

Knock I say.
Sim. Sir I should speak with an old woman that
went vp into his chamber.
Host. An old woman, the knight may be robbed,
Ile call bully knight, bully sir *Iohn.* Speake from thy
Lungs military: it is thine host, thy Ephesian calls.
Fal. Now mine Host.
Host: Here is a Bohemian tarter bully, tarries the
comming downe of the fat woman: Let her descēd
bully, let her descend, my chambers are honorable,
pah priuasie, fie.
Fal. Indeed mine host there was a fat woman with
But she is gone.   (me,
Sim. Pray sir was it not the wise woman of *Braine-*
                                          ford?
Fal. Marry was it Mussellshell, what would you?
Sim. Marry sir my maister *Slender* sent me to her,
To know whether one *Nim* that hath his chaine,
Cousoned him of it, or no.
Fal. I talked with the woman about it.
Sim. And I pray sir what ses she?
Fal. Marry she ses the very fame man that
Beguiled maister *Slender* of his chaine,
Cousoned him of it.
Sim. May I be bolde to tell my maister so sir?
Fal. I rike, who more bolde.
Sim. I thanke you sir, I shall make my maister a
glad man at these tydings, God be with you sir.
Host. Thou art clarkly sir *Iohn*, thou art clarkly,
Was there a wise woman with thee?
Fal. Marry was there mine host, one that taught
                                          Me

A pleasant Comedie, of

Me more with then I learned this 7. yeare,
And I paid nothing for it,
But was paid for my learning.
  Enter Bardolfe.
Bar. O Lord sir cousonage, plaine cousonage.
Host. Why man, where be my horses? where be
the Germanes?
Bar. Rid away with your horses:
After I came beyond Maidenhead,
They flung me in a slow of myre, & away they ran.
  Enter Doctor.
Doc. Where be my Host de gartyre?
Host. O here sir in perplexitie.
Doc. I cannot tell vad be dad,
But begar I will tell you vanting,
Dear be a Garmaine Duke come to de Court,
Has cosened all de host of *Branford*,
And *Reading*: begar I tell you for good will,
Ha, ha, mine Host, am I euen met you? *Exit.*
  Enter Sir Hugh.
Sir Hu. Where is mine Host of the gartyre?
Now my Host, I would desire you looke you now,
To haue a care of your entertainments,
For there is three sorts of cosen garmombles,
Is cosen all the Host of Maidenhead & Readings,
Now you are an honest man, and a scuruy beg-
gerly lowsie knaue beside:
And can point wrong places,
I tell you for good will, grate why mine Host. *Exit.*
Host. I am cosened *Hugh*, and coy *Bardolfe*, *Exit.*
Sweet knight assist me, I am cosened. *Exit.*
Fal. Would all the worell were cosened for me,
          For

the merry Wiues of Windsor. sc. 17

For I am cousoned and beaten too.
Well, I neuer prospered since I forswore
My selfe at *Primero*: and my winde
Were but long inough to say my prayers,
I de repent, now from whence come you?
  Enter Mistresse Quickly.
Quic. From the two parties forsooth.
Fal. The diuell take the one partie,
And his dam the other,
And theyle be both bestowed.
I haue endured more for their sakes,
Then man is able to endure.
Quic. O Lord sir, they are the sorrowfulst creatures
That euer liued: specially mistresse *Ford*,
Her husband hath beaten her that she is all
Blacke and blew poore soule.
Fal. What tellest me of blacke and blew,
I haue bene beaten all the colours in the Rainbow,
And in my escape like to a berre apprehended
For a witch of *Brainford*, and set in the flockes.
Quic. Well sir, she is a sorrowfull woman,
And I hope when you heare my errant,
Youle be perswaded to the contrarie,
Fal. Come goe with me into my chamber, Ile
heare thee.   *Exit omnes.*
  Enter Host and Fenton.
Host. Speake not to me sir, my mind is heauie,
I haue had a great losse.
Fen. Yet heare me, and as I am a gentleman,
Ile giue you a hundred pound toward your losse.
Host. Well sir Ile heare you, and at least keep your
counsell.
Fen. The thus my host, T'is not vnknown to you,
     G   The

A pleasant Comedie, of

The feruent loue I beare to young *Anne Page*,
And mutually her loue againe to mee:
But her father still againft her choife,
Doth feeke to marrie her to foolifh *Slender*,
And in a robe of white this night difguiled,
Wherein fat *Falstaffe* had a mightie fcare,
Muft *Slender* take her and carrie her to *Catam*,
And there vnknowne to any, marrie her.
Now her mother fill againft that match,
And firme for Doctor *Caym*, in a robe of red
By her deuice, the Doctor muft fteale her thence,
And fhe hath giuen confent to goe with him.
Host. Now which meanes fhe to deceiue, father or
　　mother?
Fen. Both my good Hoft, to go along with me.
Now here it refts, that you would procure a prieft,
And tarrie readie at the appointment place,
To giue our harts vnited matrimonie, (among the
Host. But how will you come to fteale her from
Fen. That hath fweet *Nan* and I agreed vpon,
And by a robe of white, fhe which fhe weares,
With ribones pendant flaring about her head,
I fhalbe fure to know her, and conuey her thence,
And bring her where the prieft abides our comming,
And by thy furtherance there be married.
Host. Well, husband your deuice, Ile to the Vicar,
Bring you the maide, you fhall not lacke a Prieft.
Fen. So fhall I euer more be bound vnto thee.
Besides Ile alwaies be thy faithfull friend.
　　　　　　　　Exit omnes.

sc.18

Enter fir Iohn with a Bucks head vpon him.
Fal. This is the third time, well Ile venter,
They fay there is good luck in old numbers,
Iune transformed himfelfe into a bull,　　And

---

the merry Wiues of Windsor.

And I am here a Stag, and I thinke the fatteft
In all *Windfor* forreft: well I ftand here
For *Horne* the hunter, waiting my Does comming.
　　Enter mistris Page, and mistris Ford.
Mis.Pa. Sir *Iohn*, where are you?
Fal. Art thou come my doe? what and thou too?
Welcome Ladies.
Mi.For. I I fir *Iohn*, I fee you will not faile,
Therefore you deferue far better then our loues,
But it grieues me for your late croffes.
Fal. This makes amends for all.
Come diuide me betweene you, each a hanch,
For my horns Ile bequeath the to your husbands,
Do I fpeake like *Horne* the hunter, ha?
Mis.Pa. God forgiue me, what noife is this?
　There is a noife of hornes, the two women runs away.

Enter fir Hugh like a Satyre, and boyes dreft like Fayries,
　　mistreffe Quickly, like the Queene of Fayries : they
　　fing a fong about him, and afterward fpeake.
　　　　　　　　　　　　　　　　　　(groues,
Qui: You Fayries that do haunt these fhady
Looke round about the wood if you can efpie
A mortall that doth haunt our facred round:
If fuch a one you can efpie, giue him his due,
And leaue no trill you pinch him blacke and blew:
Giue them their charge *Puck* ere they part away.
Sir Hu. Come hither *Peane*, go to the countrie
　　houfes,
And when you finde a flut that lies a fleepe,
And all her diffes foule, and roome vnfweps,
With your long nails pinch her till fhe crie,
　　　　　　　　　　　G 2　　　　　And

319

A pleasant Comedie, of

And sweare to mend her sluttish huswiferie.
Fal. I warrant you I will performe your will.
Hu. Where is *Peade*? go you & see where Brokers
And Foxe-eyed Seriants with their mase, (sleep,
Goe laie the Proctors in the street,
And pinch the lowsie Seriants face:
Spare none of these when they are a bed,
But such whose nose lookes plew and red.
Quic. Away be gon, his mind fulfill,
And looke that none of you stand still.
Some do that thing, some do this,
All do something, none amis.
Hir Hu. I smell a man of middle earth.
Fal. God blesse me from that welch Fairie.
Quic. Looke euery one about this round,
For his presumption in this place,
Spare neither legge, arme, head, nor face.
Sir Hu. See I haue spied one by good luck,
His bodie man, his head a buck.
Fal. God send me good fortune now, and I care
And take a Taper in your hand, (not.
And set it to his fingers endes,
And if you see it him offends,
And that he flarteth at the flame,
Then is he mortall, know his name:
If with an F. it doth begin,
Why then be sure he is full of sin.
About it then, and know the truth,
Of this same metamorphised youth.
Sir Hu. Giue me the Tapers, I will try
And if the loue venery.

They

the merry Wiues of Windsor.

They put the Tapers to his fingers, and he flurts.
Sir Hu. It is right indeed, he is full of lecheries
and iniquitie.
Quic. A little distant from him stand,
And euery one take hand in hand,
And compasse him within a ring,
First pinch him well, and after sing.

Here they pinch him, and sing about him, & the Doc-
tor comes one way & steales away a boy in red. And
Slender another way he takes a boy in greene: And
Fenton steales mistris Anne, being in white. And
a noyse of hunting is made within: and all the Fai-
ries runne away. Falstaffe palles of his bucks head,
and rises vp. And enters M. Page, M. Ford, and
their wiues, M. Shallow, Sir Hugh.

Fal. Horne the hunter quoth you: am I a ghost?
Sbloud the Fairies hath made a ghost of me:
What hunting at this time at night?
Ile lay my life the mad Prince of Wales
Is stealing his fathers Deare. How now who haue
we here, what is all *Windsor* stirring? Are you there?
Shal. God saue you sir *Iohn Falstaffe.*
Sir Hu. God plesse you sir *Iohn*, God plesse you.
Pa. Why how now sir *Iohn*, what a pair of horns
in your hand?
Ford. Those hornes he ment to place vpon my
And M. *Brooke* and he should be the men: (head,
Why how now sir *Iohn*, why are you thus amazed?
We know the Fairies man that pinched you so,
Your throwing in the Thames, your beating well,
G 3 And

320

A pleasant Comedie, of

And whats to come sir *Iohn*, that can we tell.
Mi.Pa. Sir *Iohn* tis thus, your dishonest meanes
To cull our credits into question,
Did make vs vnderrake to our best,
To turne your leaud lust to a merry Ieast.
Fal. Ieft, tis well, haue I liued to these yeares
To be gulled now, now to be ridden?
Why then these were not *Fairies*?
Mi.Pa. No sir *Iohn* but boyes.
Fal. By the Lord I was twice or thrise in the
They were not, and yet the grosnesse   (mind
Of the fopperie perswaded me they were.
Well, and the fine wits of the Court heare this,
They le so whip me with their keene Iests,
That thayle melt me out like tallow,
Drop by drop out of my grease.   Boyes!
Sir Hu. I trust me the boyes Sir *Iohn* : and I was
Also a Fairie that did helpe to pinch you.
Fal. I, tis well I am your May-pole,
You haue the flurt of mee,
Am I ridden too with a welch goate?
With a peece of toasted cheese?
Sir Hu. Butter is better then cheese sir *Iohn*,
You are all butter, butter.
For. There is a further matter yet sir *Iohn*,
There's 20. pound you borrowed of M. *Brooke* Sir
And it must be paid to M.*Ford* Sir *Iohn*,   (*Iohn*,
Mi.For. Nay husband let that go to make amends,
Forgiue that sum, and so weele all be friends.
For. Well here is my hand, alls forgiuen at last.
Fal. It hath cost me well,
I haue bene well pinched and washed.

                                                                    Enter

the merry Wiues of Windsor.

Enter the *Doctor*.

Mi.Pa. Now M. Doctor, sonne I hope you are.
Doct. Sonne begar you be de ville voman,
Begar I tincke to marry metres *An*, and begar
Tis a whorson garson lack boy.
Mi.Pa. How a boy?
Doct. I begar a boy.
Pa. Nay be not angry wife, Ile tell thee true,
It was my plot to deceiue thee so :
And by this time your daughter's married
To M.*Slender*, and see where he comes.

Enter *Slender*.

Now sonne *Slender*,
Where's your bride?
Slen. Bride, by Gods lyd I thinke there's neuer a
man in the worell hath that crosse fortune that *I*
haue : begod I could cry for verie anger.
Pa. Why whats the matter sonne *Slender*?
Slen. Sonne, nay by God I am none of your son-
Pa. No, why so?   (married.
Slen. Why so God saue me, tis a boy that I haue
Pa. How a boy? why did you mistake the word?
Slen. No neither, for I came to her in red as you
bad me, and I cried mum, and hee cried budget, so
well as euer you heard, and I haue married him.
Sir Hu. Iesu M.*Slender*, cannot you see but marrie
Pa. O I am vext at hart, what shall I do?   (boyes?

Enter *Fenton and Anne*.

Mi.Pa. Here comes the man that hath deceiued
How now daughter, where haue you bin?   (vs all:
An. At Curch forsooth.
Pa. At Church, what haue you done there?

                                                                    Fen.

A pleasant Comedie, of

Fen. Married to me, nay sir neuer storme,
Tis done sir now, and cannot be vndone.

Ford. Ifaith M. *Page* neuer chafe your selfe,
She hath made her choise wheras her hart was fixt,
Then tis in vaine for you to storme or fret.

Fal. I am glad yet that your arrow hath glanced

Ms. For. Come mistris *Page*, Ile be bold with you,
Tis pitie to part loue that is so true.

Mis. Pa. Altho that I haue missed in my intent,
Yet *I* am glad my husbands match was crossed,
Here M. *Fenton* take her, and God giue thee ioy.

Sir Hu: Come M. *Page*, you must needs agree.
Fo. I yfaith sir come, you see your wife is wel plea-
Pa. I cannot tel, and yet my hart's well eased, (sed:
And yet it doth me good the Doctor missed.
Come hither *Fenton*, and come hither daughter,
Go too you might haue staid for my good will,
But since your choise is made of one you loue,
Here take her *Fenton*, & both happie proue. (dings,
Sir Hu. I will also dance & eat plums at your wed-
Ford. All parties pleased, now let vs into feast,
And laugh at *Slender*, and the Doctors ieast,
He hath got the maiden, each of you a boy
To waite vpon yon, so God giue you ioy,
And sir *Iohn Falstaffe* now shal you keep your word,
For *Brooke* this night shall lye with mistris *Ford*.

Exit omnes.

FINIS.

322

Appendix

SEQUENCE OF SCENES IN QUARTO
AND EQUIVALENT PASSAGES IN FOLIO

Bold: Passages transferred from other scenes in F
Italics: (Quarto) Characters who do not speak
(Folio) Passages in F completely reworded in Q

Quarto	Folio
Scene no.	*Act/scene/line reference*
1 Sh. Sl. Ev. **Pa.**	1.1.1-3, 110, 127-31
Sh. Sl. Ev. Pa. Fal. Pi. Ba. Ni.	1.1.101-19, 140-73
Sh. Sl. Ev. Pa. Fal. Pi. Ba. Ni. MrsF. MrsP. AP	1.1.178-82
Sl. AP	**3.4.59-63,** 1.1.269-80, 263-8
Pa. Sl. AP	1.1.281-93
2 Ev. Sim.	1.2.1-12
3 Ho. Fal. Pi. Ba. Ni. [*Rob.*]	1.3.1-99
4 Qu. Sim.	1.4.16-21, 97-8, 89-94, **(2.2.111-12),** 1.4.3-5, 34-6
Qu. Sim. Ca. Ru.	1.4.51-84, 100-1, 116, 31-2
5 MrsP./MrsF.	2.1.4-11, 18-25, 61-3, 83-94
+ Fo. Pi. Pa. Ni. (+ Qu.)	2.1.101-3, 111-14, 119-25, 135-8, 142-50
Fo. Pa.	2.1.153-9, 164-9
Fo. Pa. Ho. Sh.	2.1.172-96, **2.3.42-5, 38-9,** 2.1.203-8, 213-14
6 Fal. Pi.	2.2.1-29
Fal. Qu.//	2.2.32-7, 48-52, 75-8, 80-91, 98-100, 111-14, 102-5
Fal. Ba.	2.2.136-9, 143-4, 130-4, 144-5
Fal. Fo.	2.2.146-50, 159-66, 175-80, 213-16, 202-13, 227-30, 241-71, 272, 274-5, 284-97
7 Ca. Ru./Ho. Sh. Sl. Pa.	2.3.11-12, 16-31, 34-5, 52-74
Ca. Ho.	2.3.75, 77-88
8 Ev. Sim.	3.1.18-21, 16-17, 30-1, 33
Ev. Sim. Pa. Sh. Sl.	3.1.38-42, 45-51, 55-64
Ev. Sim. Pa. Sh. Sl. Ho. Ca. *Ru.* [*Ba.*]	3.1.67, 70-105, 107

Appendix

Quarto	Folio
Scene no.	*Act / scene / line reference*
9 Fo./Pa. Sh. Sl. Ho. Ev. Ca. *Ru.*	3.2.45,55-7, 60-4, 68-74, **3.3.219-20**, 3.2.75-6, 78-80
10 MrsF. 2Ser./MrsF. Fal.	3.3.38-40, 43-55, 62-73
MrsP. MrsF. Fal.	3.3.97-102, 107-12, 115-20, 123-31
MrsP. MrsF. Fo. Pa. Ca. Ev. [*Sh. Sl.*]	3.3.138-40, 143-5, 156, 165-70, **4.2.97-8**, 3.3.182-3, **4.2.99-102**, 3.3.184-6, 195-7, 187, 203-4, 208-17
11 Fal. Ba./Fal. Qu.//	3.5.26-30, 4-22, 31-7, 43-8, 54-6
Fal. Fo.	3.5.57-86, 99-113, 115-28/129-31, **2.2.278-84**, 3.5.136-8
12 Qu. AP Fen.	*3.4.4-19*
Qu. AP Fen. Pa. MrsP. Sh. Sl.	3.4.65-72, 75-6, 80, 87-8, 94, 97-8
AP Sh. Sl./Qu.	3.4.51-8, 37-41, 45-9, 32-3, **3.2.50-1**, 3.4.104.6
13 MrsF. 2Ser./Fal.	4.2.103-5, 5-9
MrsF. Fal.MrsP.	4.2.19-20, 26, 38-9, 43-4, 50-3, 61-3, 69-70, 65-8, 71-4
MrsF. Fo. Pa. Sh. Ev./+ MrsP. *Fal.*	**3.3.149**, 4.2.110-12, 121-8, 133-4, 137-9, 157-69,/ 182-4, 190, 195-7, 202-3
14 Ho. Ba.	4.3.1-11
15 Pa. Fo. MrsP. MrsF. Ev. *Sh. Sl.*	4.4.*5-10*, *17-18*, 74-5, 39-41, *69-73*, 65-7, 78
16 Ho. Sim./Fal.	4.5.1-36, 51-60
Ho. Fal. Ba./Ca./Ev.	4.5.61-5, 78-83, 69-75, 85-96
Fal. Qu.	4.5.97-113, 120
17 Ho. Fen.	4.6.1-10, 23-8, 45-50, 41, 51-4
18 Fal./MrsF. MrsP.	**5.1.1-2**, 5.5.3, 12-13, 16-18, 24-8, 30
Fal. Qu. Ev. Children	5.5.*37-45*, 80-1, *84-92*
Fal. Pa. Fo. MrsP. MrsF. **Sh.** Ev.	5.5.*110-13*, *141-2*,121-5, **4.5.88-92**, 5.5.136-40, 113-4
Fal. Pa. Fo. MrsP. MrsF.**Sh.** Ev./Ca./Sl./AP Fen.	5.5.*201-6*, *197-9*, *175-96*, *211-13*, 228-9, 238-9

ABBREVIATIONS AND REFERENCES

ABBREVIATIONS

ABBREVIATIONS USED IN THE NOTES

*	indicates commentary notes involving readings that are not found in F
cf.	compare
ed.	editor, edited by
edn	edition
eds	editors, editions
mod. eds	indicates agreement of most modern editions
n.s.	new series
opp.	opposite (indicates location of marginal SD)
rev.	revised
SD	stage direction
sig.	signature
SP	speech prefix
subst.	substantially
Supp.	supplementary vols of *OED*
t.n., t.ns	textual note(s) at the foot of the page
this edn	a reading adopted or suggested for the first time in this edition
vol., vols	volume, volumes

( ) surrounding a reading in textual notes indicates original spelling, surrounding an editor's or scholar's name indicates a conjectural reading

WORKS BY AND PARTLY BY SHAKESPEARE

AC	*Antony and Cleopatra*
AW	*All's Well That Ends Well*
AYL	*As You Like It*
CE	*The Comedy of Errors*
Cor	*Coriolanus*
Cym	*Cymbeline*
E3	*The Reign of King Edward III*
Ham	*Hamlet*
1H4	*King Henry IV, Part 1*
2H4	*King Henry IV, Part 2*
H5	*King Henry V*

1H6	*King Henry VI, Part 1*
2H6	*King Henry VI, Part 2*
3H6	*King Henry VI, Part 3*
H8	*King Henry VIII*
JC	*Julius Caesar*
KJ	*King John*
KL	*King Lear*
LC	*A Lover's Complaint*
LLL	*Love's Labour's Lost*
Luc	*The Rape of Lucrece*
MA	*Much Ado About Nothing*
Mac	*Macbeth*
MM	*Measure for Measure*
MND	*A Midsummer Night's Dream*
MV	*The Merchant of Venice*
MW	*The Merry Wives of Windsor*
Oth	*Othello*
Per	*Pericles*
PP	*The Passionate Pilgrim*
PT	*The Phoenix and Turtle*
R2	*King Richard II*
R3	*King Richard III*
RJ	*Romeo and Juliet*
Son	*Sonnets*
STM	*The Book of Sir Thomas More*
TC	*Troilus and Cressida*
Tem	*The Tempest*
TGV	*The Two Gentlemen of Verona*
Tim	*Timon of Athens*
Tit	*Titus Andronicus*
TN	*Twelfth Night*
TNK	*The Two Noble Kinsmen*
TS	*The Taming of the Shrew*
VA	*Venus and Adonis*
WT	*The Winter's Tale*

REFERENCES

In references to books, the place of publication is London unless otherwise stated.

EDITIONS OF SHAKESPEARE COLLATED

Quotations and references to Shakespeare's works other than *The Merry Wives of Windsor* use the lineation, though not necessarily the spelling, of Riv (*The Riverside Shakespeare*, 2nd edn, Boston, 1997), to which the *Harvard Concordance to Shakespeare*, ed. Marvin Spevack (Cambridge, (Mass., 1973) is keyed.

Alexander	*The Complete Works*, ed. Peter Alexander, The Tudor Shakespeare (1951)
Ard[1]	*The Merry Wives of Windsor*, ed. H.C. Hart, The Arden Shakespeare (1904)
Ard[2]	*The Merry Wives of Windsor*, ed. H.J. Oliver, The [New] Arden Shakespeare (1971)
Bowers	*The Merry Wives of Windsor*, ed. Fredson Bowers, The Pelican Shakespeare, *Complete Works*, ed. Alfred Harbage (Baltimore and London, 1969)
Cam	*The Works,* ed. W.G. Clark and W.A. Wright, 9 vols. Vol. 1, ed. with John Glover. The Cambridge Shakespeare (Cambridge, 1863)
Cam[1]	*The Merry Wives of Windsor*, ed. Sir Arthur Quiller-Couch and John Dover Wilson, The New Shakespeare (Cambridge, 1921)
Cam[2]	*The Merry Wives of Windsor*, ed. David Crane, The New Cambridge Shakespeare (Cambridge, 1997)
Capell	*Comedies, Histories, and Tragedies*, ed. Edward Capell, 10 vols. Vol. 1 (1767)
Collier	*The Works*, ed. J. Payne Collier, 8 vols. Vol. 1 (1844)
Collier[2]	*The Works*, J. Payne Collier, ed. (1853)
Craig	*The Complete Works*, ed. W.J. Craig, The Oxford Shakespeare (Oxford, 1891)
Craik	see Oxf[1]
Crane	see Cam[2]
Daly	*Shakespeare's Comedy of The Merry Wives of Windsor.* Facsimile of Q1 and prompt-copy for use in Daly's theatre, with Augustin Daly's alterations (New York, 1886)
Dyce	*The Works*, ed. Alexander Dyce, 6 vols. Vol. 1 (1857)
Dyce[2]	*The Works*, ed. Alexander Dyce, 2nd edn, 9 vols. Vol. 1 (1866)

F	*Mr. William Shakespeares Comedies, Histories, & Tragedies.* The First Folio (1623)
F2	*Mr. William Shakespeares Comedies, Histories, and Tragedies.* The Second Folio (1632)
F3	*Mr. William Shakespear's Comedies, Histories, and Tragedies.* The Third Folio (1663)
F4	*Mr. William Shakespear's Comedies, Histories, and Tragedies.* The Fourth Folio (1685)
Furnivall	*The Merry Wives of Windsor*, ed. F.J. Furnivall, The Old-Spelling Shakespeare (London and New York, 1908)
Green	*The Merry Wives of Windsor*. ed. William Green, Signet Classic (New York, 1965)
Greg	conjecture reported in Cam[1], p. 134
GWW	conjecture or suggestion privately communicated by George Walton Williams
Halliwell	*The Complete Works of Shakespere*, ed. J.O. Halliwell (London and New York, 1850)
Hanmer	*The Works*, ed. Thomas Hanmer, 6 vols. Vol. 1 (Oxford, 1744)
Harness	*The Dramatic Works*, ed. William Harness. Vol. 1 (1825)
Hart	see Ard[1]
Hibbard	*The Merry Wives of Windsor*, ed. George R. Hibbard, The New Penguin Shakespeare (Harmondsworth, England, 1973)
Hudson[2]	*The Works*, ed. H.N. Hudson, revised edn, 20 vols. Vol.1 (Boston, 1871)
Irving	*The Works*, ed. Sir Henry Irving and Frank A. Marshall, The Henry Irving Shakespeare (1906)
Johnson	*The Plays . . . To which are added Notes by Sam. Johnson*, 8 vols. Vol. 2 (1765)
Keightley	*The Plays*, ed. Thomas Keightley, 6 vols. Vol. 2 (1864)
Kittredge	*The Works*, ed. George Lyman Kittredge (Boston, 1943)
Malone	*The Plays and Poems*, ed. Edmund Malone, 10 vols. Vol. 1, Part 2 (1790)
Munro	*The Works*, ed. John Munro, The London Shakespeare, 6 vols (1958)
Neilson	*The Works*, ed. William A. Neilson (Boston, 1906)
Norton	*The Norton Shakespeare*, ed. Stephen Greenblatt, with Walter Cohen and Katherine Eiseman Mars. Based on the Oxford edition (New York, 1997)
Oliver	see Ard[2]
Oxberry	*The Merry Wives of Windsor*, ed. W. Oxberry. Oxberry's New English Drama, Vol. 8 (1820)
Oxf	*Complete Works*, ed. Stanley Wells and Gary Taylor, with John Jowett and William Montgomery. The Oxford Shakespeare (Oxford, 1986)

Oxf[1]	*The Merry Wives of Windsor*, ed. T.W. Craik. The Oxford Shakespeare (Oxford, 1990)
Pope	*The Works of Shakespear . . . Collected and Corrected . . . by Mr. Pope*, 6 vols. Vol. 1 (1723)
Q	*A Most pleasaunt and excellent conceited Comedie, of Syr Iohn Falstaffe, and the merrie Wiues of Windsor. . . . By William Shakespeare*. The First Quarto. (1602)
Q2	*A Most Pleasant and Excellent Conceited Comedy, of Sir Iohn Falstaffe, and the merry Wiues of Windsor. . . . Written by W. Shakespeare*. The Second Quarto (1619)
Q3	*The Merry VViues of Windsor. . . . Written by William Shake-Speare*. The Third Quarto (1630)
Rann	*The Dramatic Works*, ed. Joseph Rann, 6 vols. Vol. 1 (Oxford, 1786)
Reed	*The Plays*, ed. Isaac Reed. Vol. 1 (1785)
Ridley	*The Merry Wives of Windsor*, ed. M.R. Ridley. The New Temple Shakespeare (1925)
Riv	*The Riverside Shakespeare*, ed. G. Blakemore Evans, 2nd edn (Boston, 1997)
Rowe	*The Works of Mr. William Shakespear . . . Revis'd and Corrected . . . by N. Rowe, Esq.*, 6 vols. Vol. 1 (1709)
Rowe[3]	*The Works of Mr. William Shakespear . . . With his Life, by N. Rowe, Esq.*, 8 vols. Vol. 1 (1714)
RP	conjecture or suggestion privately communicated by Richard Proudfoot
Singer	*The Dramatic Works*, ed. S.W. Singer, 10 vols. Vol.1 (1826)
Sisson	*The Complete Works*, ed. C.J. Sisson (1954)
Staunton	*The Plays*, ed. Howard Staunton, 3 vols. Vol. 1 (1858)
Steevens	*The Plays*, ed. Samuel Johnson and George Steevens, 10 vols. Vol. 1 (1773)
Steevens[2]	*The Plays*, ed. Samuel Johnson and George Steevens, 2nd edn, vol. 1 (1778)
Steevens[3]	*The Plays*, ed. George Steevens, 4th edn, vol. 3 (1793)
Theobald	*The Works*, ed. Lewis Theobald, 7 vols. Vol. 1 (1733)
Tollet	Conjectural emendations recorded in Steevens[2], Steevens[3]
Warburton	*The Works of Shakespear. The Genuine Text . . . settled . . . By Mr. Pope and Mr. Warburton*, 8 vols. Vol. 1 (1747)
Wheatley	*The Merry Wives of Windsor*, ed. Henry B. Wheatley (1886)
White	*The Works*, ed. Richard Grant White, 12 vols. Vol. 2 (Boston, 1857)

OTHER WORKS CITED

An asterisk (*) indicates works containing variant or conjectural readings recorded in the textual notes or discussed in the commentary.

Abbott	E.A. Abbott, *A Shakespearian Grammar*, 3rd revised edn (1870), reprinted Dover Books (1966). References are to numbered paragraphs.
Barton	Anne Barton, 'Falstaff and the Comic Community', in *Shakespeare's "Rough Magic": Renaissance Essays in Honor of C.L. Barber*, ed. Peter Erickson and Coppélia Kahn (Newark, Del., 1985), 131–48
Bracy	William Bracy, *The Merry Wives of Windsor: The History and Transmission of Shakespeare's Text*. University of Missouri Studies 25 (1952)
Bradbrook	M.C. Bradbrook, 'Royal Command: The Merry Wives of Windsor', in *Shakespeare the Craftsman*. Clark Lectures 1968 (Cambridge, 1979), 75–96
Bullough	Geoffrey Bullough, (ed.), *Narrative and Dramatic Sources of Shakespeare*. 8 vols. Vol. 2 (1959)
Burkhart, *Bad Quartos*	Robert E. Burkhart, *Shakespeare's Bad Quartos: Deliberate Abridgements Designed for Performance by a Reduced Cast*. Studies in English Literature 100 (The Hague and Paris, 1975)
Campbell, *Histories*	Lily B. Campbell, *Shakespeare's 'Histories': Mirrors of Elizabethan Policy* (1947), 3rd edn (1963)
Campbell, 'Italianate'	Oscar James Campbell, 'The Italianate Background of *The Merry Wives of Windsor*', *Essays and Studies . . . of the University of Michigan* 8 (1932), 81–117
Carroll	William Carroll, *The Metamorphoses of Shakespearean Comedy* (Princeton, N.J., 1985)
*Cartwright	Robert Cartwright, *New Readings in Shakespeare* (1866)
CD	*Comparative Drama*
Chambers, *Stage*	E.K. Chambers, *The Elizabethan Stage*, 4 vols (Oxford, 1923)
Clark	Sandra Clark, '"Wives may be merry and yet honest too": women and wit in *The Merry Wives of Windsor* and some other plays', in *'Fanned and Winnowed Opinions': Shakespearean Essays Presented to Harold Jenkins*, ed. John W. Mahon and Thomas A. Pendleton (1987), 249–67
Cohen	Walter Cohen, Introduction to *The Merry Wives of Windsor*, in The Norton Shakespeare, ed. Stephen Greenblatt, with Walter Cohen and Katherine Eiseman Mars (New York, 1977), 1225–33.
Cotton	Nancy Cotton, 'Castrating (W)itches: Impotence and Magic in *The Merry Wives of Windsor*', *SQ*, 38 (1987), 320–6

Craig, *New Look*   Hardin Craig, *A New Look at Shakespeare's Quartos* (Stanford, Ca., 1961)

*Daniel   P.A. Daniel, *Notes and Conjectural Emendations of Certain Doubtful Passages of Shakespeare's Plays* (1870)

Dean   Winton Dean, 'Shakespeare and Opera', in *Shakespeare and Music: A Collection of Essays*, ed. Phyllis Hartnoll (1964), 89–175

Dent   R.W.Dent, *Shakespeare's Proverbial Lnguage: An Index* (Berkeley, Ca., Toronto and London, 1981). References are to numbered proverbs.

Doctor Faustus   Christopher Marlowe, *The Tragical History of the Life and Death of Doctor Faustus*, ed. J.D. Jump (Manchester, 1978)

*Douce   Francis Douce, *Illustrations of Shakespeare* (1807)

ELH   *Journal of English Literary History*

Empson   William Empson, 'Falstaff', in *Essays on Shakespeare*, ed. David B. Pirie (Cambridge, 1986), 29–78

Erickson   Peter Erickson, 'The Order of the Garter, the cult of Elizabeth, and class–gender tension in *The Merry Wives of Windsor*', in Jean E. Howard and Marion F. O'Connor (eds), *Shakespeare Reproduced: The Text in History and Ideology* (1987), 116–42

Everett   Barbara Everett, 'The Fatness of Falstaff', *LRB* (16 August 1990), 18–22

Famous Victories   *The Famous Victories of Henry the Fifth* (1598), in G. Bullough (ed.), *Narrative and Dramatic Sources of Shakespeare*, vol. 4 (1962) 299–343. References are to line numbers

*Farmer   Richard Farmer, *An Essay on the Learning of Shakespeare* (Cambridge, 1767)

Fleissner   Robert F. Fleissner, 'The malleable knight and the unfettered friar: *The Merry Wives of Windsor* and Boccaccio', *SSt*, 11 (1978), 77–93

Freedman, 'Chronology'   Barbara Freedman, 'Shakespearean chronology, ideological complicity, and floating texts: something is rotten in Windsor', *SQ*, 45 (1994), 190–210

Freedman, 'Punishment'   Barbara Freedman, 'Falstaff's punishment: buffoonery as defensive posture in *The Merry Wives of Windsor*', *SSt*, 14 (1981), 163–74

French   Marilyn French, *Shakespeare's Division of Experience* (New York, 1981)

Gooch and Thatcher   B.N.S. Gooch and D. Thatcher, *A Shakespeare Music Catalogue*, 5 vols (Oxford, 1991)

Green   William Green, *Shakespeare's Merry Wives of Windsor* (Princeton, N.J., 1962)

Greg, *BEPD*	W.W. Greg, *A Bibliography of the English Printed Drama to the Restoration*, 4 vols (1939–59)
Gurr	Andrew Gurr, 'Intertextuality at Windsor', *SQ*, 38 (1987), 189–200
GWW	conjecture or suggestion privately communicated by George Walton Williams
Hart	Alfred Hart, *Stolne and Surreptitious Copies: A Comparative Study of Shakespeare's Bad Quartos* (Melbourne, 1942)
*Heath	Benjamin Heath, *A Revisal of Shakespeare's Text* (1765)
Hillman	Richard Hillman, *Shakespearean Subversions: The Trickster and the Play-text* (1989)
Hinely	Jan Lawson Hinely, 'Comic scapegoats and the Falstaff of *The Merry Wives of Windsor*', *SSt*, 15 (1982), 37–54
Hogan	C.B. Hogan, *Shakespeare in the Theatre, 1701–1800*, 2 vols (Oxford, 1952, 1957)
Honigmann, 'Oldcastle'	E.A.J. Honigmann, 'Sir John Oldcastle: Shakespeare's martyr', in *'Fanned and Winnowed Opinions': Shakespearean Essays Presented to Harold Jenkins*, ed. John W. Mahon and Thomas A. Pendleton (1987), 118–32
Hotson	Leslie Hotson, *Shakespeare versus Shallow* (1931)
Ioppolo	Grace Ioppolo, *Revising Shakespeare* (Cambridge, Mass., 1991)
Irace	Kathleen O. Irace, *Reforming the 'Bad' Quartos: Performance and Provenance of Six Shakespearean First Editions* (Newark, Del., 1994)
*Jackson	Zachariah Jackson, *Shakespeare's Genius Justified* (1819)
Johnson, '*MW*, Q1'	Gerald D. Johnson, '*The Merry Wives of Windsor*, Q1: Provincial touring and adapted texts', *SQ*, 38 (1987), 154–65
Kahn	Coppelia Kahn, *Man's Estate: Masculine Identity in Shakespeare* (Berkeley, Ca., 1981)
King, *Casting*	T.J. King, *Casting Shakespeare's Plays: London Actors and Their Roles, 1590–1642* (Cambridge, 1993)
Kinney	Arthur F. Kinney, 'Textual Signs in *The Merry Wives of Windsor*', *YES*, 23 (1993), 206–34
Knutson	Roslyn Lander Knutson, *The Repertory of Shakespeare's Company 1594–1613* (Fayetteville, Ark., 1991)
*Lambrechts	Guy Lambrechts, 'Proposed new readings in Shakespeare', in *Bulletin de la Faculté des Lettres de Strasbourg* 63 (1965), 946–7
Leggatt	Alexander Leggatt, *Citizen Comedy in the Age of Shakespeare* (Toronto, 1973)
Lilly and Colet	William Lilly and John Colet, *A Shorte Introduction of Grammar . . . for the bryngynge vp of all those that entende to atteyne the knowlege of the Latine tongue*, 1549

London Stage	*The London Stage 1660–1800*, ed. W. Van Lennep, E.L. Avery, A.H. Scouten, G.W. Stone Jr and C.B. Hogan (Carbondale, Ill., 1960–8)
Long, 'Masque'	John H. Long, 'Another masque for *The Merry Wives of Windsor*', *SQ*, 3 (1952), 39–43
Long, *Music*	John H. Long, *Shakespeare's Use of Music: 2 – The Final Comedies* (Gainesville, Fla., 1961)
LRB	*London Review of Books*
Mace	Nancy A. Mace, 'Falstaff, Quin, and the popularity of *The Merry Wives of Windsor* in the eighteenth century', *TS*, 31 (May 1990), 55–66
McDonald	Russ McDonald, *Shakespeare and Jonson, Jonson and Shakespeare* (Lincoln, Nebr., 1988)
Maguire	Laurie E. Maguire, *Shakespearean Suspect Texts: The 'Bad' Quartos and Their Contexts* (Cambridge, 1996)
Marcus, 'Levelling'	Leah Marcus, 'Levelling Shakespeare: local customs and local texts'. *SQ*, 42 (1991), 168–78
Marcus, *Unediting*	Leah Marcus, *Unediting the Renaissance: Shakespeare, Marlowe, Milton* (1996)
*Mason	J.M. Mason, *Comments on the Last Edition of Shakespeare's Plays* (Dublin, 1785)
Melchiori, *Garter*	Giorgio Melchiori, *Shakespeare's Garter Plays: 'Edward III' to 'Merry Wives of Windsor'* (Newark, Del., 1994)
Melchiori, 'Pivot'	Giorgio Melchiori, 'Pivot scenes as dramatic inclusions in Shakespeare's plays', in *The Show Within: Dramatic and Other Insets in English Renaissance Drama (1550–1642)*, ed. François Laroque (Montpellier, 1992), 1: 155–66.
Melchiori, 'Which Falstaff'	Giorgio Melchiori, 'Which Falstaff in Windsor?', *KM 80: A Birthday Album for Kenneth Muir* (Liverpool, 1987), 98–100
Met.	*Shakespeare's Ovid: Being Arthur Golding's Translation of the Metamorphoses*, ed. W.H.D. Rouse (1961)
Miola	Robert S. Miola, '*The Merry Wives of Windsor*: Classical and Italian Intertexts', *CD*, 27 (1993), 364–76
MLR	*Modern Language Review*
MSR	Malone Society Reprints
N&Q	*Notes and Queries*
Nashe	*The Works of Thomas Nashe*, ed. R.B. McKerrow, with supplementary notes by F.P. Wilson, 5 vols (Oxford, 1958)
Nosworthy *Occasional Plays*	J.M. Nosworthy, *Shakespeare's Occasional Plays: Their Origins and Transmission* (1965)
Odell	George C. Odell, *Shakespeare: From Betterton to Irving*, 2 vols (New York, 1920, reprinted 1963)

OED	*The Oxford English Dictionary*, 13 vols (Oxford, 1933), and 4 vols *Supplements* (1972–86), 2nd edn (Oxford, 1989)
Onions	C.T. Onions, *A Shakespeare Glossary*, revised by Robert D. Eagleson (Oxford, 1986)
OW	*The Oxford Dictionary of English Proverbs*, 3rd edn, revised by F.P. Wilson (1970). References are to page and column (a/b)
Parker	Patricia Parker, *Shakespeare from the Margins: Language, Culture, Context* (Chicago, 1996)
Parten	Anne Parten, 'Falstaff's horns: inadequacy and feminine mirth in *The Merry Wives of Windsor*', *SP*, 82 (1985), 184–99
Pittenger	Elizabeth Pittenger, 'Dispatch Quickly: the mechanical reproduction of Pages', *SQ*, 42 (1991), 389–408
Poole	Kristen Poole, 'Saints Alive! Falstaff, Martin Marprelate, and the staging of Puritanism', *SQ*, 46 (1995), 47–75
RES	*Review of English Studies*
Roberts, *Context*	Jeanne Addison Roberts, *Shakespeare's English Comedy: The Merry Wives of Windsor in Context* (Lincoln, Nebr., 1979)
Roberts, '*MW* Q & F'	Jeanne Addison Roberts, '*The Merry Wives* Q and F: the vagaries of progress', *SSt*, 8 (1975), 143–75
RP	conjecture or suggestion privately communicated by Richard Proudfoot
Salingar, *Traditions*	Leo Salingar, *Shakespeare and the Traditions of Comedy* (Cambridge, 1974)
Salmon	Vivian Salmon, 'Elizabethan colloquial English in the Falstaff plays', in *Leeds Studies in English*, n.s. 1 (1967), 37–70
Sams	Eric Sams, *The Real Shakespeare: Retrieving the Early Years, 1564–1594* (1995)
Schafer	Elizabeth Schafer, 'The date of *The Merry Wives of Windsor*', *N&Q* 236 (1991), 57–60
Schmidgall	Gary Schmidgall, *Shakespeare and Opera* (New York and Oxford, 1990)
Scoufos, *Satire*	Alice-Lyle Scoufos, *Shakespeare's Typological Satire: A Study of the Falstaff–Oldcastle Problem* (Athens, Ohio, 1979)
Shaheen	Naseeb Shaheen, *Biblical References in Shakespeare's Comedies* (Newark, Del., 1994)
Siegel	Paul N. Siegel, 'Falstaff and His Social Milieu' (1974), in *Shakespeare's English and Roman History Plays: A Marxist Approach* (1986), 86–92

Sir Thomas More	*Sir Thomas More*, a play by Anthony Munday and others, ed. Vittorio Gabrieli and Giorgio Melchiori (Manchester, 1990)
Slights	Camille Wells Slights, 'Pastoral and parody in *The Merry Wives of Windsor*', in *Shakespeare's Comic Commonwealths* (Toronto, Buffalo, N.Y., and London, 1993), 151–70
Smidt	Kristian Smidt, *Unconformities in Shakespeare's Early Comedies* (1986)
SP	*Studies in Philology*
SQ	*Shakespeare Quarterly*
SS	*Shakespeare Survey*
SSt	*Shakespeare Studies*
Steadman	John M. Steadman, 'Falstaff as Actaeon: a dramatic emblem', *SQ*, 14 (1963), 230–44
Taylor, 'Cobham'	Gary Taylor, 'William Shakespeare, Richard James and the House of Cobham', *RES*, 38 (1987), 334–54
Taylor, 'Expurgation'	Gary Taylor, "'Swounds revisited: theatrical, editorial, and literary expurgation', in Gary Taylor and John Jowett, *Shakespeare Reshaped 1606–1623* (Oxford, 1993), 51–106
Taylor, 'Oldcastle'	Gary Taylor, 'The Fortunes of Oldcastle', *SS*, 38 (1985), 85–100
Tiffany, 'False Staff'	Grace Tiffany, 'Falstaff's False Staff: "Jonsonian" asexuality in *The Merry Wives of Windsor*', *CD*, 26 (1992–3), 254–70
Tiffany, *Monsters*	Grace Tiffany, *Erotic Beasts and Social Monsters: Shakespeare, Jonson, and the Comic Androgyny* (Newark, Del., 1995)
Tilley	M.P. Tilley, *A Dictionary of the Proverbs in England in the Sixteenth and Seventeenth Centuries* (Ann Arbor, Mich., 1950). References are to numbered proverbs.
TS	*Theatre Survey*
TxC	Stanley Wells and Gary Taylor, with John Jowett and William Montgomery, *William Shakespeare: A Textual Companion* (Oxford, 1987)
*Tyrwhitt	Thomas Tyrwhitt, *Observations and Conjectures upon Some Passages of Shakespeare* (1766)
Urkowitz	Steven Urkowitz, 'Good news about "Bad" Quartos', in Maurice Charney (ed.), *'Bad' Shakespeare: Revaluations of the Shakespeare Canon* (Cranbury, N.J., 1988), 189–206
Vickers	Brian Vickers, *The Artistry of Shakespeare's Prose* (1968)
YES	*The Yearbook of English Studies*
*Walker	W.S. Walker, *A Critical Examination of the Text of Shakespeare*, 3 vols (1860)

Werstine | Paul Werstine, 'Narratives about printed Shakespearean texts: "foul papers" and "bad quartos" ', *SQ*, 41 (1990), 65–86

White | R.S. White, *The Merry Wives of Windsor*. Harvester New Critical Introductions to Shakespeare (Hemel Hempstead, England, 1991)

Wiles, *Clown* | David Wiles, *Shakespeare's Clown: Actor and Text in the Elizabethan Playhouse* (Cambridge, 1987)

Wilson | John Dover Wilson, *The Fortunes of Falstaff* (1953)

Woodbridge | Linda Woodbridge, *Women and the English Renaissance: Literature and the Nature of Womankind, 1540–1620* (Hemel Hempstead, England, 1984)

INDEX